THE CLINTONS'
WAR ON WOMEN

THE CLINTONS'
WAR ON WOMEN

ROGER STONE
AND ROBERT MORROW

Skyhorse Publishing

Skyhorse Publishing books may be purchased in bulk at special discounts for sales promotion, corporate gifts, fund-raising, or educational purposes. Special editions can also be created to specifications. For details, contact the Special Sales Department, Skyhorse Publishing, 307 West 36th Street, 11th Floor, New York, NY 10018 or info@skyhorsepublishing.com.

Skyhorse® and Skyhorse Publishing® are registered trademarks of Skyhorse Publishing, Inc.®, a Delaware corporation.

Visit our website at www.skyhorsepublishing.com.

10 9 8 7 6 5 4 3 2 1

Library of Congress Cataloging-in-Publication Data is available on file.

Print ISBN: 978-1-5107-0678-1
Ebook ISBN: 978-1-5107-0674-3

Printed in the United States of America

In remembrance of the seventy-six people, members of the Branch Davidian church, who died in their home at Mount Carmel, Texas, on April 19, 1993, following the decisions and actions of Hillary Clinton. The vast majority of these victims were women. Of the eighteen children younger than eight who died at Waco, Texas, two were unborn babies. Their names and ages follow.

Chanel Andrade, 1
Jennifer Andrade, 19
Katherine Andrade, 24
George Bennett, 35
Susan Benta, 31
Mary Jean Borst, 49
Pablo Cohen, 38
Abedowalo Davies, 30
Shari Doyle, 18
Beverly Elliot, 30
Doris Fagan, 51
Yvette Fagan, 32
Lisa Marie Farris, 24
Raymond Friesen, 76
Sandra Hardial, 27
Diana Henry, 28
Paulina Henry, 24
Phillip Henry, 22
Stephen Henry, 26
Vanessa Henry, 19
Zilla Henry, 55
Novellette Hipsman, 36
Floyd Houtman, 61
Sherri Jewell, 43
David M. Jones, 38
Bobbie Lane Koresh, 2
Cyrus Koresh, 8
David Koresh, 33
Rachel Koresh, 24
Star Koresh, 6
Jeffery Little, 32
Nicole Gent Little (pregnant), 24
Dayland Lord Gent, 3
Paiges Gent, 1
Livingston Malcolm, 26
Anita Martin, 18
Diane Martin, 41

Lisa Martin, 13
Sheila Martin, Jr., 15
Wayne Martin, Jr., 20
Wayne Martin, Sr., 42
Abigail Martinez, 11
Audrey Martinez, 13
Crystal Martinez, 3
Isaiah Martinez, 4
Joseph Martinez, 8
Julliete Martinez, 30
John-Mark McBean, 27
Bernadette Monbelly, 31
Melissa Morrison, 6
Rosemary Morrison, 29
Sonia Murray, 29
Theresa Nobrega, 48
James Riddle, 32
Rebecca Saipaia, 24
Judy Schneider, 41
Steve Schneider, 43
Mayanah Schneider, 2
Clifford Sellors, 33
Scott Kojiro Sonobe, 35
Floracita Sonobe, 34
Aisha Gyrfas Summers (pregnant), 17
Gregory Summers, 28
Startle Summers, 1
Hollywood Sylvia, 1
Lorraine Sylvia, 40
Rachel Sylvia, 12
Chica Jones, 2
Michelle Jones Thibodeau, 18
Serenity Jones, 4
Little One Jones, 2
Margarida Vaega, 47
Neal Vaega, 38
Mark H. Wendell, 40

"I remember one time when Bill had been quoted in the morning paper saying something she didn't like," Patterson said. "I came into the mansion and he was standing at the top of the stairs and she was standing at the bottom screaming. She has a garbage mouth on her, and she was calling him motherf—er, c—sucker, and everything else. I went into the kitchen, and the cook, Miss Emma, turned to me and said, 'The devil's in that woman.'"[1]

—Arkansas State Troopers Larry Patterson and Roger Perry, as cited by the *American Spectator* in 1994

CONTENTS

FOREWORD BY KATHLEEN WILLEY

For many years, the Clintons have been waging war on women. Now that Hillary is running for president, this war threatens to claim more casualties.

As a volunteer in the White House, I knew all too well the insincere public facade worn by the First Lady. Hillary did not think twice of boorishly "dressing down" her subordinates, male or female, in profanity-laced tirades.

In 1993, I was sexually assaulted by Bill Clinton, then president of the United States, in the Oval Office. In a professional setting where I had planned to ask him for paid employment, President Clinton put my hand on his genitals. He then proceeded to overpower me and run his hands up my skirt, over my blouse and my breasts. If not for an impending meeting for which the president was late, I might not have escaped his grasp.

On that same day, my husband, overcome with financial grief, walked into the woods in a rural Virginia county and took his own life.

Four years later, I was subpoenaed as a witness to be deposed in the Paula Jones sexual harassment case. It was then that I was treated, firsthand, to the ways Hillary tried to discredit and intimidate women who have suffered at the hands of her husband. It is my firm belief that Hillary Clinton was behind a criminal terror campaign designed to scare me into silence.

As I relate in my book, *Target: Caught in the Crosshairs of Bill and Hillary Clinton*, my children were threatened by "detectives" hired by Hillary. They threatened my friend's children. They took one of my cats and killed another. They left a skull on my porch. They told me I was in danger. They followed me. They vandalized my car. They tried to retrieve my dogs from a kennel. They hid under my deck in the middle of the night. They subjected me to a campaign of fear and intimidation, trying to silence me.

I was not the only one.

Every woman Hillary has found to be a threat to her and her husband's political capital has been subjected to choreographed investigations and terror campaigns.

I was a longtime supporter of the Clintons. I had met the up-and-coming Bill Clinton in 1989 and I thought he was a wonderful man: attractive, charming, bright, and personable. In 1992, my husband, Ed, and I raised money for Bill and I worked full-time in the "Virginians for Clinton" headquarters, which we set up in his suite of law offices. Very prominent people whom I respected, such as Ambassador Pamela Harriman, supported the Clintons. After Bill Clinton was elected president, I went to work in 1993 as a volunteer in the Social Office of the Clinton White House.

I believed in their vision of the future and their belief in the promise of tomorrow.

Hillary wants the American people to believe she is a champion of women's rights. "Women's issues are America's issues," she has said over and again, adding that "women's rights are human rights." She neglects to mention the plethora of women whose voices she silenced and whose rights she took away. She has not only enabled the behavior of her husband for almost forty years, she has engaged in a war of character assassination and caused both physical and emotional trauma to the women who were victims of her husband's depraved behavior.

In this book, you will learn that the Clintons are not the ambassadors of goodwill and progressivism you might think they are. And even though Hillary portrays herself as a champion for the rights of women and girls, she is not fighting for the best interests of women. She *is* the war on women. The stories of everyone who has been hurt by the Clintons deserve to be told.

INTRODUCTION BY ROGER STONE

Most people think they know the worst about Bill and Hillary Clinton. They're wrong. As someone who has worked on the "inside" of U.S. politics at the highest level, I've noticed that their personal lives are more stunning, lurid, and wildly dysfunctional than even their harshest critics could ever imagine.

This book doesn't focus on Monica Lewinsky, Whitewater, or the Clinton pardons. Instead, it's about the many, many ways in which the Clintons have been tied to sexual abuse, cover-ups, strong-arm tactics, drugs, lies, and the intimidation of victims. As Bill and Hillary have climbed to power, the people left in their wake have been silenced—until now.

On June 13, 2015, Hillary Clinton unveiled the broad themes of her candidacy for president in an address on Roosevelt Island, New York City. Once one of the most polarizing figures in American politics, she now shouts from the rooftops that she's an advocate for the poor, as well as for women and girls. But simply being a woman, unfortunately, does not make her the advocate that females in this country deserve.

Many in the mainstream press are quick to buy the Clintons' absurdly hypocritical narratives. Hillary Clinton is an advocate for women as long as you are not one of Bill Clinton's rape victims or girlfriends. And as Hillary rails against the excesses of wealthy hedge funders and others on Wall Street, she has used her own status as part of the power elite to bully people.

In *Clinton Cash*, Peter Schweizer recaps some of the Clintons' epic acts of greed. Now, in this book, I'm ready to shine the light on the Clintons' nonfinancial crimes. I believe in presenting the naked truth, and I am not holding back.

The Clintons have jointly abused an incredible number of people in their seemingly charmed scramble for power and money. Despite Hillary's ambition to first elect Bill president and then follow him to the White House, Bill was reckless in his epic philandering and open cocaine use during his period as attorney general and governor. It fell to Hillary to silence his victims and other witnesses, and she rationalized his outrageous behavior rather than hold accountable her sexually abusive and cocaine-driven husband.

Considering the effectiveness of the Clintons' spin machine and the bias in much of the mainstream media, it's not surprising that the public impression is that accusations of rape or sexual assault against Bill were disproven. So it is with the question of the former president's real father and his parentage of an African American child in Arkansas whom he has never acknowledged or embraced. Many Americans who have heard these accusations believe them to be false. As you shall see, the serial trail of deception, disinformation, and crime by the Clintons goes beyond what we remember from the 1990s.

Bill and Hillary are like a modern Tom and Daisy Buchanan. As F. Scott Fitzgerald wrote so eloquently almost a century ago, "They smashed up things and creatures and then retreated back into their money or their vast carelessness, or whatever it was that kept them together, and let other people clean up the mess they had made."

The Clintons have long had a loyal cadre of equally ambitious staffers who would do anything to cover up their bosses' misdeeds. Betsey Wright was famously in charge of "bimbo eruptions" whenever yet another ex-girlfriend—or sexual assault victim—would surface with details of her time with Bill. She was Bill's "cleanup woman."

Hillary Clinton positioning herself as a champion of women just doesn't measure up after a full and complete review of her public record and her connection to some of the most lurid and shocking scandals of the Clinton era. This is that story.

The Clintons have some sort of hidden, institutional immunity that maintains their viability despite the mountain of scandals connected with them. It is incredible to me that they get away with so much crap . . . until now.

The Clintons' lifelong history of lying and violating the law, seemingly without consequence or punishment, is a phenomenon known as elite deviance. Elite deviance is a condition sociologists say exists in a society when the elite of that society no longer believe that the rules apply to them. "It is not due primarily to psychopathological variables, but to the institutionalization of elite wrongdoing," says Professor David Simon in his landmark book now in its eighth printing, *Elite Deviance*.

Elite deviance is an anomaly in which a tiny few people who have enough material wealth, political influence, and personal connections can immunize themselves from considering the consequences of their most abhorrent, destructive, vile, and even criminal behavior. This describes the Clintons perfectly.

Elite deviance protects and perpetuates moral depravity and debased ethical relativism among the powerful and wealthy in our midst. It is an aberration of civil society that is only possible through the elites' cadres of supporters, sycophants, apologists, and fellow travelers in media, academia, politics, and high finance. This includes Clinton apologists James Carville, David Brock, Betsey Wright, Lanny Davis, and the now fully exposed George Stephanopoulos.

In short, elite deviance means that there are a few among us to whom the rules don't seem to apply. They can behave with impunity in ways that would otherwise incur severe, if not life-ending, repercussions for all others in the American criminal justice system. This pertains to the Bushes as well as the Clintons, as we shall see.

Hillary's decision to grasp for the presidency requires a thorough examination of the public and private records of Bill and Hillary Clinton and their adult daughter, Chelsea. The Clinton foibles did not end when Bill left the White House, though his brazen sale of presidential pardons in return for million-dollar contributions to the Clinton Foundation was a tip-off to the gusher of money and horse trading that would follow. Clinton's final days as president would be marred by the pardon he granted to international fugitive financier Marc Rich, in return for contributions from his ex-wife, Denise. Clinton would have to tell Democratic fixer Ben Barnes that he couldn't deliver a pardon for convicted Ponzi schemer Stephen Hoffenberg because "y'all got outbid by Rich."[2]

Unlike Clinton's impeachment or the semen-stained dress of Monica Lewinsky, the Clintons' use of the State Department and the Clinton Foundation to line their own pockets and the various lies they have told to bury evidence of quid pro quo has more than attracted the attention of the *New York Times,* the *Washington Post,* and the *Wall Street Journal.* Every week there are new revelations about monetary profiteering by the conniving Clintons.

Since the 1990s, many voters have come to think of Bill as the naughty, winking old uncle who gave them beer when their parents weren't looking and had a harmless weakness for women. That narrative is advantageous to the Clintons, because it's far more excusable than the truth. It works even better for Hillary, who is perfectly happy to be seen as the strong, smart woman who stood by her flawed but affable, philandering husband while launching a career to shatter the glass ceiling for women in government once and for all. But the American public needs to see past this false, dangerous narrative of a charming, goofily naïve Bubba and a poor, devoted Hillary.

In fact, despite the family image Bill and Hillary try to project to the American people, their marriage is a sham. While Bill can play an affable yokel with political skill, it is Hillary who wears the pants in the political relationship and served as a virtual co-president, steering and controlling public policy and making decisions in Waco, Texas, that would leave seventy-six dead.

The Clintons' activities have not only included Bill's physical rape of women, but also Hillary's degradation and psychological rape of women whom Bill has assaulted. Hillary, it will be seen, looks likely to authorize the heavy-handed private detectives who terrorize Bill's victims into silence. Behind the scenes, she calls them "sluts," "whores," and "bitches," blaming and shaming them for the unwanted physical attentions and violence of Bill. This is the "advocate for women and girls"?

The brave women who came forward to expose Bill Clinton's sexual abuse and assaults on them were denigrated as "trailer trash," and Clinton himself called it "trash for cash" when some of the supermarket tabloids like the *National Enquirer* and the *Globe* began paying women whose stories they found credible.

Brent Scher of the *Washington Free Beacon* produced a compelling study that showed that Hillary hasn't practiced what she preaches when it comes to female pay equality. In the U.S. Senate, the State Department, and the Clinton Foundation, women were systematically paid significantly less than men, yet Hillary makes pay inequality her battle cry. It's a glaring example of her inauthenticity. The Clintonistas floated a phony "internal analysis" to *Buzzfeed* in an attempt to discredit Scher, but close examination of both analyses shows that Hillary is a fraud on the subject of male-female pay inequality.

The Clintons' avarice is as stunning as Bill's sex crimes and Hillary's role in silencing his victims to cover them up. The Clintons are reliably estimated to have made close to $300 million since Bill Clinton left the presidency. Former President Clinton made over $200 million while Hillary made $100 million. Bill Clinton made $30 million while Hillary made $25 million last year alone. The Clintons are the 1 percent as well as the war on women.

Hillary is truly an elite, moving in rarefied air through a hushed world of luxury and deference. The former First Lady won't fly in anything less than a G5 and will stay in no hotel where she cannot get the Presidential Suite or that is not five star. The Clintons' life is one of a network of retainers, cut flowers, printed schedules, sold access, and public posturing.

This book is not about Bill Clinton's hypersexuality and consensual sex addiction. Clinton has had sex with dozens and very likely hundreds of women. In fact, to the point where former president Gerald Ford urged him to get professional help for his addiction. It is when Bill Clinton veers into rape and possibly pedophilia that the line must be drawn.

As a libertine, I think consensual sexual relationships are private business, and I had little regard for the House of Representatives' decision to impeach Clinton because he had sex with Monica Lewinsky (though Clinton's lie was the crime, not the act of receiving oral sex from the kneeling intern). I grew up during the Summer of Love and I admit to a wild sexual lifestyle in my younger years. But I stress anything I engaged in was among consenting adults and the idea of sex with children is repugnant. The most vile part of the Clinton story is about *nonconsenual* sex: rape. It's not a pretty word, but there is no other that more accurately describes Clinton's serial assaults on Eileen Wellstone, Juanita Broaddrick, Kathleen Willey, and probably dozens of others.

When the sex was nonconsensual Clinton would get physical, tearing the clothes off his victims and biting them on the lower lip, as at least three of his assault victims claimed, it constitutes a very different issue and crosses a line. Inappropriate relationships with underaged girls take the transgression to a new level. Unfortunately, Clinton has been a close personal friend of billionaire pedophile Jeffrey Epstein and others in his circle, especially during the time in his post presidency when he was linked to Epstein's hedonistic Orgy Island.

The Clintons will call this book old news. But no news is old if people haven't heard it and had a chance to consider its source. Clinton attack dog James Carville will pounce on this book. Journalists who can find no misdeed whatsoever by the Clintons in their long political career, will seek to dismiss the horrific details of the Clintons' trail of rape, drugs, cover-ups, greed, murder, and, at a minimum, the moving of the body of White House counsel Vince Foster after his suicide.

The Clintons' spin machine was adept at withholding so much of this information from the American people at the time it occurred that it bears examination.

There is much alleged about the Clintons that is not true. There is far more that is true and breathtaking in terms of the cold, cunning ambition, greed, accommodations, and power lust of Bill and Hillary Clinton.

I'm ready to tell the story I picked up from many years of insider knowledge. I had access to the exhaustive opposition research done by George H. W. Bush's presidential reelection campaign in 1992. Lee Atwater, who died of brain cancer in 1991, managed President Bush's 1988 campaign, spotting Clinton early as a threat to Poppy Bush's reelection. Atwater recognized that Clinton's Southern charm and moderation could appeal to white Democrats and return them to the Democratic fold, breaking up the mostly white coalition that had elected Bush in 1988. Atwater used his chairmanship at the Republican National Committee to begin deep opposition research on the up-and-coming Arkansas Governor.

After Atwater's death, many of the midlevel Atwater operatives in Bush's fumbled 1992 reelection campaign expressed dissatisfaction with the campaign's decision not to use this material. Campaign manager Bob Teeter, a pollster ("my god, a pollster as your campaign manager"—Richard Nixon) told the Atwater loyalists that Poppy himself had ruled out the disclosure of Clinton's drug use or his fathering of an illegitimate child who happened to be African American.

The 1992 presidential election was the only one that I professionally sat out since 1968. This book will reveal the strange and secret
working relationship between Bill Clinton and maverick billionaire
Ross Perot to deny Bush another term. In many ways, the Bush-
Clinton face-off in '92 was a "heads, I win; tails, you lose" election in
which one establishment candidate financed largely by the same interests simply outmaneuvered the other. Bush, under the tutelage of
White House Chief of Staff John Sununu, had hurt himself badly by
violating his Reagan-esque pledge not to raise taxes. Bush's inability
to notice a softening of the economy contributed to a vulnerability
exploited by Bill Clinton and abetted by the diminutive Texas eccentric. Clinton was elected with 57 percent of the vote opposing him;
he slid in with 43 percent. When George Bush plaintively glanced
at his watch in the televised debate, it was clear that he understood
that his days in the White House were limited, yet he and his family
have never shown the kind of rancor toward the Clintons that they
have with Republicans who have contested the elections of George
Bush.

Who better to expose this kabuki dance in which the Bushes and
Clintons aid each other's rehabilitation while pursuing essentially
the same policies when it comes to foreign war, the erosion of civil
liberties, massive debt, crony capitalism, and elite deviance? As
someone who spent the last forty years in the corroded rectum of
the two-party system and saw the ascent of the Bushes and Clintons
firsthand, I am the man to tell this story.

As one of the Republican Party's best-known opposition researchers, I have outlined the shocking truth about the Clintons, as
well as the Bushes, and their strange, mutually beneficial relationship in this tome. For the life of me, I can't figure out how Jeb Bush
awards Hillary a "Liberty Medal" for her actions and then runs
against her. Civility? Or shared criminality? I shall let the reader
decide.

Those who accuse me of being a Republican attack dog should
understand that I will soon publish a book on Jeb Bush and the

long history of crimes by the Bush family in January of next year. The Bush-Clinton alliance proves that the right-left divide is merely a distraction by the power elite who run America and have no ideology at all, other than the ideology of money and power. The Republican and Democratic parties have sadly morphed into one large, Wall Street–financed political establishment in which no matter which party gets elected, the erosion of our civil liberties continues and we pile up more debt, levy higher taxes on working people, and engage in endless foreign wars where America's interests are sometimes vague. The close alliance of the Bushes and Clintons shows that party is meaningless in today's political system.

Ironically, the first journalist to report extensively on the Clintons' wrongdoings was David Brock of the *American Spectator*. Brock interviewed Clinton's Arkansas State Police bodyguards who talked about Clinton's personal cocaine use, chronic infidelity, sexual assaults, and involvement with drug trafficking. The *American Spectator* stories had a profound impact. Today, Brock is a Clinton toady sucking compensation from at least three pro-Clinton front organizations. Today, Brock claims his *American Spectator* stories exposing Bill Clinton were false. He's lying.

Brock is engaging company, highly intelligent, and, like me, a bit of a dandy. He sported a monocle, cape, and gold-headed walking stick, an affectation known only to the *National Review*'s Richard Brookhiser in the past three decades. Brock let the rumor spread he was on heroin when heroin was chic. I don't think he was.

The success and impact of Brock's stories led Pittsburgh millionaire Richard Mellon Scaife to fund the Arkansas Project in which a number of journalists, including Christopher Ruddy and Ambrose Evans-Pritchard, would delve deeply into the activities of Bill and Hillary Clinton.

Ted Olson, who would later win the landmark case overturning a California anti-gay marriage proposition narrowly passed by the voters, represented George W. Bush in *Bush v. Gore*, and who would be named U.S. Solicitor General, was a board member of the

American Spectator Educational Foundation, which was the euphemistic name for the Arkansas Project. He is thought to have known about or played some role in the Arkansas Project. Olson's firm, Gibson, Dunn & Crutcher LLP, provided $14,000 worth of legal services, and he wrote or coauthored several articles that were paid for with Project funds. During Olson's Senate confirmation hearing for Solicitor General, majority Republicans blocked Democratic Senator Patrick Leahy's call for further committee inquiries on the subject of Olson's ties to the well-funded and deep-digging Arkansas Project. The Arkansas Project journalists would focus largely on the failed Whitewater real estate development and Clinton's hotel room sexual degradation of Paula Jones, but ultimately their investigations would lead to the broad panoply of Clinton crimes.

Ruddy, who wrote for the Scaife-owned *Pittsburgh Post-Gazette*, would pen a well-written book examining the mysterious death of Vince Foster. Ruddy would also publish a collection of Newsmax Media stories in book form, establishing the story of Danney Williams, Bill's alleged illegitimate African American son. Ruddy would later give $1.5 million to the Clinton Foundation, which he said he did for charitable purposes.

We have carefully sifted through the research of the Arkansas Project and its many trails and offshoots. We can report that not all of the allegations against the Clintons are true. Unfortunately for Bill and Hillary, most of the allegations involving sexual assault, drug use and trafficking, financial chicanery, the use of violence by Arkansas state troopers to silence Bill's victims, and the use of the Arkansas Economic Development Commission as a piggy bank to launder both campaign funds and graft are entirely accurate.

It is only by comparing the so-called Atwater files and the continuing opposition research conducted by the Republican National Committee after Atwater's death with the fruits of the Arkansas Project that one can pin down the truth between Bill and Hillary Clinton.

There is no question that some Clinton critics are excessive. There are widespread claims that the Clintons are responsible for the death of as many as eighty-three people whose knowledge stood in the way of their political ascent. Based on our investigation, the Clintons are only plausibly responsible for the deaths of half the people on this list. They are not responsible for the death of John F. Kennedy, Jr., as some researchers have claimed, though the number of individuals who are both knowledgeable of and pivotal to the Clintons' grasp for power who die in plane crashes defies mathematical odds. For the purpose of this book, we will focus on the deaths of teenagers Don Henry and Kevin Ives, who were most likely witnesses to the rampant cocaine-trafficking going on in Arkansas where Bill Clinton backed an inept medical examiner in a sloppy cover-up and the murder of former CIA operative and later Clinton campaign security director Jerry Parks. When Clinton tried to stiff Parks on an $83,000 invoice, Parks threatened to reveal what he knew about Governor Clinton and the drug-trafficking operating out of Mena, Arkansas, which we will examine in some detail. Parks was forced off the road near his home and riddled with bullets. Murder is very much a part of the Clinton rise to power and that's without counting the eighteen children killed in the Waco assault. Senator Arlen Specter, who headed a Senate panel investigating the Waco incident, told me that credible testimony indicated that Hillary Clinton gave the "go order" to Janet Reno and Webb Hubbell.

The second-tier hitmen for the Clintons, former conservative firebrand and left-wing entrepreneur David Brock, the overexposed Cajun James Carville, my fellow Hungarian Paul Begala, a decent fellow, and Joe Conason, will claim I am a "political dirty trickster and hitman." I admit to having a bias, and I will let the reader decide whether the case my coauthor Robert Morrow and I lay out against Bill, Hillary, and Chelsea Clinton is valid.

Based on history, we know exactly how the Clintons and their spinning machine will react to the extraordinary and deadly accurate revelations in this book. After saying it's all old news, they will blame right-wing extremists for smearing them. Finally, they will seek to discredit the authors based on our partisanship and past political activities. This book, however, is not about Roger Stone or Robert Morrow; the facts outlined and carefully sourced here speak for themselves. Let the reader decide.

Speaking of dirty tricks, I can reveal that Hillary Clinton would use her own dirty trickster. Here's what I've noticed: Sidney Blumenthal, who was giving Hillary political and intelligence advice that she passed on to her State Department staff and instructed them to follow. Blumenthal invented the fiction that the assault on our embassy in Benghazi was influenced by an anti-Islamic video aired in another country. Thus, Blumenthal invented the cover story that Hillary and President Barack Obama used to hide the fact that U.S. interests had been hit by al-Qaeda before the election. Blumenthal directed the dirty tricks campaign against Bill's critics in the impeachment scandal and played a heavy role as Hillary's henchman in the media's effort to demonize Hillary's sexual assault victims.

Blumenthal, the father of legendary anti-Israel radical Max Blumenthal, played so dirty against Obama at Hillary's direction that Obama barred him from a State Department job. Sid, who once did dirty tricks for Senator Gary Hart, vilifying those who suspected his Bill Clinton–like philanderings, never disclosed to Hillary that he was being paid by corporate entities trying to make a score in postwar Libya. Blumenthal also pushed Hillary to topple Khadafi, the eccentric madman who had changed sides, providing intelligence on Islamic terrorists to the United States and replace him with a Muslim Brotherhood puppet more to Max Blumenthal's liking. Sidney was simultaneously on the payroll of the eccentric David Brock's money-making venture, *Media Matters for America*, as well as the pro-Clinton front Correct the Record. And according to Democratic sources, he was also negotiating with American Priorities. All three are dark-money Clinton operations.

At the same time, Bill Clinton demanded that the Bill, Hillary & Chelsea Clinton Foundation pay Blumenthal ten thousand dollars per month. Why would a charity need a hitman? His real job was to coach Hillary, serving as a backchannel spin doctor. His freelancing as a Clinton flunky on Libya created the false narrative about why Americans had given their lives—pinning their murders on the notorious anti-Islamic YouTube video.

Don't get me wrong. Sid is wicked smart and charming company. I knew him well when he was a writer for the *New Republic* and a behind-the-scenes mover for Senator Hart's presidential campaign, before latching on to the Clintons. An Obama White House staffer told me that the Obama camp was aware that Blumenthal was spreading the rumor that the senator from Illinois was gay, connecting him with two members of Obama's Chicago church choir who were both viciously murdered. Blumenthal claimed to journalists that both had been former Obama lovers. He also outlined to the journalists Obama's connections to communist Frank Marshall Davis. You can see why White House Chief of Staff Rahm Emanuel enforced the Obama ban of an administration job for Blumenthal.

When the Clintonistas attack me as a dirty trickster, remember who they have working for them. Politics ain't beanbag, and the Clintons play hardball, at the same time whining when hardball tactics are used to expose their prevarications, dramas, and self-dealing. While being held to the lowest possible standard—"There is no proof of our crimes"—they continue to gripe that they are being held to a higher public standard than others.

It is also Blumenthal who has convinced Hillary to abandon the Clinton Coalition of 1992 and 1996 in which the former Arkansas governor moved his party to the center and ran competitively in the South as well as in the West by appealing to moderates, swing voters, and white Democrats. Bill Clinton became president by getting white conservative and moderate Democrats to join liberals in voting democratic. Obama turned this strategy on its ear by taking more liberal positions and winning simply by maximizing turnout in the liberal base. Obama won without competing in states like Kentucky, Louisiana, Tennessee, or West Virginia, all states won by

Bill Clinton. Obama so maximized the votes of liberals that he won even while losing among independent voters. Blumenthal has counseled Hillary, choosing to move her left on gay marriage, immigration, criminal justice, voting rights, the incredibly hypocritical call for pay equality for women, and adopting anti–Wall Street rhetoric, mostly to box out Massachusetts Senator Elizabeth Warren.

The path Sidney and Hillary have chosen is a narrow one with no room for error. Their strategy depends on a disproportionate level of support among women. It assumes the young, non-white, female vote is completely transferable to Hillary Clinton. Unlike Bill Clinton, Hillary will chase no swing voters and will concentrate on turning out greater numbers of the hardcore left. Any woman who is considering voting for Hillary should read this book.

I first met Bill Clinton on a street corner during a governor's conference in New Orleans in the 1980s. I was standing with "Big Peter Kelly," former Democrat state chairman from Connecticut and my partner in the heavy-duty lobbying firm of Black, Manafort, Stone & Kelly. He shouldn't be confused with "Little Peter Kelly" the Democratic state chairman from California who has gone on to his maker. Kelly had raised money for Clinton and knew him well. He introduced us as the governor, who was wearing cowboy boots and a huge grin, walked toward us on a Bourbon Street full of revelers. "What are you doing out here, Governor?" I asked.

"Trawling," said Bill Clinton. He would soon wander away to chat up a pair of girls who looked to be in their late teens. "That man will be president," I told Kelly.

Even then, I saw a kind of hillbilly charm and insatiable appetite in Governor Clinton. As Senator Bob Kerrey of Nebraska said, Clinton is an "uncommonly good liar."[3]

The next time I saw Clinton was at President Richard Nixon's funeral where I was invited with other Nixon friends and family as well as the former presidents and their spouses for a receiving line for the dignitaries before the president's burial. Nixon's casket loomed in the background.

"Don't think I'm crazy," my wife, Nydia, said, "but I think Clinton's giving me the eye." Indeed, the former president's eyes would follow my wife anywhere in the room as he looked over the shoulder of those whose hands he was shaking.

When he came to my wife in the receiving line, he slipped her a card that said "President of the United States" and had an extension listed. "If you are ever in Washington, look me up," he said to my Latin beauty. Mrs. Clinton wasn't so warm. "Hello, I'm Roger Stone," I said. "Yes, I know who you are," she said, coldly passing me on to the next person in line.

Far from her public image, Hillary Clinton is a violent, scheming, ambitious, foul-mouthed woman with an insatiable appetite for luxury, money, and power. Hillary is also a physically violent person, famous for hitting, scratching, and throwing things at her cheating husband. She is a classic abuser of anyone who gets in the way of her drive for power.

"Hillary Clinton doesn't play by the rules. That's not a partisan attack. It's not a talking point. It's not a fantasy. It's a fact," said veteran reporter Ron Fournier, who was the Associated Press's Washington bureau in Little Rock during Clinton's governorship and now is a senior political columnist of the *National Journal*.

Somehow, while the Clintons were extremely polarizing during Bill's stormy presidency, as Obama took over, Bill's public esteem grew. Former president George Bush would help Clinton rehabilitate his public image as the families who had moved drugs together through Mena, Arkansas, made a great show of raising money together for Haiti relief. Millions upon millions were raised, yet most went into the pockets of Bush and Clinton cronies while less than $10 million was spent for emergency housing on the Haitian isles.

Most thought it brilliant of Barack Obama to put Hillary in his cabinet, adhering to that old rule from *The Godfather*: "Keep your friends close but your enemies closer." In this way, he inoculated himself from public criticism from former President Bill Clinton. Obama was aware that Clinton had disparaged him in a conversation

THE CLINTONS' WAR ON WOMEN

with Ted Kennedy, saying, "A few years ago, this guy would have been getting us coffee."[4]

The *New York Post* reported the claim of author Ed Klein that Obama White House advisor Valerie Jarrett leaked the story about Hillary's selective erasure of more than 66 percent of her emails during her service as Secretary of State. The destruction of the evidence of the manipulation of the State Department for Clinton Foundation money-making purposes contained in Hillary's emails means the smoking gun had been destroyed when Hillary's agents, henchwoman Cheryl Mills and traveling aide and close companion Huma Abedin, sanitized Hillary's emails, deciding what would be turned over to the State Department and what would be erased forever.

But the circumstantial case is convincing that the Clintons have manipulated their control of the State Department and their charitable foundations and projects to make millions and to augment a regal and cosseted lifestyle.

As activists, Robert Morrow and I were critical of Hillary Clinton when she ran for president in 2008, but we wondered why Congressional Republicans and special prosecutor Ken Starr would bring their weakest and most controversial case against Clinton instead of exposing his more serious wrongdoing, like the laundering of Chinese money for political campaigns and his virtual sale of U.S. military secrets through the Loral Corporation in return for more Chinese campaign cash.

Clinton would experience two near-death experiences in his successful two climbs to the White House. When his consensual affair with blonde beauty Gennifer Flowers threatened to destroy his presidential candidacy in the New Hampshire primary, *60 Minutes* director Don Hewitt would allow Clinton to minimize his relationship with the sultry singer and admit on air that the incident was "causing pain in my marriage." The carefully edited "news piece" would save Clinton's candidacy. Far more important than lying on *60 Minutes* about the Gennifer Flowers affair is what happened five months later on June 26, 1992. That is when, according to many people who say they have firsthand knowledge, three goons were thought to have been sent to the condominium of Gary Johnson—who coincidentally was both the neighbor of Gennifer Flowers and also at that time the lawyer for Clinton nemesis Larry Nichols.

Three recognizable Arkansas state troopers were sent, according to sources. Their job was to retrieve a security camera videotape in the possession of Johnson that showed Bill Clinton making multiple visits to Gennifer's love nest. If that tape had been made public it could have been very damaging to the 1992 Clinton campaign.

To this day, Johnson feels traumatized by what happened. Violent men, he said, broke into his apartment and seized his VHS tape. Then, he said, they proceeded to give him a brutal Arkansas beat down. The beating was so savage that Gary Johnson never recovered physically or psychologically from what happened to him on that Friday, twenty-three years ago. Clinton's Arkansas state troopers left with the incriminating security camera VHS tape and left Johnson as a destroyed, crumpled mess, barely alive on the floor of his condominium.

For those who say the Clintons don't use violence to attain their political ends, we give you the 1992 beating of Gary Johnson.

In 1999, in the midst of the Clinton impeachment crisis, NBC would tape a chilling interview with Clinton rape victim Juanita Broaddrick. Broaddrick spoke to aggressive TV journalist Lisa Myers and she spoke about Clinton's physical assault on her as she wept. NBC pointedly sat on this tape until *after* Clinton had survived the impeachment vote. Clinton survived his second near-death experience, although Broaddrick was one of three women who described Clinton savagely biting their lower lip to both disable them and as a distinct warning to keep their mouths shut. "You better get some ice on that," Clinton said before bolting from the hotel room where the rape took place.[5]

Clinton Cash stunningly recounts how Hillary used her office to enrich herself, her husband, and the family's foundation. In fact, the

Clinton Foundation is a slush fund for grifters. Both Clintons are notorious moochers. The pizza delivery boy who recalled delivering pizza to Hillary's dorm room at Wellesley College recalled being stiffed on any tips, and Bill Clinton notoriously carried no cash, leaning on friends and associates to pick up the tabs for his meals, drinks, and revelry.[6]

"Remember, too, that neither of them ever gave up the grifter habit," wrote veteran reporter Michael Goodwin in a recent *New York Post* article. "On the way out of the White House door, they grabbed goodies like thieves in the night. And the evidence is solid that he sold a pardon to Marc Rich for cash and pardons for votes for Hillary's first Senate race involving crooked New York Hasidim and violent Puerto Rican nationalists."

"We're still seventeen months from Election Day, and already Bob Kerrey's great line comes to mind," Goodwin continued. "The former Nebraska senator and governor once accused fellow Democrat Bill Clinton of being 'an uncommonly good liar.'"[7]

The Clinton Foundation, however, is a smooth-running money machine envisioned and built initially by Doug Band, Clinton's body man who would become like a son to the former president and use the position to reap hundreds of millions for himself while still on the Foundation payroll. Because of his travels with Clinton, Band may be the man who knows too much and he bears special examination.

Also under the microscope is Hillary's closest aide and travel companion, the exotic and mysterious Huma Abedin—chic and beautiful wife of former Congressman Anthony Weiner. That Hillary and Abedin would bond is obvious by the fact that both have been publicly humiliated by their abusive husbands yet neither will split with their legal mate because it would disadvantage them in their reach for power. Abedin herself is controversial, raising suspicions that will be more closely examined here—among them, troubling ties to the Muslim Brotherhood and the special deal through which she was allowed to be on the payroll of the State Department while also being paid by Doug Band's Teneo, as Band was still collecting heavy paychecks from the Clinton Foundation.

Hillary is reportedly furious about Weiner's role in the scandal in which he sexted images of his turgid penis to women on the Internet. Hillary's greatest concern is that Weiner's foibles will remind voters of Bill Clinton's flagrant philandering and his Oval Office peccadilloes including violating Monica Lewinsky with a cigar.

The *New York Post* has reported that the adult Chelsea Clinton is like her mother: brusque, abrasive, entitled, and greedy. Chelsea's treatment of Clinton Foundation staff and her outrageous demands have caused a quick turnover at the Clinton Foundation, and those who objected to the ratios of spending in which little is used for actual charitable activity while millions are used to provide a jet-set lifestyle for the Clintons were removed by the young princess. The apple doesn't fall far from the tree.

There is more than strong circumstantial evidence that Chelsea is not the biological daughter of Bill, which would explain the extensive plastic surgery to rebuild her face in her twenties. Webb Hubbell's substantial and unique role in Hillary's life could reveal the Clintons' deepest secret. Chelsea was paid $600,000 annually by NBC to do virtually nothing. NBC's parent company, General Electric, got an enormous defense contract approved by Secretary of State Clinton right after the payoff to her daughter. Finding themselves under fire, the Clintons put out their daughter to defend the discrepancies in the Foundation's tax filing and the omissions that showed that Hillary violated her agreement with the Obama White House to carefully vet the Foundation's activities. The Clintons also used Chelsea to try to blunt criticism that the Foundation took millions from Saudi Arabia, Qatar, Oman, and the Arab Emirates, nations that brutally oppressed women, denying them education, legal rights, and the ability to control their own destinies. Chelsea could offer no defense for the Foundation's grabbing of the tainted Islamic cash. We will examine Chelsea Clinton in greater detail.

The people will be reminded of the Hillary Clinton who stole the White House furniture upon leaving the presidential residence, lied about being under sniper fire in Bosnia, and concealed the Rose Law Firm billing records in Whitewater that would show that, although all of the equity holders in the shady real estate deal lost money, the Clintons were still able to extract $800,000 in campaign funds, enough to saturate Arkansas television in 1982. There is Hillary's cattle futures windfall and of course her repetition of the claim that the attack on the U.S. facility in Benghazi was a mob incited by an anti-Islam video, when Clinton knew it was a precision military takedown tied to al-Qaeda. Hillary would repeat this lie at a memorial service for the four men killed hours after she had received a high-level briefing disproving the claim.

We will also reveal the Clintons' deepest family secrets that they are desperate to conceal from the voters in 2016. In her effort to appear human, Hillary has talked about the need to "nurture babies" in the earliest days of their existence, saying "80 percent" of brain growth occurs in the early stages of child development. This concern for children is another stunning example of Hillary's hypocrisy, as she holds complete responsibility for the cold-blooded murder in Waco.

If Hillary is concerned about babies, one must wonder about the abandonment of the man who says he is Bill's biracial, "illegitimate" son, Danney Williams, along with five grandchildren whom Clinton has refused to acknowledge or support. The false claim that a DNA test cleared Clinton of being his father is exposed here. "I just want to shake his hand," Williams once said. Incredibly, George Bush's 1992 opposition research campaign revealed the existence of Bill's son, but Bush himself ordered that the material not be used against his opponent, former fellow CIA alum Bill Clinton. Answers about Chelsea Clinton's parentage and Bill Clinton's real father are some more of the shocking facts revealed here. Let's see if you can handle the truth.

This book isn't about the Clintons' policies; it's about the Clintons as leaders, as whole people.

Since puppeteering my own election to student council almost half a century ago, I've been fascinated by the games people play in jockeying for power. I participate myself, at a high level. All the while I pay close attention, not just to white papers and policy documents, but also to how people act and dress and carry themselves and treat the people around them when they think no one important is watching.

Meanwhile my coauthor, Robert Morrow, digs dirt in the trenches. The Clintons sicken him. A Princeton graduate and consummate Southerner, he's seen the messy aftermath of the Clintons' systematic intimidation. From people too hurt and scared to speak up, who are sometimes permanently traumatized, he's heard over and over how Arkansas state troopers would do Bill's violent bidding. He's talked to women intimidated, threatened, and silenced by both Clintons. For this book, he did painstaking research and talked to an array of anonymous sources. Often what he heard made him even madder. And rightly so.

Hillary is eyeing the most powerful position in the world. She'd be the first female president, but she's not the one we deserve. Americans—including women who have been sexually attacked or intimidated, and anyone who has been bullied—deserve better. At the very least, you deserve to know more about the Clintons than mainstream media reveals. Unfortunately, the Clintons' personal history is ugly.

Bill and Hillary Clinton are the penicillin-resistant syphilis of the American body politic.

PART 1

THE WAR ON WOMEN

CHAPTER 1

THE RHODES SCHOLAR RAPIST

"Not since Moses walked through the Red Sea has a man had the ability to part everything that goes before him."

—Jaci Stephen, newspaper columnist[8]

Bill Clinton is a gifted individual.

Clinton is so intelligent that he completes the *New York Times* Sunday crossword puzzle with speed and ease in ink. Author John Gartner said Clinton has an "astounding intelligence," with an IQ "off the map, higher than we can really measure."[9]

Coupled with this daunting intellect is a powerful charisma.

British journalist and author Jenni Murray had interviewed countless politicians and celebrities, but none, in her estimation, had the magnetism of Clinton. "As he paused in front of you, he stooped slightly, engaged you fully, looked you directly in the eyes, asked you questions, listened to your answers, laughed at your witty repartee, and, yes, he twinkled," Murray recalled.

"He made you feel for those few short moments that you were the only woman in the world and he'd never met anyone as interesting or as lovely as you."[10]

Clinton charmed and influenced people, opined *Forbes* writer Mark Hughes, "because he made them feel special, he made them feel that he understood them and cared deeply about what they felt and wanted, and he made them feel that what he wanted and what they wanted were the same thing. This last aspect of his personality is the most amazing—he can convince you to go along with what he wants, while making you feel it was really what you wanted all along."

Clinton has long used his intelligence and personal charm for political power and control. He has also used these same gifts to intimidate, trick, or force women into having sex with him.

For Clinton, sex is an undying need.

Author Daniel Halper recently met with a close Clinton friend and quizzed him on just exactly how promiscuous Bill has been. "Everybody you think he fucked, he did—and the more dangerous the better. . . . All genius is flawed," the Clinton comrade said. "The great artists are addicted, whether to alcohol or they're drug addicts or whatever. His addiction is pussy."[11]

Former president Gerald Ford thought Clinton should have been admitted to a sex addiction clinic. "He's sick—he's got an addiction. He needs treatment," Ford told *Daily News* Washington bureau chief Thomas M. DeFrank. "I'll tell you one thing: He didn't miss one good looking skirt at any of the social occasions."[12]

In 1999, the political news website *Capitol Hill Blue* published an important exposé, "Juanita isn't the only one: Bill Clinton's long history of sexual violence against women dates back some 30 years." "Juanita" was Juanita Broaddrick, a former nursing home administrator who alleged that Clinton raped her in an Arkansas hotel room in the 1970s. The authors of this historically significant piece, Daniel J. Harris and Theresa Hampton, dug further back—to the behavior of Clinton at the University of Oxford.

Indeed, Clinton is one of the few Rhodes Scholars *without* a degree from Oxford. That is because at age twenty-three, Clinton was expelled from the oldest university in the English-speaking world for sexually assaulting a nineteen-year-old coed named Eileen Wellstone. Harris and Hampton discovered that Wellstone was assaulted after she "met [Clinton] at a pub near Oxford where the future President was a student in 1969. A retired State Department employee, who asked not to be identified, confirmed that he spoke with the family of the girl and filed a report with his superiors. Clinton admitted having sex with the girl, but claimed it was consensual. The victim's family declined to pursue the case."[13]

A recollection from Cliff Jackson, a lawyer who attended nearby St. John's College, provides a glimpse into Clinton's growth during his Oxford years. Clinton recounted a story to Jackson regarding President Lyndon B. Johnson, who escalated and presided over the Vietnam War, having sex with an antiwar hippie on the floor of the Oval Office. A secretary had walked in on the president and his paramour.

Clinton's reactions gave great insight into his cavalier attitude toward sexual conduct   ·

"Sure, it's a funny little story and we can all laugh," Jackson remembered. "But the impression I got was that Bill thought it was so neat that Lyndon Johnson could get away with something like that. It was just his reaction to it that made it stand out in my mind. It was like—it's just the power, the idea that Lyndon had the audacity to do something like that right in the Oval Office at the height of the war. It was something above locker-room snickering. More like, 'How slick, how neat that Lyndon could get away with this.'"[14]

The University of Oxford and the State Department, in fear of a scandal, covered up the Wellstone assault, and Clinton promptly disappeared from the prestigious institution. Even though he had an opportunity that many Americans would have killed for, he squandered it. The sexual assaults were his most damning offense, but also, according to *Capitol Hill Blue*, he was far from a good student: "The State Department official who investigated the incident said Clinton's interests appeared to be drinking, drugs and sex, not studies. 'I came away from the incident with the clear impression that this was a young man who was there to party, not study,' he said."

In his book *Unlimited Access: An FBI Agent Inside the Clinton White House*, FBI agent Gary Aldrich stated that his investigation of Clinton "reveals that after the winter of 1969, Mr. Clinton embarked on a tour of Europe, and there are suggestions that [University of Oxford] school officials told Mr. Clinton that he was no longer welcome on campus, but that could not be confirmed."[15]

A 1999 exposé of Clinton's long history of rape and sexual assault, which ran in *Capitol Hill Blue,* included some damning stories. First, the article mentioned Juanita Broaddrick, the Arkansas nursing home operator who told NBC's Lisa Myers she was raped by Clinton. NBC shelved the interview, saying it was confirming all parts of the story, but finally aired it. Broaddrick also took her story to the *Wall Street Journal*, and soon the *Washington Post* and other publications published her story of brutal rape at the hands of the future president. White House attorney David Kendall issued a public denial of the Broaddrick rape.

According to that *Capitol Hill Blue* article, Eileen Wellstone was the first of many women to be targeted by a young Bill Clinton.

In 1972, a twenty-two-year-old woman told Yale University's campus police that she was sexually assaulted by Bill Clinton, and although no charges were filed, a retired policeman confirmed the incident to *Capitol Hill Blue*. The woman herself was also tracked down and confirmed it, though she elected to stay anonymous.

Next, in 1974, a female student at the University of Arkansas complained that then law school instructor Bill Clinton tried to prevent her from leaving his office during a conference, groping her and forcing his hand inside her blouse. Although she complained to her faculty advisor, who confronted Clinton, the complaint again failed to go anywhere, as Clinton claimed the student "came on" to him. The student left the school shortly after the incident, and recently—like the Yale student—confirmed the incident but declined to go on record. According to the article, several former students at the university confirmed the incident in confidential interviews and also said there were other reports of Clinton attempting to force himself on female students.

Along with Broaddrick's claim of rape in 1978, the volunteer in Clinton's gubernatorial campaign said she suffered a bruised and torn lip when Clinton bit her during the incident. For the following two years, during Clinton's first term as Arkansas governor, the article says that state troopers assigned to protect him knew about at least seven other complaints from women who said Clinton forced himself on them sexually or attempted to do so.

One retired state trooper said in an interview that the common joke among those assigned to protect Clinton was, "Who's next?" Another former state trooper said his coworkers would often escort women to the governor's hotel room after political events, often more than one at a time.

The stories kept coming. A Little Rock legal secretary named Carolyn Moffet claimed that in 1979, she met the governor at a political fundraiser and shortly afterward received an invitation to meet him in a hotel room. She was escorted there by a state trooper. When she arrived, she said, he was sitting on a couch wearing an undershirt and nothing else. He pointed at his penis and told her to suck it. She said she didn't even do that for her boyfriend, but the governor reportedly got angry and grabbed her head, which he shoved into his lap—before she pulled away and ran out of the room.

And there were more stories, so similar and so damning that they paint a shocking picture of the future president's sexual proclivities.

Elizabeth Ward, a former Miss Arkansas who won the Miss America crown in 1982, apparently told friends she was forced by Clinton to have sex with him shortly after she won her state crown. In the late 1990s, Ward, who is now married with the last name of

Gracen (from her first marriage), told an interviewer she had had consensual sex with Clinton.

But close friends say that in private she describes it as a sexual assault. Perhaps she was intimidated into silence.

An Arkansas state employee named Paula Corbin filed a sexual harassment case against Clinton after she said the then governor exposed himself and demanded oral sex in a Little Rock hotel room. Clinton settled the case with Paula Corbin in 1998 with an $850,000 cash payment.

Sandra Allen James, a former Washington, DC, political fundraiser, told *Capitol Hill Blue* that presidential candidate-to-be Clinton invited her to his hotel room during a political trip to the nation's capital in 1991, pinned her against the wall and stuck his hand up her dress. She says she screamed loud enough for the Arkansas state trooper stationed outside the hotel suite to bang on the door and ask if everything was alright. Then, she said, Clinton released her and she fled the room.

When she reported the incident to her boss, he advised her to keep her mouth shut if she wanted to keep working. She has since married and left Washington. She later said that she since learned that other women had similar stories during Clinton's presidential run.

Christy Zercher, a flight attendant on Clinton's campaign plane in 1992, reported that he exposed himself to her, grabbed her breasts, and made explicit remarks about oral sex. A video filmed on board the plane by ABC News showed an obviously inebriated Clinton with his hand between another young flight attendant's legs. Troublingly, Zercher said later in an interview that White House attorney Bruce Lindsey tried to pressure her into not going public about the assault.

Kathleen Willey was a volunteer at the White House when Clinton grabbed her, fondled her breast, and pressed her hand against his genitals during an Oval Office meeting in November, 1993. Willey, who told her story in a *60 Minutes* interview, became a target of a White House–directed smear campaign after she went public.

It is incredibly disturbing to think about the pain and suffering caused by Bill Clinton's assaults on women throughout his political career.

And it is also disturbing to ponder the cover-ups and intimidation that often followed the sexual assault. According to that *Capitol Hill Blue* article:

> Miss James, the Washington fundraiser who confirmed the encounter with Clinton at the Four Seasons Hotel in Washington, but first said she would not appear publicly because anyone who does so is destroyed by the Clinton White House.
>
> "My husband and children deserve better than that," she said when first contacted two weeks ago. After reading the Broaddrick story Friday, however, she called back and gave permission to use her maiden name, but said she had no intention of pursuing the matter.
>
> "I wasn't raped, but I was trapped in a hotel room for a brief moment by a boorish man," she said. "I got away. He tried calling me several times after that, but I didn't take his phone calls. Then he stopped. I guess he moved on."
>
> But Miss James also retreated from public view this week after other news organizations contacted her.
>
> The former Miss Moffet, the legal secretary who says Clinton tried to force her into oral sex in 1979, has since married and left the state. She says that when she told her boyfriend, who was a lawyer and supporter of Clinton, about the incident, he told her to keep her mouth shut.
>
> "He said that people who crossed the governor usually regretted it and that if I knew what was good for me I'd forget that it ever happened," she said. "I haven't forgotten it. You don't forget crude men like that."

Like two other women, the former Miss Moffet declined further interviews. A neighbor said she had received threatening phone calls.

The other encounters were confirmed with more than 30 interviews with retired Arkansas state employees, former state troopers and former Yale and University of Arkansas students. Like others, they refused to go public because of fears of retaliation from the Clinton White House.[16]

On November 21, 2014, columnist Joan Vennochi of the *Boston Globe* wrote, "Rape allegations hurt Bill Cosby but sail past Bill Clinton." Vennochi commented on how Bill Cosby's career had just been obliterated after the rape charges against him reached critical mass, yet Bill Clinton, in 2014, had apparently skated past accusations of rape and sexual assault.

"Bill Cosby's career as a beloved comedian is in shambles in the wake of decades-old accusations of rape and sexual assault," Vennochi wrote. "In the past week alone—as more and more women come forward with allegations—NBC has called off a proposed new Cosby comedy, Netflix has canceled a 77th Cosby birthday celebration, and the cable network TV Land has pulled reruns of 'The Cosby Show.' Yet, amid media uproar, Clinton's career as revered statesman soars.[17]

"Power—who has it, who doesn't, and how it can for years insulate the holder of it—is the common thread between Cosby, Clinton, and their accusers," Vennochi wrote. "Asked why she didn't go to police, one of Cosby's accusers said she didn't think anyone would take the word of a nineteen-year-old woman over a celebrity father figure like Cosby. As she put it, 'Mr. America: Mr. Jello, as I called him.'"[18]

The Clinton legacy is left unblemished, cleansed with the classic defense that his public policies were more important than his private failings.

"Meanwhile, the Clinton spin machine did its best to portray his accusers as 'nuts or sluts,' employing the classic defense lawyer strategy against women who dare to hold men accountable for their actions," Vennochi wrote.[19]

CHAPTER 2

THE MANY ASSAULTS ON JUANITA BROADDRICK

"You will never believe what the motherfucker did now, he tried to rape some bitch!"

—Hillary Clinton on Bill, as told by Larry Nichols to Robert Morrow on June 1, 2015

On April 25, 1978, Arkansas attorney general Bill Clinton raped Juanita Broaddrick without a condom and savagely bit her top lip to subdue her.

Broaddrick was a county coordinator for Bill and a volunteer in his '78 gubernatorial campaign. She had come to Little Rock to attend a nursing conference and she was lodged at the Camelot Hotel. A week prior, Clinton, on a campaign stop, had visited the nursing home where Broaddrick worked and invited her to tour his headquarters upon arrival in the capital city. She called Clinton and asked to meet him at his office. Clinton offered the downstairs coffee shop in her hotel as an alternative. Broaddrick agreed. Clinton again called and suggested Broaddrick's hotel room as a meeting spot.

"I was a little bit uneasy," Broaddrick recalled. "But, I felt, ah, a real friendship toward this man and I didn't really feel any, um, any danger in him coming to my room."[20]

After all, Clinton at the time was the state's top law enforcement official with a bid in place to become the de facto head of Arkansas.

Once he arrived, though, it did not take Clinton long to drop any pretenses and make a hard, forceful advance.

In what would become a trademark of his sexual assaults, Clinton violently bit Juanita's upper lip and threw her on the bed. "I was just very frightened, and I tried to get away from him and I told him 'no,' that I didn't want this to happen but he wouldn't listen to me," Broaddrick recalled. Clinton "was such a different person at the moment, he was just a vicious awful person. . . . It was a real panicky, panicky situation. I was even to the point where I was getting very noisy, you know, yelling to 'please stop.' And that's when he pressed down on my right shoulder and he would bite my lip."[21]

Clinton raped Broaddrick twice within a span of thirty minutes. The first time, Bill bit her lip so hard he almost severed it. Clinton raped Broaddrick a second time after he detected a new erection. "Then he said, 'My god, I can do it again,' and he did," Broaddrick recalled. After Clinton raped her, Broaddrick said she "felt paralyzed and started to cry."

Broaddrick said she will never forget how Clinton calmly donned his sunglasses shortly after ejaculating. He then offered a suggestion for her mangled lips. "You better get some ice on that," Clinton said."[22] He told Juanita not to worry about getting pregnant because he had the mumps as a kid and was sterile. Incredibly, a few months earlier, Clinton had impregnated his mistress, Gennifer Flowers, and given her $200 to get an abortion.

Broaddrick's friend Norma Rogers-Kelsay found Juanita shaken in her hotel room. "I was sitting there crying and so upset at the time. . . . I felt like the next person coming through the door [was coming] to get rid of [my] body," Broaddrick said. "I absolutely could not believe what had happened to me."[23]

Award-winning investigative journalist John Doughtery said Rogers-Kelsay "found Broaddrick in a state of shock, her lip swollen, mouth bruised, and her pantyhose torn at the crotch." Kelsay said Juanita "told me they had intercourse against her will." Kelsay told NBC News that Broaddrick was in "quite bad shape" and her "lips were swollen, at least double in size."

Broaddrick confided in Norma Rogers-Kelsay, her then boyfriend (later husband), David, and few others. Witness Phillip Yoakum said that Rogers-Kelsay drove Broaddrick home and had to stop at regular intervals to put ice on her swollen mouth. Yoakum says that her lip was "damaged to the point of nearly being torn into two pieces."[24]

David remembered that "her top lip was black."

Broaddrick, burdened with shock, shame, and denial, put the incident behind her. In 1984, when her nursing home won an award, she received a letter from then Governor Clinton. "I admire you very much," Clinton had handwritten.[25] Broaddrick believed this meant that the Governor was grateful for her silence.

Thirteen years after the assault, in March of 1991, Clinton pulled Broaddrick out of a health-care conference. "Can you ever forgive me? That was the old me. I'm not the same now. I'm a new man," Clinton told her.[26] Candice Jackson reported that a stunned Broaddrick told Clinton to go to hell and walked away.[27] Later that year, Clinton announced his run and Broaddrick deemed his surprising apology to be a purely political gesture.

Hillary Clinton, or Hillary Rodham as she demanded to be called back then, found out very soon after the assault of Broaddrick that her husband had raped the young volunteer. Larry Nichols, a Clinton insider at that time, said Hillary rushed into a campaign office and screamed, "You will never believe what the motherfucker did now, he tried to rape some bitch!"

Instead of calling the police, she immediately began covering for her political partner. Hillary had experience with this. In 1975, as a young lawyer, she had successfully defended an accused rapist. Hillary said she was doing her "professional duty."

The victim said Clinton intentionally lied about her in court documents, and Hillary also acknowledged the attacker's guilt, laughing about it on an unearthed audio recording.

"Hillary Clinton took me through hell," the victim said. "I would say [to Clinton], 'You took a case of mine in '75, you lied on me . . . I realize the truth now, the heart of what you've done to me. And you are supposed to be for women? You call that [being] for women, what you done to me? And I hear you on tape laughing.'"[28]

In Hillary's estimation, she was just doing her job.

"When you're a lawyer you often don't have the choice to choose who you will represent, and by the very nature of criminal law there will be those who you represent that you won't approve of," Hillary said. "But at least in our system you have an obligation, and once I was appointed, I fulfilled that obligation."[29]

Following physical assault at the hands of Bill, Broaddrick was psychologically assaulted by Hillary, again fulfilling her "obligation."[30]

Decades later, in 2013, with her eyes on the presidency, Hillary would declare that the fight for women's rights was "unfinished business" and that "women's rights are human rights, and human rights are women's rights once and for all." Hillary now stumps around the country fighting for the unheard voice of women, but years ago, she fought to silence those same voices. They were victims of her husband's sexual deviance, and she fought to keep their stories suppressed.

This was perfectly illustrated at a campaign event for Bill that Broaddrick attended. Hillary made a beeline toward Broaddrick, coldly but firmly grasped her hand, and said, "We want to thank you for everything that you do for Bill." Hillary clung to and squeezed Broaddrick's hand for emphasis.[31] Broaddrick was unnerved.

When Broaddrick finally did go public about the assault in 1999, her nursing home business, in operation for decades, was audited by the IRS for the first time, and her home was broken into.[32]

In mid-January 1999, Lisa Myers of NBC's *Dateline* interviewed Broaddrick. NBC taped the interview, but it sat intentionally unaired until after Bill Clinton's impeachment trial and vote in the U.S. Senate on February 12, 1999. If the NBC interview had run before the Senate vote on impeachment, there is a chance that Clinton could have been convicted and removed from office. The interview ran a healthy two weeks after Clinton was acquitted of his impeachment charges.

In the segment, Broaddrick painfully recounted the assault and admitted she only told very few friends and her husband, David. Like many victims of rape, she thought no one would believe her and felt embarrassed that she allowed Clinton into her room. She was afraid her first husband and many others would think that she invited Clinton to her room because they were having an affair. Ashamed and worried, she even attended a Clinton fundraiser just three weeks later. Broaddrick was later appointed by then governor Clinton to a state board, but said she had promised her nursing association that she would accept it before she knew it was an appointment from him.

She also admitted lying under oath in 1997 by denying any sexual assault by Clinton, under subpoena in the Paula Jones case, for fear of drudging up the ordeal again. She told NBC that she thought about coming forward daily but was too frightened of the consequences, especially after perjuring herself to keep a lid on her story.

But after more and more stories about Clinton's serial rape of women came out, Broaddrick felt she needed to finally come forward. She was encouraged when Ken Starr, who was investigating obstruction of justice charges against Clinton, gave her immunity from prosecution for perjury. That enabled Broaddrick to speak the truth and defend the numerous other women who had been victimized and marginalized by the Clinton machine. Bill and Hillary destroyed people's lives when they got in their way and Broaddrick was reluctant to cross them for many years.

Even after coming forward, Broaddrick never filed a lawsuit against Bill Clinton, made a book deal, or financially benefitted from coming forward in any way.

It took twenty-two years for Broaddrick to finally tell Hillary what she thought of her. On October 15, 2000, during the last year of the Clinton presidency, Broaddrick wrote the following "Open Letter to Hillary Clinton." It was widely published online and began, "Do You Remember?":

As I watched Rick Lazio's interview on Fox News this morning, I felt compelled to write this open letter to you, Mrs. Clinton. Brit Hume asked Mr. Lazio's views regarding you as a person and how he perceived you as a candidate. Rick Lazio did not answer the question, but I know that I can. You know it, too.

I have no doubt that you are the same conniving, self-serving person you were twenty-two years ago when I had the misfortune to meet you. When I see you on television, campaigning for the New York senate race, I can see the same hypocrisy in your face that you displayed to me one evening in 1978. You have not changed.

I remember it as though it was yesterday. I only wish that it were yesterday and maybe there would still be time to do something about what your husband, Bill Clinton, did to me. There was a political rally for Mr. Clinton's bid for governor of Arkansas. I had obligated myself to be at this rally prior to my being assaulted by your husband in April, 1978. I had made up my mind to make an appearance and then leave as soon as the two of you arrived. This was a big mistake, but I was still in a state of shock and denial. You had questioned the gentleman who drove you and Mr. Clinton from the airport. You asked him about me and if I would be at the gathering. Do you remember? You told the driver, "Bill has talked so much about Juanita", and that you were so anxious to meet me. Well, you wasted no time. As soon as you entered the room, you came directly to me and grabbed my hand. Do you remember how you thanked me, saying "we want to thank you for everything that you do for Bill." At that point, I was pretty shaken and started to walk off. Remember how you kept a tight grip on my hand and drew closer to me? You repeated your statement, but this time with a coldness and look that I have seen many times on television in the last eight years. You said, "Everything you do for Bill." You then released your grip and I said nothing and left the gathering.

What did you mean, Hillary? Were you referring to my keeping quiet about the assault I had suffered at the hands of your husband only two weeks before? Were you warning me to continue to keep quiet? We both know the answer to that question. Yes, I can answer Brit Hume's question. You are the same Hillary that you were twenty years ago. You are cold, calculating and self-serving. You cannot tolerate the thought that you will soon be without the power you have wielded for the last eight years. Your effort to stay in power will be at the expense of the state of New York. I only hope the voters of New York will wake up in time and realize that Hillary Clinton is not an honorable or an honest person.

I will end by asking if you believe the statements I made on NBC Dateline when Lisa Myers asked if I had been assaulted and raped by your husband? Or perhaps, you are like Vice-President Gore and did not see the interview. [33]

Although she told Lisa Myers that she had no intention to, Broaddrick *did* eventually file a lawsuit against Clinton. The purpose of the suit was to obtain documents the White House may have gathered on her.

"We want to find out what information they have on her in violation of the Privacy Act and how she's been damaged by that information," Broaddrick's lawyer Larry Klayman told CNN.[i]

---

i Barrett, Ted. "Juanita Broaddrick Sues Clinton Administration over Alleged 'Smear Campaign.'" CNN. December 20, 1999.

In the midst of the lawsuit, Broaddrick's nursing home business was audited by the IRS.

Broaddrick made it clear to the *New York Post* that she did not think the audit was a coincidence.

"I do not think our number just came up," Broaddrick told the *Post*. "We've had no changes in our business, no changes in ownership, no changes in income. There have been no changes whatsoever that would trigger an IRS audit."[ii]

---

ii Blomquist, Brian. "Juanita Latest Bill Foe to be Audited." *New York Post.* May 31, 2000.

CHAPTER 3

BY FORCE IF NECESSARY

"I think [Bill] is a very dangerous, manipulative man and I've had to be very careful."

—Elizabeth Ward Gracen[34]

Governor Bill Clinton used a short list of Arkansas state troopers to act as bodyguards, for transportation, and in other, more unpleasant capacities.

"We were required to work overtime so we could sit outside some place and block the road or sit in some driveway or apartment complex while he went in to take care of his female friends," remembered state trooper Larry Patterson. "State money was utilized."[35]

Patterson, along with Roger Perry, Danny Ferguson, Ronnie Anderson, and L. D. Brown, formed the inner ring of troopers who would run security to procure and protect the sexual indiscretions of their governor.

"I saw on several occasions Bill Clinton engaging in sexual acts while I was either blocking a road or working security at the Governor's Mansion," said Patterson. "I saw this with my own eyes take place, so it is not a rumor, it is firsthand."[36]

Years later, Patterson and Perry would come forward with intimate details from the debauched lifestyle of then governor Clinton. "These two have had the courage to come forward," said Jim Johnson, "and the evidence that they have presented has not only been credible, but has been overwhelming and the truth is I'm convinced that it is just the tip of the iceberg."[37]

Arkansas state employee Paula Jones was another who came forward with dirt on Governor Clinton and his state troopers.

Governor Clinton had seen Jones working a conference table in the lobby of the Excelsior Hotel in Little Rock, where he was scheduled to speak. Clinton asked Danny Ferguson, the state trooper on his private detail that day, to summon Jones to his upstairs suite. When Jones entered the room, Ferguson carefully kept watch outside the door.

Jones said that Clinton tried to run his hands up her dress and attempted to kiss her on the lips. "I like your curves," Clinton said. "I love the way your hair flows down your back . . . I was watching you."

"His face was red, beet red. I'll never forget that look," Jones recalled.[38]

"What are you doing?" Jones asked incredulously. She escaped Clinton's grasp and quickly moved to the end of a sofa near the door. The governor followed.

"Are you married?" Clinton asked. Jones said that she had a regular boyfriend. Clinton then approached the sofa and as he sat down he lowered his trousers and underwear, exposing his erect penis. "Would you kiss it for me?" Clinton asked.

Jones became horrified, jumped up from the couch, and exclaimed that she was "not that kind of girl." She said, "Look, I've got to go," and he attempted to explain that she would get in trouble for being away from the registration desk.

"Well, I don't want to make you do anything you don't want to do," Clinton said, fondling his erect penis.[39]

Paula Blanchard, the wife of a close Clinton ally, said that Jones arrived back to the registration desk from her visit in a state of "embarrassment, horror, grief, shame, fright, worry, and humiliation."[40]

Jones's recollection of the encounter is detailed. Jones's sister Lydia Cathey said while deposed that Jones described Clinton's turgid member as "crooked and hard and gross." Debra Lynn Ballentine, a friend of Jones, said Paula ran back to her office after the incident and "she told me that [Bill] had an erection but that it was, like, bent, real bent and she asked me if I had even seen anything like that before and I said no."[41]

The incident left Jones shamed and appalled. Years later, she would file a sexual harassment lawsuit against Clinton and Ferguson, which would bring her story and many others out of the shadows and into the light.

Remember Elizabeth Ward Gracen? She said she had sex with Clinton in 1983 when she was the reigning Miss America and former Miss Arkansas. After Gracen told her good friend Judy Stokes that a forced sexual act had occurred, Stokes relayed this information to the Paula Jones investigators who were looking at Clinton's deviant sexual history. Judy Stokes was 100 percent convinced that Bill Clinton had sexually assaulted Elizabeth, based on her comments.

After years of denying an affair with Clinton, in early 1998, Gracen confirmed that she had a one-night consensual fling with the then governor. This is not what her friend said both under oath and privately. Stokes stated under oath that Gracen was in tears as she privately described Clinton pushing himself on her as she pleaded she did not want to have sex.

Gracen had mournfully told Stokes that sex with Clinton was "something I did not want to happen."[42]

Revealingly, Gracen told *Newsweek*'s Michael Isikoff that Bill, in trademark fashion, had severely bitten her lip in bed.

It is rumored that in the early 1990s, Gracen benefited from help from Bill's Hollywood friends Mickey Kantor and Harry Thomason. They landed her a miniseries job on the television show *Highlander* with no audition.

"I learned later that movie director Harry Thomason [a longtime Clinton friend] and White House bigwig Mickey Kantor sat down with my agent, Miles Levy, and worked out some kind of a deal that would have me deny anything to do with Bill Clinton, Gracen said."[43]

Later in the decade, the Paula Jones investigators were hitting pay dirt looking into Bill Clinton's violent, deviant, and criminal sexual history. Bill Clinton exposed himself to Paula Jones in May of 1991, and after her name became publicly associated with him in December of 1993, Paula sued Clinton for sexual harassment.

The Paula Jones legal team was a Dallas-based law firm that hired private investigators Rick and Beverly Lambert. In late 1997 and early 1998, Gracen was attempting to avoid contact with the Paula Jones investigators as well as dodge a subpoena in the Jones case.[44] However, Rick Lambert did find Gracen confidant Judy Stokes. "I talked to Judy Stokes for an hour and a half," said Lambert, who interviewed Stokes in December 1997. "At first, she was reluctant to burn her bridges with Liz. But I finally asked, 'Do you believe Clinton raped her?' She said, 'Absolutely. He forced her to have sex. What do you call that?' Stokes was totally convinced it was rape."[45]

Stokes said under oath in her Paula Jones deposition that Gracen was tearful when she talked about the sex that transpired with Clinton and said that it was not consensual.[46]

Miles Levy, the Hollywood agent for Gracen, told Rick Lambert the reason why Gracen did not want to get involved in the Paula Jones case was that it "would be career suicide for Liz and you know it."[47]

The case of Gracen is a textbook example of how the Clintons abuse people. There was the initial, physical assault by Bill in 1983 when she was the reigning Miss America. Then years later, in 1997, after she was subpoenaed to be a sexual harassment witness in the Paula Jones case, the psychological assault of Gracen began as the Clintons attempted to silence her. Hillary for decades has been personally in charge of the intimidation and terror campaigns to silence Bill's sex victims and former girlfriends.

In December of 1997, Gracen began to receive threatening phone calls, including a reminder that she had been subpoenaed in the Paula Jones case with the advice that she should dodge the subpoena.[48] Gracen left the country and traveled around Paris, Canada, and the Caribbean.

Gracen's belongings were ransacked by three men in suits while she was on vacation in St. Martin. Her manager, Vincent Vento, said intimidating phone had callers advised her to "keep your mouth shut about Bill Clinton and go on with your life. You could be discredited. You could have an IRS investigation."[49] Within weeks, the IRS *was* sending audit letters to the home of Gracen's parents, which was not listed on her tax filings. It is worth mentioning that the head of the IRS from 1993 to 1997 was Margaret "Peggy" Richardson, who was a longtime and college friend of Hillary Clinton. During the 1990s, four Clinton victims received IRS audits: Gennifer Flowers, Paula Jones, Juanita Broaddrick, and Gracen.[50]

In 1998, Gracen was interviewed by Steve Dunleavy of the *New York Post*.

She related that some frightening and suspicious things had been happening to her. She had started to receive "friendly" phone calls that warned her to get out of town in order to avoid a subpoena from independent counsel Kenneth Starr. There were nastier calls, too, warning of an impending character assassination. Her friends started to tell her they were being asked about a tape.

Things got even weirder when, she said, her beach cabana was ransacked while she vacationed with her boyfriend in St. Martin. Whoever did the ransacking left a Rolex and $2,000 cash; they were, apparently, looking for something.

"Yes, I was physically scared," Gracen told Dunleavy. "We are talking about the [president] of the country here, and between the friendly calls on one hand telling me to get out of town for my own good and then talking about smear tactics on the other, I got scared. Yes, physically scared. There were always veiled threats. Always. I did nothing wrong except one stupid night a long time ago. But now this last year has become very frightening."[51] Steve Dunleavy's article for the *New York Post* was titled "Elizabeth Gracen: I was a victim of Clinton's reign of terror" with the subtitle "Investigating Clinton's goons."

"I think [Bill] is a very dangerous, manipulative man and I've had to be very careful," the former Miss America told the *Toronto Star* in September 1998. "There was a lot of pressure on my family and friends, people were being staked out. I was a little bit afraid for my safety at one point. It's just not an area where you are safe."[52]

L. D. Brown described the time the Clintons, Chelsea, and his girlfriend, Becky, went to New York where Gracen was living. The Clintons went to a taping of *Sesame Street*, and young Chelsea had her picture taken with all the characters. Becky told Brown that by chance the whole Clinton entourage ran into Gracen on the streets of New York. "Becky said it was very uncomfortable and could tell Bill was a little embarrassed."[53]

Although Gracen has maintained a public denial that Clinton assaulted her, she has dropped hints that their short "affair" was not entirely consensual. "To use the word rendezvous would imply that it was romantic," Gracen said during one interview. "But it was far from romantic."

CHAPTER 4

TOSSING FLOWERS

"Bill, as always, wanted to take it a step further, so the next time I tied him to the bed, he asked me to use a dildo-shaped vibrator on him. It was exciting to see him getting so aroused, and I couldn't wait to untie him so he could use it on me."

—Gennifer Flowers[54]

In the fall of 1991, Bill Clinton announced his candidacy for president. The Clintons, aware they would have to stamp out as much of the allegations of sexual impropriety against Bill as they could, made a list of twenty-six women with whom they knew Clinton had had sex.

In January 1992, *Star* magazine ran an article about a lawsuit that accused Bill Clinton of spending state money on trysts with a series of five women including Flowers. Clinton called the story "trash," "an absolute lie," and "totally bogus." "You know the *Star* says Martians walk on earth and people have cow's heads," he added in jest.

On the night of January 26, 1992, shortly after the Washington Redskins upended the Buffalo Bills in Super Bowl XXVII, Clinton and his wife, Hillary, sat down with *60 Minutes* correspondent

Steve Kroft for another prime-time spectacle. With more than thirty million Americans tuned in, Clinton combated allegations of a twelve-year affair the then Arkansas governor and presidential hopeful had conducted with former television reporter Gennifer Flowers.

Clinton categorically denied all notions of an affair with Flowers and other women who had come forward, attributing the allegations to an overambitious and deceitful supermarket tabloid.

"It was only when money came out, when the tabloid went down there offering people money to say that they have been involved with me that she changed her story," Clinton told Kroft. "There is a recession on . . . times are tough . . . and I think you can expect more and more of these stories as long as they're down there handing out money."[55]

But Clinton stopped short of saying he had never committed adultery in his past. "You are trying to put this issue behind you," Kroft said. "And the problem with the answer is it's not a denial. And people are sitting out there, voters, and they're saying, 'Look, it's really pretty simple . . . if he's never had an extramarital affair, why doesn't he just say so?'"

Years later, *60 Minutes* producer Don Hewitt admitted that he intentionally edited the interview to portray Clinton in a more sympathetic light. "It was strong medicine, the way I edited it," said Hewitt. "He was a very sick candidate, he needed a very strong medicine and I'm not in the business of doctoring candidates, but he got up out of his sick bed that night and walked to a nomination."[56]

The real story is that Clinton was obsessed with Gennifer Flowers for approximately twelve years, from 1977 (when he got her pregnant and then paid for an abortion in early 1978) until 1989, when Bill replaced his Flowers obsession with a fixation on Marilyn Jenkins, with whom he openly carried on an affair.

Flowers said that she and Clinton were so enamored they agreed to think of each other every day at noon. "When we think of each other, let's picture ourselves in bed making wild, passionate love,"

Clinton suggested.[57] In her book, *Passion and Betrayal,* Flowers went into graphic detail regarding the sex games she and Clinton used to play.

Flowers recalled that after she had used silk scarves to tie him to her bedposts, "Bill, as always, wanted to take it a step further, so the next time I tied him to the bed, he asked me to use a dildo-shaped vibrator on him. It was exciting to see him getting so aroused, and I couldn't wait to untie him so he could use it on me."[58]

The truth is the Clintons knew, despite Bill's denial, that there was proof Clinton had regular contact with Flowers.

Flowers's neighbor Gary Johnson had video evidence that Clinton was a frequent visitor to Flowers's condo. Flowers said she did not know Johnson personally but she "had heard that he'd had a disagreement with the homeowners association of the building because he had installed a video camera overlooking the parking lot, and they told him he couldn't do that. They explained that he didn't own the exterior of the building, but he did own his portion of the interior. In response, Gary moved the camera from its perch overlooking the parking lot and placed it instead so that it had a view directly out his front door and down the hall. Because our doors were close together, he also got a very clear view of my apartment door."[59]

Silencing Johnson at all costs became priority number one for the Clintons.

"Gary let it be known that he actually had a videotape of Bill coming to my apartment," Flowers said in her book. "Big mistake. Not long after that, some large men forced their way into his place, beat him senseless and left him for dead. According to Johnson, they kept asking where 'the tape' was. Sure enough, the videotape of Bill disappeared. Johnson, it seems, was a double threat because he was also acting as counsel for Larry Nichols, the man who filed the lawsuit against Bill Clinton."

According to Nichols, some of Clinton's henchmen beat Gary Johnson to within an inch of his life and stole the incriminating tape.

"Without getting into gory details, both elbows were dislocated, his collarbones were broken, his spleen and his bladder were ruptured with holes the size of half dollars in them, his nose and sinus cavities were all crushed," said Nichols. "He had been beaten by Clinton's people."[60]

Nichols had been an ambitious young Democrat and a loyal soldier in Governor Clinton's administration. Before long, however, he would learn that the Arkansas Development Finance Authority (ADFA), a Clinton creation, was, like the Clinton Foundation decades later, a slush fund for the Clintons. The ADFA, created in 1985, had been promoted by Bill Clinton as a noble vehicle to give low-interest loans for schools, churches, and small businesses. Clinton gave "grants" to wealthy contributors with tax payer–generated money, with much of that money coming back to him in campaign contributions. Clinton himself wasn't above dipping in to get cash from the agency. Nichols ran in the same circles as Bill, Roger, Hillary, and the Arkansas political insiders.

Nichols became the man who knew too much about the Clintons' epic abuse of the ADFA, drug dealing and trafficking, Clinton's personal sex and drug abuse, and the incredible tension between Bill, who sometime preferred partying to politics, and Hillary, who was so driven for political power she would endure her husband's serial humiliations.

The Clinton spin machine would launch into high gear in an effort to discredit Nichols in the 1990s. Long before widespread video-watching on the Internet, Nichols produced a compelling documentary and book, *The Clinton Chronicles*. With some funding from evangelical minister Jerry Falwell, Nichols obtained rare footage from people who had seen Clinton's drug and sex abuse in person, one of them in prison for thirty years in connection to what she saw Bill Clinton do. The authors have gone through Nichols claims and worked hard to corroborate his inside story of the Clintons and their drive for power. Joe Conason will foam at the mouth. James Carville will be outraged and David Brock will be in full attack, but

Nichols is credible and much of the case he presents in this landmark film is both accurate and compelling. It's important to note that the production quality is hokey and the project is clearly low budget. But it is riveting and most of it, based on our research, is accurate.

After Bill Clinton dropped out of the presidential race in July, 1987, his handlers set about trying to "clean him up" for future political campaigns. Part of this process, even if Bill's womanizing could not be stopped, was to send Bill off to a drug rehab clinic. In early 1988 (or perhaps late 1987) when Larry Nichols was looking for Bill and could not find him, he was told by Clinton's chief of staff, Betsey Wright, that Bill had been sent off to a drug rehabilition clinic to get off cocaine. Nichols believes this was probably the Betty Ford Clinic in Minnesota, and Wright told Nichols that Clinton had been sent to drug rehab more than once. Nichols says that he heard an unconfirmed rumor from one of the Arkansas state troopers that Jackson T. Stephens (1923 to 2005), later a huge Clinton financial backer, was also addicted to cocaine. But Bill was the one they were supposed to get off drugs.[61]

Nichols said he went to work as the marketing director for the ADFA in summer 1988 and by December 1988, Nichols said he was kicked out after confronting Bill Clinton on the corruption in the ADFA. One of the things that Nichols noticed was that Bill's friend Dan Lasater got almost all of the ADFA's bond underwriting business. Nichols says that he started "prowling around, prowling around" to find out what was going on at the ADFA; he says that because he was "Bill Clinton's man," people such as ADFA director Wooten Epps would tell him things in confidence. Nichols says that he discovered two sets of accounting books, a classic sign of fraud, at the ADFA. Nichols says that every day at the end of work, he would make hard copies of critical ADFA documents just in case things went sour there.[62]

Nichols says that after he confronted Bill Clinton on the corruption at the ADFA, Clinton in retaliation fed derogatory information to Associated Press reporter Bill Simmons. The pretext for Nichols dismissal was that he made hundreds of phone calls on state phones in support of the Nicaraguan contras. Of course Bill Clinton was illegally facilitating the CIA drug trade in Arkansas on behalf of the Nicaraguan contras, but somehow Clinton forgot to tell AP reporter Bill Simmons about that blockbuster crime. Nichols says that he met whistleblower Terry Reed and his investigator around 1990. Combining what they knew and what he knew, Nichols says that around that point he understood the ADFA had been laundering huge amounts of cocaine money with the help of Dan Lasaster's bond company.[63]

Besides laundering drug money, the ADFA was basically a scheme set up to give dirt-cheap loans to any friend of Bill Clinton. Nichols wrote in *The Clinton Chronicles*:

> After about two weeks I went to Wooten Epps [who was running ADFA for Clinton] and I said, "Wooten, I think I've got enough background on this that we can start marketing it. Now, what is the criteria for loans?" He said, "Whoever Bill wants to get a loan." . . .
>
> We had a board meeting. In that particular board meeting I was sitting at the end of the table. James Branyan, who was chairman of the board at that time, was sitting at the head of the table. James Branyan stood up in a public restaurant, and he hollered at the Beverly Enterprises guy, Bobby Stephens, and said, "Did you get the $50,000 campaign contribution from the client that you're introducing the loan for?" He said, "Not yet."
>
> And he said, "Then, hold up the loan until you get it." I stood up, went up to James and I said, "James, don't yell stuff like that. You don't need to be yelling it in a restaurant. That sounds real bad." He was just burly and arrogant and he said, "Who cares?"[64]

Nichols says that back in the 1980s Dan Lasater would keep a big dish of cocaine in his office and that the Arkansas state troopers would often take Bill to Lasater's office (or residence) and Clinton would see Lasater for about ten minutes as he would get his cocaine hit.

Nichols told author Rodney Stich that "there was virtually no accounting of the money received by the ADFA, or the repayments of the loans. He said that money would appear in a particular account and suddenly disappear, a technique that IRS investigator William Duncan said was a zero-balance tactic commonly used in drug-money laundering."[65]

In 1992, the Clintons were so concerned about their liability in the criminality that had gone on in the ADFA that they used Terry Lenzer's Investigative International Group to snoop around and see if their political opponents were going to make a political issue of the ADFA.

Flowers and the people around her knew about the near murder of Gary Johnson. It served as a warning to anyone else in Little Rock who might possess unknown truths.

Flowers was next.

They started with breaking into her home. "A week or so after I spoke with Bill, I came home to my apartment at the Forest Place Apartments (where I had moved after Bill and I broke up) and found the dead bolt on my door locked," Flowers recalled. "Since I wasn't in the habit of locking the dead bolt I thought maybe maintenance had been in to fix something and had locked the dead bolt when they left. But when I went inside, nothing had been done. That was curious."[66]

There was no receipt from a maintenance man, yet someone had entered her apartment. Shortly after the first break-in, a similar entry occurred, except the telephone had been moved and there was a dirty shoeprint on the floor. Flowers sent her apartment office a record letter of complaint, still believing it had been a maintenance man in her apartment. A few days later, Flowers would learn these were not routine house calls.

"I came home to find the door ajar," Flowers warily recounted. "Puzzled, I pushed it open, and stepped in. I couldn't believe my eyes; my whole apartment had been ransacked—furniture turned upside down, drawers emptied onto the floor, linens stripped off the bed. I was stunned. I dropped to my knees in the doorway and started shaking uncontrollably. This wasn't maintenance that had been inside my apartment. This was something much bigger, and I knew it had to be related to Bill. It scared me out of my mind.

"For some reason, I didn't even think that someone might still be in my apartment. I just saw all the devastation and finally figured out just what was happening. I was so frightened and didn't want to be alone, so I called a friend and kept her on the phone while I started going through my things to see if anything was missing. I still shudder to think what might have happened if someone had been waiting for me!"[67]

The break-in left Flowers psychologically broken. "It horrified and angered me to think that someone had touched and inspected nearly everything I owned. What a feeling of violation!" Flowers then had a chilling thought. "As I sifted through the mess, a chilling thought hit me: The person responsible for this might *not* be looking for something on Bill and me. This could be Bill himself, looking for what *I* had on *him*."[68]

Flowers had the foresight to remove her tapes of her recordings of Clinton before the break-in. Her house had been ransacked. All her clothes were tossed on the ground, every shoe inspected, boxes of photographs on the floor, her mattress overturned. The Clinton message had been sent to Flowers. "This was not a game—it was deadly serious. I didn't know whom I could trust—including Bill. I knew then that my life was in danger."[69]

Shortly after her home invasion, Flowers called Clinton. She recorded those conversations and based on Bill's tone of voice and questions, she began to think *he* was behind the break-ins:

CLINTON: You think they were trying to look for something on us?
GENNIFER: I think so. Well, I mean . . . why, why else? Um . . .

CLINTON: You weren't missing any, any kind of papers or anything?
GENNIFER: Well, like what kind of papers?
CLINTON: Well I mean did . . . any kind of personal records or checkbooks or anything like that? Phone records?
GENNIFER: Do I have any?
CLINTON: Yeah . . . I wouldn't care if they . . . you know, I, I . . . They may have my phone records on this computer here, but I don't think it . . . that doesn't prove anything.[70]

The Clintons stayed "all in" on the cover-up of the Flowers affair for the remainder of 1992. Clinton only changed his tune years later in his deposition for the Jones case in which he admitted to exactly one tryst with Flowers. Clinton, with knowledge that he had paid for Flowers's abortion, feared she, or someone, might have records of it.

Outed by the tabloids, Flowers went public with her affair. "For twelve years I was his girlfriend and now he tells me to deny it—to say it isn't true," Flowers said.[71]

Flowers released some of her phone tapes with Clinton. The Clinton campaign countered by hiring investigator Anthony Pellicano to say the tapes had been "selectively edited."[72]

Pellicano was more a pseudo thug than a private eye whose tactics included putting a dead fish with a red rose in its mouth along with the message "stop" on the windshield of a targeted reporter's car.[73] Pellicano was eventually convicted of illegal firearms possession, wiretapping, and racketeering.

Another Clinton PI, Jack Palladino, is said to have told James Lyons that he would "impeach [Flowers's] character and veracity until she is destroyed beyond all recognition."

"Is Gennifer Flowers the sort of person who would commit suicide?" Palladino asked Loren Kirk, a former roommate of Flowers.[74]

Another former Clinton conquest abused in 1992 was Sally Perdue, whose Jeep was smashed in and shotgun shells put on the seat of the vehicle. Both Flowers and Perdue said they were in fear for their lives.

Perdue, now Sally Miller, was so scarred from the "Clinton treatment" that she refused an interview request. This is a symptom of many Clinton victims who still feel fear and watch as the Clintons are celebrated on the national and international stage. In their eyes, it is like watching Jack the Ripper receive humanitarian awards.

Perdue, another Miss Arkansas, had an affair with Bill Clinton from August to December 1983. Clinton trysted at her home twelve times, when his daughter Chelsea was only three years old. "I still have this picture of him wearing my black nightgown, playing the sax badly," Perdue recalled.[75] Clinton ceased the affair when Perdue said she wanted to get into politics and run for mayor of her town.

Throughout 1992, with Clinton running for president, the secret police were turned out in full force. They correctly estimated Perdue was a threat to "talk." Democratic operative Ron Tucker was dispatched to tell Sally to tell perdue to remain a "good little girl" in exchange for a nice federal job. However, "If I didn't take the offer then they knew I went jogging by myself and couldn't guarantee what would happen to my pretty little legs. Things just wouldn't be so much fun for me anymore. Life would get hard."[76] Perdue had a friend secretly watch the conversation with Tucker, which she later reported to the FBI.

Perdue turned down the job offer, and the Clintons turned up the terror. First, Perdue was fired from her job as an admissions officer at Linwood College. Then she received hate mail and nasty phone calls. One of her hate letters said "Marilyn Monroe got snuffed."

Perdue was so terrified of the Clintons that she left the country and headed to China before the general election. "The feature of Perdue's story that transforms Clinton's behavior toward her from mere philandering to real mistreatment is his use of smear and scare tactics to bully her into keeping quiet," wrote Candice Jackson.[77]

The mainstream media refused to cover Perdue during the 1992 campaign and also neglected the campaign waged against her. They did not cover the illegal $60,000 bribe offered to her by Ron Tucker. Perdue had interviews taped with ABC, NBC, and *Sally Jesse Raphael*, but none of them went to air. They were shelved by the networks.[78]

CHAPTER 5

ATTACK IN THE OVAL OFFICE

"[Hillary] is the war on women, as far as I'm concerned, because with every woman that she's found out about—and she made it a point to find out who every woman had been that's crossed his path over the years—she's orchestrated a terror campaign against every one of these women, including me."

—Kathleen Willey[79]

In 1993, Kathleen Willey was a volunteer in the White House Social Office in the Clinton administration. By the fall of 1993, her husband, Ed, a prominent lawyer and Democratic fundraiser, was in deep financial straits. He had stolen from his clients and was in a deep tax debt.

Willey, who had met Bill Clinton during the 1992 presidential campaign, asked for an appointment to see the president. Due to her husband's financial turmoil, Willey was seeking a paid full-time salary with the White House. The appointment took place on November 29, 1993, in the Oval Office.

Shortly after Willey arrived, Clinton suggested they get some coffee in the mini-kitchen and move to his study. The mini-kitchen was a side room where, due to its private nature, generations of presidents have engaged in amorous affairs; a sharp contrast to the large open space and prominent windows of the Oval Office. Monica Lewinsky would later remember that Clinton would use the sink in the mini-kitchen as a place to masturbate and spray his ejaculate.

Willey told Clinton about her financial woes and desperate need of a paying job. During her plea, presidential aide Andrew Friendly began knocking on the door of the Oval Office, loudly informing Clinton that he was late for his next meeting. Pressured for time, the president became more aggressive.

Clinton gave Willey a hug. The embrace lasted too long. He then started running his hands through her hair and on her neck.

The six-foot-two, two-hundred-twenty-five-pound Clinton was much bigger and stronger than the petite Willey, who stood almost a foot shorter and weighed a hundred pounds less.

"I've wanted to do this since the first time I laid eyes on you," the president said as his face reddened.

"Then he took my hand," Willey remembered. "I didn't understand what he was doing. The president put my hand on his genitals, on his erect penis. I was shocked! I yanked my hand away but he was forceful. He ran his hands all over me, touching me everywhere, up my skirt, over my blouse, my breasts. He pressed up against me and kissed me. I didn't know what to do. I could slap him or yell for help. My mind raced. And the only thing I noticed was that his face had turned red, literally beet red."[80]

Luckily for Willey, Friendly continued to bang on the door. Clinton had a big economic meeting scheduled with Treasury Secretary Lloyd Bentsen, OMB Chair Leon Panetta, and Laura Tyson, the head of the Council of Economic Advisors.

"I made a dive for the door, yanked it open, and burst into the Oval Office," Willey said. "He followed me. As I scurried across that stately room, brushing my hair with my fingertips and checking that my blouse was tucked in, Clinton walked directly to his chair.

His lechery aborted, the president of the United States concealed the remains of his arousal behind John Kennedy's desk in the Oval Office."[81]

Linda Tripp later described the condition of Kathleen as "flustered: hair messy, red face, no lipstick, an overall disheveled wreck."[82]

On the same day that Clinton was sexually assaulting Willey, Kathleen's distraught husband went out to the Virginia woods to a small marsh, put a gun in his mouth, and pulled the trigger.

Following her traumatic encounter and the death of her husband, "I still had a mountain of debt and no income," Willey recalled. "My legal and financial situation was dire. Some dear friends sent me a check that sustained me for two months, but the fact remained: I needed a job."[83] So Willey began using her lawyer, Dan, to write Bill Clinton letters—friendly letters that asked for a paying job to replace her volunteering in the White House Social Office. Eventually, Willey got a job that paid $20,000 per year plus health care for twenty-four hours of work per week.

Willey's experiences with Hillary Clinton were dreadful. "She would emerge with her entourage, cursing up a storm," Willey said. "And all day long, we heard her raised voice through the wall. Hillary always seemed to be miserable, unhappy, and angry."[84]

Other witnesses to Hillary's tantrums such as FBI agent Gary Aldrich said that it was quite a sight to see the First Lady shriek profanity at the president that ranged from "Come back here you asshole" to "Where the fuck do think you're going?"[85]

"That's the Hillary I saw," Kathleen recalled. "I've walked behind her when she was cursing an aide with a *very* foul mouth. Then she would see somebody who mattered and instantly pour it on, all sweetness and light. A doey-eyed expression on her face, she'd act so sincere. The minute they were gone, she'd turn around and explode again, cussing a blue streak."[86]

Hillary would play a big role in Willey's life after she was dragged into the Paula Jones case. By February 1997, *Newsweek* reporter Michael Isikoff had caught wind of the president's sexual assault of Willey. Isikoff told Willey that he had gotten the information from the Jones lawyers.[87] The Jones lawyers were eager to find other sexual assault victims of Clinton.

Isikoff, in hot pursuit of a scoop, was putting intense pressure on Willey to go on the record with a public account. "[Isikoff] pursued me and wouldn't let up," Willey said. "He called all the time. 'Talk to me,' he pleaded. 'Talk to me on the record!'"[88] Later in the year, the Jones lawyers were trying to get Kathleen deposed and under oath to describe what Bill had done to her. They were seeking to prove a pattern of sexual harassment by Clinton to add credibility to their case.

On July 25, 1997, the Jones team subpoenaed Willey to testify in their case. Matt Drudge posted a story about Willey regarding what she might say under oath.[89] Well aware of her impending testimony, the Clintons began to engage in witness tampering.

After the Drudge story, Isikoff wrote an article for *Newsweek*, "A Twist in the Paula Jones Case." The story quoted Clinton lawyer Bob Bennet, who said that the president "had no specific recollection of meeting" Willey.[90] After the article ran, Isikoff received an anonymous phone call from a woman claiming to be the wife of an influential Democrat. The caller said she had met the president many times at political events and that sometime in 1996, he made a heavy, overbearing pass on her in the exact same spot in the Oval Office where he had sexually assaulted Willey. She said Clinton got physical with her, tried to kiss her, and groped her breasts. The mortified woman fought the rampaging pervert off and told Isikoff "I've never had a man take advantage of me like that." Isikoff asked her what happened next. The female caller said, "I think he finished the job himself."[91] Bill, following the rejection, most likely masturbated until completion.

By mid-summer 1997, Kathleen Willey was a credible witness to Clinton's outrageous sexual behavior.

Willey did not want to testify in the Paula Jones case, but by November 1997, it was ruled that she could be deposed. When she heard the intimate details of Paula Jones's story, Willey knew it was the truth, particularly the familiar description of Clinton's flushed countenance as he advanced on Jones.

Willey was scheduled to be deposed in early January 1998.

Increasingly desperate, the Clintons and their associates took highly illegal actions.

"They threatened my children," Willey said. "They threatened my friend's children. They took one of my cats and killed another. They left a skull on my porch. They told me I was in danger. They followed me. They vandalized my car. They tried to retrieve my dogs from a kennel. They hid under my deck in the middle of the night. They subjected me to a campaign of fear and intimidation, trying to silence me."[92]

The Clintons hired detective Palladino to "investigate" Willey. Palladino would be labeled as one of Clinton's "secret police."

The Clintons paid Palladino $93,000 in 1992 to do damage control on the women who were involved with Bill Clinton.[93] Palladino was paid with campaign funds funneled through a law firm. Betsey Wright, the former chief of staff for Governor Clinton, was the "feminist" tasked to put pressure on the dozens of women who had had intimate encounters with the candidate. Wright was working hand in glove with Palladino to run suppression campaigns on these women that Michael Isikoff reported in a July 26, 1992, article, "Clinton Team Works to Deflect Allegations on Nominee's Private Life."[94]

Research into Palladino's methods of "investigation" yield horrifying results. Think digging into a target's past and present personal information and then using this information to make veiled threats and bare-knuckled attacks.

Writer Ian Halperin ran into the Palladino treatment when trying to publish a book on one of the PI's celebrity clients. Palladino visited Halperin's house and presented a long dossier he had complied on the author. "That's an intimidation tactic, when some guy starts recounting addresses where you lived 15 or 20 years ago, where you worked, your past girlfriends," Halperin recalled. "He said he could make my life miserable."[iii]

After the Clintons hired Palladino, someone started making Willey's life miserable. Three of her car tires were punctured by a nail gun. "I can remember standing at the tire place on a warm September day, waiting for them to fix my car," Willey told attorney and bestselling author Candice Jackson. "The mechanic approached her, saying 'It looks like someone has shot out all your tires with a nail gun; is there someone out there who doesn't like you?' I can hear the shiver in her voice as she says, 'That really got my attention; that's when I started getting worried.'" [95]

Not only were Kathleen's tires punctured, but the car tires of a close friend were also ruptured.

In a clear case of targeted vandalism, one of Kathleen's tires had nine nails shot in it; another tire had four nails in it; yet another tire had nine nails shot in the whitewall of it. Bullseye, Willey's cat of thirteen years, suddenly disappeared. The missing pet added to Willey's trauma.

Then, two days before Willey's deposition, a menacing stranger approached her and asked about her car tire vandalism, her missing cat, and then mentioned her children by name.

At the time, Kathleen was wearing a cervical collar around her neck. She was living in a rural part of Virginia, walking her dogs alone in the early morning on a barren country road.

Willey was about one half mile from her home when a man came jogging toward her "dressed in dark sweats, running shoes, and a plain baseball hat."[96]

Fixating his eyes on Willey, the stranger asked, "Hey did you ever find your cat?" Wiley replied that she had not. "Yeah, that Bullseye, he was a nice cat. He was a really nice old cat," the stranger replied.[97]

---

iii Rosenfeld, Seth. "Watching the Detective." *San Francisco Gate.* January 31, 1999.

The mysterious man then asked Willey if she had gotten her tires fixed. *"Whoa—how did he know my tires had been vandalized a few months back?"* Willey asked herself. "I didn't think I'd told any of my neighbors. I felt the hairs stand up on the back of my neck and a sickening feeling welled up in the pit of my stomach."

"'Who are you?' I demanded."

"And how are your children doing? How are Shannon and Patrick?"[98]

Confronted with another barrage of intimate details, Willey was overtaken by a feeling of dread.

The stranger then mentioned her friend and her friend's children by name.

"Oh God! The realization suddenly exploded into my consciousness. He means me harm! He means my loved ones harm!" Willey recalled.[99] She backed away from the man, shaken, as her legs felt almost paralyzed.

"As I backed up, he walked toward me. He was closer now. He looked at me, hardness in his eyes. He spoke deliberately and quietly.

'You're just not getting the message, are you?'"[100]

Willey, still wearing the cervical collar, broke out into a full sprint toward her home. She ran all the way home without thinking about potential damage to her neck.

"I started to understand," Willey said. "He was there to scare me, to let me know that I was being watched. But it was more than that. I realized that Bullseye's disappearance was part of it, that the damage to my tires was part of it. And the noises on my phone. It was all part of their message: *Keep your mouth shut. Don't talk about the incident in the Oval Office.*"[101]

Palladino's possible role in the Willey terror campaign invited even more suspicion in 2003 when Melanie Morgan, a conservative activist and former talk radio host, talked with Palladino and his business partner's wife, Sandra Sutherland, at the Passage Mystery Writers Conference in California.[102]

Morgan told her account of this meeting to Art Moore of *World Net Daily* in November 2007. This account is revisited in Willey's book.

Morgan, then a budding mystery author, sidled up to Palladino, engaged him in conversation and established a friendly connection. "Aren't you ashamed of yourself with the business you did for Hillary Clinton?" Morgan eventually asked Palladino. "You know, come on. That stuff with Kathleen Willey was pretty outrageous. What was that? You guys ran over her cat? What was that all about?"[103]

"Well, I'm not really going to comment about that, but let me say this," Palladino answered. "The only regret that I had about the whole thing was that Hillary did not pay me in a timely fashion."[104]

Sutherland then made some vicious comments about Hillary. As Morgan told *World Net Daily*, "It was crystal clear to me at the time that he was bragging about the fact he had done it. Literally, his body puffed up, a slow grin spread across his face. I could see conflicting emotions playing out: 'Should I say anything?'"[105]

"He definitely acknowledged that there was something that had transpired there with Kathleen Willey and her cat and that his biggest regret was that he didn't get cash up front from Hillary Clinton!" Morgan recalled. She quoted Palladino as saying "I saved Hillary Clinton's ass. You'd think she'd be more grateful to me."[106]

Willey knew that Hillary had initiated the baneful attacks. "She's worse than he is," Willey told Fox News anchor Neil Cavuto. "She's behind the secret police."[107]

For the two days before her deposition, Willey could not sleep. On January 10, 1998, she testified. The scare tactics had worked. Willey answered sixty-three times that her memory of the Clinton assault was hazy. Candice Jackson pointed out that Willey's testimony was probably indeed affected and softened by the months-long intimidation campaign directed toward her, the previous comments of Clinton's lawyer, Bob Bennett, who told Kathleen to get a criminal lawyer if she were deposed, and "the terrifying verbal threat made against Willey and her children by a thug just two days earlier."[108]

Seven days later, President Clinton gave his deposition in the Jones case and flatly denied making a hard and crude sexual pass. He said nothing about trying to kiss Willey, nothing about putting his hand up her skirt, nothing about putting her hand on his erection.

"All I can tell you is, in the first place, when she came to see me she was clearly upset," Clinton said while deposed. "I did to her what I have done to scores and scores of men and women who have worked for me or been my friends over the years. I embraced her, I put my arms around her, I may have even kissed her on the forehead. There was nothing sexual about it. I was trying to help calm her down and trying to reassure her."

The recollection by Clinton was particularly interesting when held against the statement of his lawyer, Bob Bennett, five months earlier that he had "no specific recollection" of meeting with Willey.

January of 1998 was a rough time for the Clinton presidency. Bill Clinton lied in his Paula Jones deposition about not having an affair with an intern, Monica Lewinsky; it was also when *Drudge Report* scooped the mainstream media on January 17, letting folks know that *Newsweek* was not allowing Michael Isikoff to run a story that would expose the Clinton-Monica Lewinsky affair.

On January 26, Bill, with Hillary at his side, told some forceful lies about his relationship with Lewinsky. "I want you to listen to me," Clinton professed. "I'm going to say this again: I did not have sexual relations with that woman, Miss Lewinsky. I never told anybody to lie, not a single time; never. These allegations are false. And I need to go back to work for the American people. Thank you."[109]

The next day, Hillary sat down with Matt Lauer on NBC's *Today Show*. "The great story here for anybody willing to find it and write about it and explain it is this vast right wing conspiracy that has been conspiring against my husband since the day he announced for the presidency," the First Lady said.

By late January, the Clinton presidency hung in the balance. Bill had lied in his deposition that he had never had sex with Monica Lewinsky, but the Paula Jones lawyers were aware that intern had kept a blue dress stained with the presidential semen. Clinton had not only lied in a court case, but also to the American people. A judge subsequently fined Clinton $90,000 for giving false testimony and he later had his law license suspended in Arkansas.

The Clintons decided to buckle down, maintain the lies, and try to intimidate any other women who could damage the president. In hindsight, it seems that the booming stock market and favorable economy of the late 1990s ultimately saved Clinton from either being kicked out of office or forced to resign. Most Americans thought that with the economy so flush that it was not worth having Congress impeach and convict Clinton of "high crimes and misdemeanors."

Private investigator Jared Stern said that in March of 1998 he was asked by Robert Miller (then head of a private investigation firm, Prudential Associates) to do a noisy investigation of Willey meant to scare and intimidate her—looking at her phone records, finding if she took medication, going through her trash. Miller was working at the behest of the lawyer of Nathan Landow (a huge Democratic fundraiser). Miller told Stern that the "White House" was behind the intimidation campaign request.[110]

In 2007, as Willey was writing her book, intimidation tactics turned up again. Willey's home was burglarized and nothing but the book manuscript was stolen.

World Net Daily reported in an article, "Kathleen Willey: Clintons Stole My Manuscript," at the time:

> Kathleen Willey, the woman who says Bill Clinton groped her in the Oval Office, claims she was the target of an unusual house burglary over the weekend that nabbed a manuscript for her upcoming book, which promises explosive revelations that could damage Sen. Hillary Clinton's presidential campaign.

Willey told WND little else was taken from her rural Virginia home as she slept alone upstairs–electronics and jewelry were left behind–and she believes the Clintons were behind it.

The break-in, she said, reminded her of the widely reported incident 10 years ago in which she claimed she was threatened near the same Richmond-area home by a stranger just two days before she was to testify against President Clinton in the Paula Jones sexual harassment case.

The theft of the manuscript early Saturday morning was suspicious, she told WND, coming only days after the first mainstream media mention of her upcoming book, which is expected to include accusations of campaign finance violations and new revelations about harassment and threats by the Clintons and their associates.

'"Here we go again; it's the same thing that happened before," Willey told WND. "They want you to know they were there. And they got what they wanted. They pretty much managed to terrorize me again. It scared me to death. It's an awful feeling to know you're sound asleep upstairs and someone is downstairs.'"[111]

The Powhatan County Sheriff's Department confirmed there was indeed a break-in at a home in the vicinity of Kathleen's home on early Saturday morning, September 1, 2007, and that there was an investigation.

Willey told *World Net Daily* that she believed the break-in was specifically to steal her manuscript and was designed to look like a burglary. She pointed out her home is very isolated, hard to find, and is out on a gravel road on ten acres. Willey went to bed and woke to find a missing manuscript that she had printed out and a missing purse. Her laptop, which she kept running, had been turned off. "Also her car was keyed, the antenna broken and her DirecTV satellite system was 'messed with.'"[112]

In 2008, Willey penned an open letter to Senator Barack Obama, who was challenging Hillary for the Democratic nomination for president. Willey warned the candidate about "the Clintons' secret private-investigator army, which no doubt has already been deployed to counter the threat that you present. I know that army's tactics well. They have threatened my children and my friend's children. They've threatened and killed my pets. They've vandalized my car. They've entered my home and stolen my book manuscript."[113]

CHAPTER 6

POUND OF FLESH

"It's often said, by people trying to show how grown-up and unshocked they are, that all Clinton did to get himself impeached was lie about sex. That's not really true. What he actually lied about, in the perjury that also got him disbarred, was the women. And what this involved was a steady campaign of defamation, backed up by private dicks (you should excuse the expression) and salaried government employees, against women who I believe were telling the truth. In my opinion, Gennifer Flowers was telling the truth; so was Monica Lewinsky, and so was Kathleen Willey, and so, lest we forget, was Juanita Broaddrick who says she was raped by Bill Clinton."

—Christopher Hitchens

In December of 1993, the *American Spectator* published a report by David Brock, "His Cheating Heart: Living with the Clintons: Bill's Arkansas bodyguards tell the story the press missed," which went into detail on Bill's sexual promiscuities. In the piece, a woman named "Paula" was described as meeting Clinton in a hotel room at the Excelsior. She said afterward that she was available to be Bill's regular girlfriend.

The faulty account enraged Paula Jones.

In pre-lawsuit filings, Jones did not ask for any money. Instead, "Clinton would just admit that he didn't challenge her claim that the two had met in a hotel room, state that Jones did not engage in any improper conduct, and express regret about any aspersions on her good name."[114]

After she received no apology, Jones retained more legal help and filed suit for sexual harassment just before the three-year statute of limitations ran out on her tort. In response, the White House hired Robert Bennett, who started "investigating" Jones and began a rumor campaign that targeted her as a gossipy slut.[115]

"Drag a hundred-dollar bill through a trailer park, you never know what you'll find," Clinton loyalist James Carville quipped.

When White House intern Monica Lewinsky later asked Clinton why he didn't settle the Jones case, his reply was ominous. "You don't understand. I can't. There are hundreds of them," Clinton said.[116]

Following the 1996 general election, legal journalist Stuart Taylor examined the Jones case for *American Lawyer* and concluded in a 15,000-word article that she might be telling the truth. The article prompted some members of the media to believe Jones.

The testimonies of Willey, Flowers, and Jones were not enough. The president's denials held strong until revelations about his affair with a young intern, ignored by the mainstream media, were published on a little-known political website.

Here is the post that made the career of Matt Drudge:

Web Posted: 01/17/98 23:32:47 PST -- NEWSWEEK KILLS STORY ON WHITE HOUSE INTERN
BLOCKBUSTER REPORT: 23-YEAR OLD, FORMER WHITE HOUSE INTERN, SEX RELATIONSHIP WITH PRESIDENT
　　World Exclusive

At the last minute, at 6 p.m. on Saturday evening, NEWSWEEK magazine killed a story that was destined to shake official Washington to its foundation: A White House intern carried on a sexual affair with the President of the United States!

The DRUDGE REPORT has learned that reporter Michael Isikoff developed the story of his career, only to have it spiked by top NEWSWEEK suits hours before publication. A young woman, 23, sexually involved with the love of her life, the President of the United States, since she was a 21-year-old intern at the White House. She was a frequent visitor to a small study just off the Oval Office where she claims to have indulged the president's sexual preference. Reports of the relationship spread in White House quarters and she was moved to a job at the Pentagon, where she worked until last month.

The young intern wrote long love letters to President Clinton, which she delivered through a delivery service. She was a frequent visitor at the White House after midnight, where she checked in the WAVE logs as visiting a secretary named Betty Curry, 57.

The DRUDGE REPORT has learned that tapes of intimate phone conversations exist.

The relationship between the president and the young woman become strained when the president believed that the young woman was bragging about the affair to others.

NEWSWEEK and Isikoff were planning to name the woman. Word of the story's impending release caused blind chaos in media circles; TIME magazine spent Saturday scrambling for its own version of the story, the DRUDGE REPORT has learned. The NEW YORK POST on Sunday was set to front the young intern's affair, but was forced to fall back on the dated ABC NEWS Kathleen Willey break.

The story was set to break just hours after President Clinton testified in the Paula Jones sexual harassment case.

Ironically, several years ago, it was Isikoff that found himself in a shouting match with editors who were refusing to publish even a portion of his meticulously researched investigative report that was to break Paula Jones. Isikoff worked for the WASHINGTON POST at the time, and left shortly after the incident to build them for the paper's sister magazine, NEWSWEEK.

Michael Isikoff was not available for comment late Saturday. NEWSWEEK was on voice mail.

The White House was busy checking the DRUDGE REPORT for details.

On January 18 Drudge followed up with the intern's name: Monica Lewinsky. Three days later, Drudge hit pay dirt again by pointing out that the possible existence of a "DNA trail" that could "confirm President's sexual involvement with Lewinsky":

Web Posted: 01/21/98 12:56:27 PST -- WATERGATE 1998
WORLD EXCLUSIVE
    MUST CREDIT THE DRUDGE REPORT
    CONTAINS GRAPHIC DESCRIPTIONS
    REPORT: LEWINSKY OFFERED U.N. JOB; INVESTIGATORS: DNA TRAIL MAY EXIST
    U.N. AMBASSADOR RICHARDSON OFFERED ME A JOB DURING A BREAKFAST MEETING AT THE WATERGATE HO-TEL -- WORDS WHITE HOUSE INTERN MONICA LEWINSKY, 24, ALLEGEDLY TOLD PENTAGON WORKER LINDA TRIPP LATE IN DECEMBER 1997.
    THE OFFER CAME AS LEWINSKY WAS ASKING TO RE-TURN TO THE WHITE HOUSE, THE DRUDGE REPORT HAS LEARNED, UNHAPPY IN THE PENTAGON JOB SHE HELD -- A JOB THAT SHE STARTED IN APRIL 1996 AFTER BEING RE-LEASED FROM A WHITE HOUSE POSITION.

"THEY WANTED HER OUT OF THE WHITE HOUSE DUR-
ING THE ELECTION," A SOURCE CLOSE TO THE INVESTIGA-
TION TELLS THE DRUDGE REPORT.

AMBASSADOR RICHARDSON WAS NOT AVAILABLE FOR
COMMENT.

WHITE HOUSE PRESS SECRETARY MIKE MCCURRY OF-
FERED NOTHING WHEN ASKED ABOUT THE ALLEGED
RICHARDSON JOB OFFER DURING WEDNESDAY'S PRESS
BRIEFING.

SEPARATELY, THE DRUDGE REPORT HAS LEARNED, IN-
VESTIGATORS HAVE BECOME CONVINCED THAT THERE
MAY BE A DNA TRAIL THAT COULD CONFIRM PRESIDENT
CLINTON'S SEXUAL INVOLVEMENT WITH LEWINSKY, A RE-
LATIONSHIP THAT WAS CAPTURED IN LEWINSKY'S OWN
VOICE ON AUDIO TAPE.

TRIPP HAS SHARED WITH INVESTIGATORS A CONVER-
SATION WHERE LEWINSKY ALLEGEDLY CONFIDED THAT
SHE KEPT A GARMENT WITH CLINTON'S DRIED SEMEN ON
IT—A GARMENT SHE SAID SHE WOULD NEVER WASH!

Shortly after the Drudge stories broke, former Clinton aide
George Stephanopoulos was on TV talking about impeachment.
Clinton privately told Dick Morris that he would have to lie his way
out of the mess.

On January 26, the night before his State of the Union address,
with Hillary by his side, President Clinton spoke to the nation.

"Now, I have to go back to work on my State of the Union
speech," Clinton said. "And I worked on it until pretty late last
night. But I want to say one thing to the American people. I want
you to listen to me. I'm going to say this again. I did not have sexual
relations with that woman, Miss Lewinsky. I never told anybody to
lie, not a single time—never. These allegations are false. And I need
to go back to work for the American people."[117]

Clinton later learned that Ken Starr had Lewinsky's semen-stained dress in his possession.

On August 17, 1998, Clinton admitted in a taped testimony that he had had an "improper physical relationship" with Lewinsky. That night, the president gave a nationally televised statement and admitted his relationship with the young intern was "not appropriate."[118]

Fearful that the courts would reinstate the Jones sexual harassment case, Bill decided to settle out of court on November 13, 1998. Jones never got her apology from Bill Clinton, but she did get a whopping $850,000 and credibility. Of this sum, Jones received $200,000 personally; the rest went to her lawyers. In April 1999, Judge Wright also made Bill pay an additional $1,202 to the court (for civil contempt of the court) and another $90,000 to the Jones lawyers for expenses incurred.[119]

Clinton was impeached by the House of Representatives in December 1998 and was put on trial in the Senate in February 1999.

Before he left office on January 19, 2001, Clinton also agreed to be stripped of his law license for five years and to pay a fine of $250,000 out of his legal fund.

Paula Jones had extracted her "pound of flesh" from Bill Clinton.

CHAPTER 7

ORGY ISLAND

"Well, he owes me a favor."

—Jeffrey Epstein, convicted pedophile, on Bill Clinton[120]

The post presidency of Bill Clinton was party time. Time to get away from Senator Hillary, time to earn huge money from speaking engagements, time for traveling (usually in someone else's personal jet), and time to chase women. And he kept bad company.

After he left the presidency in 2001, Bill Clinton took up friendships with some pretty questionable characters, birds of a feather, one could say. One of these men was Ron Burkle, a major Clinton fundraiser and someone who *Mediaite* called "a well-known womanizer and model hound."[121] Burkle paid Clinton at least $15 million to act as a "rainmaker" for him, and another side benefit for Clinton was that he got to hang out with Burkle and all his "pretty young things" and fly on Burkle's plane, which his aides referred to as "Air Fuck One."[122]

But that was the tip of the iceberg. Another even more questionable friend with whom Bill associated post presidency was billionaire and pedophilia ringmaster Jeffrey Epstein. If Burkle was a case of a man with a taste for "young girls," then Jeffrey Epstein would be the case of a man with a taste for "far too young girls."

Epstein was handsome, muscular, charming, and cultured. He was connected, and although he lived an opulent lifestyle, he remained low key. His address book, seized by Palm Beach police, was a cornucopia of A-list contacts, including international bankers, scientists, athletes, lawyers, and politicians. He had a palatial home on the Upper East Side of Manhattan, a cloistered Palm Beach mansion, and a high-security private island where he could conduct his late-night parties, within the U.S. Virgin Islands. FOX TV pundit Sean Hannity dubbed it "Orgy Island."

Bill Clinton in the early 2000s became quite personally close to Epstein, whom had had met while he was still president in the 1990s. Clinton took eighteen trips on Epstein's plane (which was known as the "Lolita Express" for orgies with underage girls). He also gave Epstein twenty-one ways to contact him, basically sharing the phone numbers of all key people close to him.

Hillary was not one of the contacts. Epstein was, however, wired to Hillary's closest advisors, Cheryl Mills and Ann Stock.[123]

Cheryl Mills, whose cell phone number and email address were listed in the book, was Hillary's chief of staff at the State Department after serving as senior advisor for her 2008 presidential campaign. In the 1990s, she was an associate counsel for the Clinton White House. Cheryl Mills is as inner circle with Hillary as Huma Abedin has been.

Dubbed Hillary's "henchwoman," Mills is thought to have obstructed the Benghazi investigation into the death of four Americans, vetted and erased Hillary's emails, and—incredibly—sat on the Clinton Foundation Board while she was a State Department employee. This was a stunning conflict of interest considering the staggering level of largesse the foundation took from companies and interests doing business in the armament business.

As for Stock, she was hired by Hillary to run her Social Office in the White House. Kathleen Willey, who worked as a volunteer in the Social Office, says Stock "had no sense of decorum or good taste, which was typical of the Clinton White House. She cussed like a sailor, dropping the 'F bomb' every other minute."[124] Perhaps Stock was Hillary's point of contact with Epstein for the little stuff, while heavyweight Mills was Hillary's point of contact with Epstein for the big stuff.

Bill and Hillary Clinton need to explain why the Clinton Foundation in July of 2006 accepted $25,000 from the C.O.U.Q Foundation, which was being run by Epstein.[125] This donation occurred just after Epstein had been arrested for sex crimes, but had not yet received his jaw-dropping, favorable plea bargain courtesy of Florida prosecutors and later federal prosecutors.

Epstein also had a longtime girlfriend, Ghislaine Maxwell. According to the lawsuit of victim Virginia Roberts, Maxwell was heavily involved in Epstein's activities. She is said by Roberts to have assisted Epstein in his "hobby" of having sex with underage girls. Maxwell and five other women, according to Roberts, would even go down to the Fort Lauderdale bus station as she would troll for underaged girls to be sexually pandered to her boyfriend Epstein. Ghislaine became very close to Bill Clinton and was even allowed to attend Chelsea Clinton's wedding on July 31, 2010. She had contributed $2,300 to the presidential campaign of Hillary Clinton on March 30, 2007.[126]

Maxwell was also "on a list of delegates for a Bill Clinton charity conference" and "is listed as the managing director of the New York Strategy Group, of which there seems to be little trace."[127] A question for Bill and Hillary might be: Is the Clinton Foundation shoveling money to Maxwell in return for, say, staying silent about any of Bill Clinton's sexual activities with underage girls of the Epstein entourage?

Bill Clinton has been socially close with both Epstein and Maxwell. Was Bill being provided underaged girls for sexual purposes? You gauge the odds on that. "One thing is clear," Hannity once noted, "and that is that former President Bill Clinton had a very close relationship with a shady pedophile."[128]

A Democratic mega-donor and billionaire, Epstein was linked by the FBI and Palm Beach Police to as many as thirty-five underaged girls and allegedly provided minor girls to Prince Andrew, among other VIP pedophiles.

There is currently a lawsuit by several of the child sex victims of Epstein to overturn a questionably light plea bargain that resulted in this prolific pedophile Epstein having to serve only thirteen months in jail with a sixteen-hour-a-day pass. After molesting perhaps up to one thousand girls (as Epstein confessed to his sex slave Virginia Roberts), Jeffrey Epstein was allowed to just sleep nights in the county jail while the rest of his day could be spent in luxury at his Palm Beach mansion. Based on what thirty-three child victims who have actually settled lawsuits with him have said, Epstein should be serving a twenty-year sentence in state prison.

On FOX, Coulter spoke the truth on the Epstein case. She hit the nail on the head when she said, "This is the elites circling the wagon and protecting a pederast." Let's take Coulter's observations a step further: the Epstein case is about the pedophile elite VIP friends of Epstein circling the wagons and protecting not just Epstein, but also themselves.[129]

"Elitism" is really about people who believe that because they have huge amounts of power, money, and connections, the rules of society that the common man or woman must follow do not apply to them. Jeffrey Epstein was running a well-organized sex trafficking ring that provided underaged girls for him and his pedophile friends, many of whom were VIP figures in business and politics with names you would recognize.

How Epstein, after molesting all this girls, got his "Get Out of Jail Free" card is a long and disheartening story. However, the reason for it is simple: Epstein was pandering these girls to many other VIP pedophiles, and the government, which is supposed to protect children, did not want a "political mess" (in the words of Bush Attorney General Alberto Gonzales, in this case) on its hands.

Incredibly, state and federal prosecutors originally charged Epstein with one count of soliciting a prostitute. They only added "soliciting a minor" after objections by both the Palm Beach police and the FBI.

We believe that the Epstein case was corrupted because Epstein's VIP pedophile friends leaned on the government to give a mere wrist slap to a major trafficker in young underage girls.

In 2010, the *Daily Beast* reported that Epstein's "victims alleged that Epstein molested underaged girls from South America, Europe, and the former Soviet republics, including three twelve-year-old girls brought over from France as a birthday gift."[130] Epstein also once bragged that he had "bought" a fourteen-year-old girl for his personal sexual gratification.

As of 2015, the families of thirty-three female child sex victims of Epstein have settled lawsuits with Epstein, according to journalist Nick Bryant, who has followed the Epstein case closely. Seven victims have settled lawsuits with Epstein and have received well over $1 million each for their sexual molestations by Epstein.[131] Epstein's lawyers were the high-powered Roy Black, Gerald Lefcourt, Starr (for GOP influence peddling), Guy Lewis, Martin Weinberger, and Epstein's very close personal friend Alan Dershowitz.

Virginia Roberts, known in an ongoing lawsuit as Jane Doe #3, was the precious jewel of Epstein, who sexually abused her and pimped her out to his friends. Maxwell, Epstein's pedophile girlfriend, was the one who snared Roberts into the Epstein web when she was just fifteen and working as a towel girl at a local Palm Beach spa in 1998. After being pulled in by Ghislaine, one of several adult pedo recruiters for Epstein, Roberts became a sex slave and child prostitute who worked for Epstein for the next three years. Virginia, now thirty-one and a mother of three, says that she still cries at night when she thinks of Epstein. Many of these girls, now women, still cry when they think of what Epstein and his circle of VIP pedophiles did to them—how they stole their innocence.

Roberts said Epstein trafficked children to politicians, Wall Streeters, and A-listers to curry favor, to advance his business, and for political influence. Courageous Roberts said in her lawsuit that Epstein also made her have sex multiple times with both Prince Andrew and Epstein's close friend Alan Dershowitz. It should be noted that Dershowitz vehemently denies all the accusations against him. The Palm Beach lawyer and the former federal judge who filed the lawsuit on behalf of Roberts later filed a defamation suit against Dershowitz, after he said they were lying and acting unethically by making the claims that Roberts made.

In fact, Dershowitz's high-profile client list reads like a laundry list of murderers, rapists, and pedophiles: all rich, all guilty. Dershowitz was on the legal team of director Roman Polanski after the auteur raped a thirteen-year-old girl. Dershowitz defended "Iron" Mike Tyson after the pugilist was convicted of sexually assaulting beauty pageant contestant Desiree Washington. The high-powered attorney fought for British socialite Claus von Bulow, who was accused of poisoning his wife with insulin in order to inherit her fortune. And he waged war for Brooklyn cantor Baruch Lebovits, who was convicted in 2010 on eight of ten counts of child molestation and faced up to thirty-two years in prison.

In 1994, Dershowitz wrote a column that trivialized the rape of women, proclaiming that many rape accusations were false flags. "The problem of false rape reports is a serious one," wrote Dershowitz in the *Washington Times*. "The time has come to stop patronizing calculating women who use rape accusations to serve their own selfish interests."

In 2015, Prince Andrew was savaged by the British media over a famous photo of himself with a seventeen-year-old Roberts, taken by Epstein in 2001 in London. In late 2014, Roberts had said publicly in court filings that Epstein and Maxwell had compelled her to have sex with Prince Andrew on multiple occasions, including a situation in New York City where Epstein paid her $400 to have sex with the Prince—who for years had been denying any sexual involvement with the then teenager. Roberts also said that she and eight other girls had had sex with Prince Andrew on Epstein's spread on Little Virgin Island.[132]

When Epstein and Maxwell took Roberts to England, Roberts says that on the morning of her "date" with Prince Andrew, "Ghislaine came in. She was chirpy and jumped on the bed, saying, 'Get up, sleepyhead. You've got a big day. We've got to go shopping. You need a dress as you're going to dance with a Prince tonight.' She said I needed to be 'smiley' and bubbly because he was the Queen's son. Ghislaine and I went to Burberry, where she bought me a £5,000 bag, and to a few other designer stores where we bought a couple of dresses, a pair of embroidered jeans and a pink singlet, perfume, and makeup."[133]

Roberts said, "Epstein told me to 'exceed' everything I had been taught. He emphasized that whatever Prince Andrew wanted, I was to make sure he got," and that after the tryst, Epstein debriefed her on Prince Andrew's sexual proclivities.[134]

"I told Epstein about Andy's sexual interest in feet. Epstein thought it was very funny. Epstein appeared to be collecting private information about Andy."[135]

That last comment by Roberts indicates precisely why Epstein was so dangerous not just to the young girls he was sexually abusing and psychologically scarring, but also to the compromised pedophile elites to whom he was pandering girls.

Roberts also has some interesting things to say about Bill Clinton, whom she met on two occasions. "I'd have been about seventeen at the time," she said. "I flew to the Caribbean with Jeffrey and then Ghislaine Maxwell went to pick up Bill in a huge black helicopter that Jeffrey had bought her."[136]

In an interview with the *Daily Mail*, Roberts said that Epstein and Bill Clinton were good friends and that Epstein famously said that Bill owed him a favor. Epstein's currency was providing often-underage girls to his VIP friends.

Roberts recounted:

I only ever met Bill twice but Jeffrey had told me that they were good friends. I asked, "How come?" and he laughed and said, "He owes me some favors." Maybe he was just joking but it constantly surprised me that people with as much to lose as Bill and [Prince] Andrew weren't more careful.

Bill must have known about Jeffrey's girls. There were three desks in the living area of the villa on the island.

They were covered with pictures of Jeffrey shaking hands with famous people and photos of naked girls, including one of me that Jeffrey had at all his houses, lying in a hammock.

We all dined together that night. Jeffrey was at the head of the table. Bill was at his left. I sat across from him. Emmy Tayler, Ghislaine's blonde British assistant, sat at my right.

Ghislaine was at Bill's left and at the left of Ghislaine there were two olive-skinned brunettes who'd flown in with us from New York.

I'd never met them before. I'd say they were no older than seventeen, very innocent looking. They weren't there for me. They weren't there for Jeffrey or Ghislaine because I was there to have sex with Jeffrey on the trip.

Maybe Jeffrey thought they would entertain Bill, but I saw no evidence that he was interested in them. He and Jeffrey and Ghislaine seemed to have a very good relationship. Bill was very funny.

He made me laugh a few times. And he and Jeffrey and Ghislaine told blokey jokes and the brunettes listened politely and giggled.

After dinner I gave Jeffrey an erotic massage. I don't remember seeing Bill again on the trip but I assume Ghislaine flew him back.[137]

Another Epstein masseuse (and former lingerie model), Chauntae Davies, says she was with Clinton when he flew on Epstein's airplane to Africa. Davis, who sat for an interview with *Inside Edition* in April of 2015, is adamant that she never had sex with Epstein and that she never gave Clinton a massage. "Massage" was Epstein's code word for having sex.

Conchita Sarnoff, who has written about Epstein extensively for the *Daily Beast*, said Clinton made at least seventeen trips—confirmed by flight records—with Epstein. Sarnoff, who is head of the Alliance to Rescue Victims of Trafficking, says that Random House refused to publish her book *Sex Slaves in America* because it contained damaging information about Bill Clinton. Sarnoff said, "They will not publish the book unless I take out the Clinton stuff."[138] The major book publisher refuses to expose Clinton's documented relationship with a notorious pedophile.

Roberts described what would happen on Epstein's plane, which was outfitted with a bed and had an atmosphere like that of the Playboy mansion: "It was a lot of the same things that went down on the ground. There would be sexual conduct; there would be foreplay. There was a bed in there, so we could basically re-enact exactly what happened in the house. It would start off with massaging or we would start off with foreplay. Sometimes it would lead to, you know, orgies."[139] Bill Clinton was on this plane seventeen times.

By any objective standard of typical criminal liability imposed anywhere in the United States, it is beyond question that Epstein, along with his billions and his clever, well-connected lawyers, managed to either buy, bargain, or bully his way out of any meaningful legal or moral accountability for countless sexual abuse offenses perpetrated against dozens of children for years.

As if this travesty of justice was itself not enough to sate their sense of impunity, Epstein's fellow elites have routinely praised, defended, and otherwise excused Epstein. Now, they give the same treatment to Epstein's other sex cohorts, including Bill Clinton and Prince Andrew.

Enter Michael Wolff, an Epstein confidant (Wolff now writes a regular column for British *GQ*) who recently penned a withering, faux-flummoxed attack in *USA Today* pooh-poohing the "new age" media and the American legal system, along with Epstein's persistent "Jane Doe" accusers and their pernicious Florida attorneys, Paul G. Cassell (a former federal judge) and Bradley J. Edwards.

Wolff exudes the preening condescension and huffy indignation that is the hallmark of elite, deviant cover-up artists, rushing to excuse one of their own. Wolff's somewhat flustered yet strangely navel-gazing editorial conveniently skips right over the part about his child-molesting pal Jeffrey Epstein buying himself and his confederates a free pass from any criminal punishment commensurate with the scope and extent of their heinous child sex crimes.

Wolff leaps right to the offensive against those forces, whether human or systemic, that he believes unduly besmirched Epstein's elite sex cronies. He paints the whole thing almost in conspiratorial terms: "all part of a scripted game," he writes. Wolff conveniently neglects to disclose to *USA Today*'s readers his own skin in the game, his courtesan-esque coziness and nearly two-decades-long (and presumably continuing) personal relationship with the child-molesting Epstein.

Wolff perhaps forgot the 2007 *New York* magazine piece by Jeffrey Weiss delving into Epstein's well-insulated personal fiefdom, with Wolff in the role of gushing, star-struck Epstein sycophant. The article further describes Epstein as a "discreet confidant to Wolff . . . when Wolff was involved in a bid for *New York* magazine."

"It was all a little giddy," the article quotes Wolff as saying, describing his late '90s entree into Epstein's surreal fantasy life, as he boarded Epstein's "beautiful 727" with a flight full of elites to a West Coast conference.

"Jeffrey is living a life that once might have been prized and admired and valued, but its moment has passed. . . . I think the culture has outgrown it. You can't describe it without being held to severe account. It's not allowed. It may be allowed if you're secretive and furtive, but Jeffrey is anything but secretive and furtive. I think it represents an achievement to Jeffrey."

Apparently for Wolff it is a no-no to *describe* a degenerate criminal "lifestyle" such as Epstein's, but not necessarily to actually live it. He hints that this kind of lifestyle "may be allowed," as long as it remains covert.

Not to be too obvious in exonerating Epstein with such faint damnation, Wolff is quoted as offering Epstein counsel on how to be less ostentatious about his pedophilia: "He has never been secretive about the girls. . . . At one point, when his troubles began, he was talking to me and said, 'What can I say, I like young girls.' I said, 'Maybe you should say, "I like young women."'" Surely, noble advice from a loyal friend.

Fast-forwarding to 2015, Wolff's *USA Today* editorial decrying public accusations against Epstein pals is chock full of similarly subtle, almost subliminal, sophistry. It is totally free of any supporting factual substance to boot.

For example, the Florida Jane Doe case that was recently expanded from two to four victims in its ongoing pursuit of federal criminal justice against Epstein and his child sex trafficking cohorts is dubbed "unpromising" and "the allegations do not derive from law enforcement personnel making charges related to an investigation; rather, they come entirely from someone filing a lawsuit in an effort to win compensation and damages."

He writes as if it were not a bold-faced public fact that the Palm Beach police, led by Chief Michael Reiter, publicly expressed in no uncertain terms outrage and dismay at the miscarriage of justice in Epstein's so-called prosecution and his subsequent federal "non-prosecution."

For over a year, Reiter and his department had scrupulously compiled a case against Epstein based on sworn statements establishing Epstein's repeated sexual abuse of five young girls, one just fourteen at the time of Epstein's predation, with other evidence of Epstein's abuse of up to thirty-five other underage female victims.

These "law enforcement personnel" surely would disagree with Wolff's implication that there is nothing more to the case than Epstein's one-count solicitation of a minor conviction and the negligble so-called punishment arranged for Epstein between Dershowitz and Barry Krischer, the Florida state attorney.

Wolff would do well to look into a California civil case a few years ago involving a civil defendant named O. J. Simpson who was found liable for murder where the criminal justice system found him not guilty. Should the federal government undertake the duty it has so far shirked to pursue Epstein's interstate child sex-trafficking allegations, Wolff may yet eat his words.

Given the course of the Epstein case, particularly the state and federal betrayal of underaged sex crime victims that got Epstein off practically scot-free, the problems exposed in the criminal justice system are far more grave, profound, and damaging to public trust than any journalistic lament about the wealthy and famous being done wrong in the "new" media age or even sensationalistic abuses of legal pleadings.

Nick Bryant has written several articles on the Epstein case for *Gawker*. One of those articles was titled "Here is Pedophile Billionaire Jeffrey Epstein's Little Black Book." Epstein kept a black book filled to the brim with the names of VIPs as well as the names and contact phones of numerous girls, many of them underaged, whom Epstein and his VIP friends would have sex with. The house manager, or butler, for Epstein at his Palm Beach mansion was a man named Alfredo Rodriguez, who died of cancer in late 2014. Rodriguez stole the black book of Epstein and he circled the names of the VIPs, who he thought were involved in sex with underage girls or who might be material witnesses to the pedophilia that ringmaster Epstein was orchestrating. Thirty-three names were circled, of which he suspected seven might be "witnesses" to the Epstein pedophilia and twenty-six might be "participants."

In her lawsuit deposition, Roberts said she met billionaire Donald Trump once at Epstein's Palm Beach mansion and that he was a "complete gentleman" and that she never saw him act inappropriately. Trump turned down numerous invitations to Epstein's hedonistic private island and his Palm Beach home. There is no evidence Trump did anything improper. "The one time I visited his Palm Beach home, the swimming pool was full of beautiful young girls," Trump told a member of his Club Mar Lago "'How nice,' I thought, 'he let the neighborhood kids use his pool.'" Unlike the Clintons, Trump cut Epstein and his underlings off the instant he heard about the Palm Beach police investigation. The Clinton Foundation actually took a donation from Epstein after he had a probable cause affidavit file on him by Palm Beach police in May of 2006!

Another important name circled by Rodriguez as being a potential witness to the pedophilia was Les Wexner, a billionaire and Republican mega-donor who is worth $7.2 billion as of 2015. A retail giant, Wexner owns The Limited, Victoria's Secret, and numerous other properties. Wexner is also a bigwig on the American Jewish Committee. Wikipedia says, "President George W. Bush appointed Wexner to serve on the Honorary Delegation to accompany him to Jerusalem for the celebration of the 60th anniversary of the State of Israel in 2008."[140]

Epstein's closest and dearest friend, Les Wexner was very tight with the Republican Bush family. At the same time, Epstein was a close personal friend of Democrat Bill Clinton, who also is so collegial with the Bush family that they have practically adopted him and call him "brother" and "Bubba." Isn't it easy to see how and why the Epstein prosecution got corrupted so easily in 2006 and 2007 under the presidency of George W. Bush? This is how the corroded rectum of American politics works in real life when the TV cameras are not present.

Epstein became a financial advisor to Wexner in 1985, and by the early 1990s, Epstein was allegedly worth billions. Epstein has said that the two were so close that it was as if they shared one brain. *Gawker*'s Nick Denton has speculated that Epstein and

Wexner may have been bisexual and enjoyed underage men and women.[iv]

A 1985 *New York* magazine article described Wexner as a "confirmed bachelor," though he later married and had four children. "A lot of people think because I am not married I am asexual or homosexual, but I enjoy a relationship with a woman," he said some time later. Apparently he hated to discuss this, preferring to keep his love life under wraps.[141]

As for Bill Clinton . . . Robert Morrow, while speaking with a seasoned investigator into the pedophilia of Jeffrey Epstein, opined, "With Bill's history of rape and sexual assault, I think the odds that Bill Clinton was *not* being pandered underaged girls by Jeffrey Epstein would have to be one in a million." The reply to Morrow by this investigator into Epstein was, "Make that more like one in a billion." The lawyers for some of Epstein's many victims had told this investigator that *of course* Bill Clinton was likely being provided underage girls to have sex with by Epstein.

Taking into account Bill's uninhibited and often abusive sexual rap sheet, that should have been clear: "So with his background, we are supposed to believe that [Clinton] was at this island where all this activity with young women is going on and Bill Clinton, of all people, was an innocent observer of all the activities?" Sean Hannity asked incredulously.[142]

Bill Clinton has done nothing to deserve the benefit of the doubt when it comes to a sex scandal or, more importantly, sex crimes. Clinton's serial assaults on women have been documented. At least four of his victims say he raped and/or savagely bit them, often while sporting a beet-red face, and several describe his penis as small and twisted—"like a corkscrew," one Arkansas secretary said. Remember, Monica Lewinsky said that his penis had a

---

iv A pair of articles Nick Denton wrote for *Gawker*, "Teen-Loving Epstein's Own Client" (2008) (referring to Les Wexner) and "Victoria's Secret" (2015), explore the possibility of a sexual relationship between Epstein and Wexner.

distinguishing characteristic. Epstein, whose currency was pedophilic pimping, cryptically said that Bill Clinton "owes him favors."[143] Does Maxwell have photographs of Clinton that could shatter the Clintons' 2016 bid to regain the White House?

Roberts said she did not have sex with Bill Clinton. The question is, who among Epstein's group did? Epstein told Roberts that he had been with over one thousand girls (many provided by his friend, modeling agency owner Jean Luc Brunel), so that leaves a lot of underaged girls, acquired from all over the world, who could have been pandered to a sexually unrestrained Bill Clinton.

Epstein had more ways to contact his friend Bill than he did for anyone else in his black book (except for Wexner)—a whopping twenty-one. All of Bill's contact numbers were listed under the name of Bill's top aide at the time, Doug Band, misspelled in Epstein's book as "Doug Bands." Here are all the twenty-one ways Epstein could get hold of his buddy Bill Clinton:

Bands, Doug
Office of William J. Clinton
55 West 125th St.
NY 10027, 001 212 977 112
202 320 4109 p
212 348 8882
Email: wjc@imcingular.com
(Hm) 200 West 60th
Apt. 22G
New York
Ny, 10023
212-348-6751 David Slade
202-406-8002 Mike Lee (w)
301-627-8125 Mike Lee (h)
914-806-0462 Mike Lee (car)
877-741-2905 Mike Lee (b)
Mike Lee email

mlee@uss.treas.gov
07 787 524 101 Sara Lalham
646-227-4930 Denise Diorio
Spking scheduler
212-348-0452 Joe Cashion asst director scheduling
202-236-5546 Uma
914-806-0463 Mark Galespie
202-288-5192 Mike Lee (p)
212-828-8321 Jim Morrison
212-348-9245 fax
212-348-4963 Hanna Richert
212-348-1779 Laura (Clinton's scheduler)
941-349-6467 Doug Bands h
917-887-8468 Jim Kennedy (press)
212-977-1120 (guy Doug friend h)
914-861-9380 no. 42 do not use

The last number, labeled "no. 42 do not use," was Clinton's personal cell phone number in the mid-2000s. It is indeed a cell number for Chappaqua, New York (where the Clintons have a home). However, it was long ago reassigned to someone else.

Another one of Epstein's close friends was Harvard superlawyer Alan Dershowitz. Here is what Roberts, now age thirty-one, had to say about Dershowitz in a January 2015 court filing:

24. Harvard law professor Alan Dershowitz was around Epstein frequently. Dershowitz was so comfortable with the sex that was going on that he would even come and chat with Epstein while I was giving oral sex to Epstein.

25. I had sexual intercourse with Dershowitz at least six times. The first time was when I was about 16, early on in my servitude to Epstein, and it continued until I was 19.

26. The first time we had sex took place in New York in Epstein's home. It was in Epstein's room (not the massage room). I was approximately 16 years old at the time. I called Dershowitz "Alan." I knew he was a famous professor.

27. The second time that I had sex with Dershowitz was at Epstein's house in Palm Beach. During this encounter, Dershowitz instructed me to both perform oral sex and have sexual intercourse.

28. I also had sex with Dershowitz at Epstein's Zorro Ranch in New Mexico in the massage room off of the indoor pool area, which was still being painted.

29. We also had sex at Little Saint James Island in the U.S. Virgin Islands. I was asked to give Dershowitz a massage on the beach. Dershowitz then asked me to take him somewhere more private, where we proceeded to have intercourse.[144]

Dershowitz has said that his relationship with Epstein was "entirely professional." Yet, a 2003 *Vanity Fair* piece by Vicky Ward paints a different portrait: "Alan Dershowitz says that, as he was getting to know Epstein, his wife asked him if he would still be close to him if Epstein suddenly filed for bankruptcy," Ward wrote. "Dershowitz says he replied, 'Absolutely. I would be as interested in him as a friend if we had hamburgers on the boardwalk in Coney Island and talked about his ideas.'"[145]

In the same *Vanity Fair* piece, Dershowitz said of Epstein, "I'm on my 20th book. . . . The only person outside my immediate family that I send drafts to is Jeffrey."[146]

It is clear that Epstein and Dershowitz had a close personal friendship that went far deeper than the purely professional lawyer-client relationship that Dershowitz would claim after Epstein had been exposed as a prolific child molester.

Dershowitz discussed how he first met Jeffrey Epstein: "Let me tell you how I met him. I was introduced to him by Lady de Rothschild as an academic colleague. He was friendly with Larry Summers. . . . He was in the process of contributing $50 million to Harvard for evolutionary biology." Epstein's first donation to Harvard was in 2003.[147]

However, flight logs prove that Dershowitz flew on Epstein's plane, which often was an orgy plane, as early as December 1997 and also in October 1998 and in 1999.

Dershowitz, who is being sued for defamation by Roberts and by the lawyers for the sex victims of Epstein, has made statements on national TV proclaiming that Roberts has said that she had sex with Bill Clinton and that Virginia Roberts has said that she met the Queen. Roberts, however, has repeatedly and specifically said that she has *never* had sex with Bill Clinton. However she also said that Epstein said Bill "owes him favors" and that Bill had to have known about the pedophilia because there were so many pictures of naked underage girls on the walls and tables of Epstein's residences.

In the words of Roberts in paragraph 53 of her 2015 court filing: "I have seen reports saying or implying that I had sex with former president Bill Clinton on Little Saint James Island. Former president Bill Clinton was present on the island at a time when I was also present on the island, but I have never had sexual relations with Clinton, nor have I ever claimed to have had such relations. I have never seen him have sexual relations with anyone."[148]

The Epstein Non-Prosecution Agreement says that "the United States also agrees that it will not institute any criminal charges against any potential co-conspirators of Epstein, including but not limited to Sarah Kellen, Adriana Ross, Lesley Groff, and Nadia Marcinkova." These were all women who allegedly recruited underage girls for Epstein to have sex with. A victim herself, Nadia is thought to have often had sex with Epstein and other teenage girl sex victims. Epstein's code for sex was "massage" and Sarah

Kellen in particular was thought to be one of Jeffrey Epstein's most prolific enablers of pedophilia.[149]

Nick Bryant on Kellen: "Kellen in particular was believed by detectives in the Palm Beach Police Department, which was the first to start unraveling the operation, to be so deeply involved in the enterprise that they prepared a warrant for her arrest as an accessory to molestation and sex with minors."[150]

Dershowitz, the very lawyer negotiating this egregious plea bargain, was among those "conspiring" to be pandered underaged girls by his social friend and client Epstein according to Roberts. This Non-Prosecution Agreement was done in secrecy, without informing the known thirty-plus underaged sex victims of Jeffrey Epstein, and this shameful "Get Out of Jail Free" card was then sealed by the federal prosecutors in the Epstein case because they knew there would be sharp public outrage if the terms were made public. A lawsuit by a Palm Beach newspaper finally forced a federal judge to let the public see what had gone on behind the backs of the victims.

Usually in a plea bargain, a perpetrator gets a lighter sentence in exchange for information or testimony that will lead to the prosecution of other co-conspirators. Epstein's Non-Prosecution Agreement stinks to high heaven and appears to be tailored to let Epstein's pedophile enablers (the recruiters of the girls, especially Maxwell and Kellen) off scot-free. Unsurprisingly, these women have not gone public with details about Epstein's pedophilia or what they know about the activities of his VIP pedophile cohorts. Call it a "conspiracy of silence."

As of 2015, the families of thirty-three sexual molestation victims have settled lawsuits with Epstein. Some of these settlements were in the millions, ensuring that these girls, now women, wouldn't testify as to the sexual brutality of Epstein and his wingman Jean Luc Brunel. Four of Epstein's victims are in the courts seeking justice, and it only through their courageous and detailed testimony that the stunning elite privilege and immunity from prosecution that

Epstein enjoys because of his wealth and power is exposed to all. That, and the courage of the editors at the *Palm Beach Post*.

Maxwell, the friend of Bill Clinton and the girlfriend Epstein would never marry, may have pulled an innocent Roberts into Epstein's web, according to Roberts's court filing, paragraphs 20 to 23:

20. Ghislaine Maxwell was heavily involved in the illegal sex. I understood her to be a very powerful person. She used Epstein's money and he used her name and connections to gain power and prestige.

21. One way to describe Maxwell's role was as the "madame." She assumed a position of trust for all the girls, including me. She got me to trust her and Epstein. It turned out that Maxwell was all about sex all the time. She had sex with underaged girls virtually every day when I was around her, and she was very forceful.

22. I first had sexual activities with her when I was approximately 15 at the Palm Beach mansion. I had many sexual activities with her over the next several years in Epstein's various residences plus other exotic locations. I had sex with Maxwell in the Virgin Islands, New Mexico, New York, as well as France and many other locations. I also observed Maxwell have sex with dozens of underaged girls.

23. Maxwell took pictures of many of the underaged girls. These pictures were sexually explicit. Maxwell kept the pictures on the computers in the various houses. She also made hard copies of these images and displayed them in the various houses. Maxwell had large amounts of child pornography that she personally made. Many times she made me sleep with other girls, some of whom were very young, for purposes of taking sexual pictures.[151]

By this account, Maxwell is painted as every bit as enthusiastic about child sex as was her then boyfriend Jeffrey Epstein. But even after Epstein served his time in jail, and Maxwell was invited to Chelsea's wedding, her "charity" got put on the dole of the Clinton Foundation. In fact, while the Clintons may have cut off Epstein, Maxwell remains an intimate of the Clintons and is running TerraMar, a nonprofit funded by the Clinton Foundation, according to the foundation website.

Roberts alleged that one of Maxwell's responsibilities as Epstein's right-hand woman was to photograph the billionaire's sexual abuse victims, whose photos were displayed like a pedophilic menu on a marble table in Epstein's private island retreat. Roberts testified that Clinton would certainly have seen this display. A former editor of the *National Enquirer* told us that his reporters had learned that Maxwell has retained a photo of former president Bill Clinton in a compromising position with a seventeen-year-old. Elites may snicker, but the *National Enquirer* was right about former North Carolina Senator John Edwards's sex scandal when the mainstream media refused to examine the allegations.

One could easily imagine Bill Clinton and Maxwell hopping into bed with a pair of seventeen-year-old models who Epstein had laid out as a trap for Bill Clinton. Epstein had cameras in his homes and on his airplanes; they were even in his bathrooms. This scenario is possible, maybe even probable, because Clinton, Ghislaine, and Epstein all have sexual rap sheets that are despicable.

Former Delaware Congressman Thomas B. Evans, Jr., was on the board of Towers Investors where Epstein learned at the knee of legendary Ponzi scammer Steven Hoffenberg. Evans resigned from the board and as head of the finance committee over irregularities he refused to paper over. "Epstein was handsome and virile," Evans said. "At his request I set him up with a nice Jewish girl who was a friend of my wife, Mary Page. She said later that Epstein only wanted to fuck her and showed no interest in dinner or social intercourse."[152]

Maxwell (whose father is deceased media tycoon and Mossad agent Robert Maxwell) was instrumental in introducing Epstein to an international VIP list. Robert Maxwell was the flamboyant and controversial British press lord whose mysterious death, falling off the back of his yacht, was thought by many to be faked. "He's in Israel," said Hoffenberg, who pulled off the second-largest Ponzi scheme in the country . . . second only to Bernie Madoff. Ghislaine was the glamorous, jet-setting daughter, who was expected to come up with an endless supply of young girls for Epstein.

The other person who Roberts said played a critical role in the underage sex was Jean Luc Brunel, to whom Epstein reportedly gave $2 million for his modeling agency, which is said to have been designed to funnel in underage girls for sex by Epstein and his circle. After the Epstein scandal broke open in 2006, Epstein had dozens of meetings with Brunel over the next few years. After the victim's lawsuit against the government became news again in early 2015, the relationship between Epstein and Brunel soured greatly because of devastating fallout to Brunel's modeling business.

A *Daily Beast* headline, "Model King Sues Billionaire Perv Jeffrey Epstein," and the accompanying article went on to describe the death of Brunel's modeling business. "In the lawsuit, Brunel says he can't recruit any more as the European gals know how to search his name online. In South America, moms refuse to entrust their daughters with a man who has been branded a sex trafficker."[153]

Here is a nasty but apropos description of Brunel from Michael Gross's 1995 book, *Model:*

> "Jean Luc is considered a danger," says Jérôme Bonnouvrier. "Owning Karins was a dream for a playboy. His problem is that he knows exactly what girls in trouble are looking for. He's always been on the edge of the system. John Casablancas gets with girls the healthy way. Girls would be with him if he was the butcher. They're with Jean Luc because he's the boss. Jean Luc likes drugs and silent rape. It excites him."

"I really despise Jean Luc as a human being for the way he's cheapened the business," says John Casablancas. "There is no justice. This is a guy who should be behind bars. There was a little group, Jean-Luc, Patrick Gilles, and Varsano. . . .They were very well-known in Paris for roaming the clubs. They would invite girls and put drugs in their drinks. Everybody knew they were creeps."[154]

And this from Dorothy Parker: "Jean Luc is a pimp and he was a pimp. Before Karins [his modeling agency], he took girls and sold them to agencies in Paris. I was in Ibiza with the daughter of a friend, fifteen years old, and he came to the table and wanted this girl."[155]

Here is a typical message from Brunel to Epstein, which one of Epstein's assistants left for him: "He has a teacher for you to teach you how to speak Russian. She is 2 x 8 years old and blonde. Lessons are free and you can have 1st today if you call."[156] Translation: *I have a sixteen-year-old Russian girl for you to have sex with for free. Call me and I will let you see her first.* The age of consent for sex in Florida is age eighteen; in New York, it is age seventeen; and in the Virgin Islands, it is eighteen.

Diane Sawyer and *60 Minutes* investigated Brunel as long ago as in 1988. *Jezebel* reported, "The program interviewed nearly two dozen models who said they had been sexually assaulted by Brunel and/or by his fellow agent, Claude Haddad." Even at that time, Brunel had a reputation as a man one could go to procure a "date" with a young model. CBS spoke to with five models who said that Brunel and/or his friends had drugged and raped them. Said producer Craig Pyes, "Hundreds of girls were not only harassed, but molested."[157]

Brunel's MC2 was founded in 2005. Modeling agency or pedophilia recruiting pipeline? You pick the description of Brunel's organization. "Jeff put his money up for this guy to get Jeffrey these young girls. That's a front for Jeffrey's securing more and more young girls," a longtime Epstein friend told the *Daily Beast*.[158]

This much is certain: Brunel was one of Epstein's closest friends, and both men have a very long history of ties to sex with underage girls. Brunel visited Epstein in jail sixty-seven times, according to jail logs.[159] Incredibly, Epstein only had to report to the Palm Beach jail at ten in the evening and stay till six in the morning. He was unsupervised at all hours and was allowed to travel and visit his home or office, as long as he made his ten o'clock curfew. One Palm Beach County corrections officer told Roger Stone that servants would often bring Epstein a gourmet dinner and fine wine, as "Mr. Epstein liked to dine late."[160]

Here is what Roberts had to say about Jean Luc Brunel in a court filing in January of 2015 in paragraphs 47 to 51:

> 47. I also had sexual intercourse with Jean Luc Brunel many times when I was 16 through 19 years old. He was another of Epstein's powerful friends who had many contacts with young girls throughout the world. In fact, his only similarity with Epstein and the only link to their friendship appeared to be that Brunel could get dozens of underaged girls and feed Epstein's (and Maxwell's) strong appetite for sex with minors.

> 48. Brunel ran some kind of modeling agency and appeared to have an arrangement with the U.S. Government where he could get passports or other travel documents for young girls. He would then bring these young girls (girls ranging in age from 12 to 24) to the United States for sexual purposes and farm them out to his friends, including Epstein.

> 49. Brunel would offer the girls "modeling" jobs. A lot of the girls came from poor countries or poor backgrounds, and he lured them in with a promise of making good money.

50. I had to have sex with Brunel at Little St. James (orgies), Palm Beach, New York City, New Mexico, Paris, the south of France, and California. He did not care about conversation, just sex.

51. Jeffrey Epstein has told me that he has slept with over 1,000 of Brunel's girls, and everything that I have seen confirms this claim. Epstein, Brunel, and Maxwell loved orgies with kids - that is, having sexual interactions with many young teenagers at the same time. Sometimes as many as ten underaged girls would participate in a single orgy with them. I personally observed dozens of these orgies. The orgies happened on Epstein's island in the U.S. Virgin Islands, in New Mexico, Palm Beach, and many other places. Most of the girls did not speak English. It is my understanding that the girls had been persuaded to come by Brunel offering them illegal drugs or a career in modeling. Brunel was one of the main procurers of girls.[161]

With their reputations being linked to orgies, drugs, and partying with young girls, Bill Clinton was a natural friend for Epstein and Maxwell. One could say they were on the same wavelength. Epstein even "bought" a fourteen-year-old girl from Eastern Europe, Nadia Marcinkova, who Epstein apparently said that he "had purchased her from her family in Yugoslavia. Epstein bragged he brought her into the United States to be his Yugoslavian sex slave."[162] Marcinkova later became a key facilitator and participant with Epstein when he had sex with other "too young" teenaged girls. She was skilled with Epstein's sex toys.

We find it enraging that Epstein, a close friend of Bill Clinton, got a mere wrist slap rather than many years in jail. Epstein's legal troubles belatedly began in March 2005, when a fourteen-year-old girl told her parents that she had been sexually molested by the Wall Street billionaire. Palm Beach police carefully investigated Epstein for a year and built a detailed probable cause affidavit against him that included five molestation victims of Epstein and two others they suspected. Search online for "2006 Jeffrey Epstein Probable Cause Affidavit" and you'll find this disturbing and meticulously detailed document.[163] The FBI later came in and identified over thirty under-aged sex victims of Epstein.

The Palm Beach police handed off their meticulously document-ed and airtight case to Palm Beach State Attorney Barry Krischer. At this point, we feel, the corruption in the Epstein case began. The fix was in.

Instead of a quick indictment of Epstein, followed by pressuring him with the hopes of getting him to plea bargain and give up the other co-conspirators in his massive sex-trafficking ring, Krischer made the unusual decision to call a grand jury to review the case. Barry Krischer led a grand jury by the nose to indict Epstein on just one single charge: solicitation of prostitution, the sex crime equiva-lent of jaywalking.

In Florida, grand juries are generally restricted to capital cases. Krischer presented evidence to that grand jury in 2006 and what came back was mind-boggling: a paltry one-count indictment of Epstein for solicitation of a prostitute. Nothing in the indictment pertained to sexually molesting a fourteen-year-old girl, nor was there anything about running a massive underage sex trafficking ring for VIP pedophiles. Those adults who supplied Epstein with children for the rich and powerful to molest have gone unpunished, as have the VIP pedophiles themselves. A neutral observer might conclude that Krischer had been corrupted by the pedophiles and had intentionally tanked the case behind the secrecy of a grand jury, or that Krishcher was one of the most incompetent state attorneys ever to serve in Florida.

Palm Beach Police Chief Michael Reiter had identified around five children used for the pleasure of Epstein and his friends and at least several who were procuring them. An intimidation cam-paign was waged by Epstein and his lawyers against Reiter, a good and honest man. He was being followed by strange men and "investigated" by the dark forces. Both Reiter and his top detective were being followed.

The *New York Times* in September 2006 covered the outraged reaction of Reiter: "Even before the indictment, the Palm Beach police chief, Michael Reiter, had accused prosecutors of giving Mr. Epstein special treatment and asked the state attorney, Barry E. Krischer, to remove himself from the case. In an editorial, the *Palm Beach Post* attacked Mr. Krischer, a Democrat whose post is elective, saying the public had been left 'to wonder whether the system tilted in favor of a wealthy, well-connected alleged perpetrator and against very young girls who are alleged victims of sex crimes.'"[164]

Krischer ultimately made an absurd plea bargain deal with Epstein that allowed this mega-pedophile and child sex trafficker to serve a mere thirteen months in prison and with a sixteen-hour-a-day pass to roam freely. Epstein could travel daily to his office and even took trips to New York. To say Epstein was "incarcerated" is to abuse the word. Recall that the lead lawyer negotiating this mind-blowing deal, which included immunity from prosecution for himself and others, was Dershowitz, with whom Roberts says she was forced to have sex with multiple times.

Public outrage then prompted the federal government to step in. Most believed that respected lawman Reiter had tipped off the feds to the fact that the state attorney's fix was in. Federal prosecutors were also being intimidated and investigated. The Epstein lawyers threatened the federal prosecutors that a nasty book could be written about them if they did not toe the line.

R. Alexander Acosta, the U.S. attorney who handled the Epstein case on the federal end, wrote a 2011 letter in which he described the pressure that was brought to bear on the U.S. attorneys who were prosecuting Epstein. Acosta says that after the U.S. attorneys met with the high-power Epstein legal defense team in early summer 2007, "What followed was a year-long assault on the prosecution and prosecutors. I use the word assault intentionally, as the defense in this case was more aggressive than any which I, or the prosecutors in my office, had previously encountered."[165]

Attorney Acosta complained that many of their negotiations with Epstein's lawyers were appealed to Washington, DC, over the heads of the federal Miami prosecutors. According to Acosta, Epstein's team was personally going after the prosecutors: "Defense counsel investigated individual prosecutors and their families, looking for personal peccadilloes that may provide a basis for disqualification. Disqualifying a prosecutor is an effective (though rarely used) strategy. . . . Defense counsel tried to disqualify at least two prosecutors. I carefully reviewed, and then rejected, these arguments."[166]

Acosta continued, "The defense, arguably, often failed to negotiate in good faith. They would obtain concessions as part of a negotiation and agree to proceed, only to change their minds, and appeal the office's position to Washington. The investigations into the family lives of individual prosecutors were, in my opinion, uncalled for, as were the accusations of bias and/or misconduct against individual prosecutors."[167]

Acosta's boss, then Bush Attorney General Alberto Gonzales, told the *Daily Beast* that he "would have instructed the Justice Department to pursue justice without making a political mess."[168] Gonzales's comments tell you all you need to know about the Epstein pedophile scandal because the only way to properly mete out justice in the Epstein case was to have a *very big political mess* as a side product of thorough, piercing investigations and prosecutions. It would not take long for "big names," also known as VIPs or "A-listers," to be enmeshed in any honest and complete investigation of Epstein and whom he was pandering underaged girls to.

The whole point of the sweetheart deal for Epstein (no prison time) was to avoid all that. It was to protect Epstein; and more importantly it was designed to protect scores of the elite VIP pedophiles who partook of Epstein's "Turkish Delight" (sin).

Remember, Wexner, who at one time was Epstein's "best friend forever" is a longtime billionaire Republican donor who is tight with the Bushes. Perhaps that fact clarifies why Gonzales did not want his federal prosecutors to generate a "political mess." Or perhaps it was Bill Clinton's personal friendship with the Bushes that poisoned justice in the Epstein case. Epstein gave the Clinton Foundation $25,000 after his legal troubles began in 2006. "He was manipulating currencies for the CIA," said Hoffenberg, former owner of the *New York Post* and collections business genius, who flamed out in a multi-million dollar Ponzi scam in the '80s. "His pal Larry Summers hooked him up," Hoffenberg said of the then secretary of the treasury. "He destabilizes Middle Eastern currencies to help Israel. He's protected," he told us. It is a plausible explanation as to why a Republican administration is dishing leniency to a Democratic super donor and friend of Bill. But then again, the Clinton-Bush alliance is demonstrated again and again in the true narrative of Bill and Hillary Clinton.

Israel (former prime minister Ehud Barak) and Great Britain (Prince Andrew) were two of the Bush Administration's key foreign policy allies. Prosecute those two men and you have an international political mess.

The Feds then secretly rubber-stamped the lenient deal, added immunity for Epstein's pedophile co-conspirators, and then sealed their outrageously lenient plea-bargain. Epstein's thirty-five victims were never informed of the secret Department of Justice (DOJ) deal as required by law, which is the basis for a lawsuit by the sex victims against the federal government to overturn the secretive and outrageously lenient plea bargain given to Epstein in September of 2007.

The *Palm Beach Post*, to its credit, went to court to get this wrist-slap deal unsealed. Only after two years of litigation did the public learn of the toxic terms of the secret deal. Why George W. Bush's DOJ gave Epstein a pass after a flawed state investigation seems to be a mystery.

Well, perhaps it is not a mystery when one learns of the names and social statuses of the people who were involved with Epstein.

Thanks to Epstein's butler and house manager Alfredo Rodriguez—who swiped that infamous little black book—we have a very good idea of who might have been involved with pedophilic activities with Epstein. It's always the butler.

When prosecutors found out that Rodriguez was trying to sell a copy of Epstein's book of contacts they charged him with stealing evidence and threw him in jail, and his jail sentence ended up being longer than Epstein's! Rodriguez died of cancer in late 2014. Nevertheless, he left us with a pretty good idea who some of Epstein's VIP pedophile friends were.

It should be stressed that Rodriguez was only the manager at Epstein's Palm Beach mansion. He did not know what was going on with Epstein in New York, on his New Mexico spread, the Virgin Islands, in Paris, or on Epstein's airplane, which was known for its orgies. Therefore, Rodriguez's circled names are only a fraction of the VIP friends of Epstein who may have been pandered underaged girls to molest.

Rodriguez also said Maxwell covertly took photos of the girls without their permission or knowledge and "kept the images on her computer, knew the names of the underaged girls and their respective phone numbers and other underaged victims."[169] These are the images that Maxwell would arrange on an opulent Italian marble table at Epstein's minimalist and darkly cool island retreat. One person in Epstein's phone book who visited the erudite billionaire on his island Shangri-La said the display of photos was "almost like a trophy case" that visitors could use as a menu for a future tryst.

Epstein has unloaded his Palm Beach mansion as the judicial process and the media have caught up with him. The lawsuit by Roberts and others have unearthed the lurid and brutal details that the well-connected Epstein thought had been resolved in his "arranged" guilty plea and the turnkey "incarceration" he served.

Roger Stone interviewed an Epstein neighbor who confirmed that former president Bill Clinton visited Epstein's Palm Beach compound for a party that lasted until 3 a.m. "First the presidential motorcade pulled up just as the sun was going down. There was an SUV in front, followed by a black sedan, which was trailed by a second SUV. In the backseats of the SUVs you could see men and rifle barrels as the windows were rolled down," she said.

"Two agents went into the house, presumably to sweep it as the sedan idled. Bill Clinton got out, briefly shook hands with a Cuban gardener who worked for Epstein, and entered the house," the neighbor said. "Shortly thereafter there was a virtual traffic jam of cars dropping off girls."

"I saw no couples or men, but as many as 30 very young looking girls were dropped off," this disgusted neighbor told me. "In Florida, license plates must have the county name on them. It was clear that some of these girls had come from Miami as well as Palm Beach. You could hear music and laughing until midnight, when everything got quiet, but Clinton didn't exit until 3 am and despite the fact that it was still dark, was wearing sunglasses."

It is notable that in the few instances courts have weighed in somehow on Epstein's case the result has been consistent with treatment of Epstein as the dangerous pedophile he is, rather than as some breezy good-guy philanthropist gone slightly astray.

After Epstein flew Clinton to meet the sultan in his "adult-themed private jet," the sultan has been a big donor of the Clinton Presidential Library. The government of Brunei contributed in 2002 between $1 million and $5 million to the Clinton Foundation, which said that the donation went toward the construction of the Clinton Presidential Library in Arkansas.

Clinton was picked up at a Japanese naval base by Epstein in his private Boeing 727—known to many as either the "orgy jet" or "Lolita Express"—and flown to Brunei to visit with Sultan Bolkiah, according to flight records.

Epstein is a registered sex offender who would regularly host Clinton and many others at his private Caribbean island before getting a slap on the wrist for abusing girls internationally. "This is not just a Clinton sex scandal," said political pundit and author Ann

Coulter. "This is the elites getting cozy and covering up and protecting one another."[170]

The Sultan and his brother Jefri were infamous for their sex parties and their harems composed mainly of underaged girls. In 1997, the Sultan was sued by a former Miss USA, who said she was held, drugged, and molested by both the Sultan and his brother.

Jillian Lauren, who at eighteen years of age was recruited by Jefri for his harem, said, "there's no such thing as underage among the privileged class in Brunei." Lauren was tasked with servicing the Sultan and his brother.

The Sultan has bigger problems, though.

He has been aggressive in instituting Sharia Law. Homosexuality, sodomy, adultery, and the discussion of faith by non-Muslims are now punishable by amputation of limbs, public flogging, or death by stoning. Hollywood stars have boycotted the iconic Pink Beverly Hills Hotel owned by the Sultan after Brunei adopted the anti-gay and anti-women Islamic law. The City of Beverly Hills even adopted a resolution urging the Sultan to sell his interest in the hotel.

The hotel business suffered as Jeffrey Katzenberg, Carl Reiner, David Geffen, and others called for the boycott. NBC correspondent Josh Mankiewicz, always nattily dressed, was a regular in the hotel's Polo Lounge, where he imbibed a dry martini several times a week. When Mankiewicz honored the boycott, you could tell it was over for the Sultan in Tinsletown. Ironic that sex criminal Jeffrey Epstein would fly his best buddy Bill to a tete-a-tete with another epic pedophile to pick up a check.

In December 2014, the Epstein case returned to the forefront after two more women came forward to join a Florida Jane Doe lawsuit, filed in 2008, seeking Epstein's federal prosecution for child sex trafficking. In seeking to join the two original plaintiffs, Jane Doe #3, the now-married and thirty-one-year-old mother Roberts, attempted to join a victims' lawsuit against the government for not properly informing them of the extremely lenient plea bargain terms and Non-Prosecution Agreement with Epstein and the other co-conspirators.

In April 2014, Florida Judge Kenneth Marra denied an attempt by Roberts, a.k.a. Jane Doe #3, to join a lawsuit against the federal government "for allegedly not protecting their rights in a plea deal [with] Epstein.[171]

The original victims' rights case is still grinding away in the courts, and Roberts is planning to write a book about her experiences as a child sex victim in the world of Epstein, who told Virginia that he had molested one thousand girls and as of 2015 had settled lawsuits with thirty-three victims' families.

The lawsuit to overturn the secret plea and a secondary defamation suit deal filed by a respected former judge and a Fort Lauderdale lawyer may force Dershowitz to testify and could rope in Bill Clinton. Wouldn't that turn the 2016 race upside down?

"I was speaking to one Hillary Clinton ally," said reporter Rebecca Berg from the *Washington Examiner* on *Hannity*, and "related specifically to this Epstein business, and it looks like her campaign isn't going to touch this even with the longest stick. They say Bill Clinton is not on the ballot. Hillary Clinton is her own person. We'll see if voters believe that, too."[172]

So what is kingpin sex trafficker Jeffrey Epstein's take on all this? "I'm not a sexual predator, I'm an 'offender.' It's the difference between a murderer and a person who steals a bagel."[173]

PART 2

DRUGS, MONEY, AND MURDER—CLINTON-STYLE

CHAPTER 8

BLOW, BUBBA, BLOW

"I watched Bill Clinton lean up against a brick wall. He must have had an adenoid problem because he casually stuck my tooter up his nose. . . . He was so messed up that night, he slid down the wall into a garbage can and just sat there like a complete idiot."

—Sharline Wilson, Arkansas "party girl"

Bill Clinton, as governor of Arkansas, was buried in the drug scene. When Bill's half-brother, Roger, was arrested for cocaine distribution, the Arkansas state police possessed an undercover tape of Roger involved in a drug deal. He is famously rumored to have said his half-brother had a nose like a vacuum cleaner.

Betsey Wright, who served as Governor Clinton's chief of staff for seven years, told Larry Nichols that the governor had to be sent to a drug rehab center multiple times. L. D. Brown said that while on family vacation in Boca Raton, Florida, Clinton snuck away to the bathroom and apparently was doing cocaine in a stall.

Brown, sensing something was wrong, asked, "Bill, are you okay?"[174]

"Yeah, yeah, L. D., these damned sinuses are killing me!"

Arkansas officials eventually had to cut short an investigation of Clinton's half-brother. The trail led directly to the governor. "My brother has apparently become involved with drugs, a curse which has reached epidemic proportions and has plagued the lives of millions of families in our nation, including many in our state," Clinton said following his half-brother's indictment.[175]

Governor Clinton was one of the many.

Sally Perdue said, "He [Bill] had all of the [cocaine snorting] equipment laid out, like a real pro."

Gennifer Flowers said Bill would carry marijuana joints around with him and sometimes smoke them in her presence. "I thought how foolish it was of him to carry marijuana around, but it was typical of his 'bulletproof' attitude."[176] Flowers said she never personally saw Bill use cocaine but he would talk about it and the bad effect it had on him. "He told me about a party he had been to, and said, 'I got so fucked up on cocaine at that party,'" Flowers recalled. "He said that it made his scalp itch, and he felt conspicuous because he was talking with people who were not aware drugs were at the party, and all he wanted to do was scratch his head."[177]

According to Sam Houston, a respected Little Rock doctor, in the early 1980s, Bill Clinton was admitted to the University of Arkansas Medical Center for emergency treatment for cocaine abuse and overdose and had to be cared for at the hospital on one or possibly two occasions.

"When Mrs. Clinton arrived, she told both of the resident physicians on duty that night that they would never again practice medicine in the United States if word leaked out about Clinton's drug problem," Christopher Ruddy said. "Reportedly, [Hillary] pinned one of the doctors up against the wall, both hands pressed against his shoulders, as she gave her dire warning."

Ruddy wrote an article in 1999, "Did Bill Clinton Overdose on Cocaine?" in which he said that R. Emmett Tyrrell found one of the nurses who was on the job when cocaine-inebriated Bill Clinton was brought in to the hospital. The nurse would not say anymore out of fear of losing her job.

"Dr. Suen, S-U-E-N, a doctor at the medical center here in Little Rock that's taken care of Bill Clinton for his sinus problems, which may indeed be related to cocaine use, as they destroy the sinus passages," said Dr. Houston. "Governor Bill Clinton was taken into the hospital, I believe it was the medical center, on at least one or two occasions, for cocaine abuse and overdosage, in which he actually had to be cared for at the hospital."[178]

Dan Lasater was perhaps Bill Clinton's closest and most important political contributor. Lasater was also heavily into the drug trade, and he and Bill used to party with girls as young as high-school age. One of the girls who Dan Lasater got hooked on cocaine was sixteen-year-old Patty-Anne Smith. Patty-Anne got very close to Lasaster and knew he was involved with both the drug trade and the Nicaraguan contra supply operation. She told Ambrose Evans-Pritchard that Clinton "was never acting like a governor when I saw him." Patty-Anne saw Clinton use cocaine on two or three occasions including one night in Lasater's residence: "He was doing a line. It was just there on the table."[179]

Former Saline County criminal investigator John Brown looked into the governor's "habit." "I talked to the manager and the assistant manager of the apartment complex for Roger Clinton," said Brown. "They've all said Bill Clinton did drugs, they saw him. I've talked to many other people, who have all, just like the people at the apartment complex, said 'Hey John, get us to a congressional hearing. Yes, we'll sign a sworn affidavit.' These people want to be sure that when they come forward that something is done about it, because they fear for their lives, but they really want the truth to get out."[180]

Sharline Wilson was a so-called party girl, close with Roger Clinton and other drug dealers in the 1980s. "I lived in Little Rock, Arkansas, okay?" Wilson said. "And I worked at a club called Le Bistro's, and I met Roger Clinton there, Governor Bill Clinton, a couple of his state troopers that went with him wherever he went. Roger Clinton had come up to me and he had asked me could I give him some coke, you know, and asked for my one-hitter, which a one-hitter is a very small silver device, okay, that you stick up into your nose and you just squeeze it and a snort of cocaine will go up in there. And I watched Roger hand what I had given him to Governor Clinton, and he just kind of turned around and walked off."[181]

Ambrose Evans-Pritchard gives a great recounting of the Clinton-Arkansas drug scene and the dirty deeds and cover-ups that flowed from it. "On the afternoon of December 10, 1990, her [Jean Duffey's] best informant, Sharline Wilson, walked into the U.S. District Court in Little Rock and blurted out in front of an astonished grand jury that she had provided cocaine to Bill Clinton at Le Bistro nightclub during his first term as governor."

Wilson said that one time she saw the governor so high on cocaine that he literally leaned against a wall and slid down into a trash can. "I watched Bill Clinton lean up against a brick wall," Wilson said. "He must have had an adenoid problem because he casually stuck my tooter up his nose. . . . He was so messed up that night, he slid down the wall into a garbage can and just sat there like a complete idiot. . . . I was, you know, the hostess with the mostest, the lady with the snow . . . I'd serve drinks and lines of cocaine on a glass mirror."

Wilson, who was once sexually intimate with Roger Clinton, says she and her friends would go back to the Arkansas governor's mansion and party until the early morning hours. "I thought it was the coolest thing in the world that we had a governor who got high," Wilson stated.[182]

After Wilson testified before the grand jury, the Republican-appointed U.S Attorney Charles Banks shut down his investigation. Wilson contacted investigator Jean Duffey and told her that she was terrified and that her home had come under surveillance as a result. She was dangerous to the "powers that be." She had been a girlfriend of the drug dealers, including Bill Clinton's half-brother

Roger, and she had worked "for three or four months unloading bags of cocaine at the Mena Airport in the mountains" of western Arkansas.[183]

The Clinton brothers seemed, by many accounts, to be more than just casual users.

Roger was caught bragging on a police tape to an undercover informant, "I've got four or five guys in uniform who keep an eye on the guys who keep an eye on me." Roger was dealing directly with Colombian Maurice Rodriguez, a man with ties to the Colombian drug cartels.[184]

CHAPTER 9

THE BOYS ON THE TRACKS

"Their investigation was so thorough that they left my son's foot out there for two days in plain sight."

—Linda Ives, mother of the late Kevin Ives

The small town of Mena, Arkansas, is about a four-hour drive from Dallas. The town of Alexander, thirty miles south of the Arkansas state capital, Little Rock, where Governor Clinton resided,[185] was founded as a construction camp for the railroad. Both towns had shady reputations: they were thought to be hubs of prolific illegal drug activity.

Sharline Wilson, the "party girl" described in the last chapter, would pick up loads of cocaine at the Mena Airport and "make the run down to Texas. The drop-off was at the Cowboys Stadium," she told Evans-Pritchard. "I was told that nobody would ever bother me, and I was never bothered. On Sunday morning, August 23, 1987, a Union Pacific train was making a routine run from Texarkana on that stretch of railway, when the workers manning the locomotive spotted something ahead on the tracks.

"When we were approximately one hundred feet away from this dark spot, engineer (Stephen) Shroyer yelled out, 'Oh my God!'

recalled the brakeman, Danny DeLamar. "We could tell there were two young men lying between the rails just north of the bridge, and we saw there was a gun beyond the boy who was lying to the north. There was something covering these boys from their waist to just below their knees, and I'm not sure what this object was. They were both in between the rails, heads up against the west rail, and their feet were over the east rail. Both were right beside each other and their arms and hands were to their sides, heads facing straight up. I never noticed any movement at all."[186]

The horn was sounded and the brakes were locked, but despite the deafening sounds from the futile attempts to stop the train, the boys never moved as the locomotive rolled on and over them.

"What had caught my attention at first was a big brilliant flash," said Stroyer.

"Apparently that was my headlight striking the barrel of the gun. The next thing I was totally aware of was the chest and head of that second boy, the one without the shirt. And from then on, I never took my thoughts off of him. What I focused on were his chest and his head—and how relaxed he looked. To me he looked as relaxed as a boy sunbathing on a beach."[187]

As the train ground to a halt, the men hesitantly went back to look for pieces of the boys on the tracks. What they anticipated was a large amount of fresh blood, spilled from the impact with the train; what they found made the oddity of the boy's stillness as the train bore down upon them even stranger.

There *was* blood, but not much. According to the train's conductor, Jerry Tomlin, a lifelong hunter with knowledge of how the blood will flow from a freshly wounded animal, there was "hardly any blood spilled at all. And the color of it bothered me, too. It was night, and we couldn't tell for sure, but the blood we saw was not red—not as red as you would think blood would be on a fresh kill like that. It was dark, more of a purplish color."[188]

Compounded with his earlier suspicion, the blood tipped Tomlin off. "Out there that night," Tomlin said, "I kind of smelled a rat."

Deputy Chuck Tallent and Lieutenant Ray Richmond of the Saline County Sheriff's Office, the first responders to the scene, almost immediately deemed the deaths an accident or suicide, despite the protests of the train crew or the report of Arkansas State Trooper Wayne Lainhart, who hours earlier had investigated two shots fired in the immediate vicinity.

The two EMTs on scene, Billy Heath and Shirley Raper, also noticed something wrong with the color and quantity of blood. A note attached to their official report read, "Blood from the bodies and on the body parts we observed was a dark color in nature. Due to our training, this would indicate a lack of oxygen in the blood and could pose a question as to how long the victims had been dead." Raper later told the state police, "The body parts had a pale color to them, like someone that had been dead for some time."[189]

The boys were identified as seventeen-year-old Kevin Ives and sixteen-year-old Don Henry. Linda Ives, the mother of Kevin, made finding the truth behind her son's death a lifelong mission. The evidence didn't point toward accident or suicide, yet the authorities were cavalier in their insistence. Linda knew something was wrong.

Arkansas medical examiner Fahmy Malak ruled the deaths an accident. He said the boys had smoked twenty marijuana joints and fallen into a trance on the railway tracks, side by side. How he reached this astounding conclusion was a mystery. The state crime labs had not tested the concentration of marijuana in their blood. Many in the medical world were confused by the finding.

"I know of incidents where persons smoked twenty-one marijuana cigarettes, one right after the other," said Dr. Arthur J. McBay, chief toxicologist for the North Carolina medical examiner's office. "They become euphoric, but it doesn't make them unconscious. I don't know what kind of evidence you could possibly use to conclude this. I have never heard of anyone becoming unconscious from this under ordinary circumstances." McBay added that he didn't "know who would agree with it."

In his career, Malak left a trail of perplexing medical opinions. One stood out. A ruling by Malak had once aided Governor Clinton's mother, Virginia Kelley, a nurse anesthetist. Malak gave the medical opinion that one of Kelley's patients, Susie Deer, had died of "blunt trauma" to the head when the patient was in fact determined to have died of lack of oxygen and medical malpractice by an incompetent practitioner.

Highly controversial, Malak had staunch critics. "He repeatedly lied about his credentials, misconstrued his findings, and misrepresented autopsy procedures," author Meredith Oakley claimed in her 1994 book, *On the Make: The Rise of Bill Clinton.* "In the lab, he misplaced bodies and destroyed evidence. On the witness stand, he was a prosecutor's dream."

In response to the claims of incompetence and corruption, Governor Clinton deferred the decision on Malak's future to a retired sheriff he had recently appointed.

"It didn't seem to matter what Malak did, Clinton protected him," said Linda Ives. "[Clinton] made excuses such as 'he's overworked,' 'he's just stressed out,' 'he's underpaid.' They gave him a $14 thousand raise, which was an insult to my family as well as many others in the state. I was outraged that protecting a political crony of Clinton was more important than the fact that two young boys had been murdered."[190]

Saline County Sheriff Jim Steed, complicit in the finding of an accidental death or suicide, echoed Malak's ruling and stood by the medical examiner. "Our local investigation was headed by our sheriff, Jim Steed," said Linda Ives. "He later went on television bragging about what a thorough investigation he had conducted, and that he felt very sorry for us as parents, but that he had every confidence in Fahmy Malak's ruling. Their investigation was so thorough that they left my son's foot out there for two days in plain sight."[191]

A political liability, Malak was eventually moved by the governor to a new job as head of the Arkansas state AIDS education program, which paid him three-fourths his old salary.

In April 1988, Atlanta medical examiner Dr. Joseph Burton administered a second autopsy of Ives and Henry. Dr. Burton found that Don Ives had been stabbed on the left side of the chest with "something like a large cutting edge knife."[192] Ives had damage to his skull that indicated to Dr. Burton that he had been hit in the head with the butt of a rifle. It was also discovered that the level of marijuana in the blood of the two boys was consistent with having smoked little over two joints in the hours before their death, a far cry from Dr. Malak's assertion of almost two dozen.[193]

Linda Ives, distraught with what she saw as an intentional mishandling of her sons deaths, was approached by Deputy Prosecutor Richard Garrett and, Defense Attorney Dan Harmon, who vowed to catch those responsible for her son's murder.

Linda was particularly impressed by Harmon. To Linda, Harmon was a man of integrity who "helped us when no one else would."[194]

Harmon was appointed special prosecutor to head the grand jury probe. While Harmon helped to change the ruling of the boy's deaths from a suicide to a homicide, his investigation was deeply flawed.

"He helped lead them down a path that absolutely led nowhere on this case," said former Saline County criminal investigator John Brown. "I got involved in the case and immediately Harmon tried to discredit me without even knowing me. I couldn't figure it out."[195]

Individuals who might have provided essential testimony were not called; some witnesses close to the murder, with vital information, met a far worse fate.

Keith McKaskle, bar owner of the Wagon Wheel in nearby Pulaski County, was one of those unfortunate witnesses. McKaskle had passed on a piece of information to Deputy Cathy Carty, the only Saline County deputy on the tracks the night the boys died who strongly disagreed that the deaths were an accident. "Keith told me I might want to watch Dan Harmon," Carty said, "that he was one of Saline County's largest suppliers."[196]

McKaskle knew something about Harmon that connected him with the murders of Ives and Henry. In the weeks before his death, McKaskle was treated to Clinton-style intimidation and threats. "He was always pointing out small cars, saying they were following him," a friend of McKaskle said. "[He] kept saying the law was following him."

The friend added that McKaskle repeated the belief that, "someone was going to kill him" in those last weeks.[197]

"Shortly before Keith McKaskle was murdered he knew that he was fixin' to be murdered," recalled Linda Ives. "He told his family goodbye, he told his friends goodbye."[198]

McKaskle was especially spooked by the upcoming 1988 election. If Sheriff Steed did not get reelected, McKaskle knew the information he and others possessed was incendiary.

"On the night of the elections in 1988, he took two pennies out of his pocket and put them on the bar at the Wagon Wheel and said 'If Sheriff Steed loses this election, my life ain't worth two cents' and he was murdered that night," Linda Ives recollected.[199]

Many other witnesses, close to the death of Ives and Henry, also met brutal, mysterious ends.

- In January 1989, twenty-six-year-old Greg Collins, who had been subpoenaed to testify before the grand jury after a rumor was circulated that he had been with the boys the night they were murdered, was killed by a shotgun blast to the face. His murder remains unsolved. A friend of Collins, Keith Coney, had died in a suspicious highway accident a year earlier, mere weeks after the grand jury had convened. Coney had also been called to testify.
- Only two months after Collins was brutally slain, Daniel "Boonie" Bearden disappeared. Bearden, Collins, and Coney had all been close friends.
- In April 1989, twenty-one-year-old Jeff Rhodes was murdered. Before his death, Rhodes was scared and told family he knew

too much about the other murders. "He said he had to get out of Benton, that he knew something about the Keith McKaskle murders," said Jeff's father, Eddie Rhodes. Jeff had been shot in the head and his remains set on fire in a dump.

- In July 1989, another grand jury witness, Richard Winters, was gunned down during a robbery, and it has been speculated the robbery was staged to cover his murder. His murder also remains unsolved.

It readily became apparent to Linda Ives and others that Dan Harmon was using the grand jury to dismantle the case of Ives and Henry.

"My personal opinion was that Harmon used that grand jury to find out what he could about who had information on him, and to make it appear like we were suspects, Lonoke Police Chief Ronald Jay Campbell told writer Mara Leveritt. "I believe he called us blatantly, for the sole purpose of trying to discredit us, so that in case he got arrested and charged with drugs as a result of the federal investigation, he could say it was retaliation."[200]

Indeed, in 1997 Harmon was found guilty of eleven federal felony charges including federal racketeering, extortion, and drug conspiracy, and was sentenced to eight years in prison. It was found that Harmon had used his office to procure drugs and money.

Sharline Wilson, deep in the Arkansas drug scene with the Clintons and one of the witnesses who testified, had seen Governor Clinton using cocaine with Harmon. Wilson also knew the connection between Harmon and the infamous stretch of railway.

"Every two weeks, for years, I'd go to the tracks, I'd pick up the package, and I'd deliver it to Dan Harmon, either straight to his office, or at my house," said Wilson. "Sometimes it was flown in by air, sometimes it would be kicked out of the train. A big bundle, two feet by one and a half feet, like a bale of hay, so heavy I'd have trouble lifting it. . . . Roger the Dodger [Clinton] picked it up a few times."[201]

Wilson said she and Harmon were close to the tracks the night Ives and Henry were murdered.

Wilson said that in the summer of 1987, one of the drug drops disappeared. Harmon subsequently brought his men out near midnight on August 22, 1987, to watch over the drug drop, expected to be three to four pounds of cocaine and five pounds of marijuana. While Harmon and his men went to the drug drop site, Wilson stayed back in the car, high as a kite. "It was scary," Wilson said. "I was high, very high. I was told to sit there and they'd be back. It seemed forever. . . . I heard two trains. Then I heard screams, loud screams. It . . . It . . ." and then Wilson broke into a flood of tears. "When Harmon came back, he jumped in the car and said, 'Let's go.' He was scared. It looked like there was blood all down his legs."[202]

When it comes to the boys on the tracks, the Clintons once again kept shady company.

CHAPTER 10

CLINTON, BUSH, BARRY SEAL, AND THE MENA DEAL

"You've got millions of people in this country today who just don't feel connected to the life the rest of us want them to live. You tell them to register and vote, get an education and go to work and they say, 'I may not have a job, but if I deal drugs I can make money.'"

—Bill Clinton on *The Arsenio Hall Show*, 1992[203]

For years there had been talk that the railroad tracks in Alexander, Arkansas, were a drop zone for drugs. Locals had seen small aircraft flying low, with no lights, over the area late at night.

Sure enough, Jean Duffey, former head of the Arkansas Drug Task Force, discovered that not only was Alexander a drop site for drugs, but also that the trafficking operation was spread well beyond the small town. When he made this revelation, ears were perked among many prominent government officials in Arkansas and beyond. Their response was reminiscent of many attacks previous. They lashed out against Duffey.

"I had no idea just how dangerous certain elected officials thought me to be until a brutal media campaign was launched against me," said Duffey. "For months, there were daily allegations of everything from misspending funds to ordering illegal arrests. Every attempt was made to keep me from running the drug task force. We were even shut down for several weeks during a bogus state police investigation. In spite of crippling disruptions, the task force was making significant discoveries about drug trafficking in central Arkansas, some of which led to the very people who were conducting the massive media crusade against me. We discovered that drug trafficking in Arkansas was linked to government officials in frightening proportions. A great number of people came to me with testimony about astonishing criminal activity of very high level public officials."[204]

The drug trafficking in Arkansas can be traced back to CIA drug smuggler Barry Seal, who, a year before the bodies of Kevin Ives and Don Henry were left on the tracks, on February 19, 1986, was murdered outside of a halfway house at The Salvation Army on Airline Highway in Baton Rouge, Louisiana.

With a fleet of airplanes smuggling drugs into the country, Seal operated the biggest organized drug operation in U.S. history. Seal's operations were initially conducted out of Louisiana.

"He was probably one of the biggest drug smugglers ever brought before a court in the history of our country," Louisiana Attorney General Billy Guste said. "By his own admission, he (Seal) had flown over 100 flights each bringing in between 600 and 1,200 pounds of cocaine. At a wholesale volume of an average of $50,000 a pound, he had smuggled between $3 billion and $5 billion of drugs into the United States.

"His smuggling brought dope to thousands whose lives have been adversely affected by it. He had brought enough cocaine into this country to give a 'high' to almost one hundred million users. And he earned between $60 million and $100 million by criminal activity."[205]

The planes Seal used were altered to his specifications in order to make covert drops.

"They had special cargo doors installed inside, without FAA permission, so that these doors could be opened in flight, pull 'em in and slide 'em back, and cocaine could be dropped out of sight in flight," said Arkansas State Police Investigator Russell Welch.[206]

In the 1980s, Seal moved his operations to Arkansas and struck up a personal friendship with Bill Clinton. Seal ran many of his operations out of a covert CIA landing base in Mena, Arkansas. He was protected by his employers at the CIA, Governor Bill Clinton of Arkansas, and Vice President (and former CIA director) Bush. Seal would direct planeloads of cocaine to Mena, which would then be distributed throughout the state and the U.S. The money from the drugs sold would be used to procure guns for the Contras.

"A lot of people said the Mena operation stopped in 1986 when Barry Seal was gunned down," said Saline County Criminal Investigator John Brown. "It's not true. Covert operations were still going on in Mena, Arkansas. Now if you stop and think when Bill Clinton was governor, he was asked about Mena. He said 'Well that's a federal problem, I'm not going to get involved in it.'"

What was Governor Clinton's involvement in the Arkansas drug trade?

"Every successful drug smuggling organization needs four things," Miami private eye Gary McDaniel told reporter Daniel Hopsicker, "production, distribution, transportation, and protection."

Bill Clinton, as governor, provided the protection. In the Ives and Henry case, he controlled the local police, the court system, and the medical examiner.

"One time one of the local DEA agents had told me that Barry had been arrested in Mena, Arkansas," said James Miller, a close associate of Seal. "And I ran into Barry a week or two later—at a pay telephone—and we were talking, and Barry said, let me show you something. And he showed me a piece of paper, a personal release bond, you know, the piece of paper that somebody has to sign before you can get out of jail, signed by Bill Clinton."[207]

Clinton was up to his eyeballs in CIA drug smuggling. Clinton himself has been a CIA asset, recruited at the University of Oxford in 1968 as documented by authors Roger Morris, Cord Meyer, and celebrated writer Christopher Hitchens.

Clinton's Arkansas state troopers were running some of the drugs. His biggest supporters, Dan Lasater, Jackson Stephens, and chicken king Don Tyson, were involved. Governor Clinton smoothly facilitated the drugs and money between the CIA and the Arkansas Dixie Mafia to bring billions of dollars' worth of drugs into the U.S.

At one point in the Seal-Mena operations, Governor Clinton attempted to get one of his trusted troopers, L. D. Brown, on the inside. Brown, who had specialized in undercover narcotics at the state police, believed he had a lot to offer the agency. Clinton entrusted Seal as Brown's CIA handler.

"Barry Seal was a crazy man," Brown said. "Seal telephoned me and told me he was the man I was told would call me. It was the mid-1980s and with the decadence of that time and the free-flowing cocaine, Cajun's Wharf was a hangout for the bond daddies such as Lasater and company."[208]

Brown recalled that the first words out of Seal's mouth were "How's the Guv." To Brown, "An overweight, jovial, almost slap-happy man as my contact with C.I.A. was not exactly what I expected."[209]

Brown had no idea what he was getting into. He had joined the CIA to fight communism and other political injustices in Central America and ended up running massive amounts of drugs into the U.S.

In October of 1984, Barry Seal met Brown at the Mena Airport and took him on a round-trip flight to Tegucigalpa, Honduras. Brown was paid $2,500 just for riding shotgun. Brown was unaware he was flying on a drug run.

Brown figured out what was occurring after a second flight in December 1984:

"Seal reached back to open the duffel bag in the back. He removed a manila envelope identical to the one he had given me after the first trip. I knew what was in the envelope but there was something else. He reached deeper in the bag and gave me the shock of my life.

"Seal's face had a sly, smirky, almost proud look as he removed a waxed-paper-wrapped taped brick-shaped package from the bag. I immediately recognized it as identical to bricks of cocaine from my days in narcotics. I didn't know what to think and began demanding to know what was going on. I cursed, ranted and raved and I believe I actually caused Seal to wonder if I might pull a gun and arrest him. Seal threw up his hands and tried to calm me down saying everything was all right and quickly exited my car. He removed the bag from the bag and hustled back toward the plane."[210]

Brown found out the hard way why they call the CIA the "Cocaine Import Agency."

Brown had not seen Governor Clinton since the revelation that he had been an accessory to international drug smuggling. When they next met, Brown was livid:

"[Clinton's] mouth opened and the words 'You having fun yet?' were already forming on his lips when I burst out, 'Do you know what they are bringing back on those airplanes?' He immediately threw up his hands in a halting fashion and took a couple of steps back. I know he thought he was in danger of receiving a class A state police ass-whipping. My hopes of an innocent explanation to the whole sordid affair were dashed with the now-famous line, 'That's Lasater's deal! That's Lasater's deal!' he whined as if he had just taken a tongue lashing by Hillary. 'And your buddy (HW) Bush knows about it!'"[211]

What shocked Brown is that the Governor didn't deny it. "And it wasn't like it was a surprise to him," Brown would later testify. "It wasn't like he didn't try to say, what? He was surprised that I was mad because he thought we were going to have a cordial conversation, but he didn't try to deny it. He didn't try to deny that it wasn't coming back, that I wasn't telling the truth or that he didn't know anything about it."[212]

The Clinton-Dan Lasater connection was a very important one. Dan Lasater was a young entrepreneur who in 1965 founded Ponderosa Steakhouses.[213] Lasater became successful in the restaurant business, and he later branched off into horse racing, where he was immensely successful in the years 1974, 1975, and 1976. He won the racing industry's prestigious Eclipse Award for outstanding owner.[214] "But according to a police statement by one of his employees, Lasater's success with the horses was achieved by 'putting in the boot'—fixing the races."[215]

Along the way, Dan Lasater did two other things as well: cocaine smuggling and money laundering as one of Bill Clinton's closest friends and biggest political contributors when Clinton was governor of Arkansas.

Lasater also started a bond company and in 1985, Clinton's Arkansas government awarded Lasater an exclusive $750,000 contract to sell bonds to finance a new state police radio system.[216] At this same time there was a tremendous amount of drugs being run through Arkansas. Bill Clinton and his half-brother Roger Clinton were both cocaine addicts.

Betsey Wright told Larry Nichols that Bill Clinton had had to be sent to a drug rehab multiple times. Roger Clinton had been famously rumored to say he needed to buy some cocaine because his half-brother Bill had a nose like a vacuum cleaner. It was also during the early 1980s when Roger Clinton owed some other drug dealers some big money and Lasater gave him some money to pay off the drug debt and also put Roger Clinton on his payroll to help him survive that frightening crisis.

In a nutshell, Dan Lasaster was a successful businessman, a very tight friend of Bill Clinton, and a man deep in the underworld of drug trafficking and criminal activities. "U.S. attorneys in Arkansas and Nevada as well as the Kentucky State Police suspected Lasaster had ties to organized crime; that he dealt cocaine in Arkansas and would be probed by federal undercover agents for major drug trafficking in New Mexico; that his bond brokerage was disciplined repeatedly for shady dealings with subsequent suspicions of money laundering and was nonetheless the beneficiary of millions in state commissions under the Clinton regime."[217]

The "Organized Crime Drug Enforcement Task Force concluded in 1986 that Lasaster was a major cocaine trafficker."[218]

A 1988 FBI bulletin noted that Lasater was the top supplier of cocaine to the bond and investment banking community in Little Rock. Lasater by the mid-1970s had become a key figure in Dixie Mafia cocaine trafficking. The DEA had opened a file on Lasater in 1983 and had given him the tracking number of 141475. Not only that, but one of Arkansas's top businessmen, Jackson Stephens, who later became a key Clinton donor, helped Lasater get into the bond business.[219]

In New Mexico, the authorities investigated Lasater for drug smuggling relating to planes coming in and out of his Angel Fire Resort, which has an 8,900-foot runway. At that time Angel Fire was managed by a woman named Patsy Thomasson who later got a key position in the Clinton White House in the Office of Administration. Thomasson, who used to work for Lasater, then for the Clintons, is now working as the chief of staff (Washington, DC, office) for the lobbying firm of Texas Democratic fixer Ben Barnes. Not surprisingly, Thomasson does not include her work for drug dealer Lasater in the 1980s on her resume, which is posted on the Internet.[220] She was his right-hand woman.

"New Mexico sheriffs and district attorneys were hearing reports from Angel Fire reminiscent of Mena—strange nighttime traffic, sightings of parachute drops, even hikers' accounts of a 'big military-type cargo plane' seeming to come out of nowhere and swooping low and almost silently over a deserted mountain meadow near the remote ski area."[221]

That sounds a lot like what Barry Seal was doing in Arkansas as he coordinated drug and money drops from the air.

Lasater, like Governor Bill Clinton, had a close working relationship with Seal. Lasater had bought a "horse farm," called the Carver Ranch, which drug smugglers would use to refuel the planes for their drug mule runs to Colombia. Arkansas Drug Investigator Russell Welch said, "Seal used this ranch frequently." Evans-Pritchard: "So, apparently this ranch was no horse farm. It was part of the Medellin trafficking empire."[222]

Terry Reed, who later wrote a book about the Clinton-Bush-CIA-Oliver North drug smuggling said, "The first day I met Barry Seal he was in the company of Dan Lasater and Roger Clinton. Roger was the driver for Dan Lasater at the time."[223]

With Dan Lasater and Bill Clinton it was about drugs, parties, cocaine, women, and drug money laundering. Arkansas was wide open for the drug trade: It was a diseased narco state being run by a cocaine-addled Governor Bill Clinton.

L. J. Davis wrote in the *New Republic* that "Lasater served ashtrays full of cocaine at parties in his mansion [and] stocked cocaine in his corporate jet (a plane used by the Clintons on more than one occasion)."[224] One year Lasaster flew the Clintons and friends to watch the Kentucky Derby. As for Roger Clinton, he was the lead singer in a band called Dealer's Choice.

As Victor Thorn points out in his book about the Clintons and drugs, Roger Clinton was completely out of control, constantly getting high on cocaine, boasting in an FBI transcript that he took cocaine twelve times per day, taking girls to have sex parties at the Arkansas governor's mansion, and bragging that he could buy a quarter pound of cocaine for as cheap as $10,000.[225]

One of the victims of Bill Clinton and Lasater was a young girl named Patti-Anne Smith (also Patricia Anne Smith). Bill, Roger, and Lasater were corrupting and then partying with teenaged girls. One of these victims was Patricia Anne Smith, who said, ""I was introduced to cocaine by Dan Lasater when I was 16 or 17 years old and a student at North Little Rock Old Main High School. . . . I was a virgin until two months after I met Dan Lasater. Lasater plied me with cocaine and gifts for sexual favors."[226]

Add then teenaged Smith to the list of those who have confirmed Bill Clinton's 1980 drug use: "I met Bill Clinton several times, he'd know my name and I thought he was a wonderful person, but I can tell you that he was never acting like a governor when I saw him."[227] Patti-Anne saw him take cocaine two or three times. "He was doing a line. It was just there on a table."[228]

Newsmax's Carl Limbacher did some fine reporting on the depravity of Lasater's relationship with Patti-Anne Smith and other teenaged girls: "[Patti said] I could get an eight ball [from Lasater] whenever I wanted it. I carried a vial of it around at school. After a visit to a Lasater-supplied gynecologist, who put Patti-Anne on birth control pills, Lasater was making her available for the sexual entertainment of his business colleagues. When investigators tracked her down to gain testimony against Lasater two years later, the terms they used to describe Patti-Anne were drugged-out party girl and basket case."[229]

Lasater had turned Patti-Anne Smith into a teenaged prostitute.

"Here's the police statement of Michele Cochran—nineteen years old when she met Lasater," wrote Limbacher. "He used drugs and money eventually to seduce me. As a result of the relationship I became addicted to cocaine. Another teenaged Lasater alum told police that after a few months in his orbit, she would sometimes get up and snort cocaine in order to start my day."[230]

That is who Bill Clinton was partying with in the 1980s: Dan Lasater and the teenage and even high school girls he was corrupting.

Arkansas state trooper Barry Spivey said he can remember flying Bill Clinton flying multiple times on Lasater's jet. Spivey flew to the Kentucky Derby with Lasater and Clinton. Spivey also said under oath that Clinton went to Lasater's residence many times.

While all this was going on, Lasater was using his bond business to launder the cocaine money. "One former broker told me that he never witnessed enough authentic business to justify the existence of Lasater's office at 312 Louisiana Street," said Evans-Pritchard.[231]

By the mid-1980s, the drug activities of both Roger and Lasater were attracting a lot of attention from those elements in government that were not corrupt. "Roger Clinton was indicted in 1984 by a federal grand jury on five counts of drug trafficking."[232] Roger served only a year in jail. In 2001, as he was leaving the presidency, Bill Clinton pardoned his half-brother as if it had never happened.

Lasater, a kingpin who was at the heart of CIA/Dixie Mafia drug running in Arkansas, was also indicted for cocaine possession. The FSLIC also targeted him for insurance fraud. Lasater could have been put away for twenty years or longer, but instead was given a thirty-month sentence. He served part in a halfway house and two more months under "house arrest." Then, Governor Bill Clinton pardoned him in 1990.

In *Clinton Confidential: The Climb to Power*, George Carpozi describes how Hillary got Lasater off the hook. He writes, "Hillary and Vince [Foster] huddled with Dan Lasater in discussions that are nowhere to be found in a public record. When they emerged from the dark, they announced that a deal had been struck with the defendant. He [Lasater] agreed to put up $200,000 in settlement of his $3.3 million obligation. That was paying back less than a thousandth of a cent to each of America's 250 million potential taxpaying citizens who Lasater cheated through his theft of the $3.3 million."[233]

Or one could say Lasater, still fabulously wealthy, settled for six cents on the dollar with the U.S. government. A key factor: the First Lady of Arkansas was representing the U.S. government in a case involving a close family friend, Lasater, who was friends with Bill, Hillary, Roger, and Bill's mother, Virginia Kelley, who had met Lasater at the horse racetracks. Conflict of interest, anyone?

Hillary represented the FSLIC and gave her husband's best friend the deal of a lifetime. That deal was in the best interest of Hillary, Bill, and Lasaster. As for the rest of society? Not so much.

The story of Dennis Patrick clues us in on how much criminality was involved in the Lasater operations. Ambrose Evans-Pritchard details in his book *The Secret Life of Bill Clinton* that someone tried to assassinate Patrick multiple times. Why would they do that? Perhaps because Patrick had an account at the bond firm owned by Lasater that was used to launder tens of millions in drug money. Patrick's account was being used without his knowledge to move huge amounts of drug money. When interviewed in 1994 by Evans-Pritchard, Patrick was forty-two years old. In 1985, when many of these drug laundering trades were made, he was thirty-three.

Evans-Pritchard gave a fascinating account of the murder attempts on Patrick:

"Dennis had been warned long before by a disenchanted broker at Lasater & Company called Linda Nesheim that people with ties to the firm were trying to kill him. 'Linda kept talking about Patsy Thomasson,' recalled Dennis. 'She told me that Patsy was the one in charge, that she was the one who could put an end to my whole nightmare.'

"But at the time it didn't make much sense to him. "I couldn't figure out why Lasater would do this to me. I didn't know back then that he'd run $100 million, or $150 million, or whatever it was, through my account."

Evans-Pritchard directly asked Steve Love, who used to be a bond broker for Lasater, if Lasater & Company was behind all the murder attempts on Patrick.

Love replied, "They certainly didn't want anybody to blow the whistle."[234] Love also added that Dennis Patrick was completely innocent of any wrong doing, a pure victim in this case.

One would figure that after all of this Bill Clinton would have considered Lasater radioactive. That was not the case at all. State trooper Larry Patterson, in his blockbuster exposé interview with *Newsmax*, "More Than Sex: The Secrets of Bill and Hillary Clinton Revealed," said that after Lasater got out of jail Bill Clinton asked

Larry Patterson what he thought about making Dan his chief of staff for his governor's office. That appointment never happened.[235]

If one were to summarize the Clinton-Lasater relationship, one could say that Bill Clinton provided the official political protection for the cocaine and drug smuggling, while Lasater took care of the nuts and bolts of laundering the hundreds of millions of dirty drug money. And in their spare time it was drugs, parties, and corrupting teenage girls.

In 1985, L. D. Brown received a phone call from a man named Felix Rodriguez, who said he wanted to discuss Barry Seals. Rodriguez identified himself as Seal's boss. He had traveled to Arkansas and made it clear he did not like what Seal was doing. Rodriguez had an outstanding career with the CIA, including acting as liaison officer with the Bolivian forces who captured and executed Cuban revolutionary Che Guevera. He took Che's Rolex watch as a keepsake and a transcript of his interrogation, which he liked to reenact on occasion to friends at his home in Miami. Rodriguez was a longtime confidant of George H. W. Bush.

Brown thought that Clinton had tipped off the CIA that his state trooper had gone ballistic when he found out that drugs were on that Seal plane. "Rodriguez made me feel comfortable," Brown recalled. "He had CIA credentials which he showed me. 'Don't worry about him. We'll take care of him,' is how he assured me of the 'problem' with Seal." When Brown again answered the call of the agency, he would find he was sadly mistaken.

Charles Hayes, a contract agent for the CIA, was one of the men who ran the Mena operations, and he was interviewed by a drug investigator, Jean Duffey, on July 14, 1992.

Q: Was there money laundering involved in the Mena operations?
A: Yes, the main thing about Mena was the political power and money associated with it.

Q: Would it be correct to say that the Mena operations generated 100,000,000 per week?
A: No, that's too high.

Q: Would it be correct to say that the Mena operations generated 1,000 per week?
A: No, that's too low.

Q: Would it be correct to say 10,000,000?
A: That's about right.

Q: Was there DOD involvement in the Mena operations?
A: Yes, it could not have happened without DOD involvement.

Q: Do you know Larry Nichols?
A: Yes.

Q: Larry Nichols denies that he has ever met you or Clay Lacy.
A: Nichols and Lacy have had their pictures taken together. Larry certainly knows me. If you had robbed Fort Knox, and I knew that you had done it, would you admit to knowing me?

Q: Do Lacy and ADFA have connections?
A: Yes, Lacy is associated with ADFA

Q: Do you know Wooten Epps?
A: Yes.

Q: Do you know Bob Neal?
A: Yes.

Q: Is Bob Neal associated with an underground complex at the Hope, Arkansas, airport?

A: I don't believe he owns it. You are getting into an area that I won't talk about. It's the subject of an investigation.

Q: Do you mean the recently renewed FBI investigation?
A: (Laugh) No, that's like putting the robbers in with the gold. There is another investigation that I'm talking about.

Q: Is it correct to say that the Arkansas State Police are involved in distributing cocaine derived from the Mena Arkansas operations?
A: Very definitely, and federal people as well.

Q: Do you know Buddy Young?
A: (Pause) I won't talk about Buddy Young.

Q: Do you know Jerry Montgomery?
A: I won't talk about Jerry Montgomery.

Q: Do you know David Talachet?
A: I believe I could pick him out of a crowd.

Q: Is it correct to say that David Talachet has friends in high places?
A: Sitting in the White House.

Q: Is it correct to say that Talachet has friends in very high places?
A: George Bush.[236]

Here again, it bears repeating: the Clintons associate with some extremely shady characters. The Mena drug-trafficking operations caused many people to profit from a shameful business. If this interview is accurate and the operations truly garnered ten million dollars a week, then those involved got away with an appalling crime. The link between the Clintons and this operation seems more and more suspicious upon closer inspection.

There were many Clinton men who linked the governor to the drugs. One man who tried to figure out the connections between Mena and Governor Clinton was former Arkansas Attorney General Winston Bryant.

"There was, in my opinion, more than enough evidence to prosecute a number of people for crimes regarding the Barry Seal case at Mena," said Bryant.[237] Bryant never got the chance to prosecute or properly investigate the connections of various high-ranking officials. In his bid for attorney general in 1990, Bryant attempted to raise Mena as an issue. He was subsequently confronted and warned by Clinton Aide Betsey Wright, who told Bryant "to stay away" from the matter.[238]

"The Mena investigations were never supposed to see the light of day," said William Duncan, former investigator with the Medicaid Fraud Division of Bryant's office, "Investigations were interfered with and covered up, and the justice system was subverted."[239]

A memo from Duncan in March 1992 noted that he was ordered "to remove all files concerning the Mena investigation from the attorney general's office."[240]

The money profited from the drug trade running out of Arkansas was embroiled in Iran-Contra, the high-ranking political scandal in the 1980s in which senior Reagan administration officials secretly facilitated the sale of arms to Iran, which was the subject of an arms embargo. The arms sales, it was hoped, would secure the release of several U.S. hostages and the money would also be used to fund the Contras in Nicaragua. The real scandal of Iran-Contra was not merely the Reagan administration's arms trade for hostages or the illegal arming of Nicaraguan Contras despite the congressional prohibition of the Boland Amendment. The real scandal of Iran-Contra was that the administration was running drugs to support its illegal war against the Marxist government of Nicaragua. The blame for funneling the funds to the Contras was placed on Lieutenant Colonel Oliver North, who sacrificed his career and, for a short time, his freedom. Barry Seal sacrificed his life. Those on high stayed insulated from major damage. Vice President Bush was behind the operation and the center for the drug operations operated under the watch of Governor Clinton.

"All of the drug money, and all of the trafficking of drugs sent all over the nation, came out of little Mena, Arkansas, right under the nose of little Governor Billy Clinton," said Larry Nichols.[241]

Authors Sally Denton and Roger Morris wrote a fabulous essay called the "Crimes of Mena," which was set to run in the *Washington Post* in 1995. The *Washington Post* editor, like the Bushes a Skull and Bones alumnus of Yale University, spiked the story. Denton and Morris were forced to publish the article in *Penthouse* in July 1995.

Denton and Morris pointed out that the CIA drug running at Mena had been documented to the hilt and that it implicated both Republicans and Democrats at the highest levels. The readily available article included an extensive discussion of Seal and his drug running activities and his immunity from the powers that be:

> Barry Seal—gunrunner, drug trafficker, and covert C.I.A. operative extraordinaire—is hardly a familiar name in American politics. But nine years after he was murdered in a hail of bullets by Medellin cartel hit men outside a Salvation Army shelter in Baton Rouge, Louisiana, he has come back to haunt the reputations of three American presidents.
>
> Seal's legacy includes more than 2,000 newly discovered documents that now verify and quantify much of what previously had been only suspicion, conjecture, and legend. The documents confirm that from 1981 to his brutal death in 1986, Barry Seal carried on one of the most lucrative, extensive, and brazen operations in the history of the international drug trade, and that he did it with the evident complicity, if not collusion, of elements of the United States government, apparently with the acquiescence of Ronald Reagan's administration, impunity from any subsequent exposure by George Bush's administration, and under the usually acute political nose of then-Arkansas governor Bill Clinton.

CIA operative Chip Tatum kept some careful records of his actions during Iran-Contra. One of his most revealing records was an inflight conversation on a helicopter flight to Palmerola Air Base in Honduras on March 16, 1985, between former Arkansas police captain Buddy Young and Mike Hariri of Mossad, which indicated that Seal tragically thought he had an "insurance policy" that would somehow protect him from both prosecution and physical harm. But the insurance policy was canceled in a hail of bullets on February 19, 1986, in Baton Rouge, Louisiana. Three Colombians in 1987 were convicted of the murder of Seal: Miguel Velez, Luis Carlos Quintero-Cruz, and Bernardo Antonio Vasquez. They told their lawyers that they thought they were working for Oliver North. Larry Nichols says the CIA killed Seal and those captured for his murder were the same ones he was working with in the Contra resupply efforts.

Here's our theory: The big lie is that the Medellin Cartel murdered Seal; instead, it was the bipartisan American CIA Drug Cartel that murdered him. The American CIA Cartel was running the Medellin Cartel. Seal had turned from an asset into a liability. Author Daniel Hopsicker, who wrote a biography on Seal, concluded that Lieutenant Colonel Oliver North of the National Security Council indeed used the Colombian hit team to murder Seal (though this was never officially proven).

Hopsicker interviewed Seal's well-known, highly respected Miami lawyer Richard Sharpstein. Sharpstein said that another Seal lawyer, Lewis Unglesby, was with Barry when the IRS came to seize his property for unpaid taxes on his drug dealings. Seal flat out told them that both he and they (the IRS agents) were working for the same people.

Sharpstein had strong opinions about Seal's murder.

"Unglesby was with Seal when he retired to a back room." Sharpstein stated. "He watched as Seal placed a call to Vice President Bush. He heard Seal tell Bush, 'If you don't get these IRS assholes off my back I'm going to blow the whistle on the Contra scheme.'"

Sharpstein spoke solemnly, aware of the gravity of his words. "'That's why he's dead,' is what Unglesby said."

One week after the phone conversation between Seal and Bush, Barry was sentenced to a halfway house. Two weeks later he was dead.

"Barry Seal, you mean that agent that went bad?" Gordon Novel had casually inquired, when we'd posed the question of his associations with Seal.

An agent that "goes bad," as we understand intelligence industry trade jargon, is one who contemplates talking.

"Seal was gunned down, supposedly by those Colombians," says Sharpstein. "But they were fed information by the assholes in our government who wanted him dead."[242]

Red Hall, who worked with Seal, told Hopsicker that the killers of Barry Seal were known to have worked for Oliver North.

"Chip Tatum, another covert operative who had known Seal and shared confidences with him," Hopsicker said, "listened with amusement the first time we breathlessly relayed what we'd discovered: that Oliver North is guilty in the assassination of Barry Seal . . . 'No shit, Sherlock,' he replied, laughing. 'It ain't exactly the secret of the century, I can tell you,' claimed Hopsicker."[243]

On April 19, 1986, two months after the Seal murder, Reed and his wife went out to a popular Mexican restaurant in Little Rock.

By coincidence Governor Clinton was there "partying." As Reed finished his dinner, Bob Nash approached Reed and said that the governor wanted talk with him in a security van parked outside. Reed entered the van with Clinton's head of security, Buddy Young, watching the outside. Terry Reed described the scene in his book *Compromised: Clinton, Bush, and the CIA*:

> "Bobby [Bob Nash] says you've got a problem about going to Mexico because of the deal with Barry Seal," the glassy-eyed governor began. By this time the smell of marijuana was unmistakable.

Clinton paused for a moment as if trying to sort out his thoughts. "'I can see your concern. I understand Seal was a friend of yours. His death does appear suspicious. And Bobby says you got a feeling somebody here in Arkansas may have had a motive to kill him. But nobody here had anything to do with that. Seal just got too damn big for his britches and that scum basically deserved to die, in my opinion . . .'"

With that, Clinton got up from his chair and went to the back of the van, returning with a half-smoked joint. He reseated himself. He took a long, deep drag. After holding it in until his cheeks bulged, he then exhaled slowly and deliberately.

He extended his arm and offered the joint to Reed. Terry shook his head and gestured, no thanks.

"Go on, I'm commander in chief here; you won't get busted,'" the governor said with a straight face while exhaling. . . .

[Reed said] "'No, thanks. I just want to get all of this straight. You're saying that Seal's death, from what you know, is just as the papers say, he was killed by some Colombians because of his connections to the Medellin Cartel?'"

"'Yeah. And I think you're makin' a big mistake by passing up the opportunity to go to Mexico for Cathey [Oliver North]. It sounds attractive to me. I wish I could go in your place. Terry, these guys are counting on you and they're leaning on me to get you to go. I'm not standing in your way. I just want to tell you if you wanna go to Mexico, you'd be leaving here with my blessing. There's no hard feelings about anything that has happened here. I wanted you to hear that coming from me.'"

Clinton took another deep drag [on his joint], held it and exhaled. In a raspy voice, with smoke still coming out of his mouth, Clinton added, "Sure you don't want some of this? This is good shit. We sure do grow lotsa good things besides watermelons here in Arkansas.[244]

"So what's your decision, you gonna go or aren't ya? I gotta tell Cathey [Oliver North] somethin' ASAP to get him off my ass. It's ridiculous, but he's holdin' me responsible for your vacillation."[245]

Reed told Bill Clinton that he was going to Mexico. The next month Felix Rodriguez was contacted by L. D. Brown, who prodded him to go to Mexico to murder Terry Reed.

In 1986, after the murder of Seal, L. D. Brown was again tasked by the CIA—this time with assassination.

"Rodriguez had a sense of urgency in his voice," Brown said. "He told me they had found the guy flying the second seat of the C-123 I had flown on, the plane Seal used to fly the coke into Mena. The man was to be in Puerto Vallarta, Mexico, on June 21 and I was to be there to take care of him."

In a bipartisan effort, Bush's man Rodriguez was sending Clinton's favorite state trooper down to Mexico to silence someone involved in Seal's drug flights. Rodriguez sent Brown a manual for a 7.62 rifle that Brown was supposed to pick up from a soldier at a restaurant in Puerto Vallarta. Then Brown was to assemble the rifle and find his target, who was staying at a local resort.

Before Brown left on his Mexico murder mission, he checked in with Clinton and told him he was going to "take care" of the problem there.

"That's good, L. D.," said Clinton, in compliance with the CIA-directed hit.

Supplied with a fake Arkansas driver's license, Brown went to Mexico under the alias Michael Johnson. He assembled his rifle and mentally prepared himself for the hit, which he assumed had been the co-pilot on Seal's plane. Seal himself had been murdered earlier in the year on February 19, 1986, in Baton Rouge.

Brown got to the Hotel Playa Conchas Chinas in Puerto Vallarta where his target was staying. Brown made contact with a hotel clerk who pointed out his murder target: a dark-haired man, who bore none of the characteristics of the drug runner from two years prior.

"Horror ran down my spine," said Brown. "I had never seen the man before in my life. I left the hotel with the straw bag in tow . . . I dumped the bag and gun in a ditch by the road back into town. . . . We left Puerto Vallarta that afternoon as I thought I would never see that man again. I was wrong. Ten years later I would be giving a deposition in a civil case he would bring in Little Rock, Arkansas. His name was Terry Reed."[246]

It was clear the powers that be were trying to clean up the mess of Mena.

In the summer of 1993, Clinton campaign Security Director Jerry Parks feared for his life. He would carry a pistol to check the mailbox. He would take strange routes back home to make sure he was not being followed. He was a restless sleeper at night.

Evans-Pritchard said that when he went to Arkansas to investigate the Clintons he found Jerry's son, Gary Parks, then aged twenty-three, in a state of terror. Gary Parks was "half-underground, sleeping on the floor in different houses, afraid that he too could be the target of attack." Evans-Pritchard said that the situation he discovered in Arkansas, the intimidation factor, was just like what he had found in El Salvador and Guatemala when he was covering the Central American wars of the 1980s. It should be noted that when Evans-Pritchard went to Arkansas to investigate Bill Clinton, he himself came under direct, overt, and intimidating surveillance, including a "large, corpulent, bearded, redneck wearing dark glasses" that made a point of intimidation staring at one of the witnesses who Evans-Pritchard was interviewing in an otherwise empty restaurant.[247]

Parks told Evans-Pritchard that his father who had done a lot of work for the Clintons, also was spying on Bill's infidelities. Mrs. Parks, the mother of Gary, said that Vince Foster (Hillary Clinton's law partner and lover) and Hillary had ordered the surveillance of Bill. Gary Parks said Jerry Parks was "Working on his [Bill's] infidelities. It had been going on for years. He had enough to impeach Bill Clinton on the spot." Gary said that since 1988, when he was age seventeen, he had gone with his father Jerry on four or five spying missions on Clinton. [248] After Clinton declined a run for president in 1988, his relationship with Hillary took yet another dive and they were seriously contemplating divorce.

Foster had told his brother-in-law Lee Bowman in the mid-1980s that Jerry Parks was a good pick for security work. "I was struck how insistent he was that Parks was a 'man who could be trusted,'" said Bowman.[249]

In July 1993, the home of Jerry Parks was burglarized and his womanizing files on Bill Clinton were stolen. Parks was murdered about one and one-half months later. A witness to the Parks murder told Evans-Pritchard that there were two assassins: middle-aged men with beer bellies and big shoulders, grayish hair, and in their late forties or fifties. Jane Parks, the wife of the deceased, said that her contacts in the Arkansas State police told her that "the murder was a conspiracy hatched in Hot Springs by five men who moved in the social circle of Buddy Young."[250]

In the summer of 1984, Jane Parks had been the manager of the Vantage Point apartments. Roger Clinton was placed, rent-free, in apartment B107, right next to the manager's office. When Roger was there it was drugs, partying, and girls all the time. Roger, in addition to being a big drug dealer was also in a band aptly called Dealer's Choice. Roger was filmed on police tape buying cocaine: "I've got four or five guys in uniform who keep an eye on the guys who keep an eye on me."[251]

That "four or five guys" comment by Roger pointed directly toward the official corruption in Governor Bill Clinton's administration.

Bill, aged thirty-seven in the summer of 1984, would come by apartment B107 to party with his half-brother. Bill and Roger would be smoking dope and Jane Parks could hear through the thin walls Bill yelling, "This is really good shit!"

Jane said the brothers were smoking dope and using cocaine. Roger's groupies of young women were present. She could hear loud orgasms rocketing through the walls. "The bed was pressed up against the partition wall, just a few feet from the desk of Mrs. Parks. On two occasions she heard the Governor copulating on the bed . . . some of [the visitors] appeared surprisingly young."[252]

The assistant manager of the apartment complex told Evans-Pritchard that Jane was being truthful, that you could hear the governor getting off in B107. She estimated that the girls were about age seventeen or eighteen.

Jane told Evans-Pritchard that her husband had done work for Clinton for about a decade. (And, of course, Hillary and Vince were using Parks to spy on Bill.) She said that Jerry had made trips to Mena, Arkansas, the acknowledged hub of Dixie Mafia and CIA drug smuggling in the 1980s. Jerry was a good friend of Barry Seal and had even attended Seal's funeral after his murder in 1986.

Parks was going to Mena to retrieve large sums of cash.

"[Jerry Parks] told her [his wife Jane] that he would leave his Lincoln at a hangar at the Mena airport, go off for a Coke and by the time he came back they would have loaded the money into the trunk with a forklift truck," said Evans-Pritchard. "He never touched it. When he got back to Little Rock he would deliver the money to Vince Foster in the K-Mart parking lot on Rodney Parham Boulevard, a little at a time. They used a routine of switching briefcases, a 'flip-flop mail carrier' made of leather."[253]

Jerry Parks was assassinated at 6:30 on the evening of Sunday, September 26, 1993, on the Chenal Parkway on the outskirts of Little Rock, Arkansas. Two men killed Parks and the one that did the shooting used a 9mm handgun.

Like so many others, Jerry Parks's knowledge and participation in the Dixie Mafia/CIA drug running that was going on at Mena did him in. What Parks knew threatened the Clinton presidency.

After Parks was murdered, his wife said representatives of the FBI, the Secret Service, the IRS, and even the CIA came to her home and picked it clean of evidence. Jane Parks said the FBI ransacked her place. What they confiscated included 130 tapes of phone conversations. Parks never saw the material again.[254]

Gary Parks believed Clinton was responsible for his father's death. "I believe that Bill Clinton had my father killed to protect his political career. We're dealing with a secretive machine here in Arkansas that can shut anyone up in a moment," Parks told Ambrose Evans-Pritchard in the 1990s.[255]

Robert Morrow confronted Bill Clinton about the 1993 Jerry Parks murder at a book signing in the fall of 1987. Morrow relates:

> In September 1987 Bill Clinton came to Austin, Texas, for a book signing. I decided that I would do a little bit of grassroots activism and flier his event, which was held at Book People, a destination Austin book store. Bill was hawking his book *Giving: How Each of Us Can Change the World*, which I think takes on a new meaning in light of the troubles at the Clinton Foundation.
>
> I went to Kinko's and had a thousand fliers, on bright yellow paper, made up with as much incredibly toxic Clinton dirt as I could fit on the double sided flier. I entitled the flier: *Bill and Hillary: A Lifetime of Violating People.* The flier detailed Bill's multiple rapes, sexual assaults, Hillary's facilitating this abuse and Hillary's domestic violence. I also included that fact that Bill says Hillary is a lesbian and that she had had affairs with Vince Foster and Webb Hubbell, and that the latter is unfortunately the biological father of Chelsea. Chelsea being Webb Hubbell's daughter is the Clintons' greatest shame. (I think their murdering seventy-six people at Waco in 1993 was the shameful crime that should have put them in the basement of a prison.) Let's just say the flier, like this book packed a punch.
>
> It was a nice day in late summer Austin, which is a liberal town, and a good crowd turned out to see Clinton. In fact, about 800 people lined up to see Clinton with the line extending out the store all the way to the corner of the block and then down the back sidewalk

of the property. Bill Clinton has star power. I decided that I would start flyering at the very back of the line (out of sight of management) and then work my way to the front of the line of people waiting to get their books signed. It was a crowd composed mainly of Democrats and Clinton-lovers who were nostalgic for the 1990s.

I worked the whole line and despite the liberal makeup of the crowd, many people took my flier. Some were bored standing in line and wanted something to read; others would take it and crumple it; still others would read for a bit and hand it back. All these folks had one thing in common: they were standing in line to see Bill Clinton and I was joyfully nuking the Clinton-love karma.

After I had handed out hundreds of fliers I decided to stop before I got to the front door of the bookstore and took a lunch break. I went across the street to Whole Foods for lunch while I basked in the satisfaction of a very fine job of trolling Bill Clinton's book signing. Also, I was not going to stand in line for two hours in the Texas heat just to meet a serial rapist at his book signing.

While I was munching lunch, I decided, well I did buy Clinton's book *Giving* so I am eligible to get it signed by the Rapist, so why not see what Bill has to say. The great thing is I did not have to stand in line (for very long) to see Clinton because the line had thinned down to perhaps a 30 minute wait. I flyered the rest of folks in line who I had missed and I got in line to see Clinton. When I got in the store, the security at a presidential book signing was very similar to an airport security screening. I had to leave all my metal coins, cell phone, and car keys in a drop bucket which I retrieved after the book signing. Then, like everyone else, I was wanded by the Secret Service. As you get close in line to the former president they ask you to take your hands out of your pocket.

I can't imagine why the Secret Service thinks someone would want to kill this son of a bitch. Beats me . . .

One thing that amused me while I was standing in line to see Clinton was that about every 30th person was a middle-aged woman (white or black) who when they got to meet Clinton, they would start blubbering, crying, and then collapse into his reassuring arms. These ladies as they blubbered would say stuff like, "Things were so much better when you were president, Mr. Clinton" and then they would choke up as they bawled and Bill take them in a big bear hug and say, "It's gonna be ok" as he patted the ladies on their backs.

It seemed to be some sort of cathartic therapy not just for these middle-aged ladies, but also for Bill who apparently craves this like a monkey on cocaine craves another hit. Slowly the line took me to where Bill was standing next what seemed like several stacks of perhaps 100 books. It was a small room and there were seven Secret Service agents in there who were scoping out the line. I am a well-known anti-Clinton activist and they knew exactly who I was.

I finally got up to Clinton, also known as the Rapist. Clinton was casually dressed and seemed to be wearing something similar to a Polo knit shirt and slacks. As he took my book to sign it—remember this is 2007—I said to him, "Mr. President, can I ask you a question?" Clinton replied, "Sure, go ahead."

I then asked him, "Mr. President, why did you, Hillary and Buddy Young send those three goons to beat up and nearly murder Gary Johnson [lawyer for Larry Nichols as well as the next door neighbor to Gennifer Flowers] on June 26, 1992?" It did not take long for Bill's face to get red and, by the way, he has a big head. I am standing three feet away from him. Picture a red volleyball or red basketball with a face on it.

Then Clinton said, "I do not know a Gary Johnson." Then as his face got red he started sputtering, "So are you talking about all the Jerry Falwell stuff, all that cash for trash? Is that what you are talking about?"

Later a friend told me, "Robert, he did not deny beating up Gary Johnson. He just said he did not *know* him" . . . excellent point and that is exactly how Bill Clinton approaches reality. And we know that because Larry Nichols is friends with Larry Patterson who let Nichols know that is precisely what happened on June 26,

1992. For several years Larry Nichols has confirmed that to me. Bottom line: I believe that Bill Clinton enlisted thugs to beat up people. They beat up Gary Johnson to steal a videotape that he had of Bill often entering the condominium of Gennifer Flowers. They should be rotting in jail for committing that aggravated assault.

I then had my second zinger question ready for Bill as I said, "Mr. President, did you help to organize the murder of Jerry Parks on September 26, 1993?" Now that was a big question as the Clinton-love karma of the book signing was now completely vaporized.

Clinton paused for a bit, then he answered with a very careful, "No."

As I see it, Bill Clinton and his former top goon Raymond "Buddy" Young should be treated as suspects in the murder of Jerry Parks on September 26, 1993. That is not because Jerry Parks had been hired by Hillary and Vince Foster to spy on Bill around the time period 1989–1990, but rather because it seems likely that Jerry Parks was involved in the CIA/Dixie Mafia drug trade of the 1990s. See former U.S. intelligence operative and assassin Chip Tatum for his information on Buddy Young saying that Jerry Parks was an assassin for the Arkansas drug cartel. Some people think that convicted murderer Gary Parks killed his own father Jerry Parks, but based on what Clinton/Young did to Gary Johnson in 1992, Bill Clinton must be a top suspect in the 1993 murder of Jerry Parks.[256]

After red-faced Bill Clinton had carefully told me "No" that he had not murdered Jerry Parks, I said to Clinton, "Mr. President you are a sociopath. I am done," as I turned on my heels and walked away from Clinton. That felt good. Not many people tell former or current presidents three feet from their faces that they are sociopaths. I wish more people did.

As I was leaving, Bill's reply to my labeling him a sociopath was, "Well I might be one," and he added, "but you have no right to tell these lies about me."

Bill Clinton did not challenge me when I called him out publicly as a sociopath. But we already knew that. What Clinton really is is a very dangerous psychopath with social skills. Psychopaths with social skills are the types that can fillet your gut with a carving knife, then two days later give a tear-streaked eulogy at your funeral saying how much they loved and miss you. Or rape your daughter and then speak at a rally for "women's rights." Or be addicted to drugs, facilitate a massive drug trade, take a suitcase full of drug money kickbacks and then say they *don't even know what cocaine looks like* (cokehead Clinton actually said that).

As I left a sputtering and denying Clinton, two Secret Service agents rushed up to me and asked if I consented to be "interviewed" by them. I said yes. Then they whisked me downstairs to what appeared to be a back office barely bigger than a walk in closet. They asked me why I did what I did and then I told the Secret Service agents—about three of them—that in Bill Clinton's entire public career not one person or one journalist has asked him about the 1992 beating of Gary Johnson and the 1993 murder of Jerry Parks. So it is time to hold this man accountable and I am glad to do it. One of the agents was familiar with the break in at Kathleen Willey's home, which had occurred at about that time in 2007 and it was publicized on the Drudge Report (break-ins a typical Clinton tactic).

In my dealings with the Secret Service who have checked me out a couple of times because I am so effective at skewering (and getting under the skin of the Clintons), I have found them to be polite, decent, reasonable people. In other words, *the Secret Service is everything the Clintons are not* and I get the subliminal feeling that more than one Secret Service agent just loves that I call out the Clintons for the despicable, psychopathic, criminal and trashy pond scum that they are.

CHAPTER 11

THE TWO-PARTY "SYSTEM"

"It's not the Republican's fault, of course, and it's not the Democrat's fault. Now what I'm looking for is who did it? Now they are the two folks involved, so maybe we ought to put them together —'they' did it."

—Ross Perot[257]

In 1988, highly decorated Green Beret Bo Gritz wrote a letter to George H. W. Bush in which he castigated the then vice president for the drug running of the federal government. Gritz had been tasked with finding American POWs left behind in Asia after the Vietnam War by Texas businessman and Bush associate Ross Perot. What Gritz found was a Burmese drug lord named General Khun Sa who "offered to identify U.S. Government officials who, he says, have been trafficking in heroin for more than 20 years." Gritz was incensed that when Perot brought information and evidence of the drug running to Bush's attention it was ignored.[258]

Perot's personal attorney Tom Luce, a Republican Party elder, told me that Perot had requested a meeting with the vice president to present him with evidence of the CIA's drug smuggling in Asia and the U.S. "All Ross got from Bush was a grim smile," Luce told me.

In an open letter, Gritz excoriated Bush:

Mister Richard Armitage, Assistant Secretary of Defense for International Security Affairs, is one of those USG officials implicated by Khun Sa. Nothing was done with this evidence that indicated that anyone of authority, including yourself, had intended to do anything more than protect Mr. Armitage. I was charged with 'Misuse of Passport'. Seems that it is alright for Oliver North and Robert MacFarlane to go into Iran on Irish Passports to negotiate an illegal arms deal that neither you nor anyone else admits condoning, but I can't use a passport that brings back drug information against your friends.

Please answer why a respected American Citizen like Mister H. Ross Perot can bring you a pile of evidence of wrongdoing by Armitage and others, and you, according to TIME magazine (May 4, page 18), not only offer him no support, but have your Secretary of Defense, Frank Carlucci tell Mr. Perot to 'stop pursuing Mr. Armitage'. Why Sir, will you not look into affidavits gathered by The Christic Institute (Washington, DC), which testify that Armitage not only trafficked in heroin, but did so under the guise of an officer charged with bringing home our POWs. If the charges are true, Armitage, who is still responsible for POW recovery as your Assistant Secretary of Defense ISA, has every reason not to want these heroes returned to us alive. Clearly, follow on investigations would illuminate the collective crimes of Armitage and others. . . .

I failed to realize the fullness of his meaning, or these other events, until in May 1987, Gen Khun Sa, in his jungle headquarters, named Richard Armitage as a key connection in a ring of heroin trafficking mobsters and USG officials. . . . You were Director of the CIA in 1975, during a time Khun Sa says Armitage and CIA officials were trafficking in heroin. [259]

Both Gritz and Perot, who cared about bringing United States POWs home, were stunned, shocked, and enraged to find out that the government was running drugs under the Reagan administration.

The Bushes were heavily involved in many facets of the drug trade.

The 1990 book *Blue Thunder*, by Thomas Burdick and Charlene Mitchell, goes over the close ties between Donald Aronow and Meyer Lansky. Aronow was a Mafia-associated drug smuggler. A close friend of Vice President Bush, he was also a pioneer in the building of very fast speed boats that were popular with the drug smugglers. Aronow was murdered in Miami in a professional hit while he was sitting in his car on February 2, 1987.

The authors of *Blue Thunder* present an interesting story. They write that Teagle, an imprisoned, well-connected drug smuggler, went to authorities and told them why Aronow was murdered. He told them that Bobby Young had become indebted to Colombian drug kingpins and as a payment for this debt he had to murder Aronow as a way of wiping his debt clean. Aronow had been placed on the death list, Teagle told the DEA agents, because he also had failed to pay cocaine debt with the Colombians. According to Teagle, Aronow and George Bush's son Jeb were partners in a major cocaine-smuggling operation, and they owed their Colombian suppliers $2.5 million. Jeb and Don had refused to pay.[260]

Retired US Navy Lieutenant Commander Al Martin knew that "Jeb [Bush] was extremely familiar with what these boats were actually used for, that although they were going to be gun-boats for the Panamanian Navy, they were actually going to be used for the transportation of narcotics."[261]

Martin says he had dinner with Vice President Bush, his son Jeb, and Felix Rodriguez in 1985. "But George Bush, Sr., always said that his concept of government, what he believed in, and how he had operated, was on the Big Lie principle." The Big Lie Principle is to lie so outrageously that the masses could not conceive that you would distort the truth so flagrantly. An example would be speeches made against drugs by the vice president head of the South Florida Task

Force on Drugs, while at the same time supervising a multi-billion-dollar CIA governmental drug-running operation.

Martin worked hand in glove with Jeb Bush and Oliver North during Iran-Contra. Martin most definitely was in the "belly of the beast" as high crimes were being committed in the 1980s. Martin's book has "eyewitness accounts including firsthand knowledge of US Government sanctioned narcotics trafficking, illicit weapons deals and an epidemic of fraud—corporate securities fraud, real estate fraud, banking fraud and insurance fraud."[262]

After Iran-Contra imploded and some of the criminals went to jail and others escaped completely scot free, Martin would have conversations with Jeb Bush about being taken care of. Jeb was not willing to "help out" Martin with any money and Martin highly resented this after all the things he had done to compromise himself with criminality during Iran-Contra. Martin would threaten to go public with what he knew and Jeb Bush's reply as he warned Martin to keep silent was:

"There is no constituency for the truth." Emphasis added.

In March of 2013, we asked Hopsicker about the Jeb Bush quote and Hopsicker had revealing things to say about his conversation with Al Martin: "He said this to me in a phone interview, in which he stated he had gone public because he 'didn't get his briefcase' [full of money]. It had nothing to do with morality.' There were 5,000 guys left hanging out there when Iran-Contra broke, he said. He was one of them and he was pissed. Yes. Martin told me that Jeb Bush told him, in an effort to keep Martin from going public, and becoming a whistleblower, that "'there is no constituency for the truth.'"

Hopsicker added, "It may be the truest thing Jeb Bush ever said."[263]

Oliver North had close connections with both Clinton and Jeb Bush during the period of Iran-Contra drug smuggling and murders of the 1980s. Call it the bipartisan criminal elite.

Here are former CIA counterintelligence agent Chip Tatum's notes from March 30, 1985, which allegedly memorialize what was said as he and Oliver North were inspecting some cocaine factories at some villages on the Nicaraguan-Honduran border. Vice President Bush and Oliver North were very concerned about money being lost in the chain of drug smuggling:

"Mr. North stated the following to the other passengers, 'One more year of this and we'll all retire.' He then made a remark concerning Barry Seal and Governor Clinton. 'If we can keep those Arkansas hicks in line, that is,' referring to the loss of monies as determined the week prior during their meeting in Costa Rica. I stood silently by the vat of leaves, listening to the conversation. General Alverez had gone with the Contra leader to discuss logistics. The other three—North, Rodriguez, and Ami Nir—continued through the wooden building, inspecting the cocaine. North continued, 'but he (Vice President Bush) is very concerned about those missing monies. I think he's going to have Jeb (Bush) arrange something out of Columbia,' he told his comrades, not thinking twice of my presence. What Mr. North was referring to ended up being the assassination of Barry Seal by members of the Medellin Cartel in early 1986."[264] Though North was never proven to have murdered anyone, suspicions hang over his head.

Vice President Bush and North were worried about Bill Clinton and Barry Seal stealing too much of the drug money that was going through Mena, Arkansas, which was a major transit point for the drug smuggling of Iran-Contra.

Former DEA agent Celerino "Cele" Castillo was another source to indict Vice President Bush, Oliver North, the CIA, and the Nicaraguan Contras in drug smuggling during the 1980s.

"The end of my career with the DEA took place in El Salvador," said Castillo. "One day, I received a cable from a fellow agent, saying to investigate possible drug smuggling by Nicaraguan Contras operating from the Ilopango Air Force Base.

"I quickly discovered that the Contra pilots were, indeed, smuggling narcotics back into the United States, using the same pilots, planes and hangers that the Central Intelligence Agency and the National Security Council, under the direction of Lt. Col. Oliver North, used to maintain their covert supply operation to the Contras."[265]

Castillo met Vice President Bush at a U.S. embassy party on January 14, 1986. Castillo told Bush that he was a DEA agent assigned to Guatemala and that there were some funny things going on with the Contras in El Salvador. Bush did not say anything, he just smiled and walked away.

"When Bush confronted me and then just walked away after I told him some of the evidence I had, it was obvious he knew what was going on and was involved in the illegal drug trade," said Castillo.[266]

Ross Perot knew about these government intelligence operations engaged in arms and drug smuggling. Perot knew about Mena, and he knew President Bush was involved. Perot and then president Bush had a huge falling out over the matter.

"When you look into the [Vietnam POW] cover-up, you find government officials in the drug trade who can't break themselves of the habit," Perot said. "What I have found is a snake pit (CIA drug smuggling) without a bottom. They will do anything to keep this covered up."[267]

Perot ran in the 1992 presidential race as an independent candidate. He was not running to win the presidency. Perot felt extremely strongly that Bush should lose the general election.

The eccentric Texan was not the first presidential candidate to make these accusations. Ron Paul also exposed the operation in his run for president in 1988. Paul pointed out that the U.S. was paying Panama's Manuel Noriega $200,000 per year when George Bush was head of the CIA in 1976.

"I think George Bush is deep into it," Paul said. "Well over his head. . . . I think George Bush through his office and through the fact that he was the head of the CIA, I think he was very, very close to it and he knows exactly what was happening [with regards to drug running] and I believe the rule that once a CIA member always a CIA member . . . I sadly believe that there will be very little said which means the Democrats aren't doing [anything about] it, that means they are involved, too."[268]

Ron Paul was 100 percent correct.

Ostensibly, the reason for allowing and encouraging such drug running was that Congress would not allow the Reagan administration to fund the Nicaraguan contras to stage a counter-revolution against the Marxist Sandinistas who had removed pro-American dictator Anastasio Somoza in Nicaragua in July 1979.

Tatum said that in 1992 President Bush was terrified of Perot and on the verge of having him assassinated. Bush was afraid that the billionaire would get into office and have him prosecuted for drug crimes.

Tatum's April 2, 1996, letter to Perot, which was widely reprinted on the Internet, read as follows:

Dear Mr. Perot:

As you prepare your part for the 1996 election, there is a matter of grave importance of which you should be aware.

In 1992, as the commander of a Black Operations Unit called Pegasus, I was ordered to neutralize you. Our unit was directed by President George Bush. It was determined, at some point, that the party you formed was counter to the American system of democracy. In his attempt to justify your neutralization, Mr. Bush expressed not only his concerns of the existence of your party and the threat which you posed to free America, but also the positions of other U.S. and world leaders.

I had been associated with Pegasus since its creation in 1985. The original mission of our unit was to align world leaders and financiers with the United States. I was personally responsible for the neutralization of one Mossad agent, an army Chief of Staff of a foreign government, a rebel leader and the president of a foreign government [thought to be Swedish Prime Minister Olof Palme, murdered Feb. 28, 1986].

However, all of these missions were directed toward enemies of the United States as determined by our President. And because of this, I did not hesitate to successfully neutralize these enemies.

The order to neutralize you, however, went against all that I believed in. It was obvious to me that his order was predicated on a desire to remain as President rather than a matter of enemy alignment. I refused the order. I further advised the President and others that if you or members of your organization or family were threatened or harmed in any way, I would cause information, which includes certain documents, to be disseminated from their six locations in various areas of the world, to various media and political destinations. I walked away from Special Operations that day with the knowledge that you don't just quit! I felt, however, that the time capsules protected my interests.[269]

Bill Clinton, the democratic nominee, and Perot had many phone calls and personal meetings in the summer of 1992. Perot and Clinton were jointly coordinating the takedown of Bush by stealing Republican votes in key swing and Republican-leaning states. Perot got into the 1992 race in order to defeat Bush, who he felt was committing wrongdoings. Larry Patterson, a top Arkansas state trooper of Bill Clinton, recorded a conversation with Christopher Ruddy on a cassette tape that they titled "More Than Sex" (published by *Newsmax* in 2000), saying that Ross Perot and Bill Clinton, before the 1992 campaign met in Dallas for "lunch, dinner" several times. The implication is Perot and Clinton were colluding to take down Bush.

In 1992, the mainstream media began to paint Perot as an unstable nut. In 1996 Gerald Posner, a proponent of the JFK assassination lone gunman theory, wrote a book on Ross, *Citizen Perot: His Life and Times*, designed to discredit and marginalize the billionaire.

Journalist Bob Novak interviewed Perot in 1992 and came to the conclusion that Ross was out to stick a knife in Bush. Perot told Novak that he wanted to have a one-on-one debate with then president Bush. Perot added he did not think Bush was much of a president and noted that the polls showed him ahead in three key states: California, Texas, and Florida.

Despite Bush's attempts to marginalize Perot by claiming that he had "some nutty ideas" and came "from the fringe," Perot received 18.9 percent of the popular vote, approximately 19,741,065 votes (but no electoral college votes), making him the most successful third-party presidential candidate since Theodore Roosevelt ran with the Bull Moose Party in the 1912 election.[270]

Perot was successful in siphoning votes away from Bush, but Bush was correct that a vote for Perot was a wasted vote. Perot was unwittingly kicking a Republican involved heavily in CIA drug operations out of office and helping to install a Democrat involved in the very same operations. Bubba played Ross perfectly over the phone and together they drained the votes from Bush, making Clinton a non-majority vote–elected president. Perot would come back in 1996 and play the same role, and a majority of voters voted against Bill Clinton in the two elections in which he ran. Even Nixon with his uptight manner was elected in a landslide majority in his second successful presidential election.

The Bushes and Clintons like to validate each other as good, decent, legitimate, and aboveboard political players. Drug trafficking and other covert operations were off the table in the '92 election because Bush and Clinton were in it together. Perot knew that if he raised it as an issue against Bush, it would marginalize his already tenuous standing in the race.

The Bushes and Clintons share their deepest bonds in connections with the CIA. Cord Meyer, Roger Morris, and Christopher Hitchens said that in the summer of 1968, while at the University of Oxford, young Bill Clinton was recruited by the agency to infiltrate left-wing anti-war groups in Eastern Europe and snitch on their activities to the boys at Langley.

"I think he was a double," Hitchens says. "Somebody was giving information to [the CIA] about the anti-war draft resisters, and I think it was probably him. We had a girlfriend in common—I didn't know then—who's since become a very famous radical lesbian."[271]

Washington insider Jack Wheeler related in his 1988 essay "How the Clintons Will Undo McCain" how his friend told him an important nugget about this history of Bill Clinton. He wrote:

> Back in the '90s, years after he retired, if Cord drank a little too much Scotch he would laugh derisively at those conspiracists who accused Bill Clinton of being connected with the KGB. They all darkly point to Bill's participation in anti-war peace conferences in Stockholm and Oslo, and his trip to Leningrad, Moscow and Prague while he was at Oxford. '"Who could have paid for this?" they ask. '"It had to be the KGB!'" they claim." Cord would shake his head. "What rot—we paid for it. We recruited Bill the first week he was at Oxford. Bill's been an asset of The Three Bad Words ever since."[272]

Cord passed on in 2001.

Young George Bush would be among the agency assets raising the money for the Bay of Pigs operation as early as 1963.

Zapata Oil's offshore well platforms and the company itself fronted for the CIA. Bush himself pursued politics more than he did oil deals. When George H. W. Bush said in his confirmation hearings that he had never worked for the agency, he was committing perjury, yet became the director of Central Intelligence years later. As Vice President Bush oversaw an operation to import narcotics into the United States through rural areas of Louisiana, Texas, and Arkansas. Governor Bill Clinton knew about and ordered state police to look the other way as the feds moved millions in cocaine through Mena.

Clinton would tell his bodyguard, "Bush knew all about it." The Clintons and the Bushes share the CIA tie.

The public displays of affection between the two families in the last few years is not a surprise. Both families share some of the same dark secrets.

In September 2013 Jeb Bush was presenting Hillary Clinton with a "Liberty Medal" from the National Constitution Center. "Former Secretary Clinton has dedicated her life to serving and engaging people across the world in democracy," Jeb said. "These efforts as a citizen, an activist, and a leader have earned Secretary Clinton this year's Liberty Medal."[273]

In January 2014, former First Lady Barbara Bush said in a C-SPAN interview, "I love Bill Clinton. Maybe not his politics, but I love Bill Clinton. . . . My husband, Bill Clinton and I have become friends. And Bill visits us every summer."[274]

Barbara P. Bush, the daughter of George W., said in August of 2013 that Hillary was "unbelievably accomplished" and it is her hope that Hillary runs for president in 2016.[275] George W. Bush likes to call Bill Clinton his "brother from another mother." Bush said that would make Hillary "my sister-in-law."[276]

The Associated Press reported, "Former Presidents Bill Clinton and George W. Bush, political opposites who became friends, launched a new scholars program at four presidential centers with an opening act that might have been mistaken for a comedy routine. The two former presidents shared laughs and buddy-like banter on stage Monday, talking about presidential leadership while trading stories about their famous families and life after the White House. Clinton said he and Bush laughed backstage about people coming up to them at restaurants and asking to take 'selfie' photos. Quipped Bush, 'At least they're still asking.'"[277]

The article added: "George W. Bush campaigned for president in 2000 on restoring 'honor and dignity' to the White House following Clinton's impeachment over a sex scandal. But the two former presidents have developed a bond, strengthened by their mutual admiration for the elder Bush, whom Clinton visited in Maine last week."[278]

The Bushes, the Clintons, and the LBJ Library have teamed up to form a Presidential Leadership Program. It seems like coordinated propaganda to us.

In early April of 2014 Bill Clinton and George W. Bush sat side by side in Arlington, Texas, in the luxury box of Jerry Jones to watch the NCAA college men's basketball championship. Both had big smiles on their faces as "a large crowd attending the NCAA championship game in Arlington, Texas, between Connecticut and Kentucky took a moment to loudly applaud an image displayed on the large video boards inside AT&T Stadium."[279]

The public likes these images of civility. It makes them feel good knowing that leaders of opposite parties can get along.

"I've always found the friendship between Bill Clinton and the Bush family to be very endearing," reporter John Daly wrote. "It's something genuine, positive, and quite unlikely in an American political landscape marred by bitter, hyper-partisan animosity."[280]

In 2005, Clinton and Bush, Sr., took a trip to Asia to raise money (and more importantly, polish their public relations image) for tsunami victims. "US ex-President George Bush Sr. has praised his successor Bill Clinton for letting him sleep on their plane's only bed on their tour of tsunami-hit areas," the BBC reported. "Mr. Bush, 80, told Newsweek magazine that the 58-year-old Democrat spent the night on the floor in the next room so that he could get a proper rest. Mr. Clinton was respectful of his age and 'that meant a great deal to me,' the current president's father said."[281]

Then there was "Laura Bush shows 'pure class' in message to Clintons" as blogger Joe Saunders congratulated Laura Bush for tweeting on April 18, 2014, "Congratulations @BillClinton and @HillaryClinton, grandchildren are the greatest gift. @ChelseaClinton & Marc will be wonderful parents!" The Internet erupted with many gushing that Laura Bush had "class" and "style" and "warmth" for this pedestrian well-wishing for the arrival of a baby.[282]

In October 2013 Jenna Bush-Hagar got into the act. The *Daily Mail* covered it in an article, "Jenna Bush: Hillary Clinton and I are 'related' through 'Uncle' Bill—George W Bush's 'brother from another mother.'" The subtitle was "Former first-daughter Jenna Bush-Hager joked about her Clinton family ties at a charity gala earlier this week; When former Secretary of State Hillary Clinton took the stage, she spoke about the 'special feeling of kinship' she had for Jenna."[283]

When Jenna Bush-Hagar was emceeing a gala for the Save the Children organization, she honored Hillary and Jenna stated, "I'm not sure if you know this, but Secretary Clinton and I are actually related. Yes, she's married to Uncle Bill. Uncle Bill has become so close with my grandparents and my father . . . that my dad calls him a brother from another mother."[284]

Hillary replied that she, too, felt a "special feeling of kinship" with Jenna.

In November 2014, Toby Harnden, the Washington bureau chief of the *Sunday Times*, wrote "Bush: My Sweet Dad, A Wonderful Father to Bill Clinton and Me."

"He's got a good spirit about him," said Bush, who at sixty-eight is just six weeks older than Clinton. "We're the only baby-boomer presidents. We were both Southern governors and we both like each other. He's fun to be around. I hope he would say I'm fun to be around. And we're both grandfathers."[285]

Bush talked about how he had called Clinton to congratulate him on the birth of a granddaughter and told him to get ready to be the low man on the totem pole. "And he laughed. We get along great."[286]

Bush discussed the friendship of Bush, Sr., and Clinton: "It speaks to the character of both men. Bill Clinton treated Dad with great deference and Dad has become a friend of his. There are things that are more vital in life than allowing defeat to embitter you."[287]

That was quite a change from February, 2000 when George W. Bush emphatically told John McCain in a debate before the South Carolina primary, "Whatever you do, don't equate my integrity and trustworthiness to Bill Clinton. That's about as low a blow as you can give in the Republican primary."[288]

In hacked emails the Romanian hacker Guccifer released in 2013, there was an interesting note from George W. in which he refers to Clinton as "bubba" and told his siblings that if he was going to give the eulogy at his dad's funeral rather than Clinton then he would need some help. "Hopefully I'm jumping the gun . . . But since the feeling is that you all would rather me speak than bubba, please help," Bush wrote.[289]

In December of 2014, according to political reporter Mike Allen, "[Bill Clinton] got a heads-up from the camp of President George H. W. Bush a few days before former Florida Gov. Jeb Bush made his surprise Facebook announcement in December that he would 'actively explore' a [presidential] campaign."[290]

Allen said that Clinton and Bush, Sr., "have developed a friendly bond, partly because of their work together on relief for the 2004 Asian tsusami."[291]

The bond between the Bushes and Clintons is special. It was formed on the elite level of politics where the decisions of the few are unheard by the many.

"It's a big club," said comedian George Carlin shortly before his death. "And you ain't in it. You and I are not in the big club. By the way, it's the same big club they use to beat you over the head with all day long when they tell you what to believe, what to think, and what to buy. The table is tilted, the game is rigged, and nobody seems to notice, nobody seems to care. Good honest, hardworking people continue to elect these rich cocksuckers who don't give a fuck about them at all. . . . Americans will probably remain willfully ignorant of the big red, white and blue dick that's being jammed up their assholes every day."[292]

PART 3

CRIPPLING POWER

CHAPTER 12

MADAM PRESIDENT

"Indifferent to truth, willing to use police-state tactics and vulgar libels against inconvenient witnesses, hopeless on health care, and flippant and fast and loose with national security."

—Christopher Hitchens's description of Hillary Clinton[293]

A humorous yarn was spun and spread at the beginning of the Clinton presidency. It went something like this: The Clintons were driving in Hillary's hometown of Park Ridge, Illinois. While stopping for gas, Hillary recognized the station attendant as someone she used to date in high school. Later in the day, Bill shrewdly quipped, "See, if you'd married him, you'd be working at a gas station." Hillary smugly replied, "If I'd married him, he'd be president."[294]

To the people working in Washington, there was no doubt who was on the top of The Hill.

Campaigning for the presidency in the 1992 election, Bill openly said that voters were getting "two for the price of one." During the transition phase after the Clinton-Gore ticket was elected, Hillary played a big role in vetting the cabinet of the incoming Clinton administration.

Hillary began inauguration day 1993 cursing and shrieking profanities at Bill as she demanded to have Vice President Al Gore's White House office.[295] In the spring of 1993 Hillary spearheaded the signature legislative initiative of the Clinton administration: the Task Force on National Health Care Reform, the forerunner to Obamacare.

Hillary Clinton had always been the take-charge alpha of the Clintons.

Hillary Clinton has a long history of being domestically violent with Bill. By any reasonable definition Hillary is a domestic spousal abuser, and she should have been carted off to jail a long time ago. Hillary has beaten Bill, hit him with hard objects, scratched and clawed him, and made him bleed. In 1979 the Clintons went on vacation to Bermuda. Bill told one of his new drinking buddies, "I'm going back to my cottage to rape my wife."[296]

As author Ed Klein tells the story, the next morning one of Bill's new friends, a New York investment banker, went by the Clintons' cottage. "When we get there, the place looks like World War III. There are pillows and busted-up furniture all over the place. Obviously, Hillary's got pissed off at Bill, and threw a few things across the room. I guess that's the price he paid for going back to his room and taking the initiative and demanding sex."[297]

Before David Brock wrote his December 1993 blockbuster article "His Cheatin' Heart: Living With the Clintons: Bill's Arkansas bodyguards tell the story the press missed," he spent more than thirty hours with Bill Clinton's state troopers. The stories that Brock heard were not just about Bill's flaming adultery but also about Hillary's outrageous, nasty, and even violent behavior. The troopers were in a position to know, Brock pointed out, because "the troopers functioned as chauffeurs, butlers, body-guards, errand boys, and baggage handlers" for the Clintons.[298]

State trooper Larry Patterson gave this account: "I remember one time when Bill had been quoted in the morning paper saying something she didn't like . . . I came into the mansion and he was standing at the top of the stairs and she was standing at the bottom screaming. She has a garbage mouth on her, and she was calling him motherfucker, cocksucker, and everything else. I went into the kitchen, and the cook, Miss Emma, turned to me and said, 'The devil's in that woman.'"[299]

David Brock, back when he hated the Clintons, reported on this disturbing outburst of Hillary's domestic violence: "'Even though she knew what was going on, he would hide it because he didn't want the confrontation,' [Trooper Roger] Perry said. Bill did get caught every once in a while. Generally a heavy sleeper, Hillary once woke up in the middle of the night, flicked on the bedroom light, and called down to the guard house looking for Bill. 'The sorry damn son of a bitch!' she exclaimed when told the governor had gone out for a drive. Perry grabbed the cellular phone, turning Clinton up at one of the women's homes, and told him to get back to the residence fast. 'He started saying "Oh god, god, god. What did you tell her?"' Perry recalled. When Clinton arrived soon after, Hillary was waiting in the kitchen, where, not unexpectedly, a wild screaming match ensued. When Perry entered the kitchen after the dust had settled, the room was a wreck, with a cabinet door kicked off its hinges."[300]

Author Chris Andersen describes that Bill-Hillary kitchen melee as involving "shattering glass and slamming doors. When it was over, staff members . . . [found] broken glass, smashed dishes and a cupboard door ripped off its hinges."[301]

Hillary had a habit of frequently throwing objects at Bill in the governor's limousine. The objects included "yellow legal pads, files, briefing books, car keys, Styrofoam coffee cups." And the battles were reportedly usually pitched by Hillary: "'They'd be screaming at each other, real blue-in-the-face stuff,' one of their drivers said, 'but when the car pulled up to their destination it was all smiles and waving for the crowd.'"[302]

If Bill was cowed by the domestically violent Hillary, then the Arkansas state troopers were terrified by her, and later her Secret

Service detail was appalled by her atrocious and disrespectful behavior. There was even one state trooper whom Hillary used to be so cruel with that the grown man would break down and cry. In 1984 Hillary was named "Arkansas Mother of the Year." While the Clinton entourage was waiting for the honorary ceremony to begin, one of the state troopers Ralph Parker sneered incredulously, "Mother of the Year?" and then improvised, "How about *Motherfucker* of the Year?" The eyewitness to this precious moment said that the others "looked as if they had been struck by lightning. They were scared shitless that Hillary might have heard. It was truly a great moment."[303]

Early on in Bill's first term the Clintons brought their Jerry Springer–style dysfunction to the White House. Barely a month into the nation's residence, the *Chicago Sun-Times* reported the story of Hillary smashing a White House lamp: "Seems first lady Hillary Rodham Clinton has a temper to match her hubby's. Wicked Washington whispers claim Hillary broke a lamp during a heated late night argument with the president. Not to worry: the lamp was in the family quarters, belonged to the Clintons and 'wasn't a priceless antique, or anything like that,' says a White House source."[304]

On Inauguration Day, January 21, 1993, Hillary had launched into a screaming, profane fury as she lashed out at Bill for not letting her have the West Wing office of Vice President Al Gore. White House staff and the Secret Service were appalled at these continual outbursts and they leaked the story of Hillary smashing the lamp to the press. The Clintons have referred to the Secret Service as "personal trained pigs" (source: Chelsea to her Secret Service detail).

In March of 1993, Hillary's father Hughie suffered a massive stroke that put him in a coma and on life support. Hillary, Chelsea, and her brothers flew into Little Rock to watch vigil at the St. Vincent Infirmary Medical Center. Bill was in Washington, DC, and the media reported that Barbra Streisand, who had earlier performed at the Clinton Inauguration, had stayed overnight in the Lincoln Bedroom.

Hillary "had also heard that during her absence Bill, spiffy in a black-sequined tuxedo, had escorted Streisand and his mother, who had become very friendly with the singer, to the Gridiron Dinner, an annual media-politico event. There, in a party-hardy mood, the president wailed on his sax to the Coasters' golden oldie, 'Yakety Yak.'"[305]

Upon hearing the news about Bill partying with Barbra Streisand, an enraged Hillary, while her dad was lying in the hospital (eventually dying on April 7, 1993), got on a plane and stormed back to the White House. Not long after, Bill Clinton was sporting a nasty-looking scratch on his neck. Press Secretary Dee Dee Myers said, "I'm the idiot who said he cut himself shaving before I'd seen him. Then I saw him—it was a big scratch, clearly not a shaving cut. Barbra Streisand was clearly around at the time."

Except it had not been Barbra doing the scratching. Nor was it Socks the cat. Nor was it Chelsea. It was Hillary in one of her patented "attack Bill" modes. Paul Fray, who personally bore the brunt of Hillary's rage on election night 1974, said, "Hillary left Little Rock like a rocket, went back, and caught the son of a bitch. You know who got hit in the chops, who got smacked around."[306]

Gail Sheehy described Bill's wound as a "mean claw mark along his jawline."

Let us not forget Hillary diving into domestic violence with Bill on August 13, 1999, when Hillary (supposedly) first learned about Bill's affair with Monica. Bill had to confess because the special prosecutor had a DNA match with his semen and the stains on Monica's blue dress, which proved Bill had lied under oath about not having an affair with Monica. Let us also remember that by 1999 Bill Clinton had already cheated on Hillary hundreds of times with dozens of women over the past twenty-five years. With that in mind, author Christopher Andersen describes the scene:

The President . . . weeping, begged her forgiveness. Much of what transpired next between Bill and Hillary Clinton was plainly audible to Secret Service agents and household staff members down the hall. In the past, Hillary had thrown books and an ashtray at the President—both hitting their mark . . . Hillary rose to her feet and slapped him across the face—hard enough to leave a red mark that would be clearly visible to Secret Service agents when he left the room.

"You stupid, stupid, stupid bastard," Hillary shouted. Her words, delivered at the shrill, earsplitting level that had become familiar to White House personnel over the years, ricocheted down the corridor.[307]

Hillary's friend, Linda Bloodworth-Thomasen, who was staying in the White House at the time, said she "thought it was great that Hillary "smacked him upside the head."[308]

As Glen Sacks points out: "The US Department of Justice's Office for Victims of Crime classifies these types of attacks—scratching, slapping, hitting, throwing objects, and inflicting bruises or lacerations—as physical abuse and domestic violence."[309]

There was still another Hillary assault incident during the height of the Monica Lewinsky scandal. A White House maid entered the presidential bedroom to find Bill and Hillary's bed covered with blood. As the *NY Post* reported:

The blood belonged to the president, who said publicly that he "hurt himself running into the bathroom door in the middle of the night."

But the White House residence staff believed differently. As one worker told author Kate Anderson Brower, "We're pretty sure [Hillary Clinton] clocked him with a book."

"There were at least 20 books on the bedside table for his betrayed wife to choose from," Brower adds, "including the Bible."[310]

Lieutenant Colonel Buzz Patterson, who was a military aide in the Clinton White House described what Hillary did after she got some bad news about the Whitewater investigation and her immunity:

"Every vulgar word you've ever heard poured from her mouth: 'Goddamnit,' 'you bastard,' 'it's your fucking fault,' on and on and on. What grabbed my attention was not so much that she was saying these things but the way the president reacted. He looked like a beaten puppy. He put his head down and did not try to fight back. He said, 'Yes, I understand. Yes, dear, I know.'"[311]

Lieutenant Colonel Patterson says that Hillary could be "harsh, difficult, and unpredictable" and she was the one with a temper "who could rip your heart out."[312]

Even after they left the White House, the Clintons were still having knockdown, drag-out fights. R. Emmett Tyrrell says, "Sources close to the Secret Service, however, do report that dreadful altercations have erupted several times: in September 2001, January 2002, August 2002, April 2003 and May 2004."[313]

Tyrrell's sources tell him the Clinton "verbal violence" includes "yelling, screaming, throwing of soft and hard objects, breakage of vases and glasses and just plain nastiness."[314]

In April of 2015 blogger Kristinn Taylor posted a column that asked: "Hillary Clinton: Will Dems Nominate Reported Violent Spouse Abuser for President?"[315]

Good question. We will see if the Democrats take domestic violence seriously in 2016. Not only that, if Hillary was beating up the president, why is she not in the slammer for ten years as federal law suggests? "Whoever assaults any person designated [the President] in subsection (a) (1) shall be fined under this title, or imprisoned not more than ten years, or both."[316]

Hillary was running Bill's 1974 congressional campaign even while she was on the staff of the House Judiciary Committee that was investigating Richard Nixon and the Watergate scandals. Hillary's boss, Jerry Zeifman, the general counsel and chief of staff to the House Judiciary Investigative Committee during the Watergate hearings, fired Hillary after it was uncovered that Clinton was working to impede the investigation and undermine Nixon's defense. He told Fox News that "Hillary's lies and unethical behavior goes back farther—and goes much deeper—than anyone realizes." Zeifman maintains that he fired Hillary "for unethical behavior and that she conspired to deny Richard Nixon counsel during the hearings."

When asked why he fired Clinton, Zeifman responded, "Because she is a liar." He went on, "She was an unethical, dishonest lawyer. She conspired to violate the Constitution, the rules of the House, the rules of the committee and the rules of confidentiality."

Zeifman wrote candidly about his encounter with a young Hillary Clinton when she worked for him as a staff lawyer. He mentioned a number of facts that he thought people should know about how the prospective presidential contender conducts herself. He said, "Because of a number of her unethical practices I decided that I could not recommend her for any subsequent position of public or private trust." Other Judiciary Committee staffers who worked with Clinton, such as Franklin Polk, the chief Republican counsel on the committee, have confirmed many of the details of what Zeifman has reported.

Zeifman stated, "Nixon clearly had right to counsel, but Hillary, along with Marshall, Nussbaum and Doar, was determined to gain enough votes on the Judiciary Committee to change House rules and deny counsel to Nixon. And in order to pull this off, Hillary wrote a fraudulent legal brief, and confiscated public documents to hide her deception." When Nixon was leaving the Clinton White House after a three-hour discussion with the loquacious Arkansan, Hillary greeted him as he left. "How did you find her?" I asked. "Cold, cold as ice," Nixon said.

Bill Clinton had his own strange connections to many embroiled in the Watergate caper.[v]

---

v Clinton has strange connections to the Watergate cast; Bill Clinton was interviewed and hired by Alfred Baldwin, the Watergate eavesdropper, to teach a law enforcement class at the University of New Haven in September 1971.

Clinton and Baldwin left New Haven for Washington, DC, in May 1972 to work on, respectively, the McGovern and Nixon campaigns. Baldwin apparently dated at least one woman at the DNC during his time listening in on the Watergate bug. The conversations overheard by Baldwin he described as "primarily sexual" and "intimately explicit." Baldwin was the only member of the McCord/Hunt/

In 2013, Hillary would show her disdain for Nixon in a discussion with an all-woman group over a glass of wine at a restaurant and tavern, Le Jardin Du Roi, near her palatial home in Chappaqua. "The IRS targeting the Tea Party, the Justice Department's seizure

Liddy team not indicted. The recently released names of persons overheard on the Watergate bug include people strongly linked to Bill Clinton.

Clinton was assigned to handle Wilbur Mills upon his arrival in DC in May 1972. Clinton had worked for Mills as a campaign aide and chauffeur previously. A 1972 staffer for Mills, Patsy Thomasson would become a key player in the Clinton rise to power. Wilbur Mills has been named as one of the persons overheard on the Watergate tap. Others apparently close to Bill Clinton were Severin Beliveau, Robert E. B. Allen, Spencer Oliver, and John Richardson, a State Department employee who ran the Fulbright scholarship programs. Oliver, the man whose phone was tapped, played a key role for Clinton in 1992, rebutting charges by George H. W. Bush relating to Clinton's student travels and activities. Clinton appointed Oliver to a UN/Nato Security agency upon assuming the presidency.

John Dean's ghostwriter for *Blind Ambition*, Taylor Branch, served as Bill Clinton's top aide in the Texas McGovern operation. When Dean disavowed his own book and blamed errors on Branch, the charge was met by only muted dismay from Branch. Very curious.

John Dean not only wrote the foreword to Jerry Zeifman's book *Lost Honor*, but he also appeared with Zeifman on various media outlets promoting the book. Zeifman and Dean were colleagues on the House Judiciary Committee. Their book related how their marriages failed at about the same time. Curiously, Dean has been a steadfast apologist for the Clintons over the years, despite his endorsement of the Zeifman book.

The 1971 Young Democrats of America Convention was held in November 1971 in Hot Springs, Arkansas. The YDA presidency that year was won by Robert Allen (over Steny Hoyer), a figure overheard by Baldwin on the Watergate bug. The convention site in 1971 was very close to Raymond Clinton's Vapors nightclub that offered up "party girls." The business manager of the YDA in 1971–72 was Robert Weiner, a pol who would play a prominent role in Clinton's presidency. YDA attendees in 1971 included many people pivotal to the rise of Clinton's career, such as Betsey Wright, Spencer Oliver (former YDA president), Steny Hoyer, and Jim McDougal.

James Hougan's book *Secret Agenda* detailed how Phil Bailley, the DC lawyer/pimp associated with Heidi Rikan, included "a Brigade of Young Democrats" among Bailley's partners and associates. Hot Springs was notorious for its vice. Clinton's uncle Raymond had mob connections. His mother Virginia treated the prostitutes who worked for the notorious Madame Maxine Jones. Bill Clinton even wrote about how he amused himself with prank calls to Maxine Jones as a high school student.

Additionally, at least one Wellesley classmate of Hillary Rodham was named by Bailley as a member of Heidi's ring, or said that Hillary Rodham was offered a post by her "old friend" Edward Bennett Williams after law school. Williams had multiple conflicts of interest in Watergate, not least of which is that many of his Redskin players were connected to a mob-moll Heidi Rikan.

Several authors, including Roger Morris, Richard Goodwin, and Christopher Hitchens, have alleged that young Clinton was a CIA asset. Clinton's unexpected return to Oxford in 1969–70 and his decision to co-habit with Hillary Clinton in Berkeley in 1971 might offer clues that Clinton may have been involved with either Operation Chaos and its offspring, Project Resistance, or Project Merrimac.

of AP phone records and [Fox reporter] James Rosen's e-mails—all these scandals. Obama's allowed his hatred for his enemies to screw him the way Nixon did," Hillary said.

After Bill Clinton lost his governorship of Arkansas in 1980, it was Hillary and her close friend, political operative Betsey Wright, who organized Bill's name card files, put them on a computer, and executed tremendous amounts of legwork to get Bill Clinton elected again to the position just two years later.

It was Hillary who spearheaded educational reform, the signature public policy initiative of the Arkansas Clinton Administration.

It was Hillary who shed bitter tears when Clinton announced at a press conference in the summer of 1987 that he would cast away his lifelong dream of a run for the presidency that year. Bill did not run because Gary Hart had just been knocked out of the presidential race due to the exposure of his affair with Donna Rice. Betsey Wright sat down with Clinton and told him that he would be eviscerated and crucified by the media over his epic womanizing if he dared jump into the 1988 presidential race.

It was Hillary who, in 1998, after Bill's lies under oath threatened to bring down the administration, organized the political and media defense of Bill. It was Hillary who, after hundreds of affairs by Bill over the decades, and after her own adulteries with Hubbell, Foster, and numerous women, played the role of "wronged woman" as Bill escaped being convicted with a two-thirds vote in his 1999 Senate impeachment trial.

It was Hillary who hired the private detectives to run the terror campaigns against Bill's sex victims and former girlfriends. Arkansas private investigator Ivan Duda said Hillary came to her in 1982, as Bill was trying to reclaim the Arkansas governorship, and said, "I want you to get rid of all these bitches he's seeing. . . . I want you to give me the names and addresses and phone numbers, and we can get them under control."[317]

In April 1999, the *New York Post* wrote an article entitled "Bio: Hillary Hired Snoop to Watch Bill." After interviewing Ivan Duda at length, the *NY Post* reported, "The ex-private eye, Ivan Duda, told the *Post* Mrs. Clinton didn't tell him why she wanted the dirt but that he gave her the names of fourteen women, including six who have never publicly surfaced. He declined to identify them.

Duda said Mrs. Clinton called him from a pay phone, then agreed to meet him in the parking lot of a Little Rock bar called Slick Willie's—the same nickname later given to Clinton himself.

The book says Mrs. Clinton showed no emotion except when she realized one of the women worked at the Rose Law Firm where she was a partner. Duda later lost his PI license in what he claims was an attempt by supporters of Bill Clinton to intimidate him."

It was Hillary and her boyfriend and lover Vince Foster who hired yet another private detective, Jerry Parks, to spy on Bill Clinton in the late 1980s and early 1990s when Hillary and Bill were coming very close to divorcing.[318]

Hillary was the shot-caller who made the tough decisions.

It's been said that on April 19, 1993, the Clinton administration was responsible for the deaths of seventy-six members of the Branch Davidian religious group. The Clintons used the forces of the federal government to murder these innocent people right before the eyes of the nation.

In the 1999 documentary *Waco: A New Revelation*, film director Michael McNulty told what House of Representatives investigator T. March Bell found out about who *really* ordered the final murderous assault on the Branch Davidians:

"One of the interesting things that happens in an investigation is that you get anonymous phone calls. And we in fact received anonymous phone calls from Justice Department managers and attorneys who believe that pressure was placed on Janet Reno by Webb Hubbell, and pressure that came from the first lady of the United States."[319]

Bell later told Newsmax.com that phone logs proved Hillary, Deputy White House Council Vince Foster, and Associate Attorney General Hubbell were coordinating the White House response to the Waco crisis, the U.S. government siege of the Branch Davidians home at Mount Carmel. "Those phone logs were Webb Hubbell's phone logs. There were calls from the first lady and Vince Foster to Webb Hubbell's office." [320]

This was all reported in an AFPN article in 2001: "Bell said Mrs. Clinton grew more and more impatient as the Waco standoff came to dominate the headlines during the early months of the Clinton administration. It was she, Bell's source claims, who pressured a reluctant Janet Reno to act. Reno, on the other hand, was not enthusiastic about launching the assault, said Bell. 'Give me a reason not to do this,' [Reno] is said to have begged aides."

Reno was ordered to go ahead with the murderous tank and CS gas assault that resulted in seventy-six Branch Davidians, men, women, children, babies being crushed, asphyxiated, or burned up in an inferno. Whether the Branch Davidians played a role in starting those fires as a desperate defense mechanism matters not; it was Hillary Clinton who forced the issue and who should be held responsible for the murders.

Vince Foster was greatly disturbed by the tragedy and deaths. "A special bulletin came on showing the atrocity at Waco and the [dead] children. And his face turned white, and he was absolutely crushed knowing, knowing the part he had played," said Linda Tripp, who worked in the White House Counsel's Office.[321]

CHAPTER 13

BLACK WIDOW

"Hillary Clinton is not that fascinating a person. According to those who have spent time with her, she's harsh and demanding. According to those who haven't—like her husband—she's a delight."

—Ben Shapiro, political commentator[322]

Webb Hubbell had a revealing anecdote that recounted the day before the New Hampshire Democratic primary in 1992. The Clinton-Flowers affair had become public and it appeared that something even more damaging was on the horizon:

"Suddenly I received an urgent call from Vince, asking me to come to his office right away. I practically ran down the hall and knocked on his door. When I saw his face, I closed the door behind me. He was pale, shaking. He could hardly talk. No wonder he had called me to come to him—he probably couldn't have even walked to my office.

"'What is it?' I said.

"'He finally managed to tell me. He finally managed to tell me.'"[323] The Clinton campaign had told Vince Foster that the tabloids were likely to run a story about Hillary having an affair. "He and I were the ones to be named."[324]

Foster and the Clintons shared a long history. Foster was from Hope, Arkansas, and as a child was in the same kindergarten as Bill. Foster graduated first in his class at the University of Arkansas Law School and secured the highest score in his class on the Arkansas bar exam.[325] He recruited Hillary into the Rose Law Firm in the mid-1970s, but Hillary did not make partner until 1980.

Foster's relationship with Hillary grew both emotionally and physically with their professional lives.

L. D. Brown illustrated this complicated relationship with a story regarding a small dinner party at a Chinese restaurant in Little Rock. The couples present were Bill and Hillary; Beth and Mike Coulson; and Vince and his wife Lisa Foster. A lot of drinking and partying was going on: "By this time Vince and Hillary were looking like they were in the back seat of a '57 Chevy at the drive-in. Hillary was kissing Vince like I'd never seen her kiss Bill, and the same sort of thing was going on with Bill and Beth. . . . No one seemed to notice me, except for Vince who would give the occasional furtive glance, sometimes accentuated by a wink."[326]

Then the mixed-up couples left the restaurant still carrying on. "Vince and Hillary brought up the rear as Vince was really getting a handful of Hillary's. Bill and Beth [Coulson] kissing did not bother me as much as seeing Hillary attempting to reciprocate with Vince. Vince, good looking, tall and suave obviously knew what he was doing, but Hillary looked awkward and unbalanced."[327]

Brown said Hillary loved Foster and it was amazing to him that the affair had escaped media coverage. Brown said that he and Hillary would talk about their marital problems. Hillary would often talk about Vince, that they often traveled together and once even went to London. Brown described Clinton and Foster as "soulmates."[328]

The same state troopers that used to procure girls for Bill took Hillary and Foster to a get-away cabin in the Arkansas woods (Heber

Springs) on weekends.[329] When Bill was out of town, Vince would often stop by the governor's mansion to see Hillary, staying until the early morning hours.

Former Arkansas state trooper Larry Patterson also confirmed the affair. Once at a private birthday party for Hillary, Patterson saw Foster "put his hands on her [Hillary's] breast, and then he walked by, grabbed her by the butt, looked over at me and gave me the old high sign and thumbs up." Patterson was a personal witness to Foster's frequent visits to the Arkansas governor's mansion to visit Hillary.[330]

In 1982, Hillary was using Little Rock private investigator Ivan Duda to gather information on the women Bill was having affairs with who could be potential political embarrassments. Duda turned over the names of six women to Hillary that he confirmed were having an affair with Bill Clinton.

"Bill was extremely suspicious of Hillary's relationship with Foster," Duda admitted. "When confronted, she simply denied it was a romance and claimed they were just good friends." Duda said that Bill hired a private investigator of his own who confirmed the affair.

"Bill confronted her with the information and they had several explosive arguments—screaming, shouting, red-faced blow-outs," Duda recalled. "Hillary is not meek, and while she never confessed to cheating, she aggressively reminded Bill of his numerous affairs and how he not only humiliated her but nearly wrecked their own political career with his behavior."[331]

In the late 1980s Hillary and Foster were also using a man named Jerry Parks to spy on Bill and collect dirt to use in the event of a divorce.

Lisa Parks, the former wife of Jerry, told reporter Ambrose Evans-Pritchard that Foster was using Parks to spy on and document Bill Clinton's adultery. "Jerry asked him why he needed this stuff on Clinton. He said he needed it for Hillary."[332]

Evans-Pritchard found out that "Jerry Parks had carried out sensitive assignments for the Clinton inner circle for almost a decade, and the person who gave him his instructions was Vince Foster."[vi]

Things between Foster and Clinton began to change dramatically once she reached the national stage.

In the White House, Foster was denied access to Hillary. "It's just not the same. . . . She's so busy, Hub, that we don't ever have time to talk," Foster told Hubbell.[333] Foster said that his affair had disintegrated into miserly commands from the First Lady, who would snap at him "Fix it, Vince!" or "Handle it, Vince!"

Shunned from Hillary's presence, Foster began to refer to her as the Client. Foster was put to task, "handling" and "fixing" all the legal problems that Hillary was creating.

The murders in Waco, Texas, in April 1993, had traumatized Foster. He believed he was partly responsible for the carnage.

A month later, Foster's remorse was amplified by a mass firing in the White House Travel Office. The action was instigated sub rosa by Hillary and executed on May 19, 1993. The White House Travel Office handled travel arrangements for the press corps that covered the president.

Travel Office Director Billy Dale and six other employees were canned. The business of the office was handed over to World Wide Travel, an Arkansas agency that had handled travel for the 1992 Clinton campaign and whose president, Betta Carney, was a Clinton campaign contributor.[334]

Dale had been the director of the office since 1982 and was immensely popular with the press corps. The firings caused a media firestorm, and the Clintons immediately claimed ignorance.

In truth, Hillary had spoken to both Foster and White House Chief of Staff Mack McLarty about expediting the firings.

---

vi Parks was found dead in September 1993. "'I believe my father was assassinated because he was the one link that could actually close everything and completely shut Clinton down,'" said Parks's son, Gary. "'I feel that Bill Clinton had my father killed to save his political career.'"

Five days before the firings of the White House Travel Office, Hillary told David Watkins (Clinton crony and then White House director of administration) "We need those people out—we need our people in—we need the slots."

Attorney and author Barbara Olson found that "William Kennedy III [a Hillary intimate] called the FBI and set them loose on the Travel Office staff like Dobermans to destroy Billy Dale's reputation and justify the firings. As Kennedy told the FBI: It came from the 'highest level.'"[335]

Watkins wrote a memo that he put into his files to explain what really happened. Watkins said that there would be "hell to pay" if they did not fire the seven members of the White House Travel Office.

On January 5, 1996, the *New York Times* reported the Watkins memo in a story entitled "Memo Places Hillary Clinton at Core of Travel Office Case":[336]

On Friday, while I was in Memphis, Foster told me that it was important that I speak directly with the First Lady that day. I called her that evening and she conveyed to me in clear terms her desire for swift and clear action to resolve the situation. She mentioned that Thomason had explained how the Travel Office could be run after removing the current staff–that plan included bringing in World Wide Travel to handle the basic travel functions, the actual actions taken post dismissal, and in light of that she thought immediate action was in order.

At that meeting you explained that this was on the First Lady's radar screen. The message you conveyed to me was clear: immediate action must be taken. . . . We both knew that there would be hell to pay, after our failure in the Secret Service situation earlier, we failed to take swift and decisive action in conformity with the First Lady's wishes.

At the time Hillary had said she "had no role in the decision to terminate the [Travel Office] employees."[337]

Hillary perjured herself when she repeated that statement in her answers to twenty-six questions presented to her by the General Accounting Office during their investigation. An outraged Barbara Olson, who led the Travelgate investigation, wrote, "These questions were signed by Hillary Rodham Clinton on March 21, 1996, under penalty of perjury."[338]

Hillary should have been prosecuted by the Independent Counsel for lying under oath, but when the final Independent Counsel report on the Travel Office firings was issued on June 23, 2000, there simply was not the political will to prosecute Hillary. The Independent Counsel Richard Ray concluded that "Mrs. Clinton's input into the process was significant, if not the significant factor influencing the pace of events in the Travel Office firings and the ultimate decision to fire the employees."[339] The Independent Counsel also stated that Hillary had provided "factually false" testimony about the Travel Office firings to the GAO, the Independent Counsel, and Congress. The Independent Counsel, which had proven Hillary's guilt, gave her a free pass without prosecution, but the scandal damaged both Clinton and Foster.

On June 17, the *Wall Street Journal* published an article titled "Who Is Vince Foster?" Foster, normally a composed, confidant lawyer, was pale, shaking, unable to speak, and probably could not even walk according to Hubbell.

Amid the stress, Foster was looking forward to having a reunion dinner with Hillary and the Hubbells the day before Father's Day, Saturday, June 19. Hillary, Foster, Webb, and their spouses planned to gather at the Italian restaurant Matti.

The First Lady canceled at the last minute.

"We went to dinner and Hillary soon called to say she just couldn't make it. Vince hardly said a word the rest of the evening," recalled Hubbell. "Suzy, as much as she loved Vince, thought his behavior was extremely bizarre. 'He was sulking,' she said. 'It was so uncharacteristic of him.' He pulled his chair back and turned himself away from the rest of the table. He was just like a child who had been promised quality time with a parent, only to have the parent renege when business had called him away."[340]

Foster's life continued to deteriorate personally and professionally.

Hubbell had some revealing things to say about Foster's wife, Lisa, and her thoughts on Hillary: "Lisa Foster hated that Vince would talk to Hillary, tell her things that Lisa did not know," Hubbell wrote. Hubbell recalled an internal Rose Law Firm power struggle in the 1980s. He had told his wife Suzy about it, "but this was the first Lisa [Foster] had heard of it. She hated it. And though it had nothing to do with Hillary and everything to do with Vince, I think Lisa's jealousy was mainly aimed at Hillary."[341] Lisa Foster was so angry at Vince that she refused to attend the inaugural ball with him that January.[342]

Another *WSJ* editorial focused on Foster's role defending the controversial procedures of Hillary's Health Care Task Force. The column was titled "Vincent Foster's Victory" and it had the snarky line "We suspect that Vincent Foster and Ollie North might hit it off."[343]

"He urgently asked [Hillary's tough gal fixer and confidant] Susan Thomases to meet with him. He told her he feared Hillary would be blamed for the Travel Office firings and dragged through the mud. He also confided to Thomases that he was exhausted and that his marriage was strained. He and his wife were fighting about whether to go back to Arkansas," wrote legendary journalist Carl Bernstein.[344]

"At the same time, it was increasingly hard for Foster to keep fighting tooth and nail for Hillary's interests when their relationship had degenerated, Hubbell said. . . . When he had left Arkansas for Washington, he had expected the relationship with Hillary to remain as deep as ever. The last thing he had expected is that it would turn upside down. Some days he was a flunky, some days a legal counselor, other days he was a fixer, but no longer was he her intimate."

In July 1993, Hillary had a huge disagreement with a legal objection that Foster had raised and she "humiliated Foster in front of aides."[345]

"Hillary put him down really, really bad in a pretty good-sized meeting.... She told him that he didn't get the picture, and he would always be a little hick-town lawyer who was obviously not ready for the big time," recalled FBI agent Copeland.[346] Dozens of Foster's associates would tell Copeland and other agents that "The put-down she gave him in that big meeting just pushed him over the edge. It was the final straw that broke the camel's back." [347]

On July 19, 1993, the *Wall Street Journal* ran yet another editorial slamming Vince Foster and the ethics of the Rose Law Firm lawyers who had come to Washington, DC, with the Clinton Administration. The *WSJ* also hit Hillary and Vince for being tied to the Travel Office firings.

The next day Foster took an old .38 caliber pistol, held it with both hands, and shot himself in the head in his White House office.

Ronald Kessler reported that the FBI agents' reports of their interviews with the Clintons in relation to Foster's suicide are mysteriously missing from the proper files where they should be at the National Archives.[348]

"That night, sometime between eight and nine o'clock, Mack McLarty called me at my mother's house and told me he had terrible news: Vince Foster was dead; it looked like a suicide, Hillary later wrote."[349]

Hillary told the Office of Independent Counsel while under oath that the last time she spoke to Vince Foster was before Father's Day, June 20, 1993. However, Tom Castleton was an aide to Vince Foster, and he "saw Hillary Clinton in Foster's office approximately four times during the five weeks he was employed." Castleton started working for Vince Foster after June 20, 1993.[350]

Chelsea is the spitting image of her likely biological father Webster Hubbell.
(Left: Ron Sachs/CNP/Sygma/Corbis. Right: Cynthia Johnson/Getty)

Before and After. Chelsea has had extensive plastic surgery to hide her parentage.
(R: Peter Kramer/Getty)

Bill Cosby and Bill Clinton have rape in common.

Another shot of Chelsea looking like Hubbell.

The resemblance between Chelsea and Webb Hubbell is uncanny.
(L: FORTUNE Magazine/Danuta Otfinowski)

A DNA test showed Webb Hubbell is likely Chelsea's real father.
(AKM/GSI)

Yet another shot of Chelsea looking just like her real dad.

	Aircraft Identification Mark	Points of Departure & Arrival		Miles Flown	Flight No.	Remarks, Procedures, Maneuvers, Endorsements	Number of Landings	Aircraft Ca
		From	To					AIRPLAN
31	N908JE	LGA	BED		47	JE	1/1	7
	"	BED	HPN		48	JE, JESSICA		8
	"	HPN	TEST		49	JE, GM, SK, AP CINDY LOPEZ, JOANNA, 1 FEMALE		3 4
	"	TEST	PBI		50	JE, GM, SK, AP CINDY LOPEZ JOANNA, MARY GUITY, ALEXANDRA, SARAH KELLOGG'S, 1	1/	2 6
	"	PBI	HPN		51	JE, GM, SK, AP, CINDY LOPEZ, JOANNE	1/	2 5
	"	HPN	PBI		52	JE, GM, SK, AP ALBERT PINTO, YVES PISK, ANDI, STEVE SHELDON, 1 FEMALE		2 7
	"	PBI	TEST		53	JE, GM, AP, SK, ED TUTTLE, 1 MALE, 1 FEMALE	1/	2 4
	"	TEST	JFK		54	JE, GM, SK, AP, ED TUTTLE, CINDY LOPEZ	1/	3
	"	JFK	PBI		55	JE, GM, SK, AP, 1 MALE, 1 FEMALE	1/	2 8
	"	PBI	MIA		56	JE, SK, AP		7
	"	MIA	HPN		57	BILL CLINTON, 4 SECRET SERVICE, 2 MALES, 1 FEMALE, JE, GM, SK, AP		6
	"	HPN	LFPB			2 MALES, 1 FEMALE, JE, GM, SK, AP		5
	"	LFPB	ESSA		58	JE, GM, SK, AP, FLEUR PERRY BY 3	1/	2
	"	ESSA	LFML		60	JE, SK		4
	"	LFML	EGGW		61	JE, SK		1 8
	"	EGGW	BGR		62	JE, GM, SK	2	7 2
	"	BGR	PBI		63	JE, GM, SK		3 5
98	N907JE	PBI	ABY		559	JE	1/1	1 4
	"	ABY	PBI		560	EMPTY	1/1	1

Jeffrey Epstein's flight logs. Bill Clinton was a passenger on the flight called "Air Lolita.

"Hillary Clinton *is* the war on women." - Kathleen Willey *(A. F. Branco/Legal Insurrection)*

Danney Williams, Bill Clinton's son, with his mother, Bobbie Ann Williams. *(American Media, Inc.)*

Bill's abandoned son with Mom. Clinton, who made roughly $350 million since leaving the White House, will not support his five grandchildren. *(American Media, Inc.)*

The Bush-Clinton connection. They reap money and power together. *(Kris Connor/Getty)*

Vince Foster with Hillary Clinton. After his suspicious death, Hillary ordered his body to be moved.

Future deadbeat dad Bill Clinton side-by-side with his son Danney Williams, whom he won't acknowledge or nurture. *(L: APF PHOTO FILES/Getty)*

Right-hand man Doug Band has the goods on Bill – and is estranged. *(Robert A. Cumins/Corbis)*

Kathleen Willey described her assault by Bill Clinton on national television.
(Michael Smith/Getty)

Bill Clinton victim Juanita Broaddrick circa 1978. *(Getty)*

Anthony Pellicano was hired by Hillary to silence Bill's victims. *(Michael Ochs/Getty)*

Hillary with Huma Abedin, rumored to have ties with the Muslim Brotherhood. *(Joe Raedle/Getty)*

Birds of a feather Bill Clinton and Bill Cosby. *(KMazur/Getty)*

Hillary went crazy when she learned Bill was alone with Barbra Streisand in the family quarters when she was out of town. *(Lester Cohen/Getty)*

Jeb Bush gave Hillary the Liberty Medal in 2013. They're in it together. *(Lisa Lake/Getty)*

Sex criminal Jeffrey Epstein: handsome, rich, cultured, and a close personal friend of Bill Clinton. What does he know? *(Dave Spencer/Getty)*

Sidney Blumenthal, Hillary's hitman on the Clinton Foundation payroll, is up to his knees in the Benghazi cover-up. *(Bill Clark/Getty)*

The FBI interviewed Marsha Scott, a longtime mistress of Bill Clinton and a friend and confidante of Foster who worked in the White House. The FBI report on the death of Vince Foster stated: "Scott is of the opinion that Foster committed suicide for personal reasons but commented that he didn't separate work from personal matters. He had talked about 'wanting out.' He talked about 'wanting to rest.'"[351]

CHAPTER 14

THE BODY

"Vincent Foster could not have killed himself by putting a gun in his mouth and pulling the trigger as reported in the media."

—Chris Ruddy, journalist and Newsmax Media CEO[352]

In her chronicle of life in the White House, *Living History*, Hillary Clinton admitted to some guilt over the death of Vince Foster, but a majority of the blame was shifted to the columnists who investigated crookedness in the administration.

"I would wake up in the middle of the night worrying that the actions and reactions concerning the travel office helped drive Vince Foster to take his own life," Hillary wrote. "Vince Foster was stung by the travel office affair. . . . Apparently the final blow came in a series of spiteful editorials published in the *Wall Street Journal*, which attacked the integrity and competence of all the Arkansas lawyers in the Clinton Administration. On June 17, 1993, an editorial titled 'Who Is Vince Foster?' proclaimed that the most 'disturbing' thing about the Administration was 'its carelessness about following the law.' For the next month, the *Journal* continued its editorial campaign to paint the Clinton White House and my colleagues from the Rose Firm as some sort of corrupt cabal."[353]

Conservative activist Reed Irvine ridiculed the theory as "Death by Editorial."

In truth, there was some crookedness transpiring in Foster's office on the night of his suicide, with several aides very close to Hillary securing important items. These people were White House Counsel Nussbaum (who knew Hillary since they worked on the House Watergate Committee investigating Nixon), Maggie Williams (the chief of staff for Hillary Clinton), and Patsy Thomasson.

Secret Service Agent Henry O'Neill spotted Thomasson in the office sometime after 10:42 p.m. "I saw Maggie Williams walk out of the suite and turn to the right in the direction I was standing," O'Neill subsequently said under oath, "She was carrying what I would describe in her arms and hands, as folders."[354]

Williams had a very different story to tell in her testimony. "I disturbed nothing while I was there [in Foster's office]," she declared.[355] Williams said she did not remove any documents from Foster's office; that she merely sat on the sofa.

In a 1994 press conference, Hillary denied sending her chief of staff into the office of her deceased lover. She repeated this lie to Barbara Walters on *20/20* in 1996. "I want to be very clear about this," a stern Clinton told Walters. "There were no documents taken out of Vince Foster's office on the night he died and I did not direct anyone to interfere in any investigation."[356] Foster had billing records in his office that pertained to Whitewater, a scandal that threatened the administration. At the heart of Whitewater was Madison Guaranty, a bankrupt savings and loan company that financed shady real estate transactions. The collapse of Madison Guaranty cost taxpayers $60 million. The bankrupt company was partnered with Whitewater Development Corporation, the subject of the Whitewater probe and owned, in part, by the Clintons.

Clinton later admitted to a sweep of the office.

"Since Vince's office was never a crime scene, these actions were understandable, legal and justifiable," Hillary wrote in *Living History*, offering a defense of the removal of Whitewater documents.

In the wake of Foster's suicide, phone records depicted a harried Clinton. The First Lady was engaged in a flurry of phone calls with Margaret Williams, Susan Thomases, and Bernard Nussbaum, the White House counsel.

"I know very well what we were talking about," Hillary told Barbara Walters. "We were grieving, we were supporting each other, I was asking questions about how other people who were close friends and colleagues of Vince were doing, how his family was doing, and some of those phone conversations consisted of us sobbing on the phone."[357]

Years earlier, Nussbaum was senior counsel on the House panel that drew up impeachment charges against President Nixon and supervised the work of a staff member, Hillary Rodham Clinton. In the aftermath of Foster's death, Nussbaum was working for Clinton.

"What about the First Lady? Undoubtedly she was involved in the early decision-making. There is no one else who could have volunteered the services of Margaret Williams," Michael Kellet, author of *The Murder of Vince Foster*, wrote.[358] "Given the nature of many of their dealings in Whitewater and other ventures back in Arkansas, her name was probably more exposed on the documentation in Foster's office than the former governor, and it is understandable that she would have been motivated to initiate and direct the raid. The 1995 Senate Hearings revealed that her close friend, Susan Thomases, made seventeen calls to Nussbaum and Williams over the two days following, during which the raid and search of Foster's office were being conducted. It was also revealed that Nussbaum discussed his plans and procedures for the removal of documents with Thomases, and it was revealed that it was Hillary who told Williams about Foster's death."[359]

Williams was directed by Hillary to pick Foster's office clean of any documents relating to the Clintons. Cliff Sloan, an aide of Bernie

Nussbaum, wrote a note that said "Get Maggie—go thru office—get HRC [Hillary] and WJC [Clinton] stuff."[360]

If Foster's office was not, according to Clinton, "considered a crime scene," why was it of such concern in the early hours following the death of the deputy white house counsel?

There are numerous pieces of evidence, aside from the many Clinton phone calls, that indicate Foster had indeed killed himself in his office and his body was later moved. This ensured a clean sweep of Foster's office in the aftermath of his death.

Journalist and author Marinka Peschmann discovered in her lengthy interviews with Linda Tripp that Foster was carrying his briefcase with him when he left his office in the early afternoon of July 20, 1993. This is critically important because after Foster's body was found dead, his briefcase was discovered in his office.

At the time of Foster's suicide, Tripp was working in the White House Counsel's office, seated outside of Nussbaum's office.

Had Foster left early in the afternoon with his briefcase only to return later? Upon discovery of the body, had the First Lady ordered the removal and the cleanup?

"In every investigation we were told exactly what happened and what to say, and suddenly that became the so-called truth," Tripp told Peschmann.[361]

White House intern Tom Castleton also remembered Foster carrying his briefcase when he left for lunch, a fact he related to both Tripp and to the Office of Independent Counsel.

Patsy Thomasson, former director of administration for the White House said "she saw Foster's briefcase by the desk in his office on the night of July 20" after the body had been found.[362]

When we confronted Thomasson with the theory that Foster killed himself in his office and the body was expeditiously removed by the administration, she warily replied "Where did you ever get that nutty idea?" Shortly thereafter, as Thomasson hung up the phone, it rattled unsettlingly into the cradle.

A likely scenario is that Foster left the White House just after 1 p.m. and he left with his suitcase, which is a very critical point. For the rest of the afternoon the other lawyers in the Counsel's office did not know where Foster was, and it is standard procedure to know exactly where important officials of the White House are at all times.

Foster likely returned to the White House in the late afternoon after most of the support staff had left for the day. It is reasonable to assume that Foster put his .38 caliber pistol, which he had stored in his car in an oven mitt, into his suitcase before returning to his office. He likely committed suicide in the time period of 4:30 to 5 p.m. Eastern Standard Time.

The people who are likely candidates to have found the corpse are Nussbaum, Foster's old Rose Law Firm partner William Kennedy, or Nussbaum's secretary Betsy Pond.

We can suspect that Bernie Nussbaum called the First Lady around 5 p.m. and told her about the suicide. Hillary then took action.

A cadaver in the official residence and principal workplace of the president, especially in an office with numerous sensitive and potentially incriminating documents, was poison to the administration. Hillary would have to order the body expeditiously transported off White House premises. She then likely ordered the cleanup of bodily fluids and pieces and the removal of sensitive, or incriminating, documents in Foster's office.

Kellet pointed out that two things were found all over Vince Foster's body: carpet fibers and mica, which are tiny rock particles. The carpet fibers could have come from the body rolled up in carpet, a classic means of body transportation, or it could have been fibers from the trunk of the car used during the body transfer.[363]

The carpet theory makes the most sense. The White House was in a perpetual state of interior redesign. A rolled-up carpet would raise no suspicion.

A top national Democratic operative who worked for President Clinton told Roger Stone that Clinton White House Director of Security Craig Livingstone transported Vince Foster's corpse.

Though not proven, we think it's possible that Livingstone and possibly his cohort Tony Marcea transported Vince Foster's body between 5:15 and 6 p.m.

The body was discovered by Dale Kyle shortly past 6 p.m. in Fort Marcy Park, a public park in nearby McLean, Virginia. Kyle was looking for a place to urinate in the woods that offered privacy.[364] Kyle heard no gunshot. In fact, no one heard a gunshot . . . no one in the park that day. . . . no one in the five homes within 570 feet of where the body was found, the closest of which was three hundred feet away.[365]

Foster's body had not been there long.

One of the first responders, Sergeant Rolla, "noticed blood coming from the right nostril and the right corner of his mouth down the side of his face. It appeared to still be wet, but drying. Flies were buzzing around his face, starting to—no eggs were laid yet. I think they were just making their way to do that." Rolla mentioned that Foster's blood was just beginning to gel "So it led me to believe that he hadn't been there more than a couple of hours. Again, the flies I just—he hadn't been there that long because they are fast workers."[366]

Michael Kellett called the American Entomological Association and was referred to a specialist on insects, Professor Carl Jones of the College of Veterinary Medicine. "After questioning me on the date, the temperature that day, and the approximate time of day, he stated in no more than one and a half hours, flies would have laid eggs," said Kellet.[367]

Kellet points out that the first responders were viewing the body at about 6:40 p.m. Eastern. "The egg laying-activity, or lack of it, would place the time that the body was in the park at 5:10 [p.m.] at the earliest." Vince Foster's body at Fort Marcy Park was a "fresh" corpse.[368] Foster's body was found as soon as it was dumped in the park.

Upon spotting the body, Dale Kyle immediately noticed two very important things. First, there was no gun in Vince Foster's hand. Also, there were footprints around his body.

The gun was not in Foster's hand because Kyle had interrupted individuals staging the body. They had not had the time to place the gun into Foster's hand. After Kyle went for help, a gun was later discovered in Foster's right hand. The FBI later badgered Kyle under questioning.

"CW (Confidential Witness) stated that the agents asked him '25 times' if he was sure that he didn't see a gun, and he repeatedly confirmed that he did not. Finally, they took a response from CW, a response to a hypothetical question, for which CW gave a hypothetical answer," wrote Kellet.[369]

As *Human Events* described it: "An agent asked, 'What if the trigger guard was around the thumb and the thumb was obscured by foliage and the rest of the gun was obscured by the foliage and Mr. Foster's hand?' That was all Mr. Fiske needed to suggest. CW had acknowledged that he may not have seen the gun because it was obscured by foliage. But CW did not change his story."[370]

The footprints around the body were left by the same unskilled individuals that clumsily arranged Foster's body. Kyle told Representative Dan Burton that the trampled area looked "like somebody had been walking or messing around that area."[371]

The FBI report later established that "[Kyle] stated that he stood directly over the body, looking down, for several seconds, specifically recalling that he looked at both hands. He stated that the hands were palms up. He stated that while he was not looking for a gun, he has no recollection of there being a gun in either hand. . . . He stated that as best he recalls from his vantage point on the top of the berm, the foliage and brush as the bottom of the berm or slope (approximately 15 feet below the body) was trampled down as if the individual might have been walking or pacing in that area."[372]

After Kyle found the body, he drove to the Turkey Run Maintenance Yard and told Park Service employees that there was a dead body in the park. Kyle had spent approximately ten minutes total in the park.

Kyle had discovered Foster's body lying straight, with hands hanging down his sides. He did not see much blood and he saw "no gun, no sign of a weapon. It looked like [Foster] had been placed there." And that is because Kyle "saw the leaves trampled down below" and a lot of "foot traffic at the bottom of the hill."[373]

Despite all the impressions made from footwear scattered around the body, Foster's shoes had absolutely no dirt on the bottom, even though his body was found more than two hundred yards away from the parking lot and down a trail.

After Chris Ruddy of the *New York Post* started investigating the Foster case, he published an article that included interviews with the first responders.

"The EMTs told Ruddy that there was a suspicious lack of blood around Foster's body and that the body had looked laid out on the sloping embankment, as though placed there, 'as if it was ready for the coffin,' stated historian Matthew MacAdam. One of the responders hadn't seen an exit wound in Foster's head even though he had lifted him into a body bag. Based on these descriptions, homicide investigators Ruddy spoke to speculated that Foster may have been killed elsewhere, and the body moved."[374]

There were more clues that the body had been moved. Michael Kellet later pointed out the FBI report's clear statement that " the pattern of the blood on Foster's face and on Foster's shoulder is consistent with Foster's face having come into contact with the shoulder of his shirt at some point."[375] The stain made the purported suicide in the park nearly impossible due to the position of the body. "The chin was pushed against the right shoulder which caused the contact stain," wrote Kellet.[376]

The grossly misplaced theory of the Fiske report was that someone had knocked Foster's head so that his cheek fell down on his bloody shoulder causing the contact stain. Kyle said he had not touched the body. The first responders, Sergeant Gonzalez, Todd Hall, and Officer Fornshill all "swore under oath that they did not touch the head [of Vince Foster] which they all described as 'looking up' and slightly tilted to the right as did those who arrived afterward."[377]

Kellett made a key point about Foster's blood-soaked shirt: "The only way the upper back could be soaked is if there were an enormous pool of blood found under the exit wound, not a 'fairly large' amount. It is the distribution of the blood that suggests the body was moved."[378]

There was another inconsistency between the blood found on Foster's body in relation to its position. The FBI laboratory report on Foster noted "two clearly visible blood drain tracks on Foster's face, extending from the nose and mouth, to the ear and temple."[379] In other words blood flowed out of the deceased Foster in an upside-down fashion from mouth to temple, yet Foster's body was not found upside down. Foster's body was placed on a berm in Fort Marcy Park, and it was leaned with the feet at the bottom and the head at a higher elevation on the incline of the berm. "The draining tracks suggest his head was tipped back slightly when the draining of the blood occurred," observed media watchdog Reed Irvine. "In other words, after Foster was shot, his head was tilted back or was lower than the rest of the body while the blood was draining from his mouth and nostril. He could not have been lying feet down, on a 45-degree slope. As he moved into that position following his suicide, the drainage of the blood toward the temple area occurred."[380]

Following the arrival and subsequent departure of the first responders, a crew arrived to transport the body to the morgue. EMT Corey Ashford lifted the body, with the head of the corpse on his white uniform, and placed it in a body bag. Ashford got no blood on his clean uniform and saw no blood on the ground beneath the body. Roger Harrison of Fairfax County Fire and Rescue, who helped Ashford fit the corpse into the bag, saw no blood either.[381]

"Vincent Foster could not have killed himself by putting a gun in his mouth and pulling the trigger as reported in the media," Ruddy wrote in *The Strange Death of Vince Foster: An Investigation*. "The crime scene displayed none of the telltale signs of suicide, from the amount of blood spilled to the position of the body. Foster's shoes and clothing held no grass or soil particles, despite the official determination that he walked across nearly 800 feet of grass and dirt paths before sitting on the ground and killing himself."[382]

Ruddy interviewed Joe Purvis, a longtime friend of Vince Foster. Purvis had been able to talk with one of the morticians who had worked on Foster's body up close at Little Rock's Reubel's Funeral Home. The mortician said that bullet entrance wound was a small hole in the back of Vince Foster's mouth and the exit wound was found in the back neck at the base of Foster's head.[383] Foster was leaned up against an incline on a berm, and if a bullet had come out the back of his neck it should have burrowed into the dirt. The fatal bullet that Foster used to kill himself was not found despite the fact that Robert Fiske's and Ken Starr's people made extensive searches of the area.

Foster's glasses, covered in gunpowder, were found nineteen feet away and behind the body. Both of Vince Foster's hands were found to have gunpowder on them as well. There was heavy foliage and vegetation on the berm behind Foster. The question is: did Foster throw down his glasses before he shot himself? But how could that have happened if there was gunpowder on the glasses? The report of the Independent Counsel states "This powder is physically and chemically similar to the gunpowder found in the cartridge removed from Foster's gun. . . . These facts are consistent with the eyeglasses being positioned near the gun when fired (such as Foster's face or in his shirt pocket.)"[384]

In his book *The Murder of Vince Foster*, Kellett mocked the eyeglass theory with his offer of "$10,000 TO THE WORLD'S BEST FALLING, NECK SNAPPING EYEGLASS THROWER." A .38 revolver has a sharp recoil but not one that can toss a pair of glasses nineteen feet. "According to the 'independent' counsel, the head [of Vince Foster] snapped back with such force that it caused the eyeglasses to be dislodged and thrown over the five-foot berm, plus another thirteen feet."[385]

When Vince Foster's body was found, he had no car keys on his body, according to Park Police Detective John Rolla, who conducted the initial examination. Rolla did find Foster's pager on the body but not the large mass of keys that Foster carried. Ken Starr's report speculated that Detective Rolla must not have dug deep enough into the pockets to find the large clump of keys.

"When the Park Police investigators realized they did not have Foster's car keys, they went to the morgue to research the body," wrote Marinka Peschmann. "Not only did the investigators locate Foster's car keys in his right pant pocket but they also found a second set of keys with four door and cabinet keys. Foster's right pant pocket was near 'his right waist area,' where Rolla retrieved his pager during the initial search. How could he have missed them?"[386]

Craig Livingstone and Kennedy were the two people who went to the morgue to identify Foster's body. It has been said by numerous researchers that either Livingstone or Kennedy could have planted keys on the corpse during their morgue visit.

Though Vince Foster drove a gray Honda, there is no Honda car key in the FBI photographs of the keys belonging to Vince Foster. Nor is there a Honda key listed in the evidence recovered for the Foster case. "A Park Police evidence report listed a key ring with a tab, 'Vince's Keys,' but these alleged keys were never photographed and were never on the FBI official list of evidence. Honda automobile keys are double-sided and there is no double-sided Honda key in the official photo of Foster's keys."[387]

Besides the physical incongruences, there were also problematic time issues in the "official" version of events.

In her autobiography Hillary wrote that she first heard of Foster's death "That night, sometime between eight and nine o'clock, Mack McLarty called me at my mother's house and told me he had terrible news: Vince Foster was dead; it looked like a suicide."[388] In 1993 the Clinton White House said Bill had learned about Foster's death at 10 p.m. Eastern while on a break during a *Larry King Live* interview. A CNN makeup artist told Robert Fiske that just before

9 p.m. an aide told Bill that some sort of document had been already been found in Foster's office. This is proof that Clinton was aware the search for documents had commenced.

The odds are high that by five in the evening, the Clintons knew about Foster's suicide.

Shortly after Foster's suicide, Helen Dickey, Chelsea's nanny, called the Arkansas governor's mansion and told Arkansas state trooper Roger Perry that Foster had committed suicide in the White House parking lot.

"Vince shot himself," a clearly distraught and confused Dickey told Perry. "He walked out to his car and shot himself in the head."

Perry stated that Dickey called him sometime between 4:30 and 7 p.m. Central Time. Perry then called Arkansas Governor Jim Guy Tucker and fellow trooper Larry Patterson. Patterson said that he was "fairly certain" the Perry call occurred, at the very latest, before 7 p.m. Eastern. Perry also called Lynn Davis, the former head of the Arkansas State Police, who plainly declared in an affidavit the call was no later than 7 p.m. Central.

"It was during the rush hour, before 6:00pm our time," Davis said. "He told me they'd found Vince Foster's body in his car, he's shot himself in the [White House] parking lot."[389]

At approximately the same time this series of calls was occurring, Dale Kyle stumbled upon the body. In fact, "If Patterson's memory is accurate, he learned of the Vince Foster's death fifteen minutes before the body was found by police at Fort Marcy Park," wrote Ruddy.[390] This was problematic.

Senator Alphonse D'Amato led a sham Senate investigation into Whitewater and other Clinton scandals. His Senate Banking Committee subpoenaed Helen Dickey who signed a sworn affidavit that stated that she did not learn about Foster's death until 10 p.m. *Time* magazine at the time reported that the "White House has offered D'Amato a sworn statement from Dickey in which she describes learning of Foster's suicide late that night and discussing it with a state trooper at the Governor's mansion in Arkansas."[391]

In a closed-door deposition to the Senate, Dickey couldn't remember much about the night Foster committed suicide: the time she got off work, what she did for dinner, whether she talked to the First Lady that night—she could not remember any of it.

Former Arkansas state trooper L. D. Brown confirmed that Robyn Dickey, the mother of Helen Dickey, was carrying on an affair with Clinton. Both Bill and Robyn confirmed this to L. D. Brown, and, later, Robyn went to work in the Clinton White House.[392]

Robyn's daughter Helen Dickey "worked for Marsha Scott on the illicit 'Big Brother' database that has been the subject of an investigation on Capitol Hill. She helped Hillary Clinton write *It Takes a Village*, typing up the pages every day in July and August of 1995. For two years she lived in a suite in the third floor Living Quarters of the White House, directly above the Clintons, and went in and out of their kitchens as if it were her own."

Here are the spring 1995 affidavits of Arkansas state troopers Roger Perry and Larry Patterson as well as that of Lynn Davis:

ROGER PERRY on March 28, 1995:
AFFIDAVIT
State of Arkansas }
County of Pulaski }
On this day comes before me, a Notary Public, authorized to administer oaths, in and for the County of Pulaski, State of Arkansas, Roger Perry to me well known, who being first duly sworn, says, upon oath:
On the 20th day of July, 1993, I received a telephone call from a person known to me as Helen Dickey. I was working on the security detail at the Arkansas Governor's mansion in Little Rock, Arkansas at that time. Dickey advised me that Vincent Foster, well known to me, had gotten off work and had gone out to his car in the parking lot and had shot himself in the head. I do not recall the exact time of this telephone call but am fairly certain it was some time from about 4:30 p.m. to no later than 7:00 p.m.

Dickey had previously been employed as a baby-sitter for Governor Clinton's child and at the time of the call she was working at the White House in Washington, DC. I then passed the message on to Governor Jim Guy Tucker through his wife.

During my tenure at the Governor's Mansion I received a number of calls from Jennifer Flowers to Governor Clinton.

I have been told by Danny Ferguson, another trooper who was working security detail at the time, at the Governor's Mansion, that he had talked with a young lady named Paula during a conference at the Excelsior Hotel and that he had taken her up to a room in that hotel at the direct request of then Governor Clinton. Danny has also stated that he talked with [P]aula at a restaurant in Little Rock during a chance meeting shortly before she filed her suit. He told her then, according to his conversation with me, that he would testify on her behalf if she did file suit against Clinton. I have read Danny's answer to her suit and [see] that he admitted taking Paula up to Clinton's room on that occasion.

LARRY PATTERSON on March 28, 1995:
AFFIDAVIT
    State of Arkansas }
        }
    County of Pulaski }
On this day comes before me, a Notary Public, authorized to administer oaths, in and for the County of Pulaski, State of Arkansas, Larry Patterson to me well known, who being first duly sworn, says, upon oath:

I received a telephone call from Roger Perry on the 20th day of July, 1993. Roger was working security detail at the Arkansas Governor's Mansion in Little Rock. He advised me that a lady known to both of us as Helen Dickey had telephonically [contacted] him and advised him that Vincent Foster, well known to both of us because of his relationship with Hillary Clinton and his being an advisor to Governor Bill Clinton had gotten off work and had gone out to his car in the parking lot and had shot himself in the head. I do not re-call the exact time of this telephone call but am fairly certain it was sometime before 6:00 p.m. on that date.

Dickey was employed as a baby-sitter by Governor and Hillary Clinton while in Arkansas and at the time of the call she was work-ing at the White House in Washington, DC.

I have been asked, under oath, whether Bill Clinton ever had ex-tramarital affairs while he was Governor of Arkansas. I have replied that I knew Jennifer Flowers, who has said she had an affair with Governor Clinton. I took him, on occasions to the Quapaw Towers, where she lived, and where he would meet with her. I have taken him to see other [females] with whom he had personal relationships, in-cluding one he met during the night at Chelsea Clinton's schoolyard. I worked with Danny Ferguson, another trooper who was working security detail at the Governor's Mansion. Danny told me that he had talked with a young lady named Paula Jones during a meeting at the Excelsior Hotel in Little Rock. He told me he had taken her up to a room in that Hotel after having been asked to by then Governor Bill Clinton. On one occasion I was with Governor Clinton when we met Paula Jones in the rotunda at the State Capitol. The Governor re-ferred to her as Paula as they hugged. Danny has also told me that he talked with Paula at a restaurant in Little Rock in the summer of 1994. At that time, Paula told Danny that she had learned she had been [mentioned] in a [negative] article about Bill Clinton. He told her then, according to his conversation with me, that he would testify on her behalf if she did file suit against Clinton. I have read Danny's answer to her suit and see that he admitted taking Paula up to Clinton's room on that occasion. That agrees with what I kn[o]w about that situation.

LYNN DAVIS on April 7, 1995:
(text portion of affidavit only)

This is to certify that on the 20th day of July, 1993, I received a telephone call from Roger Perry, of the Arkansas State Police, who was a member of the Arkansas Governor's security detail.

Perry advised me that he had just received a telephone call from one Helen Dickey, a [former] baby-sitter for Chelsea Clinton, who was employed at the White House and that she had advised him that Vincent Foster, known to both Perry and me, and gone to his car in the Parking Lot and had shot himself in the head.

I do not recall the exact time of the call, but I [place] it as being during the rush hour at the White House and [assumed] there must be many witnesses to the event. Perry advised me that Helen Dickey was quite upset as if the event had happened shortly before her call to him. I estimate the time at being no later that six o'clock, Central Standard Time.

Perry advised me that he had telephonically contacted Betty Tucker who had relayed the message to Governor Jim Guy Tucker.

When the D'Amato committee met, it refused to call Perry and Patterson to testify. Then the committee members made the grossly false statement that Perry and Patterson refused to testify, an outrageous lie designed to suppress the truth.

Ruddy examined the timeline when the various members of the White House were said to have discovered that Foster had committed suicide.

"The White House said that the Secret Service was initially notified of the death by Park Police at 8:30 pm—just as Park Police were wrapping up their inquiry at Fort Marcy—and that key presidential aides were only told after the president went on 'Larry King Live' at 9:00pm," wrote Ruddy. "The White House had also maintained that the president himself was not informed until about 10:00pm, when the show ended, some four hours after the Park Police first discovered Foster's body in Fort Marcy Park shortly after 6:00pm."[393]

Detective Rolla of the Park Police said in both his FBI statement and a deposition for the Senate Banking Committee that he did not find Vince Foster's identification in his car at Fort Marcy Park until about 8:30p.m.[394] Detective Rolla's statement does not appear to be accurate. There are handwritten notes by Rolla that show that he called the Secret Service at the White House at 7 p.m. or earlier to get Vince Foster's Washington address.[395]

The statements to the FBI of the paramedics who found Vince Foster indicate they knew who he was before they left Fort Marcy Park at 6:40 p.m. Fairfax Lieutenant William Bianchi said that by 7 p.m. he heard paramedics stating that the deceased had worked at the White House. Another man, Lieutenant James Iacone, confirmed Bianchi's statement.[396]

Ruddy pointed out that David Watkins was paged by the White House military communications office after 7 p.m. Ruddy also pointed out that Craig Livingstone was contacted by the Park Police around eight that night, and that Deputy Chief of Staff Bill Burton was aware of Foster's death at that time.[397]

Following the investigation, all of the crime scene photos vanished. "All of the 35 mm photos were underexposed and most of the Polaroids had disappeared. All that remained were a few close-up shot shots."[398] Somebody in the government leaked just a few Polaroids to *ABC News* in an effort to discredit Ruddy who had claimed, accurately, that "crucial" crime scene photos were missing. One of the few Polaroids leaked to the media showed a gun in Vince Foster's right hand.

In October of 1997, Ken Starr issued a report on the death of Foster. This report, drafted by Brett Kavanaugh, agreed with the Fiske report, which came to the ridiculous conclusion that Foster killed himself at Fort Marcy Park. CNN had reported earlier in the year that "The [Starr] report refutes claims by conservative political organizations that Foster was the victim of a murder plot and cover-up," but "despite those findings, right-wing political groups have continued to allege that there was more to the death and that the president and first lady tried to cover it up."[399]

"It would not take a village to alter the outcome of Foster's death, just a handful of people. And remarkably, both sides of the political aisle—were *half* right," journalist Marinka Peschmann concluded.

"Foster's death triggered a massive cover-up by the Clinton administration. This is why Hillary should not be in the White House. She should be in jail," continued Peschmann. "The Senate Whitewater Committee called [the Vince Foster investigation] a 'sham.' The Committee found that [Hillary's] counsel's office, government lawyers, 'who were supposed to protect public interest in a proper investigation and faithful execution of the laws, instead interfered and obstructed various federal investigations. Unquestionably, the Department of Justice and Park Police were authorized to conduct this investigation, and White House officials owed them a duty to cooperate. Instead, law enforcement officials were confronted at every turn with concerted efforts to deny them access to evidence in Mr. Foster's office."

Hillary's tactics and her "special treatment" of the media allowed her to dodge indictments.

Peschmann deftly illustrated her tactics concerning the media elite:

"Even though the Senate Whitewater Committee investigation's conclusion revealed that there was 'a concerted effort by senior White House officials to block career law enforcement investigators from conducting a thorough investigation' into Foster's death, and recommended that steps be taken to insure that such misuse of the White House counsel's office does not recur in this, or any future, administration, meaningful and honest reporting was still attacked," Peschmann wrote. "Journalists or investigators who dared to speak truth to power by asking legitimate and common-sense questions were sidelined, mocked, dismissed as right-wing hacks, or scolded by Hillary for inflicting 'great emotional and monetary damage on innocent people.'"

CHAPTER 15

LOOSE ENDS

"You're not going to believe what's going on here. There's a surveillance net of at least thirty people harassing Patrick [Knowlton], I've never seen anything like this in my life."

—Chris Ruddy, reporter for the *Pittsburgh Tribune-Review*, commenting on the terror campaign of Patrick Knowlton in late October of 1995

Some accounts of the Clintons' involvement in harassment and cover-up are enough to make your skin crawl.

One afternoon, when journalist Ambrose Evans-Pritchard was reading FBI interviews on the Foster case, he came across the report of a witness who was in Fort Marcy Park between 4:15 and 4:30 p.m. on the afternoon of Foster's death. Knowlton at the time was a little over forty years old and a registered Democrat. He still had a Clinton-Gore bumper sticker on his car.

Patrick Knowlton told Evans-Pritchard that he was stuck in traffic on the George Washington Parkway and, like Dale Kyle, needed a place to urinate. He pulled into the park to either find a restroom or a private spot in the woods.

In the parking lot, Knowlton noticed two cars. One was a brown Honda with Arkansas license plates and the other a blue Japanese car with a man sitting in it. When the man, who looked Middle Eastern or Hispanic, saw Knowlton he started glowering at him in a threatening manner.[400] The man got out of the car and stared at Knowlton. Knowlton, however, still needed to heed the call of nature.

"Patrick walked up toward the park," said Evans-Pritchard. "Instead of going into Fort Marcy proper, he took the logging trail to the left where the nearest trees were. That was a fortunate decision. Patrick dreads to think what would have happened if he had walked into the main body of the park [where Vince Foster's corpse was discovered]."

Knowlton told Evans-Pritchard that, "When I came back I looked at him and I thought, 'Something is going to happen to me unless I get the hell out of here.'"[401]

Knowlton left the park and went to a mountain cabin where he was staying with his girlfriend. Later that evening he heard that a high-ranking White House official had been found dead in Fort Marcy Park. Knowlton contacted the Park Police and was interviewed over the telephone by Detective Rolla about what he had seen that afternoon. Rolla did not think Knowlton's story was important, and there were no follow-up interviews.

Nine months later, the FBI contacted Knowlton and brought him in for questioning at the Office of the Independent Counsel. The FBI then tried to warp his testimony. They repeatedly showed Knowlton (approximately twenty times) a picture of a *blue* car that had Foster's license plate number (RCN-504). The FBI was trying to manufacture testimony, attempting to get Knowlton to identify Foster's car.

"I was adamant about it," Knowlton recalled. "I walked right next to the goddamn car, and it was *brown*. I saw what I saw, and I was not going to change my story. . . . I think they were just trying to screw me around. It pisses me off."[402] Foster's car was a gray 1989 Honda Accord. It was not blue and it certainly was not the brown car that Knowlton saw.

There were three other witnesses who saw "an old brown Honda" as opposed to Foster's gray-colored Honda, which was four years older: Josie, Duncan, and a "woman in the blue Mercedes" who Evans-Pritchard interviewed. Additionally, Sergeant George Gonzalez in his EMS report described a "brown Honda" with "AR tags." Even the medical examiner, Dr. Donald Haut, said he saw "an orange compact, a beat-up old thing. I was surprised anybody at the White House would be driving a car like that."[403]

The treatment of Knowlton shows that both the FBI and the Office of the Independent Counsel were in the tank. They were unwilling to hear a different point of view or to make logical conclusions based on the evidence presented.

Knowlton insists the FBI fabricated his interview with them (known as a 302 report). He told them he thought the car was an older 1983 or 1984 model and his FBI interview says it was a 1988 or 1990 model. Knowlton was called in for a second interview on May 11, 1994, designed to clear up the discrepancy between what Knowlton saw (a brown Honda) and what the FBI wanted him to have seen (Vince Foster's car).

Knowlton came under a vicious round of witness tampering, highly reminiscent of other Clinton campaigns, in October 1995, and it looks like this may have started as early as May 10, 1994.

In his lawsuit against the government, Knowlton said that Scott Jeffrey Bickett, a man with suspicious connections, had smashed the lights on Knowlton's car. Evans-Pritchard did some more investigating and discovered that Bickett had a Defense Contractor II clearance level, had been briefed at FBI headquarters, and had a very high Sensitive Compartmented Information (SCI) security clearance. "So the man who smashed the Peugeot 504 [Knowlton's car] on the night before Patrick's second FBI interview was on the roster of FBI-HQ."[404]

Knowlton also told the FBI in his original interview that he felt sure that he could identify the menacing man who was staring at him in the parking lot. The FBI wrote down that Patrick would not be able to identify the man again. "I can close my eyes and visualize this guy like it was yesterday," Knowlton said.[405]

In the fall of 1995, after Ambrose Evans-Pritchard had written about the Knowlton case in the *Sunday Telegraph*, Special Prosecutor Ken Starr issued a subpoena for Knowlton to appear before the Whitewater grand jury. Evans-Pritchard and the *Sunday Telegraph* had embarrassed both Starr and the FBI into dealing with a critical witness that they wanted nothing to do with.

Evans-Pritchard was not ready to indict every FBI agent with malfeasance in the Foster investigation. However, "it appears at least one agent was systematically altering statements, sometimes with little tweaks here and there, sometimes with outright false-hoods, as in the case of Patrick Knowlton and the Confidential Witness [Dale Kyle] . . . But once you are alert to this legerdemain by the FBI, everything comes into focus. The old tannish-brown Honda parked at Fort Marcy between 4:30 and 6:37 pm when the first team of paramedics left the scene—could not have been Vincent Foster's vehicle."[406]

The destabilization campaign aimed at Patrick Knowlton and the terror campaign unleashed on Kathleen Willey in 1997 and 1998 were both egregious examples of witness tampering. The crime of witness tampering is located at 18 US Code § 1512—*Tampering with a witness, victim, or an informant.*[407] The federal code mentions the use of physical force and also the "threat of physical force" as crimes for which the federal penalty can be up to thirty years in jail. Intimidation and threats to a witness can get the perpetrator twenty years in jail.

As Ruddy discovered, a surveillance net of perhaps thirty people was cast on Knowlton in an attempt harass, intimidate, terrify, un-nerve, and destabilize him before his testimony to the Whitewater grand jury.

The perpetrators used a variety of tactics on Knowlton. In one instance, a strange man would follow Knowlton, stop, and stare menacingly at him. "The next man was of similar vintage, with a navy blue jacket," said Evans-Pritchard. "His stare lasted about fifteen seconds. It was the same distinctive stare—one designed to provoke fear, confusion, and paranoia. And then it happened again, and again: men cutting in front of them, following them, glowering into Patrick's eyes, fixing him with the look of death wherever he turned."[408]

Then after seven or eight intimidation attempts, these agents began bumping into Knowlton and were "circling like hyenas" in the words of Evans-Pritchard. The scribe then called fellow reporter Ruddy to experience firsthand what Knowlton was going through. Ruddy said there must have been thirty people attempting to unnerve and terrify Knowlton.

It was street fascism and the terrorists did not care that reporters were witnessing the thuggery firsthand. The two reporters notified Deputy Independent Counsel John Bates (now a statist federal judge) of what was happening to Knowlton. Bates issued no response.

"Sometime after midnight, Patrick telephoned me at my home in Bethesda," recalled Evans-Pritchard. "By now he was on the verge of a nervous breakdown. Somebody had gotten inside his apartment building and was banging on the door. When he answered, there was nobody. Outside his window was a man in a green trench coat, staring up at him. The telephone kept ringing. Hang-up calls. 'I can't take it anymore. I want out of this,' [Knowlton] said.

"'Stay calm, don't let these criminals get to you,' I said. 'I'm going to come down and get you out of there. You're going to stay at my house until this nonsense is over.'"[409]

A few days later, the FBI told Knowlton that it was Ruddy and Evans-Pritchard behind the harassment campaign.

Knowlton showed up for his grand jury testimony prepared to testify to exactly what he saw (or did not see) in the parking lot. Starr's prosecutor Brett Kavanaugh (who, like Bates, is now a federal judge) questioned Knowlton before the grand jury. Kavanaugh adopted a hostile demeanor, intent on "hazing" or roughing up, disrespecting, and discrediting Knowlton. Kavanaugh asked a series of leading questions in which he attempted to paint Knowlton as a homosexual who was in Fort Marcy Park that day for a hook up. Knowlton erupted in rage at Kavanaugh as the jury laughed at the Starr prosecutors.

"Prior to going to the grand jury I was harassed and intimidated on the streets of Washington," Knowlton said. "And during that time, a three-day period, my attorney John Clarke repeatedly called the FBI and the OIC's office. They never responded to give me any protection or any help. It wasn't until the following Monday that Russell Bransford showed up at my door and he interviewed me regarding the harassment. All the time I was telling him the story, of what took place, he sat there and smiled at me. And when I asked him at one point if I could trust him? He leaned over into my face and said, 'Mr. Knowlton that is a good question, I don't know.'

"Well, I was looking forward to going to the grand jury and telling them my story about my harassment and at that time, I did not realize that the FBI and the OIC were behind it.

"I remember when I went to the grand jury. And towards the end of this two-and-a-half-hour interview, I was asked by Brett Kavanaugh to step outside of the grand jury room so the grand jurors could ask questions. When I re-entered the room, Kavanaugh first asked me if I was sure that someone else didn't see me in the park? And I replied that I hoped that someone else had seen me in the park. Then, he sarcastically asked me whether I came forward to the authorities because I was a good citizen or a good Samaritan?

"Then, John Bates who was seated behind me leaned forward and passed a note to Brett Kavanaugh, from which Kavanaugh read the following questions.

"He said, 'Mr. Knowlton did the man in the park talk to you?' And I replied, 'no.'

"He asked me, 'Did the man in the park pass you a note?' And I replied, 'no.'

"He said, 'Did the man approach you?' And I replied, 'no.'

"'Did the man in the park point a gun at you?' I replied, 'no.'

"And lastly Kavanaugh asked me, 'Did the man in the park touch your genitals?'

"I looked at him and I was in shock. I was dumbfounded. I couldn't believe he asked me such a question. Of course, I replied, 'no.'

"As I left the grand jury I was puzzled why the grand jurors would ask such questions? And as soon as I saw my attorney, John Clarke, I repeated verbatim the last questions I was asked. Now we know those questions were designed by John Bates and Brett Kavanaugh. They wanted to discredit me, and my testimony.

"Bates and Kavanaugh knew Foster's car, that gray car, was not in the parking lot when Foster was dead. They also knew that all of the other witnesses and I all saw the brown car in the small parking lot. No one in that park saw Foster's gray car.

"The press and the government claim that Vincent Foster drove to the park and shot himself. The fact is, Foster did not drive to the park."[410]

"The proceedings were out of control," said Evans-Pritchard "It had started as a charade; it had ended in a farce. At least Patrick now knew he could expect nothing from the Starr investigation. He was forced to conclude that the Office of the Independent Counsel was itself corrupt."[411]

Indeed, all three men profited heavily from their "investigation."

Starr, after being a federal judge in the 1980s as well as the solicitor general of the USA (often a stepping stone to a Supreme Court nomination) is now the chancellor and president of Baylor University. In 2007, Starr joined the legal team of notorious pedophile Jeffrey Epstein. Epstein, who had molested perhaps dozens of underaged girls, got off with a slap on the wrist, only serving thirteen months in prison. Epstein, while living a life of pedophilia with underaged girls was a close social friend of Bill Clinton.

Kavanaugh is now a federal judge on the United States Court of Appeals for the DC Circuit, the same circuit that Starr had been on. George W. Bush nominated this Yale graduate (both undergrad and law school) for a spot on the Appeals Court. Kavanaugh also was a partner at Kirkland and Ellis, the same law firm that Starr was a partner in. Kavanaugh later worked on the George W. Bush campaign for president and later joined his presidential staff. Kavanaugh's claim to fame was penning the Independent Counsel's report on the Foster death.

Bates is now a US District Judge for the United States District Court for the District of Columbia, appointed by President Bush in 2001. From 2006 to 2013, Bates served as a judge on the U.S. Foreign Intelligence Surveillance Court.

When Knowlton went to physically deliver to the Office of the Independent Counsel a Report of Witness Tampering, Bates called security and had him thrown out of the building."[412] Subsequently, in October 1996 Patrick Knowlton filed a lawsuit "alleging a conspiracy to violate his civil rights, to inflict emotional distress, and to dissuade him from testifying truthfully before a federal grand jury. In the amended complaint he named the United States of America, FBI Agents Lawrence Monroe and Russell T. Bransford, and two mysterious Jordanians, Ayman and Abdel."[413]

Knowlton was directly accusing the FBI of being part of the terror campaign that was engaged in criminal witness tampering.

John Clarke, the lawyer for Knowlton, wrote a letter that detailed the crimes that had been visited upon his witness. The judges who oversaw the Starr case ordered that the documentation of the witness tampering and harassment of Knowlton was attached to Starr's report on the Foster suicide. This became a part of the official record of the Foster "investigation" despite Starr's fierce objections.

The Federal Appeals Court eventually discarded Knowlton's suit. Nonetheless, it is interesting to read excerpts of Knowlton's motion to the court, which were attached to the Starr report. For instance:

FACTUAL BACKGROUND

Upon learning that Mr. Foster's body was found in Fort Marcy Park, Patrick Knowlton reported to authorities what he had seen in the park approximately 70 minutes before the discovery of Mr. Foster's body.

FBI Agent Lawrence Monroe interviewed Patrick Knowlton in April and May of 1994. Agent Monroe falsified Mr. Knowlton's account of the events he reported he had witnessed in Fort Marcy Park. At the time of these interviews, Agent Monroe was detailed to the office of regulatory Independent Counsel Robert W. Fiske, Jr.

Mr. Knowlton's information refutes the official conclusions that Mr. Foster committed suicide in Fort Marcy Park, primarily because Mr. Knowlton is certain (despite official conclusions to the contrary) that no car fitting the description of Mr. Foster's car was in the Fort Marcy lot approximately 70 minutes before Mr. Foster's body was officially discovered, even though Mr. Foster was dead at the time. Agent Monroe covered up this and other facts Mr. Knowlton provided to Agent Monroe. Prior to 1996, Mr. Knowlton was unaware of this state of affairs and had assumed his information was irrelevant.

When he was provided copies of his interview reports by a reporter, Mr. Knowlton discovered that Agent Monroe had falsified his account, and his account of what he had witnessed at Fort Marcy and contradictory information from his FBI interview reports were published in a London newspaper.

On the same day that this newspaper reached American newsstands, October 24, 1995, the Office of Independent Counsel under Kenneth W. Starr prepared a subpoena for Mr. Knowlton to testify before the Whitewater grand jury in this Courthouse.

That subpoena was held for service for two days, apparently to allow time for the assembly of the men who subsequently harassed Mr. Knowlton, then served by FBI Agent Russell T. Bransford. At the time of the service of that subpoena, Agent Bransford was detailed to Mr. Starr's Washington, DC, office. Agent Bransford had formerly been detailed to regulatory Independent Counsel Robert Fiske's investigation, where Agent Bransford worked with Agent Monroe.

Beginning the same day Agent Bransford served Mr. Knowlton the secret grand jury subpoena, he was harassed by at least 25 men and Agent Bransford prior to testifying before the grand jury, and one man after testifying:

(a) Eleven or more men on October 26, 1995;

(b) Twelve or more men on October 27, 1995;

(c) Two or more men on October 28, 1995;

(d) FBI Agent Bransford on October 30, 1995; and

(e) One man on November 2, 1995.

The objects of the harassment were twofold, to:

(a) Intimidate and warn Mr. Knowlton in connection with his grand jury testimony; and failing that,

(b) Destabilize Mr. Knowlton and discredit his testimony before the grand jury.

This technique of subjecting a witness to an overwhelming campaign of harassment to (i) intimidate and warn, and alternatively to

(ii) destabilize and discredit the witness, is known to federal intelligence and investigative agencies.

On Wednesday, November 1, 1995, Mr. Knowlton testified before the Washington, DC, Whitewater grand jury. Prosecutors questioning Mr. Knowlton during his grand jury appearance had been apprised prior to that appearance of his reports of being harassed by in excess of 25 men. The wrongdoers accomplished their object of discrediting him. Prosecutors did not believe Mr. Knowlton's bizarre account of having been harassed, at one point asking him to "tell us a little bit about the alleged harassment." Nor did prosecutors believe much of anything else Mr. Knowlton had to say.

On October 25, 1996, Mr. Knowlton filed a lawsuit in this District Court against FBI Agents Russel T. Bransford and Lawrence Monroe (and others), alleging that these FBI agents are vicariously liable to Plaintiff for his damages under the law of civil conspiracy for inter alia, violation of 42 U.S.C. § 1985, "Conspiracy to interfere with civil rights," part (2), "Obstructing justice; intimidating party, witness, or juror." The Plaintiff alleges he was intimidated in an attempt to obstruct justice in connection with Mr. Starr's investigation into Mr. Foster's death.

As of the date of this filing, Monroe's and Bransford's motion to dismiss and alternative motion for summary judgment is pending. See Patrick James Knowlton v. FBI Agent Russel T. Bransford, et al., Civil Action No. 96-2467.

Investigative history of the Foster death

The 1994 Senate Banking committee was precluded by the limited jurisdiction of Resolution 229 from any independent exploration of the issue of how or where Mr. Foster died, and Senator D'Amato's committee chose not to visit the issue of how or where Mr. Foster died. Therefore, save the sixteen-day US Park Police investigation, the only investigations into where or how Mr. Foster died were conducted by the FBI:

(1) First, a "preliminary investigation" in July of 1993;

(2) Second, under the auspices of regulatory;

Independent Counsel Robert Fiske; and

(3) Most recently, under the auspices of Independent Counsel Kenneth Starr.

Because of the initial FBI conclusion of "no criminal activity" in July of 1993, FBI agents who worked for Mr. Fiske the first half of 1994 would necessarily have embarrassed the Bureau had they concluded otherwise. And once the agents reported to Mr. Fiske that there was no criminal activity, there could be no abandonment of the FBI's repeated conclusion of suicide in Fort Marcy Park without a horrendous embarrassment to the FBI and possible criminal exposure to the FBI agents detailed to Mr. Fiske's investigation, some of whom subsequently were also detailed to Mr. Starr's investigation.

Given the role and the conclusion of the FBI in its first two investigations into the Foster death, it is manifest that various FBI agents and the FBI operated under a conflict of interest in the role the FBI played in Mr. Starr's investigation of the Foster death. Mr. Knowlton does not in any way seek to disparage Mr. Starr's integrity. However, the propriety of Mr. Starr's use of the FBI in his investigation of the death undermines a fundamental purpose of the Ethics in Government Act, to foster public confidence by maintaining the appearance that justice has been done. That FBI agents again investigating the death would not report to Mr. Starr their prior participation in obstructing justice was likely not lost on those who have relevant information contradicting the official conclusion, particularly in light of a steady stream of press leaks that the OIC was soon to issue a report validating earlier official conclusions.

ARGUMENT

Authority for relief requested. 28 U.S.C. § 594(h)(2) states in part:

The division of the court may make any portion of the final report filed under paragraph (1)(B) available to any individual named in such report for the purposes of receiving within a time limit set by the division of the court any comments or factual information that such individual may submit. Such comments and factual information, in whole or in part, may, in the discretion of the division of the court, be included as an appendix to such final report.

In re North, 10 F. 3rd 831, 835 (D.C. Cir. 1993), noted that one of the purposes of this section was to afford a measure of fairness to persons mentioned in the report:

To assure that the report is full and complete and to afford a measure of fairness to persons mentioned in the report, Congress authorized the court to furnish relevant portions of the report to such persons. Within a time limit set by the court, these persons may submit "comments and factual information" that the court may include as an appendix to the report. 28 U.S.C. § 594(h)(2).

Mr. Knowlton is mentioned in the Report. Mr. Knowlton must be mentioned in the subject Report in light of:

(1) Mr. Knowlton is suing an FBI agent detailed to Mr. Starr's office for conspiracy to obstruct justice in connection with the topic of the subject Report;

(2) The suit alleges an ongoing conspiracy to obstruct justice by FBI agents detailed to the Independent Counsels' investigations, and that the FBI played an integral role in those investigations; and

(3) Mr. Knowlton's information refutes the official conclusion of suicide in the park.

The As Insight on the News noted in its November 22, 1995, article "The Vince Foster Mystery": "Starr will also have to explain—or be ready to dismiss—the strange intimidation that Knowlton claims to have suffered . . ."

Mr. Knowlton's reputation is at stake and he continues to fight to clear his name. Patrick Knowlton did the right thing by calling the US Park Police in July of 1993. He was later harassed and intimidated in an effort to set him up to look like some kind of nut. Because he did not heed this warning regarding his grand jury testimony and continued to tell the truth, including the truth of the bizarre harassment he suffered, his testimony was discredited. He has been fighting for his credibility for the past 21 months. These efforts he has undertaken to establish his credibility include, inter alia:

(1) Undergoing a polygraph examination;

(2) Undergoing an extensive psychiatric examination including psychological testing;

(3) Giving a sworn interview;

(4) Obtaining sworn Affidavits of other witnesses;

(5) Assembling and publishing these documents (and photographs of two of the men who harassed him) along with a detailed description of the harassment he suffered in a 147-page Report;

(6) Avoiding affiliation with organizations known to be opposed to the Clinton administration;

(7) Avoiding obtaining funding from conservative organizations in order to avoid any appearance of political motivation or influence; and

(8) Filing his Complaint under seal of Court on October 24, 1996, because press reports of his claims on the eve of the presidential election would further undermine his credibility by the appearance of political motivation or influence.

In his opposition to defendants' pending summary judgment motion, Mr. Knowlton proffers 118 exhibits in support of his claim of an overall conspiracy, 100 of which are part of the publicly available record in the Foster case. These exhibits appear under headings in that filing which, when viewed cumulatively, fairly raise a strong inference that FBI agents obstructed justice prior to and during the time that the FBI investigated under regulatory Independent Counsel Robert Fiske.

As more of the records of the Foster death investigations are declassified and analyzed by concerned citizens, Mr. Knowlton's position that the intimidation he suffered were overt acts in furtherance of an overall FBI conspiracy to obstruct justice will slowly gain more acceptance. For example, just this week, counsel was provided with a copy of the Report of Investigation by Medical Examiner, signed on July 20, 1993, by Dr. Donald Haut, the only MD to view Mr. Foster's body in situ at Fort Marcy Park. This report (a copy of which attached hereto), found at the National Archives on July 17, 1997, was not part of the Senate Hearings Volumes made public in January of 1995 although it was found in a box indicating that it had been so released. The following is an excerpt of the entry appearing on that Medical Examiner's Report under the heading NARRATIVE SUMMARY OF CIRCUMSTANCES SURROUND-ING DEATH: ". . . gunshot wound mouth to neck . . ."

This reported "mouth to neck" circumstance surrounding Mr. Foster's death explains:

(1) Paramedic Richard Arthur's sworn testimony: "What I saw is what I saw. . . . and I saw a small—what appeared to be a small gunshot wound here near the jawline. Fine, whether the coroner's report says that or not, fine. I know what I saw."

(2) [Redacted]

(3) Why many of the crime scene Polaroid photographs mysteriously vanished;

(4) Why the FBI falsely reported all 35 millimeter photographs were "underexposed" and that despite attempts by the FBI laboratory these photographs "were of limited value;"

(5) Press reports that Miguel Rodriquez resigned from his position with the OIC after he "insisted on conducting a painstaking review of the case [but was] met with stiff opposition from FBI agents assigned to Starr's probe"—after he had the original Polaroid photographs "enhanced by a specialized lab outside the FBI";

(6) A press report that a "photograph . . . reveals that Foster suffered trauma to the right side of his neck, just below the jawline . . . it has the appearance of a small caliber gunshot wound . . . a prosecutor on the staff of Kenneth Starr . . . has shown it to individuals 'off the

record'. . . this photo was never presented to the panel of four pathologists brought in by the Fiske investigation . . ."

(7) A press report that "Joe Purvis . . . said last March that he was told by a staff member of Ruebel's Funeral Home in Little Rock that Foster had . . . an exit wound 'the size of a dime' close to the neck at the hairline"; and

(8) Why investigators stated that no autopsy X-rays were taken while inexplicably failing to investigate significant evidence the X-rays were in fact taken but mysteriously vanished.

The Medical Examiner's report that there was a gunshot exit wound in Mr. Foster's neck is inconsistent with the official conclusion that this neck wound "did not exist," and is but one of numerous records in this matter which refute the official conclusions.

CONCLUSION

Patrick Knowlton reported to authorities what he had seen at Fort Marcy Park shortly before the official discovery of Mr. Foster's body. Mr. Knowlton complied with FBI agent Larry Monroe's request that he not report his observations to the press.

After Mr. Knowlton learned from a reporter, some 27 months after Mr. Foster's death, that agent Monroe had falsified his account, his account along with contradictory information from his FBI interview reports were reported in a London newspaper. That newspaper account was the catalyst for Mr. Knowlton's being:

(1) Targeted by an orchestrated campaign of harassment and intimidation;

(2) Treated with utmost disrespect during his grand jury appearance;

(3) Attacked as a delusional conspiracy theorist;

(4) Wrongfully attacked as being a homosexual; and

(5) Attacked as an outright liar.

Mr. Knowlton did nothing to deserve this outrageous treatment at the hands of the FBI and the OIC. He did nothing to deserve being yanked into this FBI debacle, having his life turned upside down, and having to endure this fight for his reputation. Patrick Knowlton's only "crime" was reporting to the authorities what he had seen at Fort Marcy Park—consistent with his understanding of his duties as a good citizen.

Mr. Knowlton's position that the intimidation he suffered were overt acts in furtherance of an overall FBI conspiracy to obstruct justice will gain more acceptance after the release and public review of the Independent

Counsel's final report pursuant to 28 U.S.C. § 594(h)(2) and upon release and public review of other records pursuant to, inter alia, 5 U.S.C. § 552; 28 C.F.R. § 16, Subpart A; 28 U.S.C. § 594(k)(4)(B), and 28 U.S.C. § 595(a)(2). In light of significant evidence of a cover-up already in the public domain, and based upon the fact that most of the investigative records in this matter will eventually be released, it is axiomatic that the subject Office of Independent Counsel will go down in history as facilitating a fraud upon the American people by its use (perhaps unknowingly) of a federal investigative agency with a powerful vested interest in a finding of no criminal activity in the last Foster death investigation. The American people will now probably never know the truth of the events of July 20, 1993. But eventually they will be apprised of the fact of an FBI cover-up. However, this could take years. In light of the shortcomings of our press in the instant matter, it likely will not occur until after the current administration leaves office.

In the interim, Mr. Knowlton respectfully asks that the Division of the Court exercise its discretion and grant the relief prayed for. Mr. Knowlton has no remedy at law for injury to his reputation causally related to the subject investigations.

In the event the Court would be disposed to grant Mr. Knowlton's request to include his submission as an Appendix, save the 45 page opposition to Summary Judgment Motion, Mr. Knowlton respectfully asks this Court to consider including the Table of Contents of that opposition. In the event that the subject report is not a final report within the meaning of 28 U.S.C. § 594(h)(2), Mr. Knowlton respectfully asks this Court to hold the instant motion in abeyance until such time as the OIC submits its final report on the death of Vincent Foster, Jr.

The relief Mr. Knowlton requests falls squarely within the purpose of 28 U.S.C. § 594(h)(2), "to assure that the report is full and complete and to afford a measure of fairness to persons mentioned in the report . . ." In re North, Id. Mr. Knowlton merely seeks to refute allegations that he is:

(1) A liar and perjurer;

(2) A homosexual; and

(3) Mentally unstable.

If the OIC files a response hereto, Mr. Knowlton specifically asks the OIC to avoid a secret ex-parte communication and to serve counsel with a copy of any such response.

WHEREFORE, pursuant to 28 U.S.C. § 594(h)(2), Patrick James Knowlton respectfully moves the Division of the Court to furnish him relevant portions of the Report on the death of Vincent Foster, Jr., and to include as an Appendix to that Report:

(1) A letter from counsel; and

(2) A copy of Mr. Knowlton's opposition to motion for summary judgment filed in the United States District Court for the District of Columbia on June 6, 1997, filed in support of Mr. Knowlton's cause for conspiracy to obstruct justice against FBI agents in connection with the acts of FBI agents detailed to Mr. Fiske's and Mr. Starr's investigations into the death of Vincent Foster.

John H. Clarke
1730 K Street, NW Suite 304
Washington, DC 20006
(202) 332-3030[414]

In 1997 Patrick Knowlton went to the U.S. Park Police headquarters to get information on his 1994 car vandalism case. With the knowledge that his case had been closed, Knowlton wanted to see his case file. Instead of giving Knowlton a full case file, the civilian employee, upon the orders of a belligerent park police officer, gave Knowlton three documents, with the instruction that this was all he was allowed to see.

"Knowlton argued that, since the case was closed, he should be permitted to see the whole file," said journalist Joseph Farah. "When he suggested that he knew the FBI was involved, the police officer became visibly shaken. Knowlton was told he was trespassing and would have to leave."

Knowlton said that when he left the U.S. Park Police headquarters, his vehicle was followed by a squad car. After traveling about twenty-five blocks, just before he reached his home, the police car flashed its lights and pulled him over to the side of the road.

Knowlton waited with his driver's license and registration in hand. But the officer never approached the car. After a few minutes, the police car's lights went off and the officer drive away.

What would you think if this bizarre chain of events happened to you? Knowlton is persuaded that what he once believed to be a case of random vandalism was an incident perpetrated by government officials—presumably from the FBI. There is no doubt in his mind that the harassment he experienced later, when he was testifying to the grand jury in 1995, was orchestrated by FBI agents.

Farah had an opinion as to why the government was so vested in discrediting Knowlton.

"Why would the government be so concerned about Knowlton and what he saw that day in Fort Marcy Park?" Farah asked. "The only explanation is that he saw something very much in conflict with the official story—the story that, despite all evidence to the contrary, is being pushed aggressively by Starr, the Clinton administration, the FBI, the US Park Police and the establishment press.

"You have to ask yourself: If Knowlton is wrong about what he saw, why all the fuss? Why are FBI agents so concerned about a loose-cannon witness who got his facts wrong? Why would they risk their jobs, their livelihoods and their reputations on discrediting one misguided eyewitness?"

Both the government and the media (except for the courageous investigative work of Ruddy and Evans-Pritchard) refused an honest look at the Foster death.

Knowlton, his lawyer Clarke, and other activists contacted the national media and offered them a blockbuster story. They were ignored or discredited. Here are some of the replies they got from the American press and political commentators.[415]

The following is just a sampling of the journalistic non-response to the death of Vince Foster and critical witness Patrick Knowlton, who claimed he was subjected to an FBI terror campaign of witness tampering:

- George Will, Feb., 1996: "We're not interested in that [Foster case]";
- Fred Barnes, Feb. 23, 1996: "Conservatives should ignore the death of Vincent Foster and stick to the real issues . . . It was a suicide . . . No, I don't want to meet Patrick Knowlton";
- Tim Russert, Feb. 29, 1996: "I appreciate your taking the time . . . It is important to have your input";
- James Stewart, March 20, 1996: "Now I think it is too much of a coincidence that he [Foster] would be that depressed and then that somebody would somehow move in and fake some kind of crime. Life just doesn't work like that";
- Haynes Johnson, May 28, 1996: "You have raised provocative questions";
- Ted Gest, 1996: "Our magazine [*Newsweek*] covers consumer issues, that is not the kind of story we cover, try one of the daily papers";
- James Whalen (a professor of journalism at St. Paul University): "If there was anything suspicious about Foster's death, the Washington press would cover it";
- Paul Gigot (the *Wall Street Journal*), July 23, 1996: "Foster committed suicide. Everything points to that . . . No, I don't want to meet him [Patrick Knowlton] and you probably think I am part of the conspiracy";
- Michael Barone, July 30, 1996: "I'm not going to defend the coverage of Vincent Foster by *US News & World Report*, I do not know enough about the Foster story";
- Jerry Seper (*Washington Times*), Oct. 17, 1996: "I don't cover Foster, I'm covering Whitewater. Ask George Archibald, he has been assigned the Foster story";
- George Archibald, Oct. 24, 1996: "Foster is dead. I don't cover Foster . . . My time is limited";
- Eugene Meyer (*Washington Post*), Nov. 5, 1996: "No, it's not my job . . . I don't care about your friend";
- Karen Ballard (*Washington Times*), Nov. 5, 1996: "Why don't you write the story";

- William Kristol, Nov. 8, 1996: "Amazing . . . What kind of work does Mr. Knowlton do?";
- Candy Crowley (CNN), Kwame Holman, Peter Kenyon (NPR), Nov. 19, 1996: "If it was reported I would cover it . . . I have to cover other news, it's not my job";
- Carl Stern, Michael McCurry, Marlin Fitzwater, and Charles Bierbauer (CNN), Feb. 13, 1997: "We don't know anything about it";
- Cokie Roberts, April 13, 1997: "Thousands of reporters have looked into the death of Vincent Foster and everyone including the numerous investigations have concluded that his death was a suicide";
- Paul Harvey, July 16, 1997: "The death of White House counsel Vincent Foster has now been investigated four times including Kenneth Starr's most recent one and all four have reached the same conclusion. There was no conspiracy, no cover-up, it was suicide";
- Mike Wallace, July 23, 1997: "Just wait until Ken Starr's report is released, then you can apologize to me";
- Tom Sherwood, WRC-DC, July 31, 1997: "I can't believe there would be a cover-up . . . Why don't you contact Mike Isikoff";
- Michael Isikoff, Aug. 13, 1997: "[I] do not have enough evidence to go with the story about Patrick Knowlton's allegations";
- Martha Malan, (*St. Paul Press*), Oct. 12, 1997: "We don't have the resources to cover the Foster story . . . No, I don't want to talk to Patrick Knowlton";
- John Crudele (*New York Post*), Nov. 1997: "I don't believe there is a cover-up";
- Steve Labaton (*New York Times*), Nov. 1997: "The court had to attach your submission";
- Bob Zelnick, May 30, 1998: "[There isn't] any credible evidence that Vincent Foster was murdered. Can I ask to change the subject?";

- Harold Hostetler, June 25, 1998: "Mr. Knowlton does appear to be an honest and forthright person who is sticking up for his principles and beliefs. However, I do not see this as a potential story for *Guideposts*";
- Sam Fullwood (*L.A. Times*) at Sanford Ungar AU forum (with L. Brent Bozell III, Karen DeYoung, and Bill Plante), Sept. 8, 1998: "It's not my kind of story . . . Why don't you post it on the Internet then everyone will know . . . Why don't you write a book, you could make lots of money";
- Matt Drudge: "I'll read this [written materials] but I was just about ready to believe the body was moved and now you're saying he was murdered";
- Frank Sesno, Sept. 24, 1998: "I'll look at this";
- Helen Thomas, Oct. 7, 1998: "[T]his should be reported to the American people";
- Helen Thomas, April 9, 1999: "Q. I gave you the addendum to Starr's Report. Will you write about Patrick Knowlton? A. No . . . I don't have time. Q. Can I quote you? A. No. Q. You said then that his story should be reported. A. It is very unfair of you to do this to me. Just forget it."

"Attorney Clarke, Mr. Turley and I spent years calling, mailing and personally delivering this information to the Congress, to the press and to others," Knowlton recalled. "Every member of the 104th and 105th Congress was provided documented proof of the criminal cover-up. Every major newspaper and media outlet including the network news, *Dateline*, *Nightline*, *20/20*, *Larry King Live*, the *Wall Street Journal*, the *Washington Post*, the *New York Times*, the *Washington Times*, the *Los Angeles Times*, the *Chicago Tribune*, *Newsweek*, *Time*, *US News and World Report*, CNN and countless others ignored us."[416]

This provocative chain of events raises questions about the Clintons' strong-arming behavior that shouldn't be shoved under the carpet.

CHAPTER 16

WHITE HOUSE FOR SALE

"I don't think there is any doubt that some of the factors in his pardon were attributable to his large gifts. In my opinion, that was disgraceful."

—Jimmy Carter on Clinton's pardon of
billionaire swindler Marc Rich[417]

In one of his last moves in office, President Clinton cemented his reputation of being one of the most notorious grifters to ever occupy the oval office. This was of course the precursor to the Lyndon Johnson–like wheeling and dealing that would engulf the Bill, Hillary & Chelsea Clinton Foundation in 2015. President Clinton gave a pardon to billionaire swindler Marc Rich, then a fugitive. In return, Rich's ex-wife Denise gave Clinton millions of dollars for his library. It was Arkansas pay-for-play politics at its worst. The story of how it happened is breathtaking.

Convicted Ponzi-schemer Stephen Hoffenberg was vying for a pardon at the same time. Hoffenberg went down in a stunning $460 million scam and was using Democratic power broker Ben Barnes to broker the deal. Hoffenberg said Clinton let it be known that a million dollars was not enough to secure what he was after. As you will see, Rich circumvented the normal, legal review process and secured a tainted pardon.

Clinton's controversial pardon of financier Marc Rich was a move that even earned the ire of former president Jimmy Carter.[418] What did Rich need to be pardoned for and why would Clinton consider granting the pardon?

Rich was indicted by Rudy Giuliani in 1983 on sixty-five criminal counts, was accused of wire fraud, racketeering, and even trading with Iran during the hostage crisis. During his indictment, Rich was residing in Switzerland, while his wife held court stateside.[419]

Denise Rich donated large sums of money to the Democratic Party during Clinton's tenure ($1,000,000) and would go on to donate $100,000 to Hillary's Senate campaign and close to $500,000 to the Clinton Library.[420]

Hamilton Jordan, a former chief of staff to President Jimmy Carter argued in a *WSJ* editorial in 2001 that the Clintons were in fact "The First Grifters."[421]

Jordan would go on to outline the very detailed and complex process that surrounds a presidential pardon: history of the case, substantive arguments for and against the pardon, written recommendations from the prosecuting team. Mr. Jordan asserts that, due to a lack of a written history or paper trail of such a process, Clinton and his team worked outside the framework to push through the pardon of Mr. Rich.

Below is Hamilton's check list of requirements for a pardon during the Carter presidency.

- A formal, written analysis of the case by the Justice Department.
- A description of the crime and a history of the trial.
- The written statements and recommendations of the prosecuting team that won the conviction.
- A listing of the substantive arguments, for and against the pardon and a statement of any extenuating circumstances that justify the review of the case.

- The formal and written recommendations of the Justice Department (usually the attorney general in high-profile cases like Patricia Hearst or Marc Rich) and of the White House counsel.

Jack Quinn, a former White House counsel, persuaded Clinton to pardon Rich, who was now a current client. It seems as though Clinton let his decision rest solely on the recommendation of the accused attorney, bypassing the process Jordan outlined in his analysis published by the *Wall Street Journal*.

According to congressional testimony, only Deputy Attorney General Eric Holder and Mr. Quinn discussed the Rich pardon, but even those conversations were said to have been limited and obviously lopsided in scope.

Neil A. Lewis's account of the case and history surrounding presidential pardons also drew attention to Rich pardon.

"Things had plainly broken down in the last three or four months of the Clinton administration," said Margaret Love, a Washington lawyer who spent many years in the Justice Department handling pardons and served as the main pardon attorney from 1990 to 1997.

"You knew that in certain cases over the years like George Steinbrenner there was always a certain amount of persuasion going on," she said, referring to the principal owner of the Yankees, who had conspired to make illegal donations to President Nixon and was pardoned by President Reagan in his final days in office. "But just about all the pardons still went through the Justice Department," she said, including Mr. Steinbrenner's.

Mrs. Love would surmise that during each previous modern presidency, pardons with the exception of Nixon and a few other high-profile instances, would almost entirely be handled by the Justice Department and not the White House.[422]

However, during the Clinton presidency, Love argued that the White House took a much more active role in the pardon process and utilized the presidential pardon more so than other modern presidents.

This change in tides and the eventual pardon of Marc Rich put Clinton in the hotseat with the most recent Democratic president, Jimmy Carter.

Carter railed against the pardon and called it "disgraceful."

"I don't think there is any doubt that some of the factors in his pardon were attributable to his large gifts. In my opinion, that was disgraceful."

From Arkansas to Pennsylvania Avenue, the Clintons' appetite for graft and Boss Tweed–esque political quid pro quo arrangements never changed.

Trading favors, profiteering, and living outside the law are commonplace for House Clinton. Whether it's the Marc Rich scandal, or the (insert scandal list here), fellow Democrat and liberal Hamilton Jordan is spot on in proclaiming the Clintons to be the quintessential grifters. It's what they do.

Hillary's love of money would also mar the Clintons' early political career. In another example of elite deviance, Hillary would turn a one-thousand-dollar investment into a hefty return, courtesy of a wired businessman in Arkansas. This too was a precursor to the wholesale money grab that the Clintons would stage, utilizing the nexus of power at the State Department.

In one of the earliest scandals to outline Hillary and Bill Clinton's bare greed and rampant disregard for the rules, Mrs. Clinton parlayed $1,000 into over $100,000 over the course of ten months trading cattle futures.[423]

The trading began as Bill Clinton was the attorney general for the state of Arkansas and would continue until he was elected governor. The original investment was worth a market value of $12,000 dollars, but records from the Chicago Mercantile Exchange show that Clinton had only $1,000 in her account at the time of the investments.[424]

So how could someone with only $1,000 secure an investment in cattle futures worth $12,000? Relying on an experienced futures trader who was tied to one of Arkansas's biggest employers, that is how.

James Blair, a friend of Clinton, advised her on the trades and confirmed that they were processed before the paperwork was complete or approved. But Blair was not the only industry insider who was known to underwrite investments on behalf of Clinton, as she had Blair's business partner Robert L. "Red" Bone willingly approve of Blair's orders on Clinton's behalf . . . even if she did not have the cash to cover them.

Blair gloated that he had paid Bone over $800,000 in commission at the time, and that "he did not ask questions" when approached about the sweetheart deal he was brokering for Clinton, then a wife to a high-profile state official.[425]

Why would Blair go through so much trouble moving before approval of paperwork and funding Hillary's investments? During the late seventies, Blair was also the lead legal counsel to Arkansas's top employer, Tyson Foods. He claimed he advised Hillary out of friendship, but when have we known the Clintons or anyone surrounding them to do something as a "friend"? Observers rightfully acknowledged that the investment scheme was a quick way for one of the state's largest employers and companies to curry favor with the attorney general, and eventual governor.

It's extremely unusual given that the trends for that market during the time that the trades were placed were extremely volatile and unpredictable, yet Clinton walked away with a $99,000 gain. Her frequency of trades and net profit were also far outside normal returns for investors buying the same amount. Experts called the trades "unusual."[426]

A first taste of how she and her husband, Bill, could parlay elected office into financial gain, it seems.

Clinton would go on to downplay the role that Blair and his associates played in placing and underwriting her trades, but experts have debunked this and confirmed that it would be near impossible for Clinton not to have had a hand in the trades, even at a basic level that would allow her to understand the process.

The trades and the way in which they were handled speak volumes about the hypocrisy that the Clintons employ to this day. Since the start of their residence as public figures, both Bill and Hillary have long railed against the "gilded greed" of Wall Street and, more specifically, investors who trade futures.[427]

But as with nearly everything involving the well-learned grifters from Arkansas, what they say and what they do are always two different things.

Billed as one of the "Top Ten Scandals Involving Hillary Clinton You May Have Forgotten," the cattle futures debacle is something we should all be reminded of.[428]

PART 4

THE CRUDE AND CORRUPTIBLE CLINTONS

CHAPTER 17

PRISON BLOOD

"In so many ways it reminds you of Nazi Germany. . . . These guys had the power over a captive audience to make money from human beings."

—Journalist Mike Galster[429]

In the 1980s, Bill Clinton's political cronies were selling HIV- and Hepatitis C–laced prison inmate blood to the world blood market. Unscreened prisoners would sell their blood for $7 (in prison scrip) per plasma unit to politically connected blood brokers who would then put it up for sale on the world blood market for $50 per plasma unit.[430] The company that brokered the blood was Health Management Associates, Inc. (HMA).

By 1985, the business practices of HMA were coming under close scrutiny in regards to poor health assessment, record keeping, and unqualified staff hiring. Following a state investigation of HMA, the company was allowed to retain its contract because of heavy political influence and the "lobbying efforts of HMA's president, Leonard Dunn, a Pine Bluff banker who later worked on Clinton's 1990 gubernatorial campaign."[431] That contract lasted through 1986 until it was finally doomed by a critical report.

The problems with HMA were a warning flag.

Pine Bluff Biologicals took up and greatly expanded the low-cost blood acquisitions to include other Arkansas state prison units. "But donor-screening problems persisted. In 1989, a prisoner who had been forbidden to donate on account of disease was able to sell plasma twenty-three times after he transferred from the Pine Bluff Diagnostics Unit to Cummins."[432] The company was carelessly taking blood from Arkansas prisoners who had been infected with HIV and Hepatitis C, and the diseased blood was being sold on the world market, specifically to Canadians. A whopping 20,000 Canadians were infected with Hepatitis C and another 1,000 were infected with HIV from the contaminated plasma.[433]

In March 1991, reporter Mara Leveritt wrote a story for the *Arkansas Times* about the prison blood sales. Later in 1998, whistle-blower Mike Galster, under the pseudonym Michael Sullivan, wrote the novel *Blood Trail,* based on the scandal. "Although fiction, *Blood Trail* evolved from Sullivan's meditations on the true, tragic and ongoing story of a blood contamination that infected as many as 80,000 people in Canada," the inside flap read. "Thousands have died, many more have death sentences, and still more will suffer for life."[434]

In the 1980s, Galster was running orthopedic clinics in the Arkansas state prison system. Because of his access, Galster knew there were big problems.

Blood Trail was Galster's way of telling the world what really happened. In May 1999, as a reward for his honesty, Galster's clinic was burned to the ground. On the same night, the offices of a Canadian hemophiliac victims' rights group were broken into. Who was behind these crimes?

Around the time that Galster's book hit the shelves in 1998, *Salon* published a detailed article on the blood scandal by Arkansas reporter Suzi Parker. Parker's fine piece of reporting was an indictment of the Clinton administration in Arkansas, which looked the other way while political cronies were making money selling dirty prison blood to the world blood plasma market.

Parker's exposé pointed out that Arkansas was the last state in the union to allow prison blood to be brokered. The crooked business was practiced until 1994, when, after the Clinton years, the program was shut down. Parker fingered two Clinton cronies who played key roles in keeping the lucrative prison blood deal going: Leonard Dunn, a president of HMA who was very close to Bill Clinton, and a black lawyer, Richard Mays, who received $25,000 as an ombudsman for the troubled program. There were allegations that Mays's compensation was basically a bribe paid by HMA to keep the blood program alive.

"Problems with the prison plasma program were well known to Clinton throughout the 1980s," and "In 1986, Clinton's state police investigated problems at the prison and found little cause for concern, while an outside investigator looked at the same allegations and found dozens of safety violations," Parker wrote.[435]

Clinton allowed the dangerous program to continue unfettered because his cronies were making money off of it.

Parker interviewed Galster, who said the program was a "crime against humanity." Galster attested that he had seen prisoners given illegal drugs as payment for their blood plasma. Galster told Parker that he saw inmates who "appeared jaundiced and very sick. When I would ask if they had just had a blood test, they would say, 'No, I've just given plasma.' It was clear they were sick."[436]

Parker's article quoted former prisoner John Schock, who was convinced that he got Hepatitis C from a dirty needle in the "pretty shoddy" program. "They had inmates doing things they shouldn't have been doing. They would let people who was sick bleed . . . ain't no telling what they had. They didn't check all the time."[437]

The article exposed corruption and carelessness that resulted in tragic health problems for tens of thousands of innocent people. Parker pointed out that most prison plasma programs were shut down in the early 1980s especially as the AIDS crisis was picking up steam. The FDA asked companies making blood products to refrain from obtaining them from prisons and inmates because many inmates engage in risky behaviors.

Despite the FDAs warnings, Clinton allowed the prison blood program to continue. The FDA had also shut down the Arkansas plasma program for several months in 1983 because Arkansas prisoners with Hepatitis B had been allowed to donate blood.

In 1985, after the Arkansas Board of Corrections had hired the Institute for Law and Policy Planning (ILPP), an independent group, to investigate HMA, and after ILPP had issued a scathing report detailing the forty areas where HMA had violated its state contract, Clinton made sure that HMA kept getting the contract. That happened during the same year that, as stated above, Mays received $25,000 to be an "ombudsman." Some said that money was a kickback from HMA to a Clinton insider to facilitate that HMA retain its contract. Investigators never found the contract for Mays that spelled out his official duties . . . they just knew he received a large amount of quick and easy money from HMA.[438]

"In so many ways it reminds you of Nazi Germany. . . . These guys had the power over a captive audience to make money from human beings," Galster said. "This I know, without the governor's support and protection, this disease-riddled system would have been shut down by 1982."[439]

Galster's harsh words about Clinton were published in *Salon* in December 1998. When the Galster Orthopedic Laboratories later went up in flames and $200,000 in damages occurred, the firefighters who spent six hours fighting the fire suspected that it was arson.[440]

Arkansas journalist Suzi Parker was also convinced she was a victim of a Clinton-directed intimidation campaign. Parker's second story on this topic was published by *Salon* on February 25, 1999.

The article chronicled a group of Canadian victims, approximately 1,000 hemophiliacs, who had filed a $660 million class action lawsuit against the Canadian government and two Canadian companies involved in importing and supplying the tainted blood plasma to Canadians.

Parker's article had some other big news in it. The lawyer for the Canadian victims, David Harvey, "said he is seeking a deposition of President Clinton into what occurred in the Arkansas prison system while he was governor during the 1980s."

The story also revealed that the Canadian hemophiliacs were on the cusp of suing the FDA, the states of Arkansas and Louisiana, the prison systems of those two states, and the companies, such as the Clinton-connected HMA, that ran the blood plasma extraction programs for those prisons in those states. "The suit could also name the president if evidence is found that Clinton knew about repeated FDA violations and international plasma recalls, yet failed to exercise his executive power to shut down the Arkansas Department of Correction plasma industry," Parker wrote.[441]

Tens of thousands of Canadians (and others around the world) caught deadly diseases. Parker reported that 7,000 Canadians were expected to die because of their infections caused by the tainted blood. No one else in the media at the time was covering the blood scandal, and following her first piece "Parker began receiving mysterious, threatening phone calls in the middle of the night."[442]

In early 1999, Suzi Parker attended a press conference for the lawyers for the Canadian hemophiliac victims. "While attending the press conference Parker says she knew was being watched and followed, perhaps by governmental agents."[443] Parker told author Candice Jackson that "It was creepy," but she kept reporting on the blood scandal.

Jackson directly tied the firebombing of the plasma scandal whistleblower's clinic to the burglarizing of the hemophiliac group's office the same night. "The hemophiliac group had been working closely with the whistleblower to prepare the threatened lawsuit on behalf of Canadians infected with Hepatitis C and HIV from tainted Arkansas prisoners' blood. Between the intimidating phone calls she'd been receiving and the violent arson and burglary patently designed to deter investigation into this scandal, journalist Suzi Parker got the message and backed off."[444]

Parker told Jackson that she is convinced the Clintons were behind the terror tactics that successfully intimidated her from further reporting on the Clinton-Arkansas tainted prison blood scandal. In 2012, Parker again confirmed she had been a victim of a terror campaign.

We contacted Parker via email in October 2012:

> Suzi, I have a few questions about your experiences investigating the tainted prison blood scandal in Arkansas. I understand you were a victim of a harassment/intimidation campaign. Is that true? If so, do you think the Clintons were behind it? Or perhaps related business parties who were benefiting from the tainted blood trade? Would you be willing to answer some questions and/or trade information on your experiences on this story?

Parker replied quickly:

> Thanks for the email. I am sorry but that chapter of my journalism career is closed. I was the victim of such a campaign but have nothing else to say on the matter. Thanks again for your interest.
>
> Cheers,
> Suzi

All too often, we find a shroud of secrecy surrounds the Clintons' behavior. People are afraid to go public with any criticism of this powerful couple.

CHAPTER 18

CLINTON FAMILY SECRETS

"President Bush says human cloning is morally wrong. Surprisingly, this is one area where both he and former President Clinton actually agree. In fact, Clinton said today that he believes humans should be created the old-fashioned way, liquored up in a cheap motel."

—Jay Leno

In 2013, the *Globe* interviewed a twenty-seven-year-old man named Danney Williams. Williams had never met his fabulously wealthy father, one of the most famous people in the world, but the puffy eyes, the bulbous nose, and the big, mischievous smile were unmistakable. Williams told the *Globe* that he just wanted to meet his dad and shake his hand: "I read he doesn't have long to live and I want to meet him face to face before he dies. I just want to shake his hand and say 'Hi Dad,' before he dies. I'd like to have a relationship with Chelsea, too. She's my half-sister."[445]

That same year, a New York–based organization, the National Father's Day Committee, named Bill Clinton "Father of the Year." The same organization had awarded John Edwards the title a few years prior. That is the same John Edwards who cheated on his wife while she was dying of cancer. Edwards had an affair and a baby with an enthralled female supporter named Rielle Hunter.

Chelsea Clinton got up to say what a great dad Bill was. Two people not present for the ceremony were Danney Williams and his mother, Bobbie Ann.

Star reported the Danney Williams story in 1990 and then announced they would conduct a DNA test. They claimed to have DNA from Bill's semen on Monica's dress. But the Ken Starr panel never supplied Bill's DNA to anyone. Clinton, plotting a 1992 presidential run, was on high alert.

The DNA sample that was used in the paternity test was the sample that came from a book about the Lewinsky/Starr/Jones case. You could rest assured that they did not publish the correct DNA data of a sitting president. We have personally scoured the records. There was no information on record of the special prosecutor giving DNA to any "author." There was no test. It's bogus. *Time* and the *Washington Post* stories about test results being negative were planted by Clinton flacks. On January 9, the *Drudge Report* broke the news that *Time* magazine had learned that the DNA tests cleared Clinton. But *Star* announced nothing.

Interestingly, DNA experts interviewed said that it would have been "impossible" to make any definitive comparison based on the information provided in the Starr report according to *Bill and Hillary: The Marriage*, by Christopher P. Andersen, but then there was no blood sample from Starr anyway.

"We planted that *Star* piece," a veteran Clinton operative told Roger Stone over a mint julep after his man was reelected over Stone's old boss Senator Bob Dole, to whom he served as a staff assistant in the U.S. Senate. "There was no blood test." The plant was then peddled to the *Washington Post* by Clintonistas. The *Post* bit. The bogus test was recycled.

The *Washington Post* justified never having reported the true story. The *Post* and others rushed to publicize a bogus claim that DNA tests had proven that Thomas Jefferson had fathered a child by a black slave. The British journal that first published the claim has now admitted that it was inaccurate but the *Post* had given it big play. Double standard for connected elites Bill and Hillary?

The *Globe* advanced the narrative on February 18, 1992. The *Globe*'s article came a few weeks after a competing tabloid ran a blockbuster story about Bill's affair with Gennifer Flowers.

Bobbi Ann Williams recalled how she had met Clinton in 1984 and had multiple trysts with the cocaine-addled governor. The housing projects in Little Rock were located about five blocks from the Arkansas governor's mansion where Bill went for jogs. Bill Clinton was thirty-eight when he met Williams, with whom he had at least thirteen trysts.

"I was twenty-four and was working as a prostitute at the Johnson apartment building on Seventeenth and Main Street when I first met Bill," Williams recalled. "Me and some girls were walking around Spring Street near the governor's mansion when we saw him come jogging down the street in a tight T-shirt. . . . I was dressed real sexy in this tight little skirt, a halter top nothing under it, and a wig with curls. . . . The other girls were pretty excited. . . . They knew about the governor's jogging trips. He'd pick you up right there on the street. . . . My friends and me were disappointed by the governor that day. He just stopped to talk to us. . . . But about three days later, we saw him again. . . . This time, he picked me—and said that he knew a place where we could go have sex."[446]

Williams said she and Bill then trysted behind a row of bushes. She gave Bill oral sex and then he gave her $200.

"When it was done, he gave me two hundred dollars. . . . He talked all the time I was doing it [giving Clinton oral sex]. Then after he was done, he pulled up his pants and ran off jogging. . . . A couple of weeks later, he said he wanted to have an orgy. He said that he'd pay four hundred dollars apiece. There was me and two friends—and we jumped at his offer. . . . That was a lot of money for us in those days. He said he'd pick us up in a white car on the corner of Main Street at seven o'clock that night. . . . We were waiting when this big white car—it wasn't a limo, but it was a big car with tinted windows [the governor's car was a Lincoln Town Car]—drove up and stopped beside us.

"We just ran to the car, opened the door and got right in the back with the governor," Williams continued. "He knew that we liked to drink Hennessy cognac and he had a bottle and some glasses with him. . . . He was really nice. He made us drinks and we talked and laughed. He was a funny guy. He liked saying dirty things—but they were funny. . . . We called him Bill right from the start. He was like any other man. He wanted just one thing: sex. The only difference was that he paid more money—a lot more. And all we had to do was what he told us. . . . And he paid us right there in the car. That made us feel real good because we didn't have to wait for our money."

Williams remembered exactly how to get to the country cabin of Clinton's mother, Virginia Kelley.

We left on the John Barrow Road and traveled about an hour to this little house in the woods.

The house wasn't a big family place or anything. It was kind of small with a fireplace and a small bed. But it was pretty inside and nicely decorated.

The driver stayed outside smoking cigarettes. When we got in, we all just took our clothes off. Bill smiled and flopped down on his back on the bed, just laying there, stretched out naked.

He liked looking at us. We all there crawled into bed with him and started playing around. We played like that for a long time, changing positions. He liked using all the dirty words he could think of for the woman's body parts. And we could tell he liked it when we talked dirty to him.

He also watched us girls make love to each other. He told us what to do. That really got him turned on.

Finally, he was ready for straight sex and tried using a condom, but he took it off.

"I just don't like scumbags," Clinton said

I didn't care. It didn't matter to me. I guess we didn't think much about it. We were done in about three hours—and he surprised all of us with a fifty dollar tip apiece. We were really happy, and we giggled all the way back to Little Rock.[447]

Later that year, Clinton and Williams had a tryst at the downtown Little Rock Holiday Inn. Clinton would rent a room at the hotel under a fake name "William Clay." One of the Arkansas state troopers on his security detail would bring Williams to his room. Clinton paid her $200 for sex, and when they were done, Clinton would slip out the back side of the hotel while one of the state troopers would take Williams back to the housing projects.[448]

It was around that time Williams became pregnant. "I was still working the street into the fourth month I was carrying Bill's baby," recalled Williams. "And Bill got a special kick out of having sex with pregnant woman. He said that pregnancy makes gals hotter. When I told him that he was the father of my baby, he just laughed. He rubbed my big belly and said, 'Girl, that can't be my baby.' But I knew it was. I just had this kind of woman's feeling that this was his child."[449]

Danney Lee Williams, Jr.—named for the man his mother had married—was born on December 7, 1985. "When my baby was born, he was as white as any white child," said Williams in May 2013. "I told myself, 'This is Bill Clinton's baby because he's the only white man I slept with that month [when she got pregnant].'" [450]

Danney's grandmother, Sylvia Howard, in an interview with the *Globe*, said that she "told Bobbie Ann to keep her mouth shut as she could destroy Clinton's career in politics, and for doing that, he might then destroy her." Lucille Bolton, the sister of Bobbie Ann, said, "When she told me she was carrying Bill Clinton's baby, I was very skeptical. I didn't believe Bobbie Ann. But then I saw that little baby in University Hospital. He was white. That is when I started believing my sister. And as Danney got older, he started looking more and more like the governor."[451]

One of the top opposition researchers for George H. W. Bush's disastrous 1992 reelection campaign told me on the basis of anonymity that the Bush campaign had nailed down the fact Clinton was Danney Williams's father and "Bobbie Anne had intimate knowledge of the layout of Clinton's mother's home. There was no doubt," he said.

My consulting business partner Charlie Black, who emerged as a confidant and consigliere for Bushes Sr. and Jr. after helping engineer Ronald Reagan's rise from the '76 ashes to become president, told me that the Bushes knew about the biracial son and the circumstances of his birth and elected not to lob the dirtball at Bill. "The old man thinks he will beat Clinton without it," said Black. "He doesn't want to go there."

Soon after Williams gave birth to Danney in 1985, she was sent to jail for prostitution and drug crimes, and Bolton was chosen to be Danney's guardian.

"I was so furious over the situation that I went to the governor's mansion last year to talk to Clinton about Danney," said Bolton. "But I couldn't get past his aides, who listened to my story and then sent me packing. They took my name and address and asked me some questions about the boy, but I never heard another word from them."[452]

As time went on, Williams became more assured that the baby was Clinton's. "The older he got, the more he started looking like his daddy Bill," said Williams.[453]

Following Danney's birth, local Little Rock black activist and restaurant owner Robert "Say" McIntosh took it upon himself to publicize Clinton's paternity of Danney. McIntosh did it with fliers he spread all over Little Rock. McIntosh had justification for his attack. Years earlier, Clinton had made a promise to McIntosh that he did not keep. Clinton had promised McIntosh some state grant money to help develop his sweet potato pie business.

McIntosh's flier read:

The Hottest Thing Going: Bill Clinton's Dick Will Keep Him From Running for President of the United States of America.

Please help me raise money to take care of [this] black baby, the "black sheep of the family." This baby is by a black woman. This picture is furnished by the Righteous Rev. Tommy Knots. Rev. Knots is an aide to Hillary Clinton at the Rose Law Firm. After he did a six-month investigation, God told him to bring it to me. All Clinton is willing to do for the mother is keep her out of jail and prison.[454]

Newsmax later reported that "Reverend Knots became involved, according to McIntosh, after Danney's mom contacted him at the Rose Law Firm about her son. She gave Knots the photo and told him that the governor wouldn't take care of the child. Bobbie Ann Williams had sought out Knots undoubtedly hoping that the news would reach one of Rose's leading lawyers, Hillary Clinton."[455]

Despite the intersession by Reverend Knots, the Clintons would not acknowledge Danney as Bill's son nor would they pay any child support. "During the 1980 election, Clinton agreed to pay me $25,000 to have Yarnell's Ice Cream Company manufacture my pie mix," the flier also proclaimed.[456]

McIntosh had protesters follow Clinton around with signs asking for "Just One Drop" of blood so there could be a paternity test. A frazzled Clinton got his press secretary, Susie Whitacre, to meet with McIntosh in an attempt to silence him. "McIntosh said she never denied Bobbie Ann's claim."

"Bill Clinton has been with enough black women to cast a Tarzan movie. And he's got a little black son out there living in poverty," McIntosh said.[457]

In 1992, when the *Globe* first broke the story, Bobbie Ann Williams subjected herself to two lie detector tests. She passed with flying colors.

"'Little Rock is a small town in a small state," said State Trooper L. D. Brown. "Clinton was like God here and acted out all his fantasies. Buddy Young, another state trooper, was Clinton's driver. Young would take the governor and Williams to Clinton's mother's cabin. Clinton never doubted for a moment that his people would keep their mouths shut about his habits."[458, 459]

Towards the end of 1992, Steve Dinari, head of the Ross Perot campaign in Illinois, contacted Clinton's communications director George Stephanopoulos and told him that he had solid information on Clinton's spurious offspring. This story was covered well in December 28, 1998, by *Newsmax*, which has has since been scrubbed from its web archives.

Stephanopoulos put Dinari on blast. "I guarantee you that if you do this you'll never work in Democratic politics again," the communications director said. "It's completely bullshit! If you went on the radio and said that Bill Clinton is the father of an illegitimate black child, you will be laughed at. People will think you're crazy. . . . You will be embarrassed before the national press corps. People will think, nobody will believe you, and people will think you're scum."[460]

The crazy thing: the story was completely true.

The details of the story came to the attention of Tom Luce, a heavyweight Republican lawyer in Dallas. Luce was Ross Perot's personal attorney. Perot, a self-funded independent in the 1992 race, had decided to release the information publicly. A private detective for Perot confirmed that Clinton was Danney's father after Luce paid for an extensive private investigation.

Clinton operative George Stephanopoulos blocked that investigation. Stephanopoulos would assent to a top media job with ABC and skewered *Clinton Cash* author Peter Schweitzer in an ABC interview, without revealing the $75,000 he gave the Bill, Hillary & Chelsea Clinton Foundation.

Clinton froze Stephanopoulos out when the diminutive aide cashed in with a tell-all that did not flatter Bubba. "Little Cocksucker"

Hillary called him according to a Hillary staffer I socialized with in Washington. The book made him a superstar at ABC. His last contract was for $100 million. Between the money and the treatment of Schweitzer, George was trying to buy back in.

As Carl Limbacher of *Newsmax* reported:

It was the day before the 1992 election. Stephanopoulos was in Clinton's Little Rock campaign headquarters nervously anticipating the next day's returns when a secretary told him that Dinari was on the phone and "he wants to talk to someone confidentially."

Stephanopoulos' side of their conversation was captured on videotape by a film crew preparing a documentary on the 1992 Clinton-Gore campaign, which was released the next year under the title "The War Room."

Dinari was told by Stephanopoulos that the story had already been investigated and rejected by "every major national news organization," which, according to several sources close to the Danny Williams story, is altogether untrue.

Dinari informed Stephanopoulos, then campaign communications director, that he had names, addresses, and phone numbers of people who could back the story up. In a tense moment of election-eve panic, the Clinton wunderkind barked into the phone:

"It's completely bullshit! If you went on the radio and said that Bill Clinton is the father of an illegitimate black child, you will be laughed at. People will think you're crazy. . . . You will be embarrassed before the national press corps. People will think, nobody will believe you, and people will think you're scum."

Then Stephanopoulos changed tack, pointing out to Dinari that his cooperation on the Danny Williams bombshell would not go unnoticed: "If you don't do it, it will cause you some temporary pain with people who tomorrow aren't going to matter. And you have a campaign that understands that in a difficult time you did something right."

With a video camera rolling just a few feet away, Stephanopou-los was quick to qualify his hint of possible favors for Dinari's silence, adding: "I mean, it doesn't mean anything. We can't do anything for you specifically or anything like that."

Stephanopoulos would use the same tactics four years later, when similarly damaging charges surfaced in a book by a friend of mine and FBI agent who had just retired from his post at the Clinton White House. Gary Aldrich's "Unlimited Access" featured allegations of illicit presidential sex and an insider's view of an un-precedented breakdown in White House security.

George Stephanopoulos knows to this day Bill Clinton is a dead beat dad and granddad.

Newsmax also reported that "Danney's aunt, disturbed by the publicity, phoned the governor's mansion and actually got Hillary on the line. In the conversation, which lasted two or three minutes, Hillary asked, 'Is it true that he has this illegitimate child?' and gave Lucille the number of a security agency to call in order 'to get the publicity to stop.'"

Hillary's private detectives were not able to silence McIntosh, and he started to run the same exposure campaign on Bill Clinton when he ran for president in 1992. At that point the Clintons made a deal with Say McIntosh—a pardon for his son Tommy McIntosh in exchange for silence. Tommy was in jail on major drug charges and not eligible for parole until 2010. Say zipped his lips for the rest of the 1992 general election, and in early 1993, as Bill Clinton was be-ing sworn in as president, his son received his pardon by the acting governor of Arkansas, a Clinton ally.

"On January 20, 1993, the day Bill Clinton was inaugurated as President, Tommy McIntosh was pardoned," said Joyce Milton. "The papers were signed by Dr. Jerry Jewell, president pro tempore of the state senate and acting governor for the four days during which Clinton's successor, Jim Guy Tucker, was in Washington attending the inaugural festivities. Dr. Jewell, a dentist and one of Little Rock's

most prominent black political figures, later said he was just execut-
ing paperwork prepared by the governor's office."[461]

Subsequent to Tommy McIntosh's pardon in 1993, reporter Jerry
Seper of the *Washington Times* ran into Say McIntosh. He bragged
about the deal he had made with the Clintons. "Those who question
my credibility should ask themselves, 'If there was no deal, how
did this happen?' How did my son get out of prison eighteen years
before he was eligible for parole?"

After Clinton became president, the haunted Arkansan issued
a White House memorandum on the topic of responsible paternity
around Father's Day 1995:

THE WHITE HOUSE
Washington
June 16, 1995
MEMORANDUM FOR THE HEADS OF EXECUTIVE DEPART-
MENTS AND AGENCIES

SUBJECT: Supporting the Role of Fathers in Families

I am firm in my belief that the future of our Republic depends on
strong families and that committed fathers are essential to those
families. I am also aware that strengthening fathers' involvement
with their children cannot be accomplished by the Federal Government alone; the solutions lie in the hearts and consciences of individual fathers and the support of the families and communities in
which they live. However, there are ways for a flexible, responsive
Government to help support men in their roles as fathers.

Therefore, today I am asking the Federal agencies to assist me
in this effort, I direct all executive departments and agencies to review every program, policy, and initiative (hereinafter referred to
collectively as "programs") that pertains to families to:

ensure, where appropriate, and consistent with program objectives, that they seek to engage and meaningfully include fathers;

proactively modify those programs that were designed to serve primarily mothers and children, where appropriate and consistent with program objectives, to explicitly include fathers and strengthen their involvement with their children; include evidence of father involvement and participation, where appropriate, in measuring the success of the programs; and incorporate fathers, where appropriate, in government initiated research regarding children and their families.

I ask the departments and agencies to provide an initial report on the results of the review to the Vice President through the national Performance Review within 90 days of the date of this memorandum.

The information gained from this review will be combined with information gathered through the Vice President's "Father to Father" initiative and other father involvement programs to determine the direction of those programs for the future. The National Performance Review, together with the Domestic Policy Council, will recommend further action based on the results of this review.

William J. Clinton[462]

In 1998, when Danney was thirteen, his aunt Lucille Bolton told *Newsmax* that there were "no buts, there's no ifs, there's no supposes about Danny's bloodline to the president.'"[463]

Newsmax Media noted that Bolton had been the guardian of Danney Williams for years. Bolton told Limbacher that she even had a personal conversation with Hillary Clinton about Danney Williams's circumstances and she fruitlessly asked for help. On another occasion, Bolton and Danney showed up at the Arkansas governor's mansion and were turned away.

Later that year, Newsmax Media followed up with another article. Bolton declared that both she and Williams's other sister, Shirley Howard, wanted Clinton to take a DNA test to officially confirm him as the father of his abandoned son Danney. Bolton told

Newsmax that men claiming to be FBI agents (most likely impersonating them) showed up at Danney's home two days before she spoke to Newsmax.com. When Howard answered the door, the two men identified themselves as FBI agents.

"Shirley said they gave her a card and told her she should get a lawyer—and then she should contact them," said Bolton. "I asked Shirley, 'You mean they didn't show you a badge or anything?' They didn't, so she just slammed the door in their faces. So the only way she's going to do any talking is through me."

Both Bolton and Howard believed the visit was a ruse perpetrated by reporters chasing the story. What Bolton couldn't explain was why reporters would advise her sister to hire a lawyer. Moreover, as any good reporter would know, impersonating a federal agent is a felony.

On December 15, 1998, *Newsmax* published another follow-up article. Reporter Carl Limbacher interviewed Say McIntosh, who said, "If you see Danney, you can tell it's definitely his kid. I've met him, talked to him. Danney isn't black."[464]

Following the *Newsmax* articles, the Clinton administration issued an interesting press release:

December 31, 1998
STATEMENT BY THE PRESIDENT
THE WHITE HOUSE
Office of the Press Secretary
(Hilton Head, South Carolina)
For Immediate Release December 31, 1998
STATEMENT BY THE PRESIDENT

Since I became President, my Administration has waged an unprecedented campaign to make deadbeat parents pay the support their children need and deserve. Today, we have new evidence that our efforts are working: child support collections have gone up a record 80 percent since I took office, from $8 billion in 1992 to an estimated $14.4 billion in 1998. But we must do more to ensure that each and every parent honors his obligation to his children. That is why my new budget will propose new funds to help identify, investigate, and prosecute deadbeat parents. This effort will include new investigative teams in five regions of the country to identify, analyze, and investigate cases for criminal prosecution, and an eightfold increase in legal support personnel to help prosecute these new cases.

With continued commitment and this new funding, we can do even more to support our nation's children.

A simultaneous press release was issued by the government:

President Clinton Proposes New Child Support Crackdown and Announces a Record 80 Percent Increase in Child Support Collections
December 31, 1998

Today, President Clinton announced a new child support crackdown aimed at the nation's most egregious child support violators. Despite record child support collections, there are still too many parents who flagrantly ignore their obligations to their children, and the President will propose to spend $46 million to identify, investigate, and prosecute these deadbeat parents. The President took this action today as he released new evidence that his Administration's child support efforts are working: child support collections have gone up a record 80 percent since he took office, from $8 billion in 1992 to an estimated $14.4 billion in 1998.

New Record Child Support Collections

Since taking office, President Clinton has made child support enforcement a top priority, and those efforts are paying off for children across America. New figures released by the US Department of Health and Human Services today show that child support collections have gone up a record 80 percent since the President took office, from $8 billion in 1992 to an estimated $14.4 billion in 1998. Moreover, new figures show that the federal government has collected $1.1 billion this year by withholding federal tax refunds from deadbeat parents. Nearly 1.3 million families in all 50 states benefited from these tax refunds, which totaled $151 million in California, $63 million in Ohio, $52 million in Florida, and $48 million in New York (a state by state chart is available).

New Child Support Law Enforcement Initiative

To ensure that every parent pays the child support he owes, in June President Clinton signed into law the Deadbeat Parents Punishment Act, creating two new categories of federal felonies for the most egregious child support violators, a measure he had called for in his 1997 State of the Union address. Many prosecutors say they would be able to prosecute even more child support cases if they had legal staff dedicated to the issue and if they received referrals after a complete financial investigation had been conducted.

The Deadbeat Dad press release went on to tout "New Investigative Resources" and "New prosecutorial Resources." It boasted "State child support offices will refer their most serious child support cases to these sites, where trained investigative staff will locate the violator, document information needed for prosecution, and then provide the investigated case to the appropriate prosecutor" and "With this new staff, the US Department of Justice expects to increase child support prosecutions significantly."

In 1999, Jay Leno made the Bobbie Ann Williams story the topic of one of his monologues. "An Arkansas prostitute is claiming that President Clinton is the father of her son and has submitted to a DNA test to prove it," said Leno. "And today the White House said it couldn't be possible. She must have just sat on Monica's dress . . . Who do you believe? A hooker or President Clinton? For most Americans that's a tough one. . . . Only President Clinton could distract people from a sex scandal with another sex scandal. Remember those innocent times of Monica Lewinsky? It seems like a hundred years ago, those innocent times we lived in back then. . . . The White House is still trying to put a positive spin on the whole thing. Today they said, 'Hey, at least he didn't have oral sex with the woman.'"[465]

On January 6, 1999, Matt Drudge published the following special report, called "WOMAN NAMES BILL CLINTON FATHER OF SON IN SHOCKING VIDEO CONFESSION":

In a shocking new videotaped confession viewed by the DRUDGE REPORT late Tuesday, an Arkansas woman claims that President Bill Clinton is the father of her 13-year old son.

He's been told all of his life by his mother that Bill Clinton is his father, and late last month, 13-year old Danney Williams of Arkansas underwent a DNA test to find out the truth.

The story of Bobbie Ann Williams and her child Danney hit world media and rocked the White House this week after it was revealed that STAR MAGAZINE and ace investigative reporter Richard Gooding have exclusively signed Williams and his family to a paternity showdown.

Test results could not be learned Tuesday night. Gooding and Star magazine editors offered few details on the status of the story, even to their closest associates.

"It is his," Ms. Williams tells PARAMOUNT's HARD COPY in a videotaped confession recently made by the syndicated TV show. With tears rolling down her face, Williams reveals intimate details about her relationship with Bill Clinton.

"He was good to me, he gave me money," she tells HARD COPY. "No, I'm not scared."

Also interviewed on the video is Williams' sister. She tells HARD COPY how she first doubted her sister's claims.

"I thought she was joking, you know, she was running around in the streets. . . . But when the kid was born, he looked just liked Bill Clinton.

"We would go to grocery stores, people would say 'That's Bill Clinton's son!' because he looks just like him!" the woman declares.

"Now that he's older—he even looks more like him. . . .

"Bill Clinton needs to take responsibility for his son, pay child support, like everyone else."

HARD COPY executives have not decided if and when they will air the interviews, which were conducted in Arkansas.[466]

In the year 2000, just prior to Father's Day, Clinton attempted to deflect the accusation by dedicating his presidential address to the topic of fatherhood. "Good morning," Clinton began. "Tomorrow America pauses to honor the countless contributions and obligations of fatherhood. When I think back on all the titles I've held, from attorney general of Arkansas to Governor to President, none of them comes close in importance and in fulfillment to the simple title of father."[467]

In the address, Bill talked about "the critical role fathers play in their children's lives" and how important it was for parents to be involved in their children's education: "Research now confirms that involvement of both parents in a child's education makes a positive difference, and that father involvement during infancy and early childhood also contributes to a child's emotional security and enhances problem solving in math and verbal skills."[468]

Bill talked about how important it was for noncustodial parents to be involved in their kids' lives. He also underscored how important child support payments were and how great the Clinton administration was at promoting them. Bill said for seven and a half years and that his administration had made child support a top priority.

Bill talked about "caring mothers and fathers" and about a new initiative he was supporting: "Supporting responsible fatherhood is good for children, good for families, good for our Nation. It's why we propose building on our progress with a $255 million responsible fatherhood initiative called 'Fathers Work/Families Win.' The fact is, many fathers can't provide financial and emotional support to their children, not because they're deadbeat but because they're dead-broke."[469]

Bill closed with, "As we prepare to celebrate the first Father's Day of the new century, let's do all we can to help more fathers live up to that title, not just through their financial support but also by becoming more active, loving participants in their children's lives."[470]

In 2007 Andrew Young, who was supporting Hillary for president, said, "Bill is every bit as black as Barack. He's probably gone with [had sex with] more black women than Barack."[471] The Clinton campaign was mortified at Young's remarks.

The Clintons have never flat out denied that Danney is Bill's son. The media has ignored Bubba's bastard for decades. Joe Klein decided to fictionalize this important information in his book *Primary Colors*. Klein's storyline, which concerned a young Southern governor dealing with the political dangers of fathering a love child with an underage African American girl before the New Hampshire primary, was the most dangerous kind of fiction.

Today in Arkansas, based on Bill Clinton's income as a Non-Custodial Parent and the fact that the number of children he would owe money for is just one (that we know of . . .), Bill Clinton would owe an amount of $717 (in 2014 dollars) per month in child support for Danney Williams.[472]

For eighteen years of unpaid child support that would come out to 216 missed payments of $717 which equals $154,872 that Clinton would owe to Danney's guardians. More importantly, Bill Clinton has never hugged his son, never told him that he loved him, never showed any interest in his life, and never showed he cared.

In 2013, the *Cleveland Challenger* published a story that pointed out that Clinton was credibly rumored to have sexual affairs with numerous other black women—among them former Miss Arkansas Lencola Sullivan and reporter Debra Mathis (who used to work at the same TV station as Gennifer Flowers). Larry Nichols, after he had his falling out with Clinton, used to follow him around under "total surveillance." Nichols discovered that "One of the people I cornered early on, one of the people I had literally seen Clinton with, was this black lady. She was about four foot eight. Now it's going to sound like I am exaggerating, but I am not. She was about four foot eight and had, yes, blonde hair. She weighed between 250 and 260 pounds. She had one or two, I think both front teeth were gold. This is who I caught Bill Clinton with."[473]

Nichols approached this woman and got her to talk about the governor. Nichols wanted to know about any "distinguishing characteristic" that Clinton might have in his private parts area.

"And that's when she told me [Bill] had a very, very small, almost to the point of what you would call deformed, penis," Nichols said. "I mean this guy is lacking badly, if you know what I mean. She said he was 'iddy biddy,' about two inches. Then, she said he had a fetish—he was just a wild man about oral sex. I mean he was just crazy. And then she told of a mole, she called it that, but it's actually a birthmark, on the outside of his left buttock."[474]

Two state troopers corroborated Nichols's story, stating that they had taken Clinton to see this woman.

"Clinton denied he fathered Danney with Bobbie Ann just like he at first lied about Gennifer Flowers and Lewinsky," the *Challenger* article said. "He claimed not to have sexually harassed Paula Jones but yet paid her $850,000 in an out of court settlement. Sitting in front of federal Special Prosecutor Ken Starr and facing impeachment loosened Clinton's lips enough to confess to sexing it up with Lewinsky. However, because he'd only stuck a cigar tube in her vagina and she orally pleasured him, Clinton said it really wasn't a relationship."[475]

Larry Patterson said that around Christmas in 1988 or 1989 Bill ordered him to deliver some of Chelsea's Christmas presents to the household of Bobbie Ann Williams. These were presents that were sent to the Arkansas governor's mansion for Chelsea. Larry Patterson also said that there was a suspicious burglary of Williams's home when Clinton ran for president. "The thieves took only two photographs of Danney: one that had already been published in *Globe*. Patterson claimed Young (who'd driven Clinton and Bobby Ann to his mother's wooded home for sex) assisted Little Rock police in the investigation."[476] Patterson says he found it suspicious that that Arkansas state police, led by Buddy Young, would be called in to investigate this break-in. Larry Patterson, after he turned on the Clintons, became good friends with Nichols and he also gave that picture (of a young Danney) that Clinton's troopers had stolen to Larry Nichols. Larry Nichols, in turn, released it to the media.

At a White House press briefing a reporter stated that the online photos of a young Danney Williams look like Bill Clinton and what did the White House have to say about that? Joe Lockhart replied, "*Who?* That's good. And I'm an alien space baby."[477]

Just prior to Hillary's Senate bid, the Clintons floated a false flag story claiming that DNA evidence absolved Bill of being Danney's father. The story was false, but ran. This is a tactic the Clintons have used again and again. Right after Hillary announced her 2016 candidacy, her campaign floated a phony "internal analysis" to discredit a study done by the *Washington Free Beacon*'s Brent Scher that showed Hillary has consistently paid women less than men. The memo disproving Scher's story was a fraud, as was the story about Danney Williams's DNA.

While the Clintons have never laid claim to Danney Williams, it is probable that they have raised and cared for another child birthed from an affair outside of their marriage. While it may sound outrageous, there is reason to believe that Chelsea Clinton is the daughter of Hillary Clinton and Webb Hubbell. While some will reject this notion, I believe a review of the overwhelming circumstantial evidence shows that it is not beyond possibility that Hubbell is Chelsea Clinton's real daddy. And while some may believe that questioning the parentage of Chelsea is crass, she has long been part of the Clinton propaganda machine and has enjoyed enormous financial benefits as a result.

It was in June 1992, when Bill's political future was threatened by the Gennifer Flowers scandal, that the Clintons strategically placed a photo of Hillary and Bill happily posing with Chelsea on the cover of *People* magazine as a way to snooker voters into the myth of Clinton family values.

Chelsea's name and likeness has been co-opted by the Clintons in other ways. Originally, founded in 2001 as the William J. Clinton Foundation, the "philanthropic" group was rebranded as the Bill, Hillary & Chelsea Clinton Foundation in 2012. As we will show later, the foundation has been plagued by scandal.

Known to be sharp-elbowed and entitled like her mother, Chelsea was paid $600,000 by NBC in 2011 as a "special correspondent" for essentially no work whatsoever. Indeed, much like Bill and Hillary, Chelsea Clinton has become a grifter.

Although she claims that she doesn't care about money on a "fundamental level," the aura of monetary indulgence pervades the life of the young Clinton. In 2013, Chelsea doled out $10.3 million for a swanky apartment in sought-after corners of Manhattan's Flatiron District.[478] Her 2010 wedding cost $3.3 million, and she walked down the aisle in a Vera Wang dress priced at $25,000. The *National Review* noted that the $3,000 spent on alcohol for the extravagant affair was more than the average American spends on an entire wedding.[479]

Chelsea is a public figure responsible for her actions and her history is relevant to the Clinton story.

In 1977, Hillary became the first female associate at Rose Law Firm, the third oldest firm in the nation. Among the partners at Rose in the late seventies were both Vince Foster and Webb Hubbell. It was a position Hillary craved.

Hillary, Hubbell, and Bill had taken the bar exam together in Arkansas four years earlier. "I remember she had frizzy hair and thick, round glasses, and she was wearing jeans and a light blue sweatshirt with the word YALE on the front of it," Hubbell said. "Under the wild hair and behind the glasses, there was something oddly attractive about her."[480]

By 1978, Bill was gearing up for a run at the governorship of Arkansas. Around this time, in a powwow among the Clinton inner circle, Hillary inquired about the then attorney general's future plans. "Bill, what are you doing?" Hillary asked.

"Hill, I'm gonna run for governor!" Bill answered boisterously.

"Well I gotta get in Rose. . . . I'm gonna fuck Hubbell," Hillary replied without missing a beat.

In 1979, Hillary became the first woman to make full partner at Rose.[481] The married Hubbell, like Foster, was under the spell of Hillary. "Vince and I were mesmerized by her," Hubbell said. "She was like nobody we had ever been around before. Bill wasn't much of a presence in our lives."

On February 27, 1980, Chelsea Clinton was born. As she grew, she bore none of the distinct features of Bill that Danney Williams had, but curiously many facial similarities to Hubbell.

The genetic giveaway is the protruding large lower lip that both Hubbell and Chelsea possess. Even after going through extensive plastic surgery in her twenties, this feature is still noticeable. The large rubbery Hubbell lips are especially noticeable in pictures of a teenage Chelsea.

In her twenties, Chelsea reportedly had "gotten a nose job and may have also gotten a chin augmentation or implant to give her a stronger jawline," according to Dr. Jennifer Walden, a Manhattan plastic surgeon. "Chelsea, who wore braces on her teeth during her youth, is now also sporting a less gummy smile and has straightened her naturally curly hair."[482]

In Dr. Walden's estimation, "Clinton also underwent dental work and received Juvederm—a dermal filler—to disguise her 'gummy' smile."[483]

Manhattan plastic surgeon Dr. David Shafer said that Chelsea has improved over the years and now has a nose that fits her face thanks to her surgeon.

Melrose Larry Green, author of the book *Why the Clintons Belong in Prison*, was one of the first to point out the strong resemblance between Hubbell and Chelsea.

"I present it to you as rumor, not a fact," Green wrote. "I am the first to admit that without DNA or blood type analysis, this story must unfortunately be considered an allegation, not a fact. I heard this allegation from many people. According to a woman who has worked for a Republican US Senator for 18 years, the rumor has been around Capitol Hill for years. People who knew and worked with the Clintons in Arkansas have told me they heard the rumor. I am reminded of the maxim: 'A picture is worth a thousand words.' Look at the picture of Webb Hubbell in David Brock's book and judge for yourself."

Hillary has always been protective of Hubbell. When Clinton was elected president in 1992, Hillary tried to make Bill promise to appoint Hubbell to the U.S. Supreme Court if a vacancy opened. Hillary ordered the newly elected president to give Webb an interim appointment as chief justice of the Arkansas Supreme Court: "Well goddam it Bill, he's my friend, you can appoint him by law, so do it!" said Hillary according to L. D. Brown.

After Bill was sworn in, Hillary made sure that Hubbell was placed in the number three spot at the Justice Department. Hubbell himself clearly saw Chelsea as one of his greatest achievements.

"On summer evenings, I could sip a drink in my big living room and look out at children—including the Fosters' and the Clintons', when Chelsea got big enough—bouncing happily on a trampoline in the shade of my big oak trees," Hubbell wrote in his account of the Clintons, *Friends in High Places*. "Such a scene made me feel successful."[484]

CHAPTER 19

HILLARY'S FIGHT FOR WOMEN

"At last we have a First Lady in the White House that we can fuck!"

—A lesbian activist at the 1993 March on Washington for Lesbian Gay and Bisexual Rights and Liberation rally[485]

Hillary Clinton has long had close ties to the lesbian community. And over the years, many in the media have speculated about her own sexuality. She hasn't commented on it publicly. Meanwhile, the Clinton Foundation has a sketchy record when it comes to gay rights.

Hillary is a graduate of Wellesley, a women's college with a long history of having a sizeable lesbian contingent. In the early days of Wellesley: "So many of the college's female professors lived together in lesbian relationships that a union between two women came to be known as a 'Wellesley marriage' or a 'Boston marriage.'"[486]

Two of Hillary's closest friends at Wellesley became lesbians: Eldie Acheson and Nancy Wanderer. Hillary roomed for four years with Acheson, the granddaughter of Dean Acheson, secretary of state for Harry Truman.

"The notion of a woman being a lesbian was fascinating to Hillary," said one of Hillary's Wellesley friends. "But she was much more interested in lesbianism as a political statement than a sexual practice. . . . Hillary talked about it a lot, read lesbian literature, and embraced it as a revolutionary concept."[487]

In Arkansas politics during the 1970s and 1980s, Clinton's friends, taking note of and concerned about Bill's risky womanizing, would ask a question: "Bill, what does Hillary think about you running around with all these women?" It's been rumored that Bill would just brush it off and say that Hillary "probably has eaten more pussy than I have."

In 1974 Hillary's supposed lesbianism was a campaign issue that the Clintons had to handle. "Hillary's drab appearance and her brusque manner fueled rumors in both Democratic and Republican circles that she was a lesbian," said author Chris Andersen. He wrote:

> So persistent was the gossip that Paul Fray finally asked Bill point blank if Hillary was indeed gay. When Bill simply shrugged, Fray went straight to Hillary.
>
> "There have been all these rumors, Hillary. Is it true?" he asked.
>
> "It's nobody's goddamn business," she snapped back.
>
> Fray pressed on. "Maybe so," he said, "but we can't ignore this—all those rumors are hurting Bill."
>
> Hillary would have none of it. "Fuck this shit!" she yelled, then stormed off.[488]

The stories went further. In her book *Passion and Betrayal,* Gennifer Flowers recounted the time when she asked Bill if his wife was a lesbian:

> "There's something you need to know. I've been hearing tales around town that Hillary is having another thing with another *woman.*" I watched his face to see his reaction, and couldn't believe

it when he burst out laughing. I was stunned! I asked him what was so funny. "Honey," he said, "she's probably eaten more pussy than I have." Bill said he had known for a long time that Hillary was attracted to women, and it didn't really bother him anymore. His first clue came from her lack of enjoyment of sex with him. He said she was very cold and not playful at all in bed. She didn't like to experiment and insisted on the missionary position and nothing else. Because she wasn't enjoying herself, neither was he. Sex with her became a duty; nothing more.[489]

In a September 2013 interview with *Mail Online*, Flowers reiterated Bill's confession. "I don't know Huma or the Weiners," Flowers said in reference to the scandal that involved former New York Congressman Anthony Weiner and his wife Huma, who was rumored to have carried on a tryst with Hillary. "I just know what Bill told me and that was that he was aware that Hillary was bisexual and he didn't care. He should know. He said Hillary had eaten more pussy than he had."[490]

Longtime GOP insider Jack Wheeler, a well-connected DC politico, was hearing from his Secret Service sources right out of the starting gate of the Clinton administration that Hillary was a promiscuous lesbian. Wheeler wrote in his *Strategic Investment* newsletter, dated February 10, 1993: "My sources indicate that Hillary Clinton is bisexual and fools around more than her husband. The stories you hear from the Secret Service, detailed to guard her, are mind boggling. . . . It is Hillary that is pushing the White House's homosexual agenda." Wheeler put these well-sourced revelations into print a mere twenty days into the Clinton administration.

Later that year, at the 1993 March on Washington for Lesbian Gay and Bisexual Rights and Liberation rally, Nancy Pelosi read to the marchers a letter of support from President Clinton titled "Statement of the President on the Occasion of the 1993 March on Washington" for gay rights. Bill Clinton's first order as president had been to allow gays to openly serve in the military.

At one point in the proceedings a lesbian activist stood on the main stage—in front of thousands of gay rights activists on national television and joyfully said that Hillary was a fellow lesbian. "I'm going to tell you a secret," the activist shouted. "Hillary Clinton has had a lesbian affair. At last we have a First Lady in the White House that we can fuck!"[491] Washington was buzzing about the revelation, and Hillary did not issue any denials from the White House.

Two former deep Clinton insiders say Hillary is a lesbian: Dick Morris and Larry Nichols. Dick Morris was a key advisor to the Clintons from the late 1970s to the mid-1990s when he helped Bill Clinton get back into the White House for a second term. Fox News contributor Morris who was in the "belly of the beast" of the Clinton machine has, for decades, touted that Hillary is a closeted lesbian.[492]

David Martin, known as DC Dave on the Internet, lives in Washington, DC, and has been a close observer of the Clintons for decades. In his essay titled "Is Hillary Clinton a Lesbian?" he recounted the story of a DC veterinarian called to the White House to treat the Clintons' cat Socks and then walking in on Hillary having sex with another woman, precisely the kind of sexual activity the Secret Service was telling Jack Wheeler about in early 1993. Martin explained how he initially heard the story:

> The person who told me was a business contact of some years' standing. I don't know anything about his political leanings; we never discussed politics. His overall credibility was important, because he was engaged in selling my organization on a product that his organization has developed, with millions of dollars in the balance. He was leaving my office at the end of the day and introduced the subject in an offhand sort of way. His sister, he said, was a Washington-area veterinarian who has a friend who is another Washington-area veterinarian. That friend had told her that she had received a call from the White House requesting someone to come treat the Clintons' sick cat. She sent a female assistant, who had difficulty locating the cat. In her search, she happened to open

what must have been Hillary's bedroom door, and there in the bed were two women, one of whom she took to be Hillary. She told her boss about the incident, the boss told her friend, the friend told her brother, and the brother told me.

On May 3, 2004, the *Globe* published a piece about Eldie Acheson titled "Hillary's Gay Roommate." Eldie Acheson was very much that bawdy lesbian in college and she was extremely close to Hillary:

Since College, Hillary has become a champion of gay and lesbian rights, appearing at a gay Democrats rally in New York in 2000, where she gave lengthy speech.

According to the rumors, Hillary's alleged lovers included a younger woman who often traveled with her, a popular TV and movie star, the daughter of a top government official and a stunning model who got a career boost after sleeping with Hillary.

A Washington insider says there were stories that Hillary used the presidential retreat at Camp David for romps with her gay friends during the Clinton White House years.

"A witness claimed he was making a night security round when he heard laughter and went to investigate," says the insider. "He was shocked when he say Hillary and a brunette woman frolicking in the pool and quickly walked away."

"It's political dynamite," says a source. "It's very, very powerful stuff."

Despite the rumors, Eldie has been Hillary's most trusted friend since both women were teenagers and Hillary was a clueless virgin, say the sources.

"Eldie is the person Hillary most trusts in the world," says a source. "She taught Hillary about life when they were roommates."

"They have as close a relationship as it's possible to have. They finish each other's sentences."[493]

When Hillary came out (publicly) for gay marriage in 2013, American Family Association radio show host Sandy Rios said:

> If you think that her support of lesbian and gay rights is something new, I'm sorry, she has repackaged herself so successfully but if you just do a little research on Hillary Clinton you know that her love of homosexuality goes back a very long way. I remember even when she was First Lady, that would be, not the beginning of her support for this, but this would be one of the more notable things, on the UN Convention on the Rights of Women, she oversaw the whole thing, the Beijing conference. It was shocking. This was a shocking thing. I think it was in '94, I remember interviewing women that I knew who came back from the conference and I have mentioned this on the air before but I have to mention it again, under Hillary's leadership there were even tents on lesbian lovemaking, they were making sure that people defined gender; there were five genders, not just two genders. . . .
>
> All I can tell you is that rumors abound and I guess since it doesn't matter anymore then it doesn't matter anymore, does it? So if you think this is like a seismic shift for Hillary Clinton I can guarantee you this is not a seismic shift. She has always, as far as I know back to college, endorsed and embraced all things lesbian and gay, that is her history on this so that shouldn't be too shocking. She has played the role of wife and cookie-making mother, I'm sorry but this is just the reality of things. We are being caught in this vortex of homosexual advocacy, it's just amazing.[494]

Bryan Fisher of the anti-gay American Family Association said on his radio show Focal Point in 2013, "The bottom line is that if Hillary Clinton becomes president in 2016, she will not only be our first female president, she could be our first lesbian president." However, Fisher is highly confident that if Hillary runs, the United States will not "elect an old woman to the Oval Office . . . She's just going to be too old, going to be too saggy, gravity will have done too much of its mojo on her; she's just going to look old and tired next to virtually anybody that the Republicans run out there."[495]

Was or is Hillary Clinton having an affair with her top aide Huma Abedin? There's been no evidence and certainly no confession from either party. But with Hillary's close ties to the lesbian community coupled with her unusual relationship with her aide, speculation has abounded. Michael Musto, the well-known gay gossip columnist for the *Village Voice* chimed in:

As I recently said on MONICA CROWLEY's radio show, whisper campaigns are claiming that HILLARY CLINTON is GAYLE KING-ing her aide-de-camp, the glamorous HUMA ABEDIN, an Indian/Pakistani goddess from Kalamazoo, Michigan. In other words, Hillary may be putting Huma out there in the press and purposely making her more visible as a preemptive strike that amounts to her hiding in plain sight. This way, no Republican can later say, "Who is this gorgeous babe who spends so much intimate time with Hillary that the Observer called her Hill's 'body person'? Was GENNIFER FLOWERS's book right about Hillary's sexual taste?" And does either of this couple have the balls to bottom?

Of course that whole scenario can't possibly be true, since Bill and Hill have been so lovey-dovey lately for the cameras, and besides, whenever he's been serviced by an intern—or by anyone—he's clearly been thinking of his wife. (They're that close.) But suddenly, Huma—a sort of Muslim SALMA HAYEK—has that spread in Vogue and the accompanying write-up notes that she "oversees every minute of Senator Clinton's day." Every single minute? Even Gayle King takes a break now and then! (PS: If I called for comment, Hillary's camp would surely say, "Just because two powerful women are closer than sardines doesn't make them dykes." And that's so true. Look at MATT and BEN. But now that Crowley has dubbed me the head of Huma Resources, I'm going to pursue this story with every cojone I've got.)

The Hillary-Huma rumor was taken further by an anonymous source for the political gossip site *BigHeadDC*: "We're still a bit incredulous on this one, but a top level US Department of Justice official is telling Big Head DC that Michael Musto's rumor about Hillary Clinton fooling around with one of her top female aides Huma Abedin is based in reality!"

"I am close enough to Hillary and Huma to tell you that this 'rumor' is true," the source said. "It is well known inside her campaign that Hillary and Huma are an item. If you call Hillary's residence in DC first thing in the morning, Huma answers the phone. Same thing late at night and on the road. It's a closely guarded secret that Hillary's inner circle guards at all costs."

Blogger Luke Ford on October 30, 2007, expressed his own suspicions: "Within a couple of hours of reading Mickey Kaus's report above [about the *LA Times* sitting on a sex scandal story], I blitzed more than 30 sources (most of them journalists) for what they know about this matter. None of them could identify the purported *LA Times* story. My dialogue with my sources left me with no doubt Tuesday night (Oct. 30) that Hillary's made passes at women and that Muslim Huma Abedin is Hillary's most likely source of romantic and sexual love."[496]

Michelle Cottle wrote in the August 13, 2007, edition of *New York* magazine: "Huma Abedin, Hillary's beautiful, enigmatic 'body person,' spends nearly every waking minute with Hillary and so has the best sense of her daily rhythms and routines."[497]

Throughout the 1990s the Clintons scrupulously avoided support for gay marriage, even while the LGBT community became more influential in Democratic Party circles. Hillary would *evolve* into a supporter of same-sex marriage by 2015. That did not, however, prevent Mrs. Clinton's foundation with her husband from taking $10 million from a bizarre African church that advocates the torture and death of gays.

The *London Daily Mail* reported that the Cameroon Baptist Convention believes that being gay "contradicts God's purpose" and likens homosexuality to the Devil.

The *New York Post*'s Michael Goodwin reported that, "The church only has about 100,000 members, so where did it get so much money? And why is it shipping millions to the Clintons when Cameroon is one of the poorest countries on Earth, with child labor a scourge and only one doctor for every 5,000 people? Life expectancy is reported as 55. Moreover, Cameroon is extremely corrupt, with human-rights organization claiming that criminal suspects, gays and political activists are routinely tortured."[498]

If Hillary Clinton *is* gay or bisexual, or even if she considers herself a fighter for the rights of lesbians, then her hypocrisy is stunning.

CHAPTER 20

LIKE MOTHER, LIKE SON

"Dr. George Wright was Bill Clinton's father. Everyone in town knew that."

—an anonymous resident of Hope, Arkansas [499]

The debate over who is the biological father of Bill Clinton has gone on for a long time. In 1995, almost twenty years ago, David Maraniss was writing about this mystery in his book *First in His Class: A Biography of Bill Clinton*. Clinton's mother, Virginia Kelley had married Billy Blythe on September 3, 1943, just before Blythe shipped out for World War II. Blythe got out of the military on December 7, 1945, and David Mariniss estimates that there was no way Blythe could have reunited with Virginia until December 10, 1945.

"This is inconsequential except for one thing: the timing of the conception of William Jefferson Blythe III," wrote David Maraniss. "For years afterward, there were whispers in Hope about who little Billy's father was, rumors spawned by Virginia's flirtacious nature as a young nurse and by the inevitable temptation of people to count backwards nine months from the birth date to see who was where doing what.

"Nine months before August 19, 1946, Bill Blythe was still in Italy. Virginia heard the talk. Her answer was that Billy was born a month early. He had been induced weeks ahead of schedule because she had taken a fall and the doctor was concerned about her condition."[500]

Clinton biographer Nigel Hamilton also investigated Bill Clinton's real father. He said that relatives and friends of Kelley would shrug their shoulders or go silent when asked who Bill's real father was. But when they spoke to Hamilton off the record, "Not a single one in confidence believed Bill Blythe had been the child's father."[501]

So one might wonder why conventional knowledge had deemed Blythe the father of Clinton. There is no credible Clinton biographer who still believes Blythe was Clinton's dad.

"Flirtatious" does not do justice to Virginia Kelley's true nature. Kelley, Bill's mother, was an industrial-grade slut, often hopping in the beds of the married doctors with whom she worked, as well as many others.

"Like Bill, Virginia had a long string of adulterous affairs that till now have been undisclosed," wrote psychologist John D. Gartner. "Her liaisons, including her five marriages (she had four husbands, but married Roger Clinton twice), were often impulsive, and usually showed poor judgement. The extent of her promiscuity was one of the most surprising findings in my research."[502] Gartner says extramarital sex was a "lifestyle" for Bill's mother, even "an addiction."

It has been determined by Gartner that Bill Clinton's *real* "biological" father is the deceased Dr. George Wright of Hope, Arkansas.

Gartner found the nurse, Wilma Rowe Booker, who helped deliver Clinton. "I was the first person to spank Bill Clinton's butt, ha ha . . . But I wasn't the last," Booker said.[503] Gartner also found Richard Fenwick, a friend of Bill's mother, who "held Bill Clinton in the hospital the day he was born."

Bill was not a premature baby according to Booker: "he was a big, pink, healthy-looking full-term baby. There was absolutely no way he was premature."[504]

Jim Blair, the former husband of Diane Blair, very close to the Clintons, said he did not believe Blythe was the father of Bill Clinton. Joe Purvis grew up with Bill Clinton and he asked his dad one time who Bill's real father was, "He just smiled and said: 'Gosh, we just don't know.' But I could tell he knew a lot he wasn't saying."[505]

Kelley had told a friend Virginia Heath that she had in fact had an affair with a doctor in Hope, Arkansas, at a time that would line up with Bill's conception. There were not too many doctors in tiny Hope around the time Clinton was born. A longtime reporter on the Clintons told Gartner that he tried to interview a doctor in Hope but the doctor sounded "real nervous and jumpy" and canceled the interview at the last moment. David Mariness told Gartner that he had been trying to interview Dr. George Wright of Hope, Arkansas, when he wrote his biography of Clinton.[506]

The reporters and biographers of Clinton had been circling around the Dr. George Wright–Bill Clinton connection for decades, but it is our opinion that John Gartner is the one who has finally hit pay dirt with his conclusion that Dr. George Wright is the biological father of Bill Clinton.

Gartner went to the Hope public library and ran into a woman in her eighties as he was looking over Bill's high school yearbooks. She told Gartner that she knew who Clinton's real dad was. Gartner asked her if he might be kin to a Larry Wright who was a school age friend of Clinton and the son of Dr. George Wright:

"As a matter of fact, it does. Dr. George Wright was Bill Clinton's father. Everyone in town knew that."

"Everyone knew? I heard that there were lots of different rumors about a variety of suspected fathers."

"Oh, no. There were not lots of different rumors. There was one rumor, and it was no rumor. Everyone in Hope knew it was Dr. Wright."

"How did you know it was Dr. Wright?"

"I had personal knowledge."

"Personal knowledge?" I asked, trying to imagine what they could possibly be.

"One of Dr. Wright's best friends told me that Wright said to him: 'I'm Billy Blythe's father.'"[507]

Gartner found others who confirmed this old lady's story, an "open secret" in the little town of Hope, Arkansas.

Gartner interviewed George Wright, Jr., the half-brother of Bill Clinton. Wright said that he grew up with Clinton and that Kelley helped his father Dr. George Wright set up his medical practice in Hope in May of 1946. Kelley was pregnant with Bill at the time. Dr. George Wright had come to Hope, Arkansas, before he moved there to check out the town. It is very likely that is when he hopped in bed with the "hot to trot" Kelley.

When Bill was a young kid, Kelley and Roger Clinton were often guests of the Wright family and even when they moved away to Hot Springs, Dr. Wright would rent a summer lake house and Bill would visit.

"Every summer, young Bill would spend a large part of the Wright's vacation living with them on the lake," wrote Gartner. If Bill Clinton was the biological child, Dr. Wright had cleverly found a way to have annual visitation with his son without anyone being the wiser."[508] George Wright, Jr., was well aware of the rumors regarding Bill's true father.

Gartner dug up another bombshell, saying that Bill's half-brother Roger was not the son of Roger Clinton, Sr. John Gartner interviewed Virginia Heath, who was a friend of Kelley: "Uncle Roger told me that little Roger wasn't his. Roger senior said he knew because he couldn't have children. And he told me who the daddy was, I just never have told anyone his name. He's a doctor here in town." Is it even surprising, at this point, that yet another layer of secrecy and sketchiness is added to the Clintons' personal lives?

CHAPTER 21

THE QUOTABLE CLINTONS

"Get fucked! Get the fuck out of my way! Get out of my face!"

—First Lady Hillary Clinton

One should never be surprised what comes out of the mouths of the Clintons, especially Hillary. Pro-life activist Lurleen Stackhouse went to a pre-inauguration prayer service at the AME Church in Washington, DC, on January 21, 1993, a few hours before Bill was to be sworn in as president. After the service concluded, Lurleen gave her anti-abortion message to the Clintons. Stackhouse relayed the story to *Washington Week*:

> When the service concluded we were asked to stay seated until the President and Mrs. Clinton departed for the White House. However, as they walked down the aisle I stood and reached out for Mr. Clinton. "Mr. Clinton, America must stop killing babies." He looked at me with a blank stare on his face. I repeated this statement to him.
>
> Hillary (not hearing my comment) then came to give me a hug and I said (in a voice only audible to her), "Hillary, it is against God's law to kill babies." She stepped back, shaking and trembling,

and then grabbed my arm. Her countenance transformed from a pleasant demeanor to the appearance of being possessed. Her eyes were enraged as [Hillary] replied, *"It is God's law to kill babies."*

I drew back in shock at this blatant and revealing statement. I fully expected her to say, "It is God's law for women to have a choice," or other pro-death rhetoric. But no, she was bold and blatant. I would not have believed it if I had not heard it with my own ears. I walked out with General Colin Powell. As the Clintons got into their limousine I approached the car. Through the glass I continued to plead with Mr. Clinton to stop killing babies. Again, he had a troubled stare.[509]

Hillary had started out that morning by yelling at Bill what a "motherfucker" he was because he would not let her have Vice President Al Gore's office in the White House. Gary Aldrich, in his *Unlimited Access*, has documented Hillary's profane fury as she trailed Bill Clinton through the White House on day one, cussing him out every step of the way, wanting the vice president's office as her own.

Hillary is known for her cruel and vicious tongue as well as her often nasty demeanor. According to author Ron Kessler, Secret Service agents considered it "punishment" to be assigned to her detail because she is so rude and disrespectful towards them.

Here is a sampler of some other Hillary quotes over the years:

1) "Where is the goddamn fucking flag? I want the goddamn fucking flag up every fucking morning at fucking sunrise."
—Hillary to Arkansas state troopers at the guardhouse as she was pulling out of the governor's mansion on Labor Day, 1991 (*The First Partner*, p. 192).

2) "Fuck off! It's enough that I have to see you shit-kickers every day. I'm not going to talk to you, too. Just do your goddamn job and keep your mouth shut."

> —Hillary to her Arkansas state trooper bodyguards, after one of them told her "good morning" (*American Evita*, p. 90).

3) "[You] fucking idiot."

> —Hillary to a state trooper who was driving her to an event (*Crossfire*, p. 84). Larry Gleghorn, a former state trooper, said: "She was a bitch day in and day out" (*The First Partner*, p. 119).

4) "That sorry son of a bitch." According to Larry Patterson, this was a common phrase that Hillary used to describe Bill back when he was governor of Arkansas.

5) Former FBI agent stationed to the White House Gary Aldrich said, "[Hillary] had a clear dislike for the agents (US Secret Service), bordering on hatred. . . . Two Secret Service agents heard Hillary's daughter Chelsea refer to them as 'personal, trained pigs.' . . . The agent on the detail tried to scold Chelsea for such disrespect. He told her . . . he believed that her father, the president, would be shocked if he heard what she had just said to her friends. Chelsea's response? 'I don't think so. That's what my parents call you'" (*Unlimited Access*, p. 90).

6) "If you want to remain on this detail, get your fucking ass over here and grab those bags."

> —Hillary to a Secret Service agent who is trained to keep his hands free at all times to protect his boss. According to countless witnesses, this kind of demanding and demeaning behavior and attitude is very common for Hillary over the years. CNBC host Chris Matthews commented on *Hardball* on July 17, 2001, as quoted on *Newsmax* in August 2001, that he had seen the Secret Service carry bags for Senator Hillary on the train. "Who in the Senate gets a sherpa to carry their bags for them? Who pays the airfare for this

guy? Who pays for his life-style? Who pays his salary to walk around carrying her bags? This looks pretty regal."

7) "Get fucked! Get the fuck out of my way! Get out of my face!"
—A typical comment from Hillary to Secret Service agents throughout the 1990s (*Hillary's Scheme*, p. 89).

8) "Stay the fuck back, stay the fuck away from me! Don't come within ten yards of me, or else! . . . Just fucking do as I say, okay?"
—Hillary to her Secret Service detail (*Unlimited Access*, p. 139). Author Ron Kessler wrote, "Secret Service agents assigned at various points to guard Hillary during her campaign for the Senate were dismayed at how two-faced and unbalanced she was" (*A Matter of Character*, p. 2).

9) "What the fuck is going on?"
—Hillary to a Secret Service agent after reading an article, written by a UC Berkeley student, which was critical of Chelsea Clinton, a new high-profile Stanford undergrad. The student was subsequently interrogated by the Secret Service (SFGate.com, November 26, 1997).

10) "Bimbos," "sluts," "trailer trash," "rednecks," and "shit-kickers."
—Terms Hillary commonly used to describe Arkansans (*American Evita*, p. 139).

11) "Goddamn, L. D., did you see that family right out of *Deliverance*? Get me the hell out of here."
—L. D. Brown, Bill's favorite state trooper, while at a county fair in Arkansas in the early 1980s. They had just spoken to "salt of the earth" country Arkansans who wore bib overalls and cotton dresses. Brown also said that Hillary would reduce grown men state troopers such as Trooper Mark Allen to tears with her vicious attacks (*Crossfire*, p. 85).

12) "This is the kind of shit I have to put up with."
     —Hillary to a friend after a well-meaning supporter gave her earrings shaped like Arkansas Razorbacks (*Blood Sport*, p. 105).

13) "Motherfucker," "cocksucker."
     —Two of Hillary's favorite names for Bill (*Boy Clinton*, p. 278).

14) "You goddamn stupid fucking fool."
     —Hillary to Bill while in the presence of Chelsea, then a toddler (*Newsmax*, July 15, 2000).

15) "I want you to do damage control over Bill's philandering. . . . Bill's going to be president of the United States. . . . I want you to get rid of these bitches he's seeing. . . . I want you to give me the names and addresses and phone numbers, and we can get them under control."
     —Hillary instructing Ivan Duda in 1982, a full sixteen years before the Monica Lewinsky scandal broke (*The Truth About Hillary*, pp. 98–99).

16) "Goddamn it, Bill, you promised me that office."
     —Hillary literally was the de facto co-president with Bill Clinton and she demanded to have Vice President Al Gore's office, which was in proximity to the Oval Office. Gore told Clinton that he would go public with it and embarrass the new administration if Hillary got that office space. Hillary, despite her screaming and profanity-laced fits throughout Inauguration Day, did not win this battle (*Bill & Hillary*, p. 258).

17) "You fucking asshole."
     —Hillary, while demanding Al Gore's office on Inauguration Day (*Hillary's Choice*, p. 223)

18) "You stupid motherfucker."

—Hillary to Bill in front of the media on Inauguration Day (*The Seduction of Hillary Rodham*, p. 321).

19) "Gentlemen, I have looked at your proposal, and it's pure bullshit! Now you've had your meeting! Get out!"

—Hillary to insurance executives who had just given their input on the Clintons' health-care bill. (*Unlimited Access*, p. 88).

20) "What the fuck are you doing up there? You get back here right away."

—Hillary on the phone excoriating President Clinton because he had suggested a health-care proposal that differed from hers (*The Survivor*, p. 118).

21) "Come back here, you asshole! Where the fuck do you think you're going?"

—Hillary, enraged (*Unlimited Access*, p. 192).

22) "How could you be so damn stupid? How could you do that?"

—Hillary chewing out the president in front of guests (*US News & World Report*, February 5, 1996).

23) After Hillary had heard some bad news about Whitewater, Lieutenant Colonel Buzz Patterson describes the scene: "As soon as the elevator closed, she exploded at the president with a spew of four-letter words. Every vulgar word you've ever heard poured from her mouth: 'Goddamnit,' 'you bastard,' 'it's your fucking fault.'" Patterson said Bill just hung his head, took the abuse while the Secret Service agents and a doctor looked on mortified. (*Dereliction of Duty*, p. 68).

24) "You stupid fucking moron. How could you risk your presidency for this?"

—Hillary to Bill during the Monica Lewinsky scandal in 1998 (Newsmax.com, December 9, 2001).

25) "Fuck him, Bill. He's Reagan's goddamn vice president!"

—Hillary talking about Vice President Bush in approximately 1984 while the Clintons and Bushes were facilitating the CIA drug trade of the 1980s (*Crossfire*, p. 69).

26) "That'll teach them to fuck with us."

—Hillary said to aides right after her comments to Matt Lauer in January 1998 that a "vast right-wing conspiracy" was out to get the Clintons (*The Case Against Hillary Clinton*, p. 162).

27) "These women are all trash. Nobody's going to believe them."

—Hillary on Bill's accusers (*Bill & Hillary*, p. 220).

28) "What the fuck do you think you're doing? I know who that whore is. I know what she's here for. Get her out of here."

—Hillary spotting one of President-elect Clinton's girlfriends on the day before they were heading to Washington, DC, from Little Rock in early 1992 (*Inside the White House*, p. 245).

29) "The sorry damn son of a bitch."

—Hillary's reaction when finding out that Bill was missing from the Arkansas governor's mansion one night. (*Inside the White House*, p. 240).

30) "Goddamn it, Bill, how long do you expect me to put up with this shit?"

—An exasperated Hillary (*Bill & Hillary*, p. 202).

31) "You are a real shit, do you know that, Bill? Christ, a real shit."
—Hillary, angry again (*Bill & Hillary*, p. 132).

32) "Come on, Bill, put your dick up. You can't fuck her here."
—Hillary to Governor Clinton as he was hitting on an attractive woman at a campaign event in Arkansas (*Inside the White House*, p. 243).

33) "Bill has talked so much about Juanita."
—Hillary in spring 1978 to her chauffeur just weeks after Bill had raped Juanita Broaddrick (then Hickey).

34) "I am proud that my husband has stood up as president to confront the violence and to protect American women."
—Hillary on Clinton's position on the issue of violence against women (Issues2000.org January 21, 2003).

35) "You sold out, you motherfucker, you sold out!"
—Hillary to Joseph Califano who was representing clients and interests averse to her, circa 1970 (*Inside: A Public and Private Life*, p. 213).

36) "I want to get this shit over with and get these damn people out of here."
—Hillary, over the Arkansas governor's mansion intercom as preschoolers who had been invited to the governor's mansion were posing on the lawn for a photograph (*The First Partner*, p. 192).

37) "We have to destroy her."
—Hillary on Gennifer Flowers (*The Final Days*, p. 13).

38) "Just keep smiling until these assholes get their pictures."
—Hillary telling Bill how to pose for photographers (*American Evita*, p. 114).

39) "Who in the hell asked you?"

—Hillary snapping at a staffer expressing a contrary viewpoint (*American Evita*, p. 125).

40) "She's a short, Irish bitch."

—Hillary on *New York Times* columnist Maureen Dowd (*Newsmax* quoting the *New York Post*, July 25, 2000).

41) "You fucking Jew bastard."

—Hillary to campaign manager Paul Fray on the night of Bill's loss in his 1974 congressional race (*The State of a Union*, p. 153).

42) "[You] Jew bastard! . . . [You] Jew motherfucker!"

—Hillary and Bill would often call *each other* these slurs, according to former Arkansas state trooper Larry Patterson (*The State of a Union*, p. 155).

43) "[You] motherfucking Jew."

—Hillary (*Bitter Legacy*, p. 11).

Here are a few Bill Clinton quotes to balance things out.

44) "What's all the fuss about? It was just a goddamn motherfucking pig."

—Bill Clinton seeing people at the funeral of a black Arkansas state trooper, according to Larry Patterson on an audiotape interview called *More Than Sex*, which was produced by *Newsmax*.

45) "What does that whore think she's doing to me? . . . [She's] a fucking slut."

—Bill on Gennifer Flowers (*High Crimes & Misdemeanors*, p. 80).

46) "That little Greek motherfucker!"

—Bill on Michael Dukakis at the 1988 Democratic convention. He was mad that the Dukakis people had given him a long-winded speech to read (*Partners in Power*, p. 439).

47) "He couldn't get a whore across a bridge."

—Bill on Ted Kennedy in reference to Chappaquiddick (*Bill & Hillary*, p. 238).

48) "Larry, unless they have pictures of me with a goat, I'll deny it."

—Bill telling state trooper Larry Patterson what he would do if anyone brought up any of his sexual affairs. Bill also told Patterson that he liked to "sin at the foot of the cross" (*More Than Sex: The Secrets of Bill and Hillary Clinton Revealed!* via *Newsmax*).

49) "Larry, it's kind of like *Beauty and the Beast,* isn't it?"

—Bill, while hugging Paula Jones in the Rotunda of the Arkansas Capitol (*More Than Sex*, Larry Patterson).

50) "Larry, I am the governor of the state of Arkansas. I work really hard and the laws that apply to everyone else shouldn't apply to me."

—Bill (*More Than Sex*, Larry Patterson).

51) "I can do any goddamned thing I want. I'm the president of the United States. I take care of my friends and I fuck with my enemies. That is the way it is."

—Bill to his staff who challenged him after he said he wanted every member of the Independent Counsel's office audited by the IRS.

52) "'Kill' is what Bill Clinton often said about what he wants to do with his enemies."

—Doug Thompson (*Capitol Hill Blue*, April 8, 1999).

53) "Write down the name of that motherfucker. When I'm back in office, he's a dead man."

—Bill after he was called a "two-bit" politician during the 1982 Arkansas governor's campaign (*Capitol Hill Blue*, April 8, 1999).

54) "I can see your concern. I understand [Barry] Seal was a friend of yours. His death does appear suspicious. And Bobby [William Barr] says you got a feeling somebody here in Arkansas may have had a motive to kill him. But nobody here had anything to do with that. Seal just got too damn big for his britches and that scum basically deserved to die, in my opinion."

—Bill to Terry Reed on the murder of Barry Seal (*Compromised: Clinton, Bush and the CIA*, pp. 264–265).

55) "Everyone knows I never wear a condom. They could have heard that anywhere."

—Bill to Dolly Kyle Browning (*Perjuries of the Heart*, p. 51).

56) "If you cooperate with the media, we will destroy you!"

—Bill to Dolly Kyle Browning. Clinton used Dolly's brother Walter Kyle to deliver this message. Dolly had been a longtime friend of Bill since they were about twelve years old. They also had been lovers for decades (*Perjuries of the Heart*, p. 9).

And now for a final word from Miss Emma, the cook at the Arkansas governor's mansion, referring to Hillary during one of Hillary's wild cursing fits (Ronald Kessler, *Inside the White House*, p. 246):

"The devil's in that woman."

PART 5

OLD DOGS

CHAPTER 22

PUBLIC SERVANT, PRIVATE SERVER

"Looking back, it would have been better if I'd simply used a second email account and carried a second phone, but at the time, this didn't seem like an issue."

—Hillary defending the use of a private email server while secretary of state[510]

As U.S. secretary of state from 2009 to 2013, Hillary Clinton waged a war on government transparency and electronic security. In a clear breach of regulations from the National Archives and Records Administration, Clinton was found to have conducted her email correspondence as secretary of state through a private email account. This in itself was egregious.

"It is very difficult to conceive of a scenario—short of nuclear winter—where an agency would be justified in allowing its cabinet-level head officer to solely use a private email communications channel for the conduct of government business," said Jason R. Baron, a lawyer at Drinker Biddle & Reath who is a former director of litigation at the National Archives and Records Administration.[511]

The Benghazi Select Committee, conducting an open-ended inquiry on the 2012 terrorist attacks in Benghazi, made a request for

Hillary's emails. The request was a fair one. As secretary of state, Clinton was accused of not doing enough to address concerns about inadequate security at the diplomatic outpost in Benghazi, Libya, that was attacked, of responding too slowly to reports of the attack, and of covering up information. At first Clinton said the incident was merely a protest that had gotten out of hand. In fact, this was a political maneuver to avoid public exposure of the fact that U.S. interests had been hit by an al-Qaeda–affiliated group only weeks before a presidential election. This head fake kept Republican presidential challenger Mitt Romney flatfooted, as he too tried to learn the truth about what happened in Benghazi.

We now know, thanks to the House Committee investigating Hillary, operative Sidney Blumenthal first suggested the false narrative that the attack on our facility in Benghazi was a mob uprising caused by public reaction to an anti-Islamic video that appeared briefly on YouTube. The secretary of state forwarded Blumenthal's political spin to her top deputies.

Thanks to *Daily Caller* writer Patrick Howley, we now know that this misdirection was the brainchild of Blumenthal's radical blogger son, Max Blumenthal:

Left-wing writer Max Blumenthal helped inspire Hillary Clinton's debunked talking point that an obscure YouTube movie called "Innocence of Muslims" was responsible for the deadly terrorist attack on the US consulate in Benghazi, Libya, in 2012.

The son of Clinton's longtime political adviser and informal Libya consultant, Max Blumenthal pushed his conspiratorial theories onto the secretary of state in the hours after Ambassador Chris Stevens and three others were killed.

The *Daily Caller* reported in December that Hillary Clinton received the "Youtube video" talking points before the rest of the Obama administration. Clinton was the first administration official to suggest that the violence in Benghazi was caused by spontaneous reaction to the anti-Muslim video, rather than by a terrorist group affiliated with al-Qaeda.

Clinton first mentioned the video publicly on the morning of Sept. 13, 2012. Obama's White House speechwriter Ben Rhodes, an NYU-educated fiction writer who was initially blamed for crafting the talking points, didn't mention the video until Sept. 14, when he sent around a memo preparing Susan Rice and others for Sunday-show appearances to discuss the attack.

Now we know that Hillary became aware of the video on Sept. 12, the day after the attack, through her political adviser Sidney Blumenthal—Max Blumenthal's father.

Sidney Blumenthal served as the Clintons' political hatchet man during the Monica Lewinsky scandal, helping to tar Lewinsky's credibility. He served as Hillary's anti-Obama hatchet man during the 2008 Democratic primary, which was why David Axelrod and other Obama officials denied him an official State Department adviser job under Clinton.

So Blumenthal acted as an informal adviser to Clinton, citing his own personal sources and unclassified information to feed Clinton 25 memos on Libya during Clinton's disastrous military intervention in the country.

In the hours after the deadly terrorist attack on Clinton's consulate, Sidney Blumenthal rushed political guidance to the secretary.

"During the afternoon of September 11, 2012, new interim President of Libya Mohammed Yussef el Magariaf spoke in private with senior advisors, including the members of the Libyan Muslim Brotherhood, to discuss the attacks by demonstrators on US missions in Tripoli and Benghazi," Blumenthal reported to Clinton in a memo dated Sept. 12 at 12:50 a.m.

"During this session, a senior security officer told Magariaf that the attacks on that day were inspired by what many devout Libyans viewed as a sacrilegious internet video on the prophet Mohammed originating in America. The Libyan attacks were also inspired by and linked to an attack on the US mission the same day," Blumenthal said.

At 2:11 p.m. on Sept. 12, Hillary Clinton personally forwarded a link to an article about "Innocence of Muslims" to a colleague. That article was posted on MaxBlumenthal.com, and was written by Sidney Blumenthal's son Max, who is now the senior writer for the far-left website AlterNet.

Max Blumenthal's article was entitled "Meet the Right-Wing Extremist Behind Anti-Muslim Film That Sparked Deadly Riots." In the piece, he implicated anti-Muslim activist Steve Klein as a consultant on the Hollywood-produced film.

"Pls print," Hillary Clinton wrote to her colleague, referring to Max Blumenthal's article.

Where did Hillary get the link from originally? That part is redacted.

Max Blumenthal spent that day feverishly promoting the obscure film's role in the Benghazi violence.

He also appeared that day on Al-Jazeera English to discuss the YouTube video.

On Sept. 13, hours after Hillary Clinton first publicly acknowledged the video, Max Blumenthal published an article for the *Guardian* about the YouTube video, again focusing on Klein's involvement.

Max Blumenthal was memorably confronted by the late Andrew Breitbart and Larry O'Connor at CPAC for smearing conservative filmmaker James O'Keefe as a racist. Breitbart accused Blumenthal of "fighting your father's battles."

Max Blumenthal's highly-private email address was not located by press time. He did not return a request for comment on social media.[512]

Hillary's most egregious sin in the Benghazi affair was her brazen lying to the parents of the civil servants and U.S. citizens murdered in the U.S. compound. Only hours after being told in an

NSA briefing that the narrative supplied by Blumenthal through his father, Clinton hitman Sidney Blumenthal, was false, she still told the parents, "We will apprehend the people who made that video." Quite clearly, Secretary Clinton knew at this time that the assault on the facility was a precision military operation conducted by highly skilled commandos who quite clearly knew the floorplan of our consulate. It is also noteworthy that the CIA facility, only two miles down the road, did receive the security upgrades they requested and repelled the attacks on that compound.

Later it was discovered that at the time an intelligence report was being circulated by the Defense Department that detailed that the attack was planned by an al-Qaeda–linked group, Hillary still maintained her false narrative of the attack.[513] When her email records were requested by the State Department last year, Clinton answered with the deliberate erasure of her private email server. Her top aide, Cheryl Mills, purposely obstructed the release of information requested by the House Committee. Stunningly, Committee Chairman Trey Gowdy noted that there were no emails whatsoever in Clinton's records on the actual day of the attack on U.S. interests in Libya. How likely is that?

For those who want to understand more about Hillary's dereliction of duty and lies about the Benghazi affair, Roger Stone has written a full exposé published with the stunning, bipartisan report of the U.S. Senate Select Committee on Intelligence.[vii]

The comparison can therefore be made, in all fairness, between Hillary Clinton and former president Richard Nixon's actions in the scandal of his time, Watergate. Nixon, as those of age will remember, had amassed hundreds of hours of tape recordings. The tapes would show a record of his conversations with his inner circle and most importantly could reveal what he knew and when he knew of illegal acts carried out by men hired by the White House. Nixon felt that the tapes belonged to him and him alone. He viewed any

---

vii http://www.amazon.com/Benghazi-Report-Terrorist-Facilities-September/
    dp/1629148113.

requests by the Justice Department, the Congress, and the Senate to hand over the tapes as an invasion of privacy. Nixon looked guilty of withholding evidence relevant to an investigation. On these grounds, the articles of impeachment were drawn and proceedings to impeach Nixon were put in motion. Nixon, however, never destroyed the recordings.

Hillary, on the other hand, permanently deleted her emails, up to 55,000 pages of them, in direct violation of requests to hand them over. Guilty? If the emails showed no misdeeds, then why not give them up? Since she professed no wrongdoing, and the emails could have proved that, it seems odd that she would destroy her only proof. Or, logically, the emails would have shown something completely different; that she was engaged in unlawful and unethical activities in her role as secretary of state.

Hillary's connection with Nixon goes back to Watergate. Believe it or not, Hillary Clinton worked on the Watergate investigation when she was twenty-seven years old. In a revealing article that was first published in 2008, the Clinton trend for dishonesty goes back to her work for the House Judiciary Committee in 1974.

Jeff Zeifman, now-retired general counsel and chief of staff of the House Judiciary Committee, supervised Hillary when she worked on the Watergate investigation. Zeifman was a lifelong Democrat and no fan of Nixon. Hillary was hired by the committee thanks to a recommendation from her law school professor, Burke Marshall, who was also Senator Ted Kennedy's chief counsel in the Chappaquiddick scandal. But when the Watergate investigation was over, Zeifman fired Hillary and refused to even give her a letter of recommendation.

Zeifman was disgusted by Hillary's fraudulent and outrageous assertion that the president was not permitted legal counsel during the investigation. Young Hillary worked with Marshall, Special Counsel John Doar and Senior Associate Special Counsel (and future Clinton White House counsel) Bernard Nussbaum to deny Richard Nixon the right to counsel, despite the precedent of Supreme Court

Justice William O. Douglas, who faced an impeachment attempt in 1970 and was allowed to retain legal counsel. They feared putting E. Howard Hunt on the stand to be cross-examined by counsel to the president. Hunt, Zeifman said, knew too much about secret activities going back to the Kennedy presidency, including Kennedy's complicity in the attempted assassination of Fidel Castro. After Zeifman told her about the Douglas precedent, Hillary went ahead in writing a legal brief that ignored it and physically took all the records of the Douglas proceedings into a private office she controlled. Hillary's astonishing attempt to deceive the committee and hide a critical legal precedent shocked and disgusted Zeifman.

Nixon's resignation rendered the entire issue moot, ending Hillary's career on the judiciary committee staff in a most undistinguished manner. Zeifman says he was urged by top committee members to keep a diary of everything that was happening. He did so, and still has the diary to maintain the veracity of his story. Certainly, he could not have known in 1974 that diary entries about a young lawyer named Hillary Rodham would be of interest to anyone thirty-four years later.

Zeifman's diary details Hillary's dastardly attempt to cover up the Douglas precedent for legal counsel during an investigation, as well as other deceitful actions. She even tried to have the rules of committee changed to deny the president legal counsel, to not hold any hearings, take any live depositions, or conduct any of its own investigation of the Watergate incident or any other potentially impeachable offenses on Nixon's part but to rely solely on evidence compiled by other committees and by the Justice Department's special Watergate prosecutor. This would have, Zeifman explains, allowed Hillary and the few far Leftist cohorts on the impeachment committee staff and in Congress who supported such underhanded tactics to go after Nixon without worrying about someone like Hunt spilling the beans on the covert actions of the Kennedy White House. It would also have prevented Gerald Ford from recovering the morale of the GOP and pave the way for a liberal Democrat, like Senator Ted Kennedy, to be elected in 1976.

Hillary, at twenty-seven years old, drafted memoranda and advocated for these rule changes despite Zeifman (her boss, to whom she lied about drafting them) telling her not to because most Congressional leaders were firmly against changing any of the rules at the time of a major national scandal. Hillary's unauthorized, fraudulent proposals were voted down in the House.

Zeifman's diary also tells of an unauthorized study of Nixon's wrongdoings and set of standards against which to judge them, conducted by Hillary, liberal professors, and some of her impeachment committee pals. The study was kept secret from Congress and later published and made available for sale in bookstores. It was never found whether Hillary or anyone involved with the unauthorized study received royalties for the publication.[514]

The *New York Post* conversely explored the dichotomy between the email deletion of Clinton and the taped conversations held by the notoriously paranoid Nixon. As the *Post* comments, Clinton at least learned something from Watergate: destroy potentially threatening evidence whenever you can. Nixon never burned his White House Tapes, though he could have. Clinton had her private email server wiped clean after Congress and the State Department issued subpoenas for her emails. Only selected emails were handed over, so her attorneys could try to claim compliance. The hacking of longtime Clinton pal Sidney Blumenthal's email points to intelligence information about Benghazi being sent from Blumenthal to Clinton, several weeks before the attacks. But with Clinton's email server cleaned out, the nation will never know what happened. If only it had been so easy for Nixon. As the *Post* says, he'd be jealous.[515]

The *National Review* examined further the parallels between Hillary and "Tricky Dick," also pointing out that Nixon never erased his tapes while Clinton had her entire email server wiped. They also point out that many in the GOP had concerns about Nixon but they were ignored because of what seemed like a sure victory.

The victory was short lived and did tremendous, extensive damage to the Republican Party brand for many years. Democrats seem to have reached the same moment with Hillary. Many Democrats have their doubts but are being told she is the inevitable candidate.[516]

The end result of Nixon's presidency was to stain the Republican Party as untrustworthy. It would take years to clean up the damage.

Standard operating procedure for State Department officials is to use high-security government-run servers to send electronic communications such as emails. By this method all electronic correspondence is automatically protected and saved in high-security government files. There are several reasons for this.

First is security. As secretary of state, the bulk of Clinton's emails would pertain to classified, sensitive but unclassified, and non-personal correspondence related to the State Department. We don't want anyone hacking in on what could be classified or sensitive communications. Many of the government's foreign policy strategies are configured and communicated within other government agencies. Those communications are not for general public scrutiny.

A second important issue related to using government servers falls into what is called "transparency." This means that in the future, these protected emails can potentially be accessed by anyone, in the government or citizenry, if those emails are part of an investigation or request under the Freedom of Information Act. The concern over Hillary's sidestep of these two issues is troubling at the least, and may constitute the worst breach of Federal Records Act regulations as well as State Department policy. The Foreign Affairs Manual was codified by the State Department, which ruled in 2005 that employees could only use private email accounts for non-governmental correspondence except in emergencies and then only if they were turned over to be entered into government computers. That ruling also forbade State Department employees from including "sensitive but unclassified" information on private emails except for some very narrow exceptions.[517]

According to the U.S. Code of Federal Regulations, if an agency allows its employees to use a personal email account, it must ensure that the emails are preserved in the appropriate agency record-keeping system.

The beginning of the disclosure that Secretary of State Clinton was bypassing federal regulations came during the Benghazi hearings when the Congressional committee investigating the Benghazi attack asked the State Department for all relevant emails. In turn, the State Department asked for Clinton to turn over all of her non-personal emails from her time as secretary. In late 2014, she handed over 55,000 pages of emails. This initiated a landslide of questions that pertained to why Hillary would violate existing rules and protocols by sending official State Department business over her private email.

The idea that Hillary Clinton was innocent of violating federal regulations can be answered by a quote from Hillary herself. In the midst of the 2008 presidential race, she took a jab at the Bush administration's use of non-governmental email accounts by stating that "Our Constitution is being shredded. We know about the secret wiretaps. We know about secret military tribunals, the secret White House email accounts." There is another fascinating recording of Hillary's understanding of emails and their potential use as evidence. In 2000, Hillary was recorded telling a donor that she didn't like using email. Home video footage from 2000, shot at a fundraiser by a donor, Peter Paul, showed then Senator Clinton talking about how she had chosen to avoid email for fear of leaving a paper trail. "As much as I've been investigated and all of that, you know, why would I?—I don't even want—Why would I ever want to do email?" she said. "Can you imagine?" she then asked.

Hillary Clinton, in her own defense, has stated that her use of personal emails stemmed from the fact that she didn't want to carry two cell phones, yet in March 2015, she admitted that she had carried four devices. She has also stated in her defense that because her emails were sent to people with ".state" and ".gov" addresses, she was in the clear because those addresses would have been saved on government servers. This, however, is not true. The State Department disclosed that it had no way of routinely preserving senior officials' emails. Instead, the department relied on individual employees to decide if certain emails should be considered public records, and if so, to move them onto a special record-keeping server, or print them out and manually file them for preservation. Since then, the State Department began using a system that automatically keeps the emails of the department's highest-ranking officials—like the deputy secretary of state, and under assistant secretaries.[518]

ABC News has now identified at least two ways in which Clinton may have broken federal rules. During her tenure at the State Department she appears to have violated an existing 2005 rule. And after her tenure, it appears that she did not heed a 2013 rule change that may have put her in violation.

Let's review the timeline of Clinton's history with email.

2000

Hillary Clinton was recorded telling a donor that she didn't like using email.

Home video footage from 2000, shot at a fundraiser by a donor, Peter Paul, showed then Senator Clinton talking about how she had chosen to avoid email for fear of leaving a paper trail.

"As much as I've been investigated and all of that, you know, why would I?—I don't even want—Why would I ever want to do email?" Clinton said.

"Can you imagine?" she asked.

2005

The Foreign Affairs Manual was codified by the State Department, which ruled in 2005 that employees could only use private email accounts for official business if they turned those emails over to be entered into government computers.

That ruling also forbade State Department employees from including "sensitive but unclassified" information on private email, except for some very narrow exceptions.

2007

In the midst of the 2008 presidential race, Clinton took a jab at the Bush administration's use of non-governmental email accounts.

"Our Constitution is being shredded. We know about the secret wiretaps. We know about secret military tribunals, the secret White House email accounts," Clinton said in a 2007 campaign speech.

2008

Much of the mystery surrounding Clinton's emails came from the fact that an IP address associated with the clintonemail.com domain she is believed to have used was registered to a person named Eric Hoteham on Feb. 1, 2008. No public records matching that individual can be found and it is possible that it was simply a misspelling of the name Eric Hothem, a former aide to Clinton while she was first lady. An Eric Hothem is now listed as an employee at JP Morgan in Washington, DC. The IP address for clintonemail.com, along with others registered in Hoteham's name, are all connected to the Clintons' address in Chappaqua, New York.

2009

Justin Cooper, a longtime aide to former president Bill Clinton, registered the clintonemail.com domain on Jan. 13, a little more than a week before Hillary Clinton took office as secretary of state on Jan. 21.

Questions remain about what the National Archives considers an "appropriate agency record keeping system" and if they believe Clinton, who did not hand over any emails until last year, was in compliance with it.

2012

Clinton was not the only one in the diplomatic service to use a personal email account, but it appears that someone else got in trouble for their habit.

As part of a 2012 report by the Office of the Inspector General, the then ambassador to Kenya Scott Gration was reprimanded for using private email and other issues.

The report suggested his "use of commercial email for official government business" amounted to a failure to "adhere to department regulations and government information security standards."

2013

Clinton stepped down from the State Department on Feb. 1.

Later that year, the National Archives updated their guidelines to say that agency employees should generally only use personal email accounts in "emergency situations." If an employee does use a personal account, all of the emails must be preserved in "accordance with agency record-keeping practices."

2014

In late November, President Obama signed the Federal Records Act into law, requiring the head of each agency to "make and preserve records containing adequate and proper documentation of the organization, functions, policies, decisions, procedures and essential transactions of the agency."

The realization that Clinton's emails were not recorded at the State Department appears to have been made in two steps. According to a timeline from the *New York Times*, first, the Congressional Committee investigating the Benghazi attack asked the State Department for all relevant emails. At that point, the State Department asked for Clinton to turn over all of her non-personal emails from her time as secretary.

She handed over 55,000 pages of emails late in 2014.

The State Department also asked other former secretaries of state to turn over government-related emails for preservation.

2015

The *New York Times* reported that, in mid-February, Clinton handed over more than 300 emails to the House committee investigating the Benghazi consulate attack.

Clinton's use of a private email address did not become public knowledge until the *New York Times* reported on it Tuesday, March 3. Clinton's team insisted she acted in the spirit of the laws governing email use. Citing the labor required to review the emails, the State Department said the emails would not be released for "several months."[519]

Hillary's complete disregard of protocol was enabled by the fact that there seemed to have been no one in charge of monitoring Hillary's use of a private email account. According to existing rules, that job fell upon the office of a permanent, independent inspector general. The problem is that for five years, including all of Clinton's time as secretary, the State Department's Office of Inspector General never had a confirmed inspector.[520]

The Inspector General Act of 1978 established independent watchdog offices for every major federal agency, led by an official nominated either by the president or the agency. There are currently eleven inspector general positions open.[521] It could be that either President Obama or the agency have yet to nominate, or because a presidential nominee has yet to be confirmed by Congress. The Office of Inspector General has had its own problems. In 2007, the State Department's Inspector General, Howard J. Krongard, resigned over allegations that he'd impeded investigations into Blackwater and corruption in Iraq. By September 2013, several months after Clinton left State, the department finally had a permanent inspector.[522] A little too late? In view of Hillary's blatant disregard for the law, it probably wouldn't have made much difference.

Longtime Clinton retainer James Carville openly boasted about Hillary's intent to maintain a private server to avoid congressional oversight. "I suspect," Carville said, "she didn't want [Republican Congressman] Louis Gohmert rifling through her emails, which seems to me to be a kinda reasonable position to take."[523]

The erasure of Hillary's emails of course buried the roadmap of the nexus between the secretary of state's office and the Clinton Foundation, leading Bill Clinton to claim that there was not one shred of evidence proving specific quid pro quos between contributions to the foundation and State Department decisions and policies.

"There's just no evidence," the former president said to reporter Christiane Amanpour when asked about *Clinton Cash*, an exposé on the shady connection between the Hillary's office and the foundation. "Even the guy that wrote the book apparently had to admit under questioning that, 'We didn't have a shred of evidence for this, we just sort of thought we would throw it out there and see if it flies.' And it won't fly."

This is a common Clinton tactic, turn a credible allegation into an incredible attack. "This is not the fault of a vast right-wing conspiracy, sexism, or unfair media coverage," wrote journalist Ron Fournier. "It's the result of actions taken by an experienced and important public servant whose better angels are often outrun by her demons—paranoia, greed, entitlement, and an ends-justify-the-means sense of righteousness."[524]

Clinton knows that, unlike Nixon, Hillary has erased the evidence of her crimes, but the avalanche of money speaks for itself.

"The gusher of money flowing their way also offers an explanation for the email scandal, in which Hillary claimed to have deleted more than 30,000 emails from her private server," Michael Goodwin wrote in the *New York Post*. "What did she know about money coming into the foundation? What did she know about who was paying her husband to speak? How much coordination was there? She claims the emails she deleted were purely personal, and her lawyer says the server was 'wiped clean.' That's not something that can ever be said about their reputation."

"It is Tammany without the charm," Goodwin concluded.

CHAPTER 23

CONFLICT OF INTEREST

"I've got to pay our bills."

—Bill Clinton, who has earned an estimated $300 million since
leaving the presidency[525]

B enghazi was a sideshow, but it led to the government's demands
for Hillary's emails. This turned a focus on a money-making
machine designed to line the Clintons' pockets, underwrite their
luxury travel, pay a coterie of aides and courtiers, and in a few places, pay also for the silence of those who know too much about Bill
and Hillary Clinton.

Former president Nixon declined to sit on corporate boards or
take any honoraria for speeches, living on the proceeds of six *New
York Times* bestsellers. Not since the days of Lyndon Johnson has any
U.S. president cashed in the way the Clintons have.

The media had long struggled with document requests from
Hillary's State Department, which now all made sense. "If there
wasn't something to hide, Hillary Clinton wouldn't have deleted
tens of thousands of emails from her secret email server and the
State Department wouldn't be dragging its feet on virtually every

public records request that comes their way," said one Capitol Hill staffer who worked on the Gowdy Committee.[526]

Did she realize when she conducted official business through her private emails that she was in violation of the Freedom of Information Act? Daniel Metcalf, the former top FOIA (Freedom of Information Act) official, says that Hillary was well acquainted with those issues. "I have no doubt whatsoever based upon firsthand knowledge that she is quite familiar with the requirements and potential disclosure risks of the FOIA. I happen to know this from the work I did during the Clinton administration on the more than two dozen scandals that erupted then, and the records controversies and information policy issues that arose in connection with them. I daresay that her familiarity with the FOIA is what animated this unique arrangement. In other words, she knew what she was getting out of."[527] Clinton's statement that she set up her own private email system and server for convenience didn't persuade Metcalf. "What she did blatantly circumvented the Freedom of Information Act," he said. "By managing to obtain what truly was an unprecedented arrangement with the State Department's administrative officials, she effectively insulated her emails from FOIA's reach, categorically so, from 2009 until now. And she relegated to herself unilateral control over the process, unlike anything that any other department head has managed to do in recent memory."[528]

In circumventing federal regulations by using her own off-the-books server, she gained control over who had access to her emails. This also helped to make the release of the emails an issue of personal privacy. Clinton said that it was understandable that she wouldn't want other parties privy to her email server, some of which she said contained "personal communications from my husband and me."[529] This statement regarding Bill's personal emails proved to be irrefutably false. In fact, her husband had only sent two emails in his life, both as president. One email was to former senator and astronaut John Glenn, the other to U.S. troops serving in the Adriatic.[530]

It is of importance to note that just one week before Hillary Clinton took office Justin Cooper, a longtime aide to former president Bill Clinton, registered the clintonemail.com domain that Hillary would use as secretary of state. This action lends further credence to the theory that the use of a private server for official government communication was more than a sinless lapse in judgement. The private email address Hillary used on the server was hdr22@clintonemail.com. Recently, a second email address Secretary of State Clinton used for official business was found on the server. When discovered, Clinton's lawyer stated that the email address, Hrod17@clintonemail.com was never used when Hillary was secretary of state. This was later proven to be false.[531]

Although it can't be proven, Hillary's lines of communication between big-money donors to the Clinton Foundation and her influence on issues that had a positive outcome for those donors would not be hard to find in the thousands of destroyed emails.

The foundation has always been something Hillary has had interest in. Hillary, according to the *New York Times*, served "an important role in shaping both the foundation's organization and the scope of its work."[532]

The foundation is essentially a luxury travel service for the former president and his wife and their daughter. It spent $8.5 million for luxury travel in 2013, while only spending $9 million on actual charitable deeds.

The foundation also serves as a broker between big business and political donors when they engage in influence peddling. For money, the Clintons will give cover to dictators and human rights abusers and enrich our nation's oldest enemies. They will accept donations from convicted pedophiles as well as Islamic regimes that oppress women.

Shrewd observers thought President Barack Obama put Hillary in his cabinet to mute criticism by Bill. In actuality, Obama handed them the keys to the candy store. As insurance to the administration, the Clintons agreed to disclose the names of and seek approval on donations. This accord was briskly violated.

"Ultimately, there is no conflict between the foreign policy of the United States and the efforts of the Clinton Foundation seeking to reduce human suffering and increase opportunity for people in need," Hillary said assuredly.[533] This proved to be patently untrue.

At first, the Clinton Foundation did publish what they said was a complete list of the names, more than 200,000 donors, and has continued to update it. But in 2010 the foundation's flagship health program stopped making the annual disclosure. The health program, called the Clinton Health Access Initiative (CHAI), spends more money than all the other programs combined.[534] A spokesperson for Hillary declined to comment and former president Clinton could not be reached due to his extensive traveling demands. The White House declined to answer questions about whether the Obama administration was aware of this breach of promise. In a second breach of promise, Hillary Clinton assured President Obama that the State Department would be able to review any new or increased contributions to CHAI by foreign governments while she served as the nation's top diplomat. This, however, was also a lie. The State Department said it was unable to cite any instances of officially reviewing or approving new money from any foreign governments. This is because none of the seven government donations had been submitted to the State Department. CHAI spokesperson Maura Daley confirmed this apparent flub adding that "not doing so was an oversight which we made up for this year."[535]

The web of VIP donors with corporate interests and the sheer number of donors who were lobbying the State Department for *something* in itself stinks of corruption and a clear conflict of interest. Even Stevie Wonder could connect the dots.

A recent study found that many of the donors to the foundation also spent money swaying the State Department while Clinton ran the agency. "Roughly 65 percent of foundation donors among the Fortune 100 also spent money on lobbying the State Department," wrote Sarah Westwood in the *Washington Examiner.* "By contrast, just 31 percent of companies that declined to give to the Clinton Foundation from the same group also lobbied the agency. What's more, many corporations that gave to the charity also funneled resources into other State Department projects as lobbyists worked to further their interests at the agency."[536]

Though the Clintons have steadfastly maintained their innocence in the face of any and all accusations, there are several glaring instances in which the actions of the State Department benefited the immediate interests of the Clinton Foundation:

- According to the *National Journal,* a New York developer donated $100,000 to the foundation at about the same time Hillary helped secure millions of dollars in federal assistance for the businessman's mall project.[537]
- Chevron donated between $500,000 to $1 million to the Clinton Foundation and in the same year contributed more money to the State Department than any other federal agency. With the help of the State Department, the American energy corporation was able to secure natural gas leases to drill on six continents.[538]
- In 2001, when the State Department decided on which products and services would be included in expanded sanctions of Iran, Swedish telecom company Ericsson was spared. Iran was a major market for the company. Later in the year, Bill was paid $750,000 by Ericsson for a single speech.[539]
- In 2013, it was found that a Chinese firm with strong ties to China's internal intelligence department was one of the largest donors to the Clinton Foundation, with a $2 million pledge to the foundation's endowment.[540] The firm, Rilin Enterprises, spent $1.4 million since 2012, lobbying Congress and the State Department. Rilin Enterprises owns a strategic port along the

border with North Korea and was also the contractor that built the Chinese embassy in Washington, DC.[viii]

- San Jose, California, networking giant Cisco Systems invested $16 billion in the Chinese market when suddenly they faced congressional scrutiny over their alleged complicity in building the infamous Great Firewall that helps China's brutal regime censor information and spy on its citizens. In 2008, Cisco endured a high-profile Senate hearing about its Chinese policy and reaffirmed its commitment to China. At the company's annual meeting in 2009, a group of investors stormed the meeting and demanded a shareholders resolution that would prevent the Chinese government from using Cisco technology to engage in its widespread human-rights abuses. Secretary of State Hillary Clinton stepped in on behalf of the giant company and supported Cisco's opposition to the shareholder resolution. The State Department honored Cisco as a finalist for "outstanding corporate citizenship, innovation and democratic principles." The following year the company won the award. Although the honors were for Cisco's work in the Middle East, the award and recognition gave Cisco the image as a company on the forefront of human rights.[541]

What Clinton did not say at the State Department award ceremonies was that Cisco had been pumping money into her family's foundation. Though the foundation will not release an exact time line of the contributions, records reviewed by International Business Times show that Cisco had by December 2008 donated from $500,000 to $1 million to the foundation. The company had hired lobbying firms run by former Clinton aides. After the money flowed into the foundation,

---

viii This recent connection with Chinese donations brings to mind former President Bill Clinton's many campaign finance scandals involving illegal Asian money. The Democratic National Committee was ultimately forced to return $2,825,600 after the Senate Governmental Affairs Committee, led by then chairman Senator Fred Thompson, uncovered strong evidence of illegal or improper donations from the People's Republic of China.

Clinton's State Department not only lauded Cisco's human rights record, it also delivered millions of dollars' worth of new government contracts to the company. Asked by the IBT for comment, the State Department, the Clinton Foundation, and Hillary's presidential campaign all declined.

On February 19, 2015, the *Wall Street Journal* reported that, during her time as secretary of state, Hillary Clinton helped promote the interest of other large U.S. corporations, many of which have donated large sums of money to the Clinton Foundation: "Among recent Secretaries of State, Hillary Clinton was one of the most aggressive global cheerleaders for American companies, pushing governments to sign deals and change policies to the advantage of corporate giants such as General Electric, Exxon Mobile, Boeing, and Microsoft Corp."

At the same time, those companies were among the many that gave to the Clinton Foundation. At least sixty companies that lobbied the State Department during her tenure donated a total of more than $26 million, according to a *Wall Street Journal* analysis of public and foundation disclosures. The *Journal* went on to say that "As Mrs. Clinton prepares to embark on a race for the Presidency, she has a web of connections to big corporations unique in American politics—ties forged both as Secretary of State and by her family's charitable interests. Those relationships are emerging as an issue for Mrs. Clinton's expected Presidential campaign as income disparity."[542]

According to an article in the *Federalist* posted on March 2, 2015, by Sean Davis, Oman, Qatar, Kuwait, and Algeria all funneled cash to the Clinton Foundation while each country had business pending before the U.S. government. The *Post* went on to report that "In one instance, Foundation officials acknowledged they should have sought approval in 2010 from the State Department ethics office, as required by the agreement for new government donors, before accepting a $500,000 donation from the Algerian government." The money was given to assist with earthquake relief in Haiti, the foundation said. At the time, Algeria, which has sought a closer relationship with Washington, was spending heavily to lobby the State Department on human-rights issues. Most of the contributions were possible because of exceptions written into the foundation's 2008 agreement, which included limits on foreign-government donations.

As secretary of state, Hillary devoted much of her time in 2010 to the Haitian recovery and the Clinton Foundation led the fundraising efforts for relief in the third-world country. Millions upon millions of dollars were raised, yet only 900 homes were rebuilt. Protesters later gathered at the Clinton Foundation to complain of missing money from the Haiti recovery. Daniel Halper, author of *Clinton Inc.: The Audacious Rebuilding of a Political Machine,* wrote that the protesters were angry that the money "meant to help rebuild Haiti did little to help the country after the devastating earthquake. And that much of the money went to non-Haitian companies."

If one looks closely at the Clintons' work in Haiti, the promises they have made, the money that has been thrown around, who it benefits, and what makes Haiti so important, you'll see that the small, destitute island country is a victim of the Clinton agenda. As *Politico* magazine's Jonathan M. Katz has exhaustively documented, both Clintons have had their unsavory hands buried deep in Haiti's politics.

"The island nation, in many ways, represents ground zero for the confusing and often conflict-ridden intersection of her State Department, the Clinton family's foundation, and both of their foreign policies," wrote Katz. "Five years after the hemisphere's deadliest single natural disaster, when both Clintons assumed leading roles in the rebuilding efforts, little progress has been made on many core problems in Haiti, and the government that Hillary Clinton helped put in power during that January 2011 trip—and that both Clintons have backed strongly since—has proven itself unworthy of that trust. Economic growth is stalling, and the nation's politics look headed for a showdown in the next year that could once again plunge the country into internal strife."

The Clintons were the crucial brokers of the response effort. They were involved in every phase of the relief attempt including a UN donors conference at which 150 nations and organizations pledged an astonishing $9 billion.[543] The Clintons set themselves up to have control of this vast fortune and use it to benefit their foundation and their friends. By controlling the money flow, the Clintons controlled who received lucrative contracts on the small island. It was a cash grab.

As Fox News reported, "What quickly became apparent to many people was that if you . . . wanted to do business in Haiti, you had to have relationships with a Clinton." One of the big investments was the new Caracol Industrial Park, a $300 million investment the Clinton State Department projected to create 65,000 jobs. To date the project has delivered fewer than ten thousand jobs. The Clintons also neglected to reveal that the anchor tenant of the park, a Korean manufacturer, is a Clinton supporter. The company VCS Mining received a gold permit to extract mineral wealth in Haiti. After the permit was issued, VCS put Hillary Clinton's brother, Tony Rodham, on its board and in position to profit. It should be noted that Rodham did not have a background in mining or a history in Haiti. The global communications provider Digicel, run by Irish billionaire and Clinton confidant Denis O'Brien, made millions in revenue in Haiti. Not surprisingly, O'Brien subsequently plied the Clinton Foundation with money and facilitated profitable speeches for Bill.[544]

Hillary's State Department and the Clinton Foundation worked together to enrich the few insiders with capital enough to curry favor with both agencies.

"You don't have to be a conspiracy theorist to know that foreign companies and countries expected something in return for donating to the Clinton foundation rather than the countless other charities not connected to the US presidency. You don't have to be a lawyer to know the Clintons violated ethics rules. You don't have to be a historian to know their ethical blind spot has decades-old roots. You don't have to be a political scientist to know this behavior contributes to the public's declining trust in its leaders," wrote Ron Fournier.[545]

Governments and corporations involved in arms deals approved by Hillary Clinton's State Department have given between $54 million and $141 million to the Clinton Foundation as well as hundreds of thousands of dollars in payments to the Clinton family. This is according to the *International Business Times*. These figures far surpass anything that involved the Bush administration.

Between 2009 and 2012, Hillary's State Department approved of $165 billion worth of commercial arms sales to twenty nations whose governments have given money to the Clinton Foundation.[546] In addition, the Clinton State Department also authorized $151 billion of separate Pentagon brokered deals for sixteen countries that donated to the Clinton Foundation.[547]

Many of these arms deals went to countries whose human rights abuses have been publicly criticized by the very same State Department. Countries like Algeria, Saudi Arabia, Kuwait, the United Arab Emirates, Oman, and Qatar, all donated heavily to the Clinton Foundation and were given clearance to buy caches of American-made weapons.

Under federal law, foreign governments seeking to buy weapons from the United States are prohibited from making campaign contributions. The Clintons have been using the foundation as a conduit to accept these illegal payments under the guise of their charitable foundation.

In addition, the Clinton Foundation accepted donations from six companies benefiting from U.S. State Department arms export approvals. They are as follows:

Defense Contractor Donation Min. Boeing $5,000,000
General Electric $1,000,000
Goldman Sachs (Hawker Beechcraft) $500,000
Honeywell $50,000
Lockheed Martin $250,000

United Technologies $50,000[548]

One arms contractor that got millions from Hillary was General Electric. General Electric owned 49 percent of NBC. NBC hired Chelsea Clinton for $600 thousand just prior to their enormous contract, approved by the State Department. Chelsea, who is a fully matured adult, has become a grifter like her mother. Those who are shocked by the likelihood that she is Webb Hubbell's daughter must also realize that she is in on the scam. Loud and demanding, she has offended top staff at the Clinton Foundation, causing substantial turnover. She is opinionated and aggressive. Staffers call her "the Princess" behind her back.

The cooperation between the foundation and the State Department provided a financial windfall for the Clintons. In one particular case, this conflict of interest led to a dangerous agreement, where a Russian state-owned energy company acquired a major foothold in the nuclear energy market with the State Department-sanctioned sale of major U.S. uranium deposits. Because of this deal, over 20 percent of U.S. uranium is now owned by the Kremlin. Treason, anyone?

CHAPTER 24

URANIUM ONE

"I hope that the US media can start to focus on the real challenges of the world and US society. Focus on poverty, homelessness, infrastructure, health care, education, or fractious world politics. You are a great country."

—Frank Giustra, Canadian mining tycoon/Clinton crony[549]

The name Frank Giustra has popped up before in dealings and donations with the Clinton Foundation. Giustra is a Canadian mining executive whose company UrAsia Energy sought mining concessions from Kazakhstan. According to the *New York Times*, former president Clinton, Frank Giustra, and Kazakhstan dictator Nursultan Nazarbeyev met in 2005 and concluded a deal for the transfer of uranium assets to UrAsia Energy.

In 2009, Mukhtar Dzhakishev, a Kazakh official intimately involved in the transfer, claimed that then Senator Hillary Clinton put the screws to the Kazakhs, threatening to cancel an important diplomatic meeting unless a deal was reached. Dzhakishev said that Kazakh Prime Minister Karim Massimov "was in America and needed to meet with Hillary Clinton but this meeting was cancelled. And they said that those investors connected with the Clintons who were working in Kazakhstan have problems. Until Kazakhstan solved those problems, there would be no meeting, and all manner of measures would be taken."[550]

Months after the deal, Giustra transferred $31.1 million to the Clinton Foundation and announced a multi-year commitment to donate $100 million to the foundation, as well as half of the future profits.

In addition to Giustra, the *New York Times* confirmed that a host of Clinton Foundation donors were connected to the uranium deal, including:

- Frank Holmes, a shareholder in the deal who donated between $250,000 and $500,000 (the Clinton Foundation doesn't report exact amounts, only in ranges) and is a Clinton Foundation adviser
- Neil Woodyer, Frank Giustra's colleague who founded Endeavor Financial and pledged $500,000 as well as promises of "ongoing financial support"
- Robert Disbrow, a Haywood Securities broker, the firm that provided "$58 million in capital to float shares of UrAsia's private placement," gave the Clintons' family foundation between $1 and $5 million, according to *Clinton Cash*
- Paul Reynolds, a Canaccord Capital, Inc., executive who donated between $1 million and $5 million. "The UrAsia deal was the largest in Canaccord's history," reports Schweizer
- GMP Securities Ltd., a UrAsia Energy shareholder that pledged to donate a portion of its profits to the Clinton Foundation
- Robert Cross, a major shareholder who serves as UrAsia energy director who pledged portions of his future income to the Clinton Foundation
- Egizio Blanchini, "the Capital Markets vice chair and Global co head of BMO's Global Metals and Mining group, had also been an underwriter on the mining deals. BMO paid $600,000 for two tables at the CGS-GI's March 2008 benefit"

- Sergei Kurzin, the Russian rainmaker involved in the Kazakh-stan uranium deal and a shareholder in UrAsia Energy, also pledged $1 million to the foundation
- Uranium One chairman Ian Telfer committed $2.35 million

Following the acquisition by Giustra, UrAsia Energy began to merge with the company Uranium One. In 2009, the Russian state-owned energy company, Rosatom, began purchasing large stakes in Uranium One. In 2010, Rosatom purchased 51 percent of Uranium One, a $610 million transaction that required approved by Hillary Clinton's State Department.

In April of 2015, the *New York Times* ran an article titled "Cash flowed to Clinton Foundation amid Russian Uranium Deal." The article recounted an earlier piece published in January 2013, on the Russian website *Pravda*, which detailed how Rosatom had taken over a Canadian company with uranium mining holdings stretch-ing from Central Asia to the American West.[551] The deal may sound innocuous, but the takeover gave the Russians control over 1/5 of the uranium mining in North America. That the Russians have con-trol of any uranium mining in North America is unthinkable, when one considers uranium a primary material in the manufacture of nu-clear weapons. Rosatom is now one of the world's largest uranium producers and Russian President Vladimir Putin is much closer to having a monopoly on much of the world's uranium.

"Experts consider highly enriched uranium the terrorists' nucle-ar explosive of choice," wrote Douglas Birch and R. Jeffrey Smith in the *Washington Post*. "A bomb's worth could fit in a five-pound sack and emit so little radiation that it could be carried around in a back-pack with little hazard to the wearer. Physicists say a sizable nuclear blast could be readily achieved by slamming two shaped chunks of it together at high speed."[552]

Because uranium is considered a U.S. strategic asset with im-plications for national security, this deal had to be approved by a several U.S. government agencies, including the State Department.

It's no surprise that Hillary Clinton also served on the Committee on Foreign Investment in the United States (CFIUS), which evaluates investment transactions that might have a direct effect on U.S. national security. When the CFIUS approved of the deal in 2010 it was projected that half of the uranium output would be in the hands of the Russians by 2015.[553]

Senator Rand Paul, running on the 2016 GOP platform, has suggested that former secretary of state Clinton should be investigated for her role in what is a shady and dangerous deal. Paul is also pushing for a Congressional investigation as well.[554] Why is Paul seeking an investigation of Clinton for a Russian-Canadian uranium purchase deal? Because as confirmed by the *New York Times*, at the same time the purchase deal went through, investors whom would profit from the deal "donated" an astounding $145 million to the Clinton Foundation!

These donations occurred at the same time former president Clinton was paid hundreds of thousands of dollars in speaking fees by Kremlin-connected businesses. Included in the donations were $2.35 million in hidden contributions from Canadian Ian Telfer, chairman of Uranium One.

"There is every appearance that Hillary Clinton was bribed to grease the sale of, what, 20 percent of America's uranium production to Russia, and then it was covered up by lying about a meeting at her home with the principals, and by erasing emails," Mitt Romney said. "And you know, I presume we might know for sure whether there was or was not bribery if she hadn't wiped out thousands of emails. But this is a very, very serious series of facts, and it looks like bribery."[555]

Those contributions were not disclosed to the Obama White House publicly. This was a direct violation of the agreement that Hillary made with the Obama administration. This is not only dangerous, it is treasonous. Rosatom is one of Putin's gems, used to show the power and might of Russia.

"Much of Rosatom's success can be ascribed to the strong support provided by the Russian government," Hannah Thoburn reported. "Moscow recognized roughly ten to fifteen years ago that Rosatom's work enables Russia to add another energy-related means of extending its long-term political influence throughout the world. Unlike oil or gas projects, Russia's nuclear developments need not be in neighboring countries or even in its region—a fact that broadens the Kremlin's investment options."[556]

As the *New York Times* reported, "Amid this influx of Uranium One–connected money, Mr. Clinton was invited to speak in Moscow in June 2010, the same month Rosatom struck its deal for a majority stake in Uranium One."

The *Times* added that "The $500,000 fee—among Mr. Clinton's highest—was paid by Renaissance Capital, a Russian investment bank with ties to the Kremlin."

CHAPTER 25

HIRED HANDS

"If something's on the other side of a brick wall and the Clintons need it, she'll find a way to get to it: over, around, or through."

—an anonymous White House source speaking about Clinton consiglicre Cheryl Mills[557]

The story of Doug Band's rise to become Clinton's gatekeeper is a tale of a premeditated obsession with power and greed, by any means necessary. A visit by Bill Clinton way back in 1992 to a campus must have flashed in young Band's brain like an atom bomb. Band came to Washington, DC, in 1995 and interned in the Clinton White House. Band tried hard to ingratiate himself with anyone in Clinton's office, learning the names of even the lowliest workers. He was considered to be on the bottom rung. In the next five years, Band worked his way up the chain to become Clinton's "body man." Among presidential aides, the "body man" is often referred to dismissively as "the butt boy." Band, however, was positioning himself in the very position that gave him the most access to his target. Band observed that "It's a strange and surreal existence to be both the least important guy in the room and at the same time, the person that spends the most time with the President of the United States." According to Band, "Heads of State and corporations throughout the world know you by your first name, because, wherever the President is, that's where you are." Soon, those very same heads of state would realize that if you wanted an audience with the President of the United States, you would have to go through Doug Band. If someone wanted to talk with Clinton, Doug had the power to grant the interview for a price, or not. This quickly became a financial "cash cow."

After Clinton left the White House, Band was there to distract the ex-president from the depression that engulfed him. They quickly became inseparable and Bill cherished his new found "best friend." He was with Clinton at his bedside during his heart bypass surgery in 2004. Band developed an uncanny sense about his master and seemingly could read his body language down to the minutest detail. He could tell when his boss was in a mood to receive guests or not. He would know when it was the right time for Mr. Clinton to rest or read, and he told his boss so. Clinton relied on Band's "mothering" and allowed Band to take total control over his scheduling, including appointments, dinner engagements, social events, even scheduling visits with Hillary. Without ever actually asking Clinton who he would grant an audience with, Band became the gatekeeper for all things Clinton and thus he became the most powerful person in his life. When Band called someone for any reason, they automatically assumed it was on behalf of the former president.

Band often used "us," or "we" in his phrasing, subtly deepening a client's perceived notions about Band and Clinton. Band soon started presenting his own opinions and choices as if they were Clinton's, and nobody challenged it. According to former White House chief of staff John Podesta, "The President gets a zillion requests to do stuff, and Doug is the guy who has the power to say no to nine hundred and ninety nine percent." Towards the end of Clinton's second term, Band was offered a position at Goldman Sachs and turned it down. Clinton was fully hooked by the ever crafty Doug Band.

In July of 2001, when Clinton opened an office in Harlem, Band was there to engage any needs, business or otherwise that his master had. In reality, Band had now seemed more like the master. Band soon was elevated from trusted aide to essential companion, staying with Clinton around the clock. It wasn't all serious business for the pair. Being Clinton's best buddy had its perks. One of which was Doug's entrance into Clinton's billionaire boys' club and other postpresidential social circles. Soon the two were jet-setting around the globe from one party to the next. Supermarket mogul Ron Burkle supplied his Boeing 757 to the pair after he took Clinton on as a partner. The massive plane was dubbed "Air Fuck One!" Band was now considering himself an equal to Bill and acted as such. His influence with the ex-president was known and acknowledged by all. His position was so strong that when in 2004 Hillary's former chief of staff Maggie Williams, at Hillary's request, informed Band that he had to leave, Band, backed by Bill, refused to go!

At some point Band hit upon the idea of turning Clinton's power to bring people together into a money-making enterprise, one in which Doug Band was the man with power to grant face time with Bill. Band already knew that dozens of CEO's and millionaires wanted to present Clinton with various money-making enterprises. What could be better that having an ex-president as a spokesperson for your company? Certainly Bill had a charm and a way with bringing opposing sides together. It was Bill's soft Arkansas drawl that disarmed even the most rigid temperament. Clinton was ready for an image remake, and Band was just the guy to do it. It was to this end that in 2005 the Clinton Global Initiative (CGI) was conceived and born.

Most charities dispense money. Not the CGI. Instead, it acted to bring corporations together, with Clinton as partner to solve problems of a global nature. In the past eight years, CGI has secured pledges worth $74 billion. Clinton's bruised ego was now a thing of the past and he had his best buddy, Doug Band, to thank. The setting became a series of one-on-one meetings between billionaires and celebrities. For example, he might get $30 million from Dow Chemical to finance clean water utilities in India, or $100 million for small businesses in developing countries in Africa. Through these initiatives, Bill Clinton was reborn in the eyes of the world. From a lying womanizer and sex deviant to the humanitarian of unequaled position. With Clinton's new persona and old connections, corporations like Dow or Coca Cola would come to him for advice, and who was the man in control? Who had the power to determine who got to be on stage with Bill, and for how long? Who would get to ride on the plane? And who got to be in the photo shoots? Doug Band. Band saw the entrepreneurial opportunities embedded within CGI. He was the one who kept tabs and cut deals.

Band flourished under these conditions, buying a $2.1 million condo in the Metropolitan Tower, one of the swankiest real estate locations in New York. For Band, whose salary was a modest $100,000 a year, this was something of a miracle. In reality, Band had been supplementing his income for some time, receiving payments from Burkle's Yucaipa company through a Florida company Band had set up named SGRD. There were other signs that Band had been working independently while using his position with Clinton. When a company wanted Clinton to speak at a conference, Band explained that the company should pay a certain sum to Clinton's speaker's agency, as well as pay him for having made this happen, and in addition, donate a sum to Clinton's CGI. Band, controlling the gate, was letting people of questionable backgrounds gain access to Clinton. One such person was Victor Dahdaleh, a London business man who donated around $5 million to the foundation in 2010.

Probably the most embarrassing association was with Italian business man Raffaello Follieri. Making a big splash in New York's social scene by dating actress Anne Hathaway, Follieri let it be known that he was interested in writing a generous check to Clinton's foundation. Follieri claimed that he had been delegated by the Vatican to develop some of the Catholic Church's choicest North American properties to help offset the cost of defending the church in sex scandal cases. During a meeting with Band and Burkle, Follieri somehow managed to get Burkle to put in as much as $105 million in Follieri's church deal. Through another Clinton contact supplied by Band, another $6 million was added to the church development scheme. The donor was Michael Cooper, head of Toronto-based Dundee Realty Corporation. After this investment, Follieri wired $400,000 to Band via one of his partnerships. Band claimed the money was a finders fee for making the introduction and that Follieri insisted on it. According to Band, he sent an invoice to Follieri for the $400,000, which he claims Follieri never paid. At the 2006 CGI summit, Clinton publicly announced that Follieri would fund an effort to provide Hep A vaccines to 10,000 Honduran children to the tune of $50 million. Neither the $400,000 or the $50 million were ever fulfilled. On top of that Follieri was sued by Burkle's company for misappropriating $1.3 million for his personal use. Follieri had spent the money living a lavish lifestyle while bragging to friends of his close ties to Clinton via Doug Band. This fiasco created embarrassment for Clinton. Still, he did not abandon his friend.

It was around this time that Band set up a company of his own. With all his Clinton connections in his arsenal, he launched Teneo, offering investment banking, restructuring advice, and business intelligence when dealing with "global disruptors." Teneo resembled an extension of Band's relationship with Clinton and in fact took Clinton on as a paid advisor. A number of Teneo clients were also closely involved with Clinton's foundation. The Rockefeller Foundation gave Teneo a $3.4 million contract to propose "tangible solutions to global problems." Pretty good for a new company. Teneo's monthly fees are as high as $250,000. All things were not well, for in 2011, it emerged that the company had been paid $125,000 per month in consulting fees by MF Global, the brokerage firm that lost $600 million of its investors' money. Hillary was upset. There were conflict of interest problems with Teneo's overseas clients and Hillary's work in the State Department.

In 2012, Bill announced he would no longer accept payments from Teneo. This had been a problematic situation for some time. Band was working for Clinton, and at the same time, Clinton was working for Teneo (Band). Teneo's rise to the top was based on Band's connection to Clinton, which had started long ago, and which everyone knew was the only reason Teneo was ever successful. Band had been milking his friendship with Bill for his own personal standing and importance. Clinton was getting wind of these conflicts and finding out that Band had been saying that Clinton supported prospective clients to use Teneo for their business dealings. When Clinton went to Ireland to speak, Declan Kelly, also speaking, turned to Clinton and said that it was Teneo who brought Clinton to Ireland. Clinton went ashen! He was furious. Clinton continued to receive reports about the demands that Band had set in place. The donors had been convinced by Band that Clinton gave his full support to the outrageous financial demands that were being levied on them. Many left with a bitter taste in their mouths and a feeling that they were being extorted.

As Band's relationship with Clinton deteriorated, Band tried desperately to show the world that he was still in charge of Bill Clinton. In September 2011, the Obama White House let it be known that they would be agreeable to Clinton's participation in Obama's reelection campaign. Clinton was thrilled that Obama wanted to deploy him to their advantage. This seemed like a simple enough deal, until Band stepped in. He demanded that Obama's team help pay off Hillary's 2008 campaign debt as a condition of Bill's assistance. He objected to some of the locations that Obama wanted Clinton to visit. People in the Obama campaign got word to Clinton that Band had gone too far and he was "poison." Eventually the Clinton foundation stopped paying him, although he remained on its advisory board until mere weeks before Hillary kicked off her campaign when he quietly left. Insiders speculated that the addition of Chelsea to the foundation, whom many saw as inexperienced and tyrannical, ultimately ended Band's days with the company.[558] These days

Clinton and Band rarely see or speak to one another. One wonders what Doug Band's role, if any, may be in Hillary's presidential campaign. Band is the man who knows too much. He could no doubt reveal information both strikingly damaging and illuminating.

The Clintons are notoriously disloyal.

History proves that their close confidantes will be discarded at a moment's notice. Some even conveniently die under shadowy circumstances. One Clintonista, however, who does not have to worry about disappearing is Huma Adebin.

Hillary's long relationship with Huma began during Bill's presidency. Serving as an intern to then First Lady Hillary in 1996, incidentally at the same time Bill was having affair with Monica Lewinsky, Huma developed a close, secretive, and personal relationship with Hillary. Some have even speculated that they have had an affair.

While a student at the George Washington University, Huma maintained her contacts with Hillary. She also began to advocate for her Islamic religion. She also served as editor of the *Journal of Muslim Minority Affairs*. As Andy McCarthy explains in a 2012 interview, this journal is linked to the Muslim Brotherhood and its offshoot al-Qaeda:

> Huma Abedin served for a dozen years as the assistant editor of the Journal of Muslim Minority Affairs, publication of which was the main business of the Institute of Muslim Minority Affairs. Both the institute and the journal were founded by Abdullah Omar Naseef, a wealthy and influential Saudi academic who became a financier of the al-Qaeda terror network as well as the secretary-general of Muslim World League—one of the most significant joint ventures of the Muslim Brotherhood and the Saudi government in terms of spreading Islamic supremacist ideology. Naseef recruited Huma Abedin's parents to run the journal when it started in the late seventies, and it has been an Abedin family venture since that time, with Naseef remaining closely involved.[559]

Abedin's ties to the Muslim Brotherhood are incontrovertible. Born in Kalamazoo, Michigan, at the age of two, her parents moved to Jeddah, Saudi Arabia, where she was raised until the age of eighteen. Abedin's mother has remained in Saudi Arabia. This begs the question: how did Huma get security clearance to be Hillary's intern when her parents had strong ties to an al-Qaeda financier?

Abedin later worked for Hillary during Hillary's Senate term. She was Hillary's travelling chief of staff and "body woman" during the failed 2008 presidential bid. Abedin went on to serve as Hillary's deputy chief of staff at the corrupt Clinton Foundation. And of course Hillary brought Huma to State during Hillary's disastrous tenure. And as this book is being written, Huma is Hillary's sole traveling companion across Iowa and New Hampshire during her 2016 bid.

The Muslim Brotherhood rose in regional influence and orchestrated a coup in Egypt against longtime American ally Hosni Mubarak while Huma was a consultant for private clients at Teneo Holdings and an aide to the Clinton Foundation. The Muslim Brotherhood were of special interest to Hillary, who views them as moderates. During Obama's Cairo Speech, in which he proclaimed it was his duty as President of the United States to protect the defamation of Islam worldwide, representatives from the Brotherhood were seated as special guests in front rows of Cairo University's auditorium, including Huma's mother, who travelled from Jeddah to witness the speech.

The Brotherhood visited the Obama White House and State Department while Clinton was secretary of state. And Clinton negotiated a failed Israeli-Hamas ceasefire with Egyptian President Mohammed Morsi, which Clinton celebrates in her failed book *Hard Choices*.

In 2012, five U.S. Congressmen sent a letter to the State Department's deputy secretary general alerting him that Huma's mother, brother, and deceased father were members of the Muslim

Brotherhood and that Huma "too may be working on the Muslim Brotherhood's behalf." This letter was quickly attacked by the Washington elite and press core. Some Republicans even came to her defense, including Ed Rollins, who incidentally is also an employee of Teneo Holdings, the same firm Huma worked for while working for State.

Huma's other jobs came under scrutiny by Iowa Senator Chuck Grassley. Senator Grassley raised concerns that Huma was holding three jobs while working for Hillary in State. The State Department responded that Huma was given a special exception and did not disclose any sensitive information to her private clients. Senator Grassley found the letter "unresponsive."

Huma's employment by the Clinton Foundation at this time raises legitimate questions of financial impropriety. As we know from Peter Schwiezer's *Clinton Cash*, Bill Clinton received exorbitant speaking and consulting fees from countries and clients who either received preferential treatment at the same time from the State Department.

Perhaps the most notorious is Bill Clinton receiving the $500,000 speaking fee in 2010, a year after Hillary's "reset" with Putin, by a Russian bank with ties to the Russian government. As we know, in that time period the Russian atomic energy agency was approved by the State Department to control over 20 percent of American uranium mines. At the same time, a number of Uranium One investors gave donations to the Clinton Foundation. And Huma was working at the Clinton Foundation and State Department during this very period, a clear conflict.

Further, Huma is intimately connected to Hillary's email scandal. Against government policy, Hillary held two private email accounts during her State Department tenure with all emails stored on a private server located in Bill and Hillary's Chappaqua manor. The server was destroyed immediately after Hillary's tenure. It is well known in the reporting and political world that Huma often wrote emails on behalf of Hillary from her own account. All of Huma's correspondences during this time have also been destroyed on the same server. We will never know if and when Huma was communicating with the Muslim Brotherhood on behalf of Hillary and what was communicated.

Huma and Hillary also share a close personal bond. Both their husbands have publicly humiliated them with extramarital affairs. With Hillary, it was Monica Lewinsky. With Huma, it was multiple porn stars.

During Huma's pre-wedding celebration to then Queens Congressman Anthony Weiner, Hillary said she had one daughter. "But if I had a second daughter, it would [be] Huma." Huma and Weiner, who was predicted by many to succeed Michael Bloomberg as New York's mayor, were married in July 2010, with Bill Clinton performing the wedding ceremony. Less than a year later, in June 2011, Weiner resigned in disgrace when it was discovered that he had been sexting through Twitter to porn actress Ginger Lee, among others.

Weiner, however, was quick to attempt a political comeback. In April 2013, he ran for the Democratic nomination for New York City mayor. Through Clintonesque hubris, Weiner believed that New Yorkers would give him a second chances. Second chances are only deserved if you learn your lesson, and Weiner did not. Under the alias "Carlos Danger," Weiner had continued his sexting a year after his resignation and up until his mayoral announcement with Sydney Leathers. Due to her notoriety, she also became a porn actress.

In the run up to the mayoral race, Huma and Weiner did a *People* magazine family profile. Huma was quoted, "[i]t took a lot of work to get to where we are today, but I want people to know we're a normal family." About as normal as the Clintons.

How has Hillary Clinton managed to stay as far away from being indicted as she has when you consider the absolutely brazen way in which she carries out her various crimes? Talk about transparency! One could almost call her a criminal exhibitionist.

Hillary can't be given all the credit: she has a partner, a sidekick, a co-dependent accomplice who worships the very ground she walks on. A mystery person who watches her back, covers her ass, and takes some heat. This person enables Hillary to continue with her criminal exhibitionism by serving as her protector and cover-up specialist. Her name is Cheryl Mills.

Since the 1990s, Mills has been at Hillary's side—first as her White House lawyer, then as her closest and most loyal adviser in the State department, and now as a key member of the Clinton Foundation board. It happens that the board is under fire for raking in hundreds of millions of dollars from questionable foreign sources in alleged influence-peddling deals.

Mills has proven her worth many times through quite a few of Hillary's scandals. During her stint as White House deputy counsel, Mills ordered Commerce Department officials to "withhold" from investigators email and other documents detailing then president Bill Clinton's and First Lady Hillary's illegal selling of seats on foreign trade junkets for campaign cash. In sworn statements by Commerce's former FOIA chief Sonya Stewart Gilliam, "Ms. Mills, in her position as deputy counsel to the president, advised Commerce officials to withhold certain documents." Gilliam called Mill's actions "highly irregular."

During the Monica Lewinsky and "Filegate" scandals, Mills was entrusted with locating and recovering 1.8 million emails under subpoena after they were discovered to be missing. The emails were relevant to investigators. Mills made "the most critical error" in recovering them and in her testimony regarding the lost emails, she claimed she had "no recollection" so many times, it sounded like an interview with an amnesia patient. The emails were never found! She took the heat, protecting her masters like a good watchdog.

In yet another scandal, Mills brazenly withheld and concealed so many subpoenaed emails and documents detailing illegal fund raising activity between the White house and the Democratic National Committee that the Justice Department demanded she be charged with obstruction of justice and perjury! Yet, nothing happened. Mills was right in the thick of it as she sorted through key

Benghazi documents, deciding which ones to withhold and which ones to show the independent review board. She also brokered the deal that Hillary made (and couldn't keep) with President Obama regarding rules for foreign donations.

CHAPTER 26

THE SINS OF THE FOUNDATION

"I regret it. It was inartful."

—Hillary Clinton, in response to her claim that she and her husband left the White House "dead broke"[560]

In May 2015, Peter Schweizer released *Clinton Cash*, an exposé on the many shady affairs of the Clinton Foundation. A week before the release, George Stephanopoulos interviewed Schweizer under the veneer of "objective journalism." Stephanopoulos laid into Schweizer, opining that the book had "partisan interest" and contained no "smoking gun." Later it was discovered that Stephanopoulos had his own partisan interest—he had donated $75,000 to the Clinton Foundation.[561]

The Clintons would have you believe that the Clinton Foundation was founded as a purely philanthropic endeavor, designed to enrich and aid the vulnerable populations of the world. The foundation, according to Clinton Global Initiative CEO and former Goldman Sachs executive Robert Harrison, "works across the globe to expand opportunity and help millions of people live their best life story."[562]

In truth, the Clinton Foundation is organized crime hiding just behind the guise of tax-deductible fundraising. A peek behind the curtain shows bribery, kickbacks, and political favors. It is the familiar story of wealthy liberal elites and the poor minorities they are "helping." The more people there are to "help," the more money there is to plunder.

The Clintons essentially work as middlemen between lucrative contracts and high moneyed individuals or businesses. Repayment comes in the form of donations to the foundation or filtered directly to the Clintons in the form of "speech fees." Six-figure paydays for single speeches are not granted specifically to Bill. Since January 2014, Hillary has given fifty-one speeches for a total of $11.7 million.[563] In the original ethics agreement between President Obama and Hillary, the important issues of disclosure and not accepting foreign donations were set in place to provide transparency and prevent conflict of interest issues with regards to Hillary as secretary of state and the massive amounts of cash coming in from the same foreign countries that were lobbying the State Department for various contracts. As described earlier in the book, a large percentage of "donors" were host to either Bill or Hillary Clinton, and paid huge sums for speeches they gave. Since January 2014, the Clintons have earned $25 million from speeches.

According to the *Washington Post*, there was one entity clearly associated with a foreign government that provided speaking fees of $250,000 to $500,000 for a speech by Bill Clinton: The energy Ministry in Thailand. The U.S. Islamic World Forum also provided $250,000 to $500,000 to the foundation for a speech by Bill Clinton, according to the new disclosure. The event was organized in part by the Brookings Institution with support from the government of Qatar. In addition, the list is studded with overseas corporations and foundations. They included the South Korean energy and chemicals conglomerate Hanwha, which paid $500,000 to $1,000,000 for a speech by Bill Clinton. China Real Estate Development Corp. paid the foundation between $250,000 and $500,000 for a speech by the former president. The Qatar First Investment Bank, now known as the Qatar First Bank, paid fees in a similar range. The bank is described by Persian Gulf financial press as specializing in high-net-worth clients. The Telmex Foundation, founded by Mexican billionaire Carlos Slim, provided between $250,000 and $500,000 for a speech by Hillary Clinton.[564]

It came as no surprise when on May 21, 2015, the *Washington Post* reported that the Clinton Foundation had neglected to report $26 million it had received from major corporations, universities, foreign sources, and other groups.

As Hillary Clinton continues to say she is anxious to have all her emails examined and that she feels strongly about "transparency," an oversight of this proportion does not fit in with the statements she makes.

The error or oversight in this lack of disclosure was due to the fact that the foundation viewed the $26 million as "revenue" rather than donation. This may be a valid distinction to the Clintons, however most Americans just don't buy it. If I wanted to cloak a donation, I might be inclined to list it as a "payment." Conversely, if the IRS was looking into my income, I might be inclined to list the $26 million as "donations."

Revelations like this and others underscore the public's growing weariness with the Clintons' insatiable concern with money. Hillary continues to look wide-eyed into the camera and smile, just as if there was nothing inappropriate in her and her husband's activities.

"The story of the Clinton rulebook is a long and Gothic yarn, with its roots in the loam of human nature: lust, money, ambition, idealism," wrote prolific journalist David Von Drehle in a recent exposé for *Time*. "The mix of those last two—ambition and idealism—put the young Bill and Hillary Clinton on the path of politics a half-century ago. The first two—lust and money—posed significant obstacles in their way.

"Because the Clintons did not have wealth of their own to fund their ambitions, they had to become adept at coaxing it from others," Von Drehle continued. "Indeed, they may be the most adept in American history, having coaxed billions of dollars from a multitude of donors—which requires a degree of flexibility in one's choice of benefactors. As the saying goes: Beggars can't be choosers."[565]

Last July, Corning, Inc., a New York glass company, gave a lump sum of $225,000 to Hillary for one speech.[566] Years earlier, Secretary of State Clinton had convinced the Chinese government to lower tariffs on the company.[567] In true pay-to-play nature, Corning also donated six-figure sums to the foundation.[568]

Hillary claims she donates payments from universities to the foundation, but has not provided evidence to support that claim. For her memoir, *Hard Choices*, she received $14 million from Simon & Schuster. In light of such huge financial gains, it's strange to hear Hillary bemoan the "fact" that she was "broke" and could barely afford the mortgages on her many houses.

Then there is a concern about the foundation accepting foreign donations.

Since 2013, when Hillary stepped down from her position as secretary of state, $262 million has come in from foreign entities. The largest share of donations from the financial services sector has been from those contributors with close ties to Wall Street. A third of foundation donors who have given more than $1 million are foreign governments or other entities based outside the United States, and foreign donors make up more than half of those who have given more than $5 million.

"The role of interests located in countries such as Saudi Arabia, Qatar, and Argentina may spur questions about the independence of a potential commander in chief who has solicited money from foreign donors with a stake in the actions of the US government."[569] This, of course, ignores the fact that these Islamic nations brutally oppress women denying them the right to vote, drive a car, get an education, choose their own husbands, or show their face in the public square.

Foreign nationals are banned by law from contributing to American politicians' campaign coffers. They are not, however, banned from contributing to private foundations. According to

Ken Thomas of the *Washington Post*, "Republicans contend that foreign governments donating to a foundation led by a potential US president creates unacceptable conflicts of interest."[570] The laws that dictate the exclusion of foreign nationals from donating to the campaigns of American politicians were put there for a reason; to keep foreign influence from dictating U.S. foreign policy.

The constitutional ban on foreign cash payments to U.S. officials is known as the Emoluments Clause and originated from Article VI of the Articles of Confederation. The text of the clause:

> No Title of Nobility shall be granted by the United States:
> And no Person holding Office of Profit or Trust under them, shall, without Consent of the Congress, accept of any present, Emolument, Office, or Title, of any kind whatever, from any King, Prince, or foreign State.
> (Article 1, Section 9 of the US Constitution)

These questionable contributions also come with the caveat that some of the countries they are accepting from are deplorable on human rights, an issue aligned with the "mission" of the foundation. The *Wall Street Journal* reported that from 1999 to 2014, the foundation received $7.3 million from Saudi Arabians.[571] Saudi Arabia is a country known to deny freedoms of speech, religion, and political association to it citizens. It is also a country known for its restrictive social code, which suppresses women's rights.

"In countries that stone people to death for adultery and imprison people for adultery, this is the kind of thing you would think someone for women's rights would be standing up against, instead of accepting thinly veiled bribes," said Rand Paul.[572]

Earlier this year, a government-owned Moroccan company donated one million dollars to the foundation.[573] Former president Clinton heaped praise upon the country and its leadership. Unfortunately, as Kenneth Vogel wrote in *Politico*, the workers of OCP Corporate, the mining company that donated the money, "had seen a very different side of Morocco's government and OCP. They say the company, formerly called the Office Chérifien des Phosphates, forced them to retire early and slashed their pensions, leaving them struggling to scrape by while hiring ethnic Moroccans for more senior jobs. The miners also told me how they had witnessed first-hand multiple examples of the 'arbitrary and prolonged detention' and 'physical and verbal abuse' that the US State Department says Moroccan authorities mete out to Sahrawis advocating for independence in Moroccan-occupied Western Saharas."

"Hillary Clinton sold her soul when they accepted that money," declared Mohamed Lahwaimed, "And now we are concerned that if Hillary Clinton wins the presidency of the United States of America, she will take the side of Moroccans even more," Lahwaimed said through an interpreter.

Added fellow former miner Lahbib Salhi, "All the tainted money that Morocco has gathered from taking away our rights has been used to bribe the Clinton Foundation and the international community."[574]

Yet another scandal involved a Clinton spinoff in Sweden that collected $26 million in donations while Sweden was trying to persuade Hillary Clinton's State Department not to sanction major national firms doing business with Iran. The *New York Post*'s Michael Goodwin summed it up. "The *Washington Times* broke the story and says the spin-off was never disclosed to federal ethics officials, 'even though one of its largest sources of donations was a Swedish government sanctioned lottery,'" Goodwin wrote.

"Two results: No Swedish firms were sanctioned, and one of them, telecommunications giant Ericsson AB, paid Bill Clinton $750,000 for a speech," Goodwin continued. "The *Times* reports that Ericsson was trying to sell tracking technology to Iran that could be used by the mullah's security services."[575]

Indeed, it seems the Clinton Foundation will take money from anyone with pockets, regardless of purpose or ethical standards.

The issue of travel has also come up recently, as the figure of $8.4 million for travel costs incurred by the Clintons in 2013 gave rise to questions of overlapping travel: how much was legitimate for the foundation versus primarily for the benefit of Hillary's political campaign. According to documents reviewed by *America Rising,* "The Clinton Foundation has raised hundreds of millions that it claims is for charitable causes, but clearly overlaps with Hillary Clinton's political ambitions. The Foundation must be transparent in all spending so voters can see how it used charitable funds to subsidize expensive air travel, a lavish personal lifestyle, the courting of political donors, or other campaign related travel." *America Rising's* executive director, Tim Miller, went on to say, "With 10 percent of the Clinton Foundation spending going towards 'travel,' and the Foundation's acknowledgment that it approves charted private jet flights for Bill and Hillary Clinton, it's past the time for self-described 'most transparent person in public life' to provide a detailed accounting of how her family foundation spends the money that it raises." The travel expenses were nearly double what they were a year ago.[576]

In its released IRS Form 990 for 2013, the Clintons' travel bill showed the $8.4 million. Yet Clinton's only political travel in 2013 was related to Terry McAuliffe, the Clintons' longtime friend who won the West Virginia governorship that year. The rest of her travel was for paid speeches, which were covered by the entity she spoke for. In previously uncovered speaking contracts it is clear that the venues normally covered the cost of travel. So how did Hillary spend $8.4 million in that year for travel? The Clinton Foundation responded by charging that the accusations made by *America Rising* were false. "There was no overlap. Period." Hillary's spokesman charged that "The accusation is patently, but not surprisingly given its source, false." According to the *New York Post,* "the Clintons have spent nearly $50 million in travel costs over the past decade." Reports by the *New York Post,* based on internal tax documents, show the foundation logged a $4.2 million travel bill in 2011. We have yet to see how much Hillary will spend on travel in 2014. Money has been streaming in, but there are many cracks in the foundation.

According to credible sources, many "operators" associated with the Clinton Foundation have either been charged or convicted of financial crimes, including bribery and fraud.[577]

One such scoundrel, now serving a lengthy (twelve-year) federal prison sentence, is Florida's own Claudio Osorio. Clinton's pal Osorio is a sociopathic conman of such guile and greed that he was featured for a full hour on CNBC's exposé show *American Greed*. Osorio, like the Clintons, exploited ostensibly charitable vehicles to line his own pockets. A good chunk of Osorio's ill-gotten money managed to make its way into both the Hillary 2008 campaign coffers and the Clinton Global Initiative.

The earthquake-ravaged Haitians were a particularly disturbing target for Osorio's frauds. Osorio had acquired federally backed money after the 2010 earthquake there, to the tune of tens of millions of dollars to build hundreds of homes for the displaced and homeless. Osorio never constructed a thing and simply pocketed the money to support his lavish lifestyle.

Vinod Gupta, the founder and chairman of the database firm InfoUSA and a major Clinton financial supporter was charged in 2008 with fraud by the Securities and Exchange Commission (SEC) for using company funds to support his lavish lifestyle. Allegedly he spent more than $9.5 million in corporate funds to pay for personal jet travel, his yacht, personal credit card expenses, and the twenty or more cars he owns. Eventually he settled with the SEC for around $4 million. Bill Clinton managed to get some of that money for himself to the tune of $3 million for consulting fees.[578]

A foundation trustee named Sant Chatwal, has convictions for illegal campaign financing, obstruction of justice, and other related charges. The Clintons pocketed millions from Chatwal in supposed speaking fees and in donations to the foundation. Chatwal was convicted in federal district court in 2014 for giving almost $200,000 in various illegal campaign donations to candidates for U.S. federal offices, one of whom was none other than Hillary Clinton. Chatwal also pled guilty to tampering with witnesses in the course of the investigation into his illegal campaign activities. Chatwal's convictions earned him no jail time, only fines, probation, and community service. Indian officials arrested Chatwal in 2001 on charges that he defrauded the Bank of India in a $9 million loan he obtained in the early 1990's. Chatwal skipped town (skipped the country, really) to avoid this prosecution. Indeed, a trustworthy "trustee" worthy of Clinton-style ethics.

Another Indian, a politician named Amar Singh, got hooked up with the Clinton graft machine starting with his sponsorship of a Bill Clinton visit to India in late 2005. Singh was rewarded with personal access to the Clintons at their private dinner table that same year, in recognition of millions of dollars Singh gave to the Clinton Foundation. Singh met disgrace in India in late 2011, driven from the country's political scene after being charged with corruption for trying to bribe members of India's parliament during proceedings involving U.S.-Indian nuclear secrets.

Victor Dahdaleh, another foundation trustee was charged by the Serious Fraud Office (SFO) in Great Britain with paying more than 25 million pounds in bribes to executives in Bahrain to win contracts worth more than 2 billion pounds. Then there's Rolando Gonzales Bunster, another trustee who has been named in a fraud case in the Dominican Republic.[579]

Rounding out this sordid summary of a few top Clinton crony-funders is Gilbert Chagoury, another Clinton/Democratic Party fundraiser with a bad reputation. During Bill Clinton's presidential re-election bid, Chagoury has been accused of funneling nearly half a million dollars to a supposed Democrat voter-registration outfit in Florida. Chagoury is a million-dollar donor to both the Clinton Foundation and the Clinton Global Initiative, which even honored Chagoury and his "Group" for supposed efforts in "sustainable development." Chagoury has been linked to trying to take advantage of a third-world military dictatorship to line his pockets, specifically the Abacha regime in Nigeria. That regime raped the Nigerian people for billions. Chagoury, and the Clintons, reaped the benefits. Topping it off, Chagoury could be found on the U.S. terrorism no-fly list as recently as five years ago.

Many of those who haven't broken with the foundation due to their criminality, have left due to the increasingly difficult and demanding Chelsea, who came aboard as vice chairman in 2011.

"A lot of people left because she was there. A lot of people left because she didn't want them there," said a foundation insider. "She is very difficult."[580]

This follows a familiar pattern for the entitled Chelsea. Coworkers at her previous places of employment, NBC News and McKinsey, were told they were not to approach her.

"If someone wanted to talk to Chelsea about something, they had to go through a producer," a source claimed.[581]

Indeed, the next generation of Clinton doesn't seem to be any better than the last.

CHAPTER 27

THE COVER-UP QUEEN

Can the Clintons seize power for four more years? Will the 2016 election offer us a "heads we win, tails you lose" election between Hillary and Jeb Bush?

One thing to take into consideration is the advanced age of the Clintons. Senator Mitch McConnell recently quipped that Hillary's prospective run would be a "rerun of *The Golden Girls*."[582] Political commentator Matt Drudge speculated that Hillary was holding onto a walker for her 2014 *People* magazine cover photo.[583] When Hillary tried to tap into the youth vote by announcing her candidacy on social media, the decision was greeted with derision by many in the Twitterverse. @faughtd tweeted "@ReadyForHillary we don't let Grandma touch the TV remote. Why would we let Hillary have access to our nuclear armament? She's too OLD." @libertynowUSA joined the masses asking "Why is Hillary wasting everyone's time with trust worthy ratings below 35%. She needs to go away. We need leadership not an old bag that lies."[584]

Given the trail of intimidation, lies, campaign finance manipulation, self-dealing, perjury, and the use of violence to beat witnesses, the Clintons have dodged many bullets. One would think they would take their riches, public esteem, and money and ride off into the sunset.

Had Lance Armstrong retired he would have kept his money, fame, and reputation intact. Like the Clintons, when his involvement with drugs began to leak, he used heavy-handed detectives to silence those who could give him up. Lance reached for the gold one time too many. And so it is with Hillary Clinton.

In fact Bill himself may be the driving force behind the 2016 bid that Hillary herself has reservations about. "He says he can roll her," a longtime Clinton advisor told me. "What do you mean?" I asked. "Run the government, take over," he said.

So what drives the Clintons comeback attempt to win the White House for a sixty-seven-year-old grandmother? The answer is greed and power lust. They can't resist another grab for the trappings and opportunities of power, and Hillary feels that the prize that eluded her in 2012 is rightfully hers. Hillary is the inspiration for Claire Underwood, the bloodless and ambitious wife of President Frank Underwood in Netflix's original series *House of Cards*. It has always been her intention to succeed her husband in the White House. Kevin Spacey's character is mostly based on Lyndon Johnson, and the directors use vivid LBJ imageries in paintings and signed photos in the background of the Underwood White House to telegraph this fact.

Even Bill, always sharp-witted and quick to parry a point or stance, has stumbled and shown his age recently.

The former president attacked Peter Schweizer's exposé, exclaiming there was "not a shred of evidence" of unscrupulous dealings in the Clinton Foundation when malfeasance and corruption was evident. Clinton's ill-timed parry was quickly pointed out as such by the media. When Bill was questioned about his unprecedented speaking fees, he unwisely stated that he needed to keep making speeches "to pay the bills." This from a man who with his wife has earned $25 million from speeches in the last year and a half.

A recent article revealed that the odd missteps by the notoriously slick discourser are a result of dementia. "The truth is Bill has lost it," a longtime Clinton family friend told the *Globe*. "There are days when he believes he's still President and gives his aides orders to place calls to leaders around the world—then he completely forgets doing it. Other days, he can't remember ever being President! He frequently asks his driver to take him home to the White House, but Hillary has issued explicit orders to ignore him and just take him to their house in Chappaqua. On his last visit to his presidential library in Little Rock where he has a luxury apartment, he couldn't remember that he was once the governor of Arkansas. It's all very sad."[585]

The magazine also exposed one of Hillary's dark secrets in another recent edition: her thirst for the bottle.

"Hillary's drinking got totally out of control," said one of Hillary's friends, whom the presidential hopeful turned to for help. "The stress of her high-pressure political career, never-ending scandals and her worsening health have sent her into life-threatening booze hell. She turned to drink to drown her fears. Hillary tries to hide her problem like she lies about so many things. But she has repeatedly suffered blackouts. When she comes around, she has no idea where she has been or what she has said or done. She's not fit to be President."

These are not the nimble liars of the '90s. Yet they are still crafty.

Hillary is the queen of the cover-up and her experience hiding evidence, destroying documents, and lying almost defies belief. The erasure of the hard evidence that she was granting governmental favors, trade agreements, and multi-million dollar defense contracts to the big donors of the Clinton Foundation are undeniable. Unlike Richard Nixon, she has destroyed the evidence.

Let's review Hillary's game of "keep away" when it comes to covering up her misdeeds.

Hillary's "Thwarted Record Requests." The *Times* reported that Clinton used her private email address to avoid turning over documents to Congressional committees investigating the Benghazi, Libya, terror attack of September 11, 2012. According to the *Times*, "It was one of several instances in which records requests sent to the State Department, which had no access to Mrs. Clinton's emails, came up empty." The State Department did the same routine with regard to a Freedom of Information Act request asking for correspondence between Hillary and former political hit man Sidney Blumenthal; in 2010, the AP said its FOIA requests had gone unanswered by the State Department on the same grounds; the same holds true with regard to FOIA requests from conservative group Citizens United.

Hillary's First Emailgate. According to Tom Fitton of Judicial Watch, Hillary's top woman, Cheryl Mills—you remember her from Benghazi—"helped orchestrate the cover-up of a major scandal, often referred to as 'Email-gate.'" Over the course of years, the Clinton Administration allegedly withheld some 1.8 million email communications from Judicial Watch's attorneys, as well as federal investigators and Congress. Judicial Watch says that when a White House computer contractor attempted to reveal the emails, White House officials "instructed her to keep her mouth shut about the hidden email or face dismissal and jail time."

Hillary's Missing Whitewater Documents. In 1996, a special Senate Whitewater committee released a report from the FBI demonstrating that documents sought in the Whitewater investigation had been found in the personal Clinton quarters of the White House. The First Lady's fingerprints were on them. The documents had gone mysteriously missing for two years. Mark Fabiani, special White House counsel, immediately stated that there was no problem, according to the *Times*: "He added that she had testified under oath that she had nothing to do with the documents during the two years they were missing and did not know how they ended up in the family quarters." Hillary remains the only First Lady in American history to be fingerprinted by the FBI. Those weren't the only missing Whitewater documents later found in the Clinton White House. Rose Law billing records were found years after being sought "in the storage area in the third-floor private residence at the White House where unsolicited gifts to the President and First Lady are stored before being sorted and catalogued."

Hillary's Missing Travelgate Documents. In 1996, just before the Whitewater documents emerged—literally the day before—a two-year-old memo emerged, according to the *New York Times*, showing that Hillary "had played a far greater role in the dismissal of employees of the White House travel office than the Administration has acknowledged." Oops.[586]

Although Hillary's handlers believe she can still be elected president with the minority of voters believing she is honest and truthful, in fact her credibility is her principal problem in 2016.

When Hillary Clinton or her cronies attack this book as partisan or "old news" or seek to dismiss the very serious charges against them they will whine that they are being held to a higher standard. But in fact, particularly in the case of Jerry Parks, they may be getting away with murder.

As Hillary's now-infamous email scandal demonstrates, where Madam Secretary purposely used private email to conduct government business and escape disclosure requirements, telling the truth is outside her DNA. For instance, during the sole time Hillary publicly addressed this issue at the UN press conference, she claimed that some of the deleted emails were between Bill and her. Yet the *Wall Street Journal* reported only hours before the press conference that the impeached former president has "sent a grand total of two emails during his entire life." She also got busted lying about having one computer device when she used two.

Hillary's lies caught up to her during her failed 2008 campaign. In the heat of the primary against Obama, Hillary repeatedly said in a March 17 speech and several interviews that she was caught under sniper fire in 1996 as First Lady and "ran for cover under hostile fire shortly after her plane landed in Tuzla, Bosnia." Eight days later, a video became public that showed "Clinton arriving on the tarmac under no visible duress, and greeting a child who offers her a copy of a poem." Further, more than "100 news stories from the time documented no security threats to the First Lady."

In January 2001, a scandal broke when Hillary was caught taking artwork and furniture from the White House. She claimed that these items were given to Bill and her as gifts during their years in the White House. However, less than a month later on February 8, Hillary agreed to return $28,000 worth of gifts to the White House and pay in restitution $86,000 for china, flatware, rugs, televisions, sofas, and other items, which was only half of the value.

If Hillary was able to make an $86,000 vanity purchase in February 2008, then why did she describe herself as "dead broke" upon leaving the White House?

Of course, Hillary has often lied about her biography for convenience as well. Since at least 1995, Hillary claimed that her mother named her after Sir Edmund Hillary, the first climber to reach the summit of Mount Everest. Bill even mentioned this anecdote in his autobiography. The only problem, Hillary was born in 1947 and Sir Edmund did complete his historic feat until 1953. Perhaps Hillary's mother was clairvoyant?

As Roger Stone revealed in his book *Nixon's Secrets*, Hillary was fired from the 1974 House Impeachment Committee shortly after she took, and failed, the DC bar examination. Hillary authored memos demanding Nixon yield his tapes (a little irony there?) and that the president was not entitled to a lawyer in the impeachment proceeding. Asked why she was fired, Majority Staff Director Jerry Zeifman said, "Because she was a liar. She was an unethical, dishonest lawyer. She conspired to violate the Constitution, the rules of the House, the rules of the committee and the rules of confidentiality."

Hillary has no credibility for her denial when confronted with her real record, and that's a problem. As a serial liar she will get caught lying again.

Reporters like the *New York Times'* Amy Chozick mistakenly think that Hillary Clinton has a lock on women voters that will send her to the White House. As a veteran reader of polling data, I think this is incorrect. More than 50 percent of voters were not alive during the Clinton presidency and their impression of Hillary is generally favorable but not very deep. I believe that when women learn about Hillary's war on women they will turn on her.

The Clintons' rapid response and standard MO is denial and counterattack. Hillary and her hysterical female supporters will claim that any attack that is launched on her by a mom is misogyny and sexist. That is why it is crucial that those women violated by Bill Clinton and then violated again in the cover-up must speak. Paula Jones was assaulted by Bill Clinton in a Little Rock hotel room. When she refused Clinton's advances he dropped his trousers pointed at his erect penis and said, "Kiss it." Jones was paid $850,000 not to discuss the case publicly.

The *Daily Mail* reported that Paula Corbin Jones surfaced in 2015. This is a woman Hillary Clinton called a "whore" because she was unfortunate enough to have been sexually assaulted by Hillary's husband.

In an exclusive interview with the *Daily Mail Online,* Jones delivers her own verdict on Hillary's bid to become president, saying that her husband's attitude towards women disqualifies Bill from re-entering the White House—while what she calls Hillary's "lies" disqualify her from the Oval Office. "There is no way that she did not know what was going on, that women were being abused and accosted by her husband," she says. "They have both lied."

Jones, forty-eight, as we have seen, became a national figure when in 1994 she sued President Clinton for sexual harassment after an incident in an Arkansas hotel room three years earlier. Her lawsuit led to Clinton's affair with Monica Lewinsky being uncovered and led to Clinton being impeached, accused of lying about the nature of his relationship with the White House intern.

But with Hillary Clinton vying for the Democratic nomination, Jones has come out swinging with her own personal take on the White House bid. "She should not be running with the terrible history they have," she told the *Daily Mail Online*. She continued, "They have both lied. He does not have a right to be in the White House to serve the people the way he treated women, sexually harassing women. There were many women that came out and spoke out about what he did to them. He does not have a place in the White House to serve the American people."

Jones became the central figure in the extraordinary scandal that engulfed the Clinton White House and almost led to his removal from office when she accused him of sexual harassment. The incident had taken place in 1991 when Clinton was governor of Arkansas and Jones a twenty-four-year-old clerk with the Arkansas Industrial Development Commission. She claimed he propositioned her in a hotel room at the Excelsior Hotel in Little Rock, dropping his trousers and asking her for oral sex.

She had asked to meet him because it would be "exciting" to meet the governor, and she hoped it might lead to promotion. Instead, she said in court, she found herself telling him she was "not that kind of girl." It was a brief encounter, and she alleged that Mr. Clinton took her hand, pulled her towards him, then said: "I love your curves." She tried to walk away, she said in a deposition, but "Mr. Clinton then walked over to the sofa, lowered his trousers and underwear, exposed his penis (which was erect) and told me to 'kiss it.'"

Jones told her sisters and mother about the incident but took no further action. It wasn't until two years later, in 1993, when former Clinton bodyguards spoke in a magazine interview about escorting a woman called "Paula" to his room in May 1991 that she was advised to go public.

She hired a lawyer and in 1994 sued Clinton and asked for $700,000 in damages, claiming she suffered emotional trauma. Clinton denied the claims, or even that he had met Jones. He dismissed her as an opportunist out for money and to damage him politically.

He asked that the civil suit be put off until he left the White House, but in January 1997 an appeals court ruled the trial should go ahead.

A year later, Judge Susan Webber Wright tossed out Jones's case, saying she had not suffered any damages. She ruled that even if Clinton's behavior had been "boorish and offensive" it did not amount to sexual harassment under the law.

Jones appealed and the Supreme Court reinstated her case leading to the unprecedented step of President Clinton being forced to make a deposition.

While working on the Paula Jones investigation, independent prosecutor Kenneth Starr uncovered Clinton's alleged affair with White House intern Monica Lewinsky. Clinton was asked if he had sex with Lewinsky—and he denied it. He would make the now infamous statement: "I did not have sexual relations with that woman, Monica Lewinsky," but would later go on TV to admit to an inappropriate relationship with the twenty-one-year-old.

Hillary stood by him, although former White House staff have recently said she used a book kept on her bedside to bash her husband around the head so hard it caused him bleed. Staffers told Kate Andersen Brower for her book *The Residence: Inside the Private World of The White House* how they heard loud arguments coming from the private quarters of the White House around the time of the Lewinsky affair.

During the Clinton sex scandal Jones became a side show as Linda Tripp produced a semen-stained blue dress and audiotapes of she secretly recorded of her conversations with Lewinsky.

It was the president's original statement to lawyers for Jones that almost led to his downfall, as he had denied any improper relationship with Lewinsky, which was found to be untrue. Having been accused of perjury, charges were drawn up and impeachment proceedings begun. Although Democratic leaders preferred to censure the president, Congress began the impeachment process against Clinton in December 1998.

A divided House of Representatives impeached him on December 19 and the issue then passed to the Senate, where after a five-week trial, he was acquitted.

Clinton survived the political fallout what became known as the "Lewinsky affair." His marriage to Hillary also survived. By the time Lewinsky was headline news, Jones had already reached an out-of-court settlement with the president. Despite denying her claims he agreed to pay her $850,000, but did not offer an apology. One of his attorneys said it was simply to end the case, and move on with his life.

Legal fees ate up over $600,000 of the award, and the pressure of being in the spotlight for almost four years caused her first marriage to end.

It also resulted in Clinton agreeing to be stripped of his license to practice law in Arkansas starting five years after he left the White House, having been found in contempt of court in 1999 for misleading testimony and reported to the state bar over the finding.

Her experience is likely to shape her views of the Clintons—especially her view of the nature of their marriage. "He is going to be telling her what to do," she said. "It is a partnership. They have a political relationship, that is all it is."

While countless books and articles have been written about the dynamics of the Clinton marriage, Jones is insistent that Hillary was fully aware of what her husband was like, saying, "I believe she knew all about it. Theirs was a political relationship and not a normal relationship that a man and a wife have. They did not have a normal relationship. . . . If she is for the everyday person why did she not stand up for the women when she knew what her husband did?"

There is no way that she did not know what was going on, that women were being abused and accosted by her husband. "She knew what was happening and just to ignore it. It was a political relationship and suited them both," Jones said.

Jones added: "The Clintons don't care what they do, who they run over to get to the top. It is all about political status."

Unsurprisingly, Jones has little respect for Bill Clinton, as she maintains he is a liar who was happy to pay her close to $1 million but would not apologies for his actions. Her scorn for his wife is equally ferocious, and she shudders at the thought of Bill back in the White House—even if it is as playing Hillary's helpmate. Wiley Bill has told at least one senior Democrat advisor that he will co-opt and control a Hillary presidency. "He assured me he could handle Hillary and take control to provide a third term for William Jefferson Clinton," the advisor told Roger Stone.

EPILOGUE

At the time *The Clintons' War on Women* went to press, legitimate concerns had begun to arise in the Clinton campaign. The controversy that arose over Clinton's emails is now much more than a "witch hunt" concocted by the GOP.

Major newspapers have begun to pursue the story with fervor, and Democratic Party heavyweights are questioning her legitimacy as a candidate. The Obama administration's Justice Department has also opened up an official investigation into what was contained on Clinton's private server. A slow panic has crept into the campaign itself.

"They're worried about it," a longtime Clinton adviser told the *Washington Post*. "They don't know where it goes. That's the problem."[ix]

On August 11, the media reported that two emails on HRC's private email address were classified as "Top Secret" information. Clinton also admitted in an affidavit that Huma Abedin had an account on her personal server. Abedin, as we know, worked several assignments of interest for the Clintons aside from her official job at the State Department. The most notorious of these was Abedin's

---

ix Helderman, Rosalind, Tumulty, Karen, and Leonning, Carol. "Clinton's Team Went from Nonchalant to Nervous over Email Controversy." *Washington Post.* August 14, 2015.

designation as a consultant to Teneo, a New York–based firm of which Bill Clinton's former personal assistant Doug Band is founding partner and president. This, of course, opened the door to many potential conflicts of interest.

One juicy tidbit garnered from the Abedin emails thus far is the revelation of a dinner Huma arranged between Declan Kelly, a Teneo executive, Hillary Clinton, Clinton Foundation donors, and State Department officials during an official State Department trip to Ireland in late 2012. Abedin had previously stated in a letter that she "was not asked, nor did [she] provide, insights about the Department, my work with the Secretary, or any government information to which I may have had access."[x]

Unsurprisingly, despite this unsavory and questionable arrangement, Abedin has denied any and all wrongdoing.

The other three aides who have turned over emails are Cheryl Mills, Philippe Reines, and Jake Sullivan.[xi]

On August 12, Clinton "finally produced to the FBI her server and three thumb drives. Apparently, the server had been professionally wiped clean of any useable information, and the thumb drives contain only what she selectively culled."[xii] The server was originally located in the Clintons' Chappaqua estate. It was "wiped clean in June . . . but nonetheless stored at a data center in New Jersey."[xiii] The data center is Platte River Networks, which also set up Clinton's server.

On August 14, the Associated Press reported that the two classified emails "deemed 'top secret'" include a discussion of a news

---

x   MacGuill, Dan. "Irish-run company at centre of Hillary Clinton controversy." Thejournal.ie. April 19, 2015.

xi   Kumar, Anita, Taylor, Marisa, and Gordon, Greg. "'Top Secret' emails found as Clinton probe expands to key aides" *McClatchy.* August 11, 2015.

xii   Powell, Sidney. "Hillary finally hands over her server–after it's been professionally wiped clean." *Infowars.* August 14, 2015.

xiii   Ross, Chuck. "If Hillary's Server Was 'Blank,' Why Was It Kept At A Data Center In New Jersey?" *Daily Caller.* August 14, 2015.

article detailing a U.S. drone operation and a separate conversation that could point back to highly classified material in an improper manner or merely reflect information collected independently."[xiv]

That same day Jon Karl, the chief White House correspondent for ABC News, reported that the most recent batch of released emails show "Clinton asking to borrow a book called *Send: Why People Email So Badly and How to Do It Better*, by David Shipley and Will Schwalbe. Clinton has not said why she requested the book, but it includes some advice that is particularly interesting in light of the controversy over her unconventional email arrangement at the State Department and her decision to delete tens of thousands of emails she deemed to be purely personal."[xv] One chapter "advised that to truly delete emails may require a special rewriting program 'to make sure that it's not just elsewhere on the drive but has in fact been written over sixteen or twenty times and rendered undefinable.'"

Also on August 14, former attorney general Michael Mukasey wrote an opinion piece in the *Wall Street Journal* that outlined the severity of the crimes that Clinton may have committed:

> It is a misdemeanor punishable by imprisonment for not more than a year to keep "documents or materials containing classified information . . . at an unauthorized location." Note that it is the information that is protected; the issue doesn't turn on whether the document or materials bear a classified marking. This is the statute under which David Petraeus—former Army general and Central Intelligence Agency director—was prosecuted for keeping classified information at home. Mrs. Clinton's holding of classified information on a personal server was a violation of that law. So is transferring that information on a thumb drive to David Kendall, her lawyer.

---

xiv Klapper, Bradley and Ken Dilanian. "We know what those 2 top-secret Clinton emails were about." Associated Press. August 14, 2015.

xv Karl, Jonathan. "Tips on Deleting Emails From Email Book Hillary Clinton Wanted to Read." ABC News. August 12, 2015.

The Espionage Act defines as a felony, punishable by up to 10 years, the grossly negligent loss or destruction of "information relating to the national defense." Note that at least one of the emails from the small random sample taken by the inspector general for the intelligence community contained signals intelligence and was classified top secret.

To be sure, this particular email was turned over, but on paper rather than in its original electronic form, without the metadata that went with it. If other emails of like sensitivity are among the 30,000 Mrs. Clinton erased, that is yet more problematic. The server is now in the hands of the Federal Bureau of Investigation, whose forensic skills in recovering data in situations like this are unexcelled.

The highest step in this ascending scale of criminal penalties—20 years maximum—is reached by anyone who destroys "any record, document or tangible object with intent to impede, obstruct or influence the proper administration of any matter within the jurisdiction of any department or agency of the United States . . . or in relation to or contemplation of any such matter."[xvi]

On August 16, Platte River Networks, the company that set up Hillary's server, said it is "highly likely" that a full backup was made.[xvii]

It was also reported by the *Washington Times* on August 16 that "the total number of her private emails identified by an ongoing State Department review as having contained classified data has ballooned to 60."[xviii]

It is certain that the Clinton campaign is in turmoil. The cavalier dismissal of the email controversy by Hillary Clinton early on in her

xvi Mukasey, Michael. "Clinton Defies the Law and Common Sense." *Wall Street Journal.* August 14, 2015.

xvii Twitchy. "'HUGE!' ABC News reports that it's 'highly likely' a backup server of Hillary's emails was made [video]." August 16, 2015.

xviii Solomon, John. "Number of Hillary Clinton's emails flagged for classified data grows to 60 as review continues." *Washington Times.* August 16, 2015.

campaign has turned serious as the egregious mishandling of government property is threatening her presidential aspirations.

Adding to the turmoil in the Clinton campaign, we have also learned there has been a concerted effort by Hillary and Chelsea to distance Bill from the campaign. A highly placed Democrat in Hillary's entourage told us that Bill is slipping mentally and has been sidelined as a result. This is coupled with new information that DNA lab samples suggest that Chelsea Clinton may indeed be the daughter of Clinton law partner Webb Hubbell.[xix]

Despite the Left's and Hillary's claims of a "war on women" by Republicans, the real war on women has been from the Clinton tag team. Bill abuses them physically, often in freakishly violent ways. Hillary abuses them mentally.

No one knows the devastating effects of Bill and Hillary's war on women better than Kathleen Willey. "This woman wrote the book on terrorizing women, on terrorism," said Willey. "Her tactics and the things that she set in motion against all the women like me, the ones you have heard of and the ones you haven't heard of, and the ones who are so scared that they fled the country, are terrorist tactics like I've never seen before. I went through them. I lived through them. And I know exactly what I am talking about. She is the war on women. I don't care what anybody says."[xx]

Willey took great exception to comments made by Hillary on the campaign trail in August of 2015, in which she compared the GOP's treatment of women to that of Islamic terrorists. Willey fired back, "This is a woman who is comparing the Republicans to terrorists. Terrorists who behead women, who deface women, who burn women alive. . . . And I can tell you, knowing what I know, and reading what I've read, and having talked to people, other women, who have been in the same boat that I have been in, basically in the crosshairs of the Clintons. The one difference between me and the

xix   Montero, Douglas and Butterfield, Allen. "Clinton's Paternity Scandal." *National Enquirer.* July 15, 2015

xx   WND. "Kathleen Willey: Hillary 'wrote the book on terrorizing women." August 30, 2015.

poor women who are the victims of ISIS and all the other terrorist groups is that our heads are still attached. That's the difference."[xxi]

The many victims left in the wake of both Clintons would no doubt take gratification in the toppling of Hillary at what could be her brightest moment. The Visigoths are at the gate and it is seemingly only a matter of time until it is busted open.

xxi   Ibid.

ENDNOTES

1. David Brock. "Living with The Clintons." *American Spectator.* January, 1994.
2. Author interview with Stephen Hoffenberg. February 21, 2015.
3. Neil Snyder. "Bill Clinton is an Unusually Good Liar and Hillary is no Slouch." *American Thinker.* February 2, 2013.
4. Helen Kennedy. "Bill Clinton told Ted Kennedy that Obama 'Would be getting us coffee' a few years ago: 'game change.'" *Daily News.* January 10, 2010.
5. Candice Jackson, *Their Lives: The Women Targeted by the Clinton Machine*, p. 226.
6. Melrose Larry Green. "Why the Clintons Belong in Prison." p. 85
7. Michael Goodwin. "The Kevlar Clintons." *New York Post.* March 31, 2015.
8. "How it feels to fall under the spell of the Seducer In Chief: Vain and amoral, yes. But here, four women who (very briefly) succumbed reveal the sheer power of Bill Clinton's charm." *Daily Mail.com.* February 6, 2014.
9. John Gartner, *In Search of Bill Clinton*, p. 81.
10. "How it feels to all under the spell of the Seducer In Chief: Vain and amoral, yes. But here, four women who (very briefly) succumbed reveal the sheer power of Bill Clinton's charm." *Daily Mail.com.* February 6, 2014.
11. Daniel Halper, *Clinton, Inc.: The Audacious Rebuilding of a Political Machine*, p. 55.
12. Tracy Connor. "Newser's Book: Ford saw Clinton as a Sex 'Addict.'" *Daily News.* October 28, 2007.
13. Daniel J. Harris and Teresa Hampton, *Capitol Hill Blue* "Juanita isn't the only one: Bill Clinton's long history of sexual violence against women dates back some 30 years," 1999. http://web.archive.org/web/20070516192906/http://chblue.com/Feb1999/022599/clintonwomen022599.htm accessed September 24, 2014.
14. Meredith Oakley, *On the Make: The Rise of Bill Clinton.* p. 68.
15. Gary Aldrich, *Unlimited Access: An FBI Agent Inside the Clinton White House*, p. 221.
16. http://web.archive.org/web/20070516192906/http://chblue.com/Feb1999/022599/clintonwomen022599.htm accessed November 24, 2014.

17. Joan Vennochi. "Rape allegations hurt Bill Cosby but sail past Bill Clinton." *Boston Globe*, December 21, 2014. http://www.bostonglobe.com/opinion/2014/11/21/rape-allegations-hurt-bill-cosby-but-sail-past-bill-clinton/YTIsUoXS2uxrW1mW2JSuRM/story.html.

18. Joan Vennochi, "Rape allegations hurt Bill Cosby but sail past Bill Clinton," *Boston Globe*, December 21, 2014.

19. Joan Vennochi, "Rape allegations hurt Bill Cosby but sail past Bill Clinton," Boston Globe, 12-21-14.

20. "The War On Women: Juanita Broaddrick and Bill Clinton." *Breitbart News*. October 23, 2014.

21. Candice Jackson, *Their Lives: The Women Targeted by the Clinton Machine*, p. 226.

22. Candice Jackson, *Their Lives: The Women Targeted by the Clinton Machine*, p. 226.

23. John Dougherty. "Broaddrick Details Alleged Rape By Clinton." *World Net Daily*. June 11, 2003, http://www.wnd.com/2003/06/19242/ accessed September 25, 2004.

24. http://web.archive.org/web/20030708072307/http://www.papillonsartpalace.com/janedoe.htm accessed September 26, 2014.

25. "The War On Women: Juanita Broaddrick and Bill Clinton." *Breitbart News*. October 23, 2014.

26. David Schippers, *Sellout: The Inside Story of President Clinton's Impeachment*, p. 131.

27. Candice Jackson, *Their Lives: The Women Targeted by the Clinton Machine*, p. 228.

28. Josh Rogin. "Exclusive: 'Hillary Clinton Took Me Through Hell,' Rape Victim Says." *Daily Beast*. June 20, 2014.

29. Liz Kreutz. "Hillary Clinton said she had 'obligation' to defend accused rapist." *ABC News*. July 7, 2014.

30. Ibid.

31. Juanita Broaddrick, An Open Letter to Hillary Clinton, August 15, 2000. http://www.apfn.org/apfn/Juanita.htm accessed on September 26, 2014.

32. "What's the difference between Bill Cosby and Bill Clinton?" The National Review. December 2, 2014. http://www.nationalreview.com/article/393521/wall-women-tim-cavanaugh/page/0/2 accessed December 9, 2014.

33. http://www.apfn.org/apfn/juanita.htm.

34. *Toronto Star*. September 17, 1998.

35. Interview with Larry Patterson, *The Clinton Chronicles*.

36. Ibid.

37. Interview with Jim Johnson, *The Clinton Chronicles*.

38. Ambrose Evans-Pritchard, *The Secret Life of Bill Clinton*, p. 358.

39. http://whatreallyhappened.com/WRHARTICLES/pearl/www.geocities.com/Pentagon/6315/strange.html accessed January 2, 2015.

40. Ambrose Evans-Pritchard, *The Secret Life of Bill Clinton*, p. 359.

ENDNOTES

41. http://whatreallyhappened.com/WRHARTICLES/pearl/www.geocities.com/Pentagon/6315/strange.html accessed January 26, 2015.
42. Carl Limbacher, *Hillary's Scheme*, p. 200.
43. Steve Dunleavy. "Elizabeth Gracen: I was a victim of Clinton's reign of terror." *New York Post*. September 27, 1998.
44. http://web.archive.org/web/20030708072307/http://www.papillonsartpalace.com/janedoe.htm accessed September 26, 2014.
45. http://web.archive.org/web/20030708072307/http://www.papillonsartpalace.com/janedoe.htm accessed September 26, 2014.
46. Candice Jackson, *Their Lives: The Women Targeted by the Clinton Machine*, p. 27.
47. http://web.archive.org/web/20030708072307/http://www.papillonsartpalace.com/janedoe.htm accessed September 26, 2014.
48. Candice Jackson, *Their Lives: The Women Targeted by the Clinton Machine*, p. 27.
49. "Actress Who Claimed Sex with Bill Says IRS Is Hounding Her." *New York Post*. January 13, 1999.
50. http://www.freerepublic.com/focus/news/1547995/posts accessed September 26, 2014.
51. Steve Dunleavy. "Elizabeth Gracen: I was a victim of Clinton's reign of terror." *New York Post*. September 27, 1998.
52. *Toronto Star*, September 17, 1998.
53. L. D. Brown, *Crossfire: Witness in the Clinton Investigation*, p. 80.
54. Gennifer Flowers, *Passion and Betrayal*, p. 75.
55. *60 Minutes*. January 26, 1992.
56. Interview with Don Hewitt, *The Clinton Chronicles*.
57. Gennifer Flowers, *Passion and Betrayal*, p. 70.
58. Gennifer Flowers, *Passion and Betrayal*, p. 75.
59. Gennifer Flowers, *Passion and Betrayal*, p. 94.
60. Interview with Larry Nichols, *The Clinton Chronicles*.
61. Robert Morrow interview with Larry Nichols, June 1, 2015.
62. Ibid.
63. Ibid.
64. *The Clinton Chronicles*.
65. Rodney Stich, *Defrauding America*, p. 457.
66. Gennifer Flowers, *Passion and Betrayal*, pp. 95–96.
67. Gennifer Flowers, *Passion and Betrayal*, pp. 96–97.
68. Gennifer Flowers, *Passion and Betrayal*, p. 97.
69. Gennifer Flowers, *Passion and Betrayal*, p. 98.
70. Candice Jackson, *Their Lives: The Women Targeted by the Clinton Machine*, p. 73.
71. Candice Jackson, *Their Lives: The Women Targeted by the Clinton Machine*, p. 76.
72. http://www.joeclarke.net/2008/05/sleazy-investigator-anthony-pellicano.html *NewsMax*, November 12, 2003 accessed September 29, 2014.

73. Cruz, G. "Anthony Pellicano." *TIME*. December 14, 2008. http://en.wikipedia. org/wiki/Anthony_Pellicano.

74. Candice Jackson, *Their Lives: The Women Targeted by the Clinton Machine*, p. 80.

75. Candice Jackson, *Their Lives: The Women Targeted by the Clinton Machine*, p. 43.

76. Candice Jackson, *Their Lives: The Women Targeted by the Clinton Machine*, p. 44.

77. Candice Jackson, *Their Lives: The Women Targeted by the Clinton Machine*, p. 49.

78. http://www.freerepublic.com/focus/f-news/1155295/posts accessed January 25, 2015.

79. Brent Scher. "Hillary Clinton's Long History of Targeting Women." *Washington Free Beacon*. March 9, 2015.

80. Kathleen Willey, *Target: Caught in the Crosshairs of Bill and Hillary Clinton*, p. 61.

81. Kathleen Willey, *Target: Caught in the Crosshairs of Bill and Hillary Clinton*, p. 62.

82. Kathleen Willey, *Target: Caught in the Crosshairs of Bill and Hillary Clinton*, p. 63.

83. Kathleen Willey, *Target: Caught in the Crosshairs of Bill and Hillary Clinton*, p. 82.

84. Kathleen Willey, *Target: Caught in the Crosshairs of Bill and Hillary Clinton*, p. 83.

85. Gary Aldrich, *Unlimited Access: An FBI Agent Inside the Clinton White House.*

86. Kathleen Willey, *Target: Caught in the Crosshairs of Bill and Hillary Clinton*, p. 84.

87. Kathleen Willey, *Target: Caught in the Crosshairs of Bill and Hillary Clinton*, p. 95.

88. Kathleen Willey, *Target: Caught in the Crosshairs of Bill and Hillary Clinton*, p. 97.

89. Candice Jackson, *Their Lives: The Women Targeted by the Clinton Machine*, p. 151.

90. Candice Jackson, *Their Lives: The Women Targeted by the Clinton Machine*, p. 151.

91. Michael Isikoff, *Uncovering Clinton: A Reporter's Story*, p. 162.

92. Kathleen Willey, *Target: Caught in the Crosshairs of Bill and Hillary Clinton*, pp. ix–x.

93. Kathleen Willey, *Target: Caught in the Crosshairs of Bill and Hillary Clinton*, p. 209.

94. https://www.judicialwatch.org/archive/ois/cases/filegate/Exhibits/EXHIBIT-13.pdf accessed October 8, 2004.

95. Candice Jackson, *Their Lives: The Women Targeted by the Clinton Machine*, p. 153.

96. Kathleen Willey, *Target: Caught in the Crosshairs of Bill and Hillary Clinton*, p. 119.

97. Kathleen Willey, *Target: Caught in the Crosshairs of Bill and Hillary Clinton*, p. 119.

98. Kathleen Willey, *Target: Caught in the Crosshairs of Bill and Hillary Clinton*, p. 120.

99. Kathleen Willey, *Target: Caught in the Crosshairs of Bill and Hillary Clinton*, p. 120.

100. Kathleen Willey, *Target: Caught in the Crosshairs of Bill and Hillary Clinton*, p. 120.

101. Kathleen Willey, *Target: Caught in the Crosshairs of Bill and Hillary Clinton*, p. 121.

102. Art Moore. "PI 'Admits' Hillary Paid Him to Harass Willey." *World Net Daily*. November 7, 2007. http://www.wnd.com/2007/11/44416/.

103. Kathleen Willey, *Target: Caught in the Crosshairs of Bill and Hillary Clinton*, p. 211.

104. Art Moore. "PI 'Admits' Hillary Paid Him to Harass Willey." *World Net Daily*. November 7, 2007. http://www.wnd.com/2007/11/44416/.

105. Art Moore. "PI 'Admits' Hillary Paid Him to Harass Willey." *World Net Daily*. November 7, 2007. http://www.wnd.com/2007/11/44416/.

106. Kathleen Willey, *Target: Caught in the Crosshairs of Bill and Hillary Clinton*, p. 212.

ENDNOTES

107. Fox, Cavuto, Willey Part 1 November 8, 2007. https://www.youtube.com/watch?v=KUB9PAX8wGc.

108. Candice Jackson, *Their Lives: The Women Targeted by the Clinton Machine*, p. 155.

109. http://en.wikipedia.org/wiki/Lewinsky_scandal accessed September 30, 2004.

110. Michael Isikoff, *Uncovering Clinton: A Reporter's Story*, p. 381.

111. "Kathleen Willey: Clintons Stole My Manuscript." *World Net Daily*. September 5, 2007. http://www.wnd.com/2007/09/43383/

112. "Kathleen Willey: Clintons Stole My Manuscript." *World Net Daily*. September 5, 2007. http://www.wnd.com/2007/09/43383/.

113. Parker Jennifer. "Kathleen Willey warns about the Clintons." ABC News. January 30, 2008.

114. Candice Jackson, *Their Lives: The Women Targeted by the Clinton Machine*, p. 112.

115. Candice Jackson, *Their Lives: The Women Targeted by the Clinton Machine*, p. 112.

116. http://whatreallyhappened.com/WRHARTICLES/pearl/www.geocities.com/Pentagon/6315/strange.html accessed January 25, 2015.

117. Bill Clinton. Response to the Lewinsky Allegations, Miller Center of Public Affairs, January 26, 1998.

118. Bill Clinton. "Address to the Nation." August 17, 1998.

119. http://en.wikipedia.org/wiki/Paula_Jones accessed January 26, 2015 .

120. Maureen Callahan, "Bill's Libido Threatens to Derail Hillary–Again." *New York Post*. February 14, 2015

121. http://www.mediaite.com/print/ron-burkle-throws-bill-clinton-under-the-bus/ accessed January 29, 2015.

122. http://www.mediaite.com/print/ron-burkle-throws-bill-clinton-under-the-bus/ accessed January 29, 2015.

123. Jeffrey Epstein book of contacts, https://www.documentcloud.org/documents/1508273-jeffrey-epsteins-little-black-book-redacted.html.

124. Kathleen Willey, *Target Caught in the Crosshairs of Bill and Hillary Clinton*, p. 43.

125. Scher, Brent. "Clinton Foundation Got $25,000 From Pedophile Epstein in 2006." *Free Beacon*. January 8, 2015. http://freebeacon.com/politics/clinton-foundation-got-25000-from-pedophile-epstein-in-2006/.

126. http://www.opensecrets.org/pres08/search.php?cid=ALL&name=&employ=&cycle=2008&state=&zip=10022&amt=a&sort=A&page=18.

127. http://www.dailymail.co.uk/news/article-1363247/Unsavoury-association-How-Robert-Maxwells-daughter-procured-young-girls-Prince-Andrews-billionaire-friend.html.

128. Sean Hannity. "Will Bill Clinton's Epstein Connection Hurt Hillary in 2016?" Fox News. February 12, 2015.

129. Interview with Ann Coulter. http://www.realclearpolitics.com/video/2015/01/07/coulter_lambastes_media_over_epstein_rape_case_this_is_what_media_thought_uva_rape_case_was.html.

130. http://www.thedailybeast.com/articles/2010/07/20/jeffrey-epstein-billion-aire-pedophile-goes-free.html.

131. http://www.thedailybeast.com/articles/2010/07/20/jeffrey-epstein-billion-aire-pedophile-goes-free.html.

132. http://www.mirror.co.uk/news/uk-news/prince-andrew-sex-allegations-slave-5020094.

133. http://www.dailymail.co.uk/news/article-2900787/Prince-Andrew-Heidi-Klum-Hookers-Pimps-party-New-York-socialite-accused-procuring-underaged-girls-billionaire-pedophile-Jeffrey-Epstein.html.

134. http://www.nydailynews.com/new-york/alleged-sex-slave-didn-sex-bill-clinton-article-1.2087614.

135. http://www.nydailynews.com/new-york/alleged-sex-slave-didn-sex-bill-clinton-article-1.2087614.

136. http://www.dailymail.co.uk/news/article-1363452/Bill-Clinton-15-year-old-masseuse-I-met-twice-claims-Epsteins-girl.html#ixzz3Oj8MgbuM.

137. http://www.dailymail.co.uk/news/article-1363452/Bill-Clinton-15-year-old-masseuse-I-met-twice-claims-Epsteins-girl.html#ixzz3Oj8MgbuM accessed January 29, 2015.

138. Richard Johnson. "Author Faces Off Against Bill Clinton." *New York Post.* November 5, 2014. http://pagesix.com/2014/11/05/author-faces-off-against-bill-clinton/?utm_medium=twitter&utm_source=twitterfeed.

139. Lia Eustachewich. "Sex Slave Claims Bill Clinton Visited Epstein's 'Orgy Island.'" *New York Post.* January 26, 2015. http://nation.foxnews.com/2015/01/24/sex-slave-claims-bill-clinton-visited-epstein-s-orgy-island.

140. http://en.wikipedia.org/wiki/Les_Wexner.

141. Julie Baumgold. "The Bachelor Billionaire: On Pins and Needles with Leslie Wexner." *New York* magazine, August 5, 1985.

142. "Illegal Emails, Shady Donations and a Billionaire Pedophile." https://www.youtube.com/watch?v=9snfK8ndPho.

143. Deposition of Virginia Roberts.

144. https://www.dropbox.com/s/65bpx6kew9n7q27/Doe%20v.%20United%20States%20of%20America%20-%20291.pdf?dl=0

145. Vicky Ward. "The Talented Mr. Epstein." http://www.vanityfair.com/society/features/2003/03/jeffrey-epstein-200303.

146. Vicky Ward. "The Talented Mr. Epstein." http://www.vanityfair.com/society/features/2003/03/jeffrey-epstein-200303.

147. "Harvard to Keep Epstein Gift." *Harvard Crimson.* September 13, 2006. http://www.thecrimson.com/article/2006/9/13/harvard-to-keep-epstein-gift-after.

148. https://www.dropbox.com/s/65bpx6kew9n7q27/Doe%20v.%20United%20States%20of%20America%20-%20291.pdf?dl=0.

149. "In re: Investigation of Jeffrey Epstein: Non-Prosecution Agreement, dated 9-24-07, between the U.S. attorneys and Jeffrey Epstein."

150. Nick Bryant. "Flight Logs Put Clinton, Dershowitz on Pedophile Billionaire's Sex Jet." *Gawker*. January 22, 2015.

151. Declaration of Virginia Roberts, January 19, 2015, Case No. 08-80736-CIV-MARRA, United States District Court, Southern District of Florida https://www.dropbox.com/s/65bpx6kew9n7q27/Doe%20v.%20United%20States%20of%20America%20-%20291.pdf?dl=0.

152. Interview with Thomas B. Evans, Jr. October 12, 2013.

153. http://www.thedailybeast.com/articles/2015/03/26/model-king-sues-billionaire-perv-jeffrey-epstein.html.

154. http://jezebel.com/5603638/meet-the-modeling-agent-who-trafficked-under-aged-girls-for-sex Michael Gross, *Model*, p. 527.

155. Michael Gross, *Model*, p. 527.

156. http://www.buzzfeed.com/kenbensinger/clinton-epstein-innuendo#.ihMX-4qabg accessed October 29, 2015.

157. Jenna Sauders. "The Sex Trafficking Model Scout." *Jezebel*. August 4, 2010. http://jezebel.com/5603638/meet-the-modeling-agent-who-trafficked-under-aged-girls-for-sex.

158. http://www.thedailybeast.com/articles/2015/02/13/the-dead-model-and-the-dirty-billionaire.html.

159. http://www.examiner.com/article/jerry-epstein-underaged-models-supplied-by-jean-luc-brunel-says-court-documents accessed January 29, 2015.

160. Interview with Palm Beach correction officer. March 5, 2015.

161. https://www.dropbox.com/s/65bpx6kew9n7q27/Doe%20v.%20United%20States%20of%20America%20-%20291.pdf?dl=0.

162. http://gawker.com/190625/exclusive-jeffrey-epsteins-sex-slave.

163. http://1984arkansasmotheroftheyear.blogspot.com/2014/04/2006-probable-cause-affidavit-for-mega.html.

164. http://www.nytimes.com/2006/09/03/us/03epstein.html?pagewanted=print&_r=0.

165. Conchita Sarnoff. "Behind Pedophile Jeffrey Epstein's Sweetheart Deal." *Daily Beast*. March 25, 2011. http://www.thedailybeast.com/articles/2011/03/25/jeffrey-epstein-how-the-billionaire-pedophile-got-off-easy.html accessed February 19, 2015.

166. http://www.thedailybeast.com/articles/2011/03/25/jeffrey-epstein-how-the-billionaire-pedophile-got-off-easy.html.

167. http://www.thedailybeast.com/articles/2011/03/25/jeffrey-epstein-how-the-billionaire-pedophile-got-off-easy.html.

168. Conchita Sarnoff. "Billionaire Pedophile Goes Free." *Daily Beast*. July 20, 2010. http://www.thedailybeast.com/articles/2010/07/20/jeffrey-epstein-billionaire-pedophile-goes-free.html.

169. http://www.palmbeachdailynews.com/news/news/lawsuit-documents-link-jeffrey-epstein-to-modeling/nMGzH.

170. "Ann Coulter on Bill Clinton's Possible Connection to Epstein." https://www.youtube.com/watch?v=xzP8kK7miik.
171. http://www.people.com/people/package/article/0,,20395222_20913690,00.html.
172. Sean Hannity. "Will Bill Clinton's Epstein Connection Hurt Hillary in 2016?" Fox News. February 12, 2015.
173. http://www.independent.co.uk/news/world/americas/who-is-jeffrey-epstein-a-study-of-the-man-linked-to-worlds-of-celebrity-politics--and-royalty-9954397.html.
174. L. D. Brown, *Crossfire: Witness in the Clinton Investigation*, p. 54.
175. Mara Leveritt, *The Boys on The Tracks*, p. 223.
176. Gennifer Flowers, *Passion and Betrayal*, p. 42.
177. Gennifer Flowers, *Passion and Betrayal*, p. 42.
178. http://www.freerepublic.com/focus/fr/1155472/posts accessed December 15, 2014.
179. Ambrose Evans-Pritchard, *The Secret Life of Bill Clinton: The Unreported Stories*, p. 290.
180. Interview with John Brown, *The Clinton Chronicles*, 1994.
181. http://www.freerepublic.com/focus/fr/1155472/posts accessed December 15, 2014.
182. Ambrose Evans-Pritchard, *The Secret Life of Bill Clinton: The Unreported Stories*, p. 262.
183. Ambrose Evans-Pritchard, *The Secret Life of Bill Clinton: The Unreported Stories*, p. 259.
184. Ambrose Evans-Pritchard, *The Secret Life of Bill Clinton: The Unreported Stories*, p. 239.
185. Ambrose Evans-Pritchard, *The Secret Life of Bill Clinton: The Unreported Stories*, p. 264.
186. Leveritt, Mara, *The Boys on the Tracks*, p. 2.
187. Leveritt, Mara, *The Boys on the Tracks*, p. 3.
188. Leveritt, Mara, *The Boys on the Tracks*, p. 5.
189. Leveritt, Mara, *The Boys on the Tracks*, p. 8.
190. Interview with Linda Ives, *The Clinton Chronicles*, 1994.
191. http://idfiles.com/salvid.htm#1.
192. Ambrose Evans-Pritchard, *The Secret Life of Bill Clinton: The Unreported Stories*, p. 267.
193. Ibid.
194. Leveritt, Mara, *The Boys on the Tracks*, p. 71.
195. Interview with John Brown, *The Clinton Chronicles*, 1994.
196. Leveritt, Mara, *The Boys on the Tracks*, p. 84.
197. Leveritt, Mara, *The Boys on the Tracks*, p. 90.
198. Interview with Linda Ives, *The Clinton Chronicles*, 1994.

199. Interview with Linda Ives. *The Clinton Chronicles*. 1994.
200. Mara Leveritt and Max Brantley. "Out of Control in Lonoke County." *Arkansas Times*. June 22, 2006.
201. Ambrose Evans-Pritchard, *The Secret Life of Bill Clinton: The Unreported Stories*, p. 263.
202. Ambrose Evans-Pritchard, *The Secret Life of Bill Clinton: The Unreported Stories*, p. 264.
203. Bill Clinton on *The Arsenio Hall Show*, November 22, 1992.
204. Interview with Jean Duffey, *The Clinton Chronicles*.
205. Letter of LA Attorney General William Guste to US Attorney General Ed Meese. March 3, 1986. http://whatreallyhappened.com/RANCHO/POLITICS/MENA/letter_to_edwin_meese_iii_3-3-86.html.
206. Interview with Russell Welch, *The Clinton Chronicles*.
207. Daniel Hopsicker, *Barry & the Boys: The CIA, the Mob and America's Secret History*, p. 268.
208. L. D. Brown, *Crossfire*, pp. 102–103.
209. L. D. Brown, *Crossfire*, p. 104.
210. L. D. Brown, *Crossfire*, pp. 113–114.
211. L. D. Brown, *Crossfire*, p. 116.
212. Roger Morris, *Partners in Power*, p. 40.
213. http://en.wikipedia.org/wiki/Ponderosa_Steakhouse_and_Bonanza_Steakhouse.
214. http://en.wikipedia.org/wiki/Eclipse_Award_for_Outstanding_Owner.
215. Ambrose Evans-Pritchard, *The Secret Life of Bill Clinton: The Unreported Stories*, p. 291.
216. http://articles.latimes.com/1992-03-23/news/mn-3134_1_state-police.
217. Richard Poe, *Hillary's Secret War: The Clinton Conspiracy to Muzzle Internet Journalists*, p. 113.
218. Gary Webb, *Dark Alliance, the CIA, the Contras, and the Crack Cocaine Explosion*, p. 117.
219. Victor Thorn, *Hillary and Bill: The Drugs Volume*, p. 164.
220. http://www.benbarnesgroup.com/resume/PatsyT_digitalResume.pdf.
221. Victor Thorn, *Hillary and Bill: The Drugs Volume*, p. 173.
222. Victor Thorn, *Hillary and Bill: The Drugs Volume*, p. 164.
223. Barbara Olson, *The Final Days*, p. 147.
224. L. J. Davis. "The Name of the Rose." *New Republic*. April 4, 1994.
225. Victor Thorn, *Hillary and Bill: The Drugs Volume*, p. 165.
226. *Insight on the News*. November 6, 1995.
227. Ambrose Evans-Pritchard, *The Secret Life of Bill Clinton: The Unreported Stories*, p. 289.
228. Ambrose Evans-Pritchard, *The Secret Life of Bill Clinton: The Unreported Stories*, p. 290.

229. http://www.freerepublic.com/focus/f-news/1155368/posts.

230. http://www.freerepublic.com/focus/f-news/1155368/posts.

231. Ambrose Evans-Pritchard, *The Secret Life of Bill Clinton: The Unreported Stories*, p. 292.

232. Victor Thorn, *Hillary and Bill: The Drugs Volume*, p. 168.

233. George Carpozi, *Clinton Confidential: The Climb to Power*, p. 261.

234. Ambrose Evans-Pritchard, *The Secret Life of Bill Clinton: The Unreported Stories*, p. 309.

235. Larry Patterson, *More Than Sex: The Secrets of Bill and Hillary Clinton Revealed!*, NewsMax.

236. http://www.idfiles.com/menatarget2.htm accessed December 17, 2014.

237. Interview with Winston Bryant, *The Clinton Chronicles*.

238. Micah Morrison. "The Mena Coverup." *Wall Street Journal*. October 18, 1994.

239. Ibid.

240. Ibid.

241. Interview with Larry Nichols. *The Clinton Chronicles*.

242. Daniel Hopsicker, *Barry & the Boys: The CIA, the Mob and America's Secret History*, p. 375.

243. Daniel Hopsicker, *Barry & the Boys: The CIA, the Mob and America's Secret History*, p. 376.

244. Terry Reed, *Compromised: Clinton, Bush and the CIA*, pp. 264–265.

245. Terry Reed, *Compromised: Clinton, Bush and the CIA*, p. 265.

246. L. D. Brown, *Crossfire*, p. 130.

247. Ambrose Evans-Pritchard, *The Secret Life of Bill Clinton*, p. 244.

248. Ambrose Evans-Pritchard, *The Secret Life of Bill Clinton*, p. 236.

249. Ambrose Evans-Pritchard, *The Secret Life of Bill Clinton*, p. 245.

250. Ambrose Evans-Pritchard, *The Secret Life of Bill Clinton*, p. 237.

251. Ambrose Evans-Pritchard, *The Secret Life of Bill Clinton*, p. 239.

252. Ambrose Evans-Pritchard, *The Secret Life of Bill Clinton*, p. 243.

253. Ambrose Evans-Pritchard, *The Secret Life of Bill Clinton*, p. 247.

254. Ambrose Evans-Pritchard, *The Secret Life of Bill Clinton*, p. 250.

255. Ambrose Evans-Pritchard, *The Secret Life of Bill Clinton*, p. 236.

256. http://whatreallyhappened.com/RANCHO/POLITICS/MENA/TATUM/tatum.html.

257. Presidential Debate with George H. W. Bush, Bill Clinton & Ross Perot. October 15, 1992.

258. http://www.serendipity.li/cia/gritz1.htm.

259. http://en.wikipedia.org/wiki/Richard_Armitage_(politician).

260. Thomas Burdick, *Blue Thunder: How the Mafia Owned and finally Murdered Cigarette Boat King Donald Aronow*, p. 351.

261. Al Martin, *The Conspirators, Secrets of an Iran-Contra Insider*, p. 240.

262. http://www.amazon.com/Conspirators-Secrets-Iran-Contra-Insider/dp/097100420X/ref=sr_1_1?ie=UTF8&qid=1418922522&sr=8-1&keywords=al+martin+conspirators.

263. March 2013. Facebook PM exchange between Robert Morrow and Daniel Hopsicker.

264. http://whatreallyhappened.com/RANCHO/POLITICS/MENA/TATUM/tatum.html accessed December 18, 2014.

265. Greg Szymanski. "Former DEA Agent Wants George H. Bush, Negroponte and Other Higher-Ups Held Accountable for Illegal Drug Smuggling." March 5, 2006. http://rense.com/general69/eVE.HTM accessed December 18, 2014.

266. Greg Szymanski. "Former DEA Agent Wants George H. Bush, Negroponte and Other Higher-Ups Held Accountable for Illegal Drug Smuggling." March 5, 2006. http://rense.com/general69/eVE.HTM accessed December 18, 2014.

267. Richard Bernstein. "Ross Perot Will Not Like this Book." *New York Times*. August 7, 1996.

268. "FLASHBACK Ron Paul on CIA Drug Trafficking (1988)." https://www.youtube.com/watch?v=CyzsW8qIGug.

269. http://www.leopoldreport.com/Pegasus.html.

270. Douglas Jehl. "Bush Calls Votes for Perot Wasted." *Los Angeles Times*. October 23, 1992.

271. Lloyd Grove. "Bill Clinton a CIA Spy?" *Washington Post*. February 4, 2003.

272. Jack Wheeler. "How the Clintons Will Undo McCain." http://www.wnd.com/2008/02/45867.

273. http://www.breitbart.com/Big-Government/2013/09/09/Jeb-Bush-To-Award-Hillary-Clinton-Liberty-Medal.

274. "Barbara Bush: I love Bill Clinton." http://www.politico.com/story/2014/01/barbara-bush-bill-clinton-102418.html.

275. "Bush daughter hopes Hillary Clinton runs in 2016." CBS News. August 15, 2013. http://www.cbsnews.com/news/bush-daughter-hopes-hillary-clinton-runs-in-2016.

276. http://news.yahoo.com/george-w-bush-garner-clinton-jeb-interview-190705340.html.

277. "Are Bill Clinton and George W. Bush best buds now?" Associated Press, December 13, 2014.

278. "Are Bill Clinton and George W. Bush best buds now?" Associated Press, December 13, 2014.

279. John Daly. "Why It's Sad to Watch the Bush/Clinton Friendship." April 8, 2014. http://bernardgoldberg.com/sad-watch-bushclinton-friendshi.

280. John Daly. "Why It's Sad to Watch the Bush/Clinton Friendship." April 8, 2014. http://bernardgoldberg.com/sad-watch-bushclinton-friendship.

281. "Elder Bush hails 'polite' Clinton." BBC, March 7, 2005. http://news.bbc.co.uk/2/hi/asia-pacific/4325585.stm.

282. http://www.bizpacreview.com/2014/04/19/laura-bush-shows-pure-class-in-message-to-clintons-113718 accessed December 13, 2014.

283. "Jenna Bush: Hillary Clinton and I are 'related' through 'Uncle' Bill." *Daily Mail*, October 4, 2013. http://www.dailymail.co.uk/news/article-2443961/Jenna-Bush-Hillary-Clinton-related-marriage-uncle-Bill--George-W-Bushs-brother-mother.html.

284. "Jenna Bush: Hillary Clinton and I are 'related' through 'Uncle' Bill." *Daily Mail*, October 4, 2013.

285. "Bush: My Sweet Dad, a Wonderful Father to Bill Clinton and Me." Tony Harnden. *Sunday Times*. November 18, 2014. http://www.realclearpolitics.com/articles/2014/11/18/bush_my_sweet_daddy_a_wonderful_father_to_bill_clinton_and_me_124685.html.

286. "Bush: My Sweet Dad, a Wonderful Father to Bill Clinton and Me." Tony Harnden. *Sunday Times*. November 18, 2014.

287. "Bush: My Sweet Dad, a Wonderful Father to Bill Clinton and Me." Tony Harnden. *Sunday Times*. November 18, 2014.

288. http://www.nytimes.com/2000/02/16/us/2000-campaign-excerpts-television-debate-among-3-remaining-gop-candidates.html.

289. "The Four most interesting revelations from the hacked Bush emails." *Salon*. February 8, 2013. http://www.salon.com/2013/02/08/the_four_most_interesting_revelations_from_the_hacked_bush_emails.

290. Mike Allen. "Inside Hillary Clinton's 2016 Plan." *Politico*, January 26, 2015. http://www.politico.com/story/2015/01/hillary-clinton-2016-elections-114586.html accessed January 26, 2015.

291. Mike Allen. "Inside Hillary Clinton's 2016 Plan." *Politico*, January 26, 2015. http://www.politico.com/story/2015/01/hillary-clinton-2016-elections-114586.html accessed January 26, 2015.

292. George Carlin. *It's Bad for Ya!* HBO 2008.

293. Christopher Hitchens. "The Case Against Hillary Clinton." *Slate*. January 14, 2008.

294. Rebecca Mead. "Hillary for President: No Joke." *The New Yorker*. April 14, 2015.

295. Gary Aldrich, *Unlimited Access: An FBI Agent Inside the Clinton White House.*

296. Edward Klein, *The Truth about Hillary*, p. 90.

297. Edward Klein, *The Truth about Hillary*, p. 91.

298. David Brock. "His Cheatin' Heart: Living With the Clintons: Bill's Arkansas bodyguard tell the story the press missed." *American Spectator*, January 1994. http://www.shwiggie.com/articles/clintons.html.

299. David Brock. "His Cheatin' Heart: Living With the Clintons: Bill's Arkansas bodyguard tell the story the press missed." *American Spectator*, January 1994.

300. David Brock. "His Cheatin' Heart: Living With the Clintons: Bill's Arkansas bodyguard tell the story the press missed." *American Spectator*, January 1994.

301. Christopher Andersen, *American Evita: Hillary Clinton's Path to Power*, p. 89.

302. Christopher Andersen, *American Evita: Hillary Clinton's Path to Power*, p. 89.

303. Christopher Andersen, *American Evita: Hillary Clinton's Path to Power*, p. 90.

304. *Chicago Sun-Times*. February 19, 1993.

305. http://sweetness-light.com/archive/flashback-hillary-and-barbra-streisand.

306. http://sweetness-light.com/archive/flashback-hillary-and-barbra-streisand.

307. Glenn Sacks. "Is There a Batterer in the US Senate?" May 7, 2002. http://www.ifeminists.com/introduction/editorials/2002/0507a.html.

308. http://www.ifeminists.com/introduction/editorials/2002/0507a.html.

309. http://www.ifeminists.com/introduction/editorials/2002/0507a.html.

310. Larry Getlen. "Hillary Clinton hit Bill in the head with a book after Monica affair." *New York Post*. April 5, 2015.

311. Buzz Patterson, *Dereliction of Duty*, p. 68.

312. Buzz Patterson, *Dereliction of Duty*, p. 63.

313. R. Emmett Tyrrell, Jr., *The Clinton Crack-Up: the Boy President's Life after the White House*, p. 65.

314. R. Emmett Tyrrell, Jr., *The Clinton Crack-Up: the Boy President's Life after the White House*, p. 65.

315. http://www.thegatewaypundit.com/2015/04/hillary-clinton-will-dems-nominate-reported-violent-spouse-abuser-for-president.

316. http://www.thegatewaypundit.com/2015/04/hillary-clinton-will-dems-nominate-reported-violent-spouse-abuser-for-president.

317. Ed Klein, *The Truth about Hillary*, p. 99.

318. Marilyn Rauber. "Bio: Hillary Hired Snoop to Watch Bill." *New York Post*. April 22, 1999.

319. Hillary Directed Waco. February 10, 2001. APFN http://www.apfn.org/apfn/hillary_waco.htm accessed September 24, 2014.

320. Hillary Directed Waco. February 10, 2001. APFN http://www.apfn.org/apfn/hillary_waco.htm accessed September 24, 2014.

321. Hillary Directed Waco. February 10, 2001. APFN http://www.apfn.org/apfn/hillary_waco.htm accessed September 24, 2014.

322. Ben Shapiro. "Hollywood Goes Hoo-Hoo for Hillary." CNSNEWS.COM. August 1, 2013.

323. Webb Hubbell, *Friends in High Places*, p. 157.

324. Webb Hubbell, *Friends in High Places*, p. 157.

325. http://en.wikipedia.org/wiki/Vince_Foster accessed November 2, 2014.

326. L. D. Brown, *Crossfire: Witness in the Clinton Investigation*, p. 63.

327. L. D. Brown, *Crossfire: Witness in the Clinton Investigation*, p. 63.

328. L. D. Brown, *Crossfire: Witness in the Clinton Investigation*, p. 64.

329. Ronald Kessler, *Inside the White House*, p. 245.

330. http://www.mega.nu/ampp/foster.html accessed November 2, 2014. Also Larry Patterson, *More Than Sex: the Secrets of Bill & Hillary Clinton Revealed!* January 2000, NewsMax.

331. *National Enquirer*, January 26, 1999 and Barbara Olson, *Hell To Pay*, p. 211.
332. Ambrose Evans-Pritchard, *The Secret Life of Bill Clinton: the Unreported Stories*, p. 246.
333. Webb Hubbell, *Friends in High Places*, p. 234.
334. Toni Locy. "For White House Travel Office, A Two-Year Trip of Trouble." *Washington Post*. February 27, 1995.
335. Barbara Olson, *Hell To Pay, The Unfolding Story of Hillary Clinton*, p. 243.
336. David Johnston. "Memo Places Hillary Clinton at Core of Travel Office Case." *New York Times*. January 5, 1996.
337. Barbara Olson, *Hell To Pay, The Unfolding Story of Hillary Clinton*, p. 245.
338. Barbara Olson, *Hell To Pay, The Unfolding Story of Hillary Clinton*, p. 245.
339. http://en.wikipedia.org/wiki/White_House_travel_office_controversy accessed November 11, 2014 .
340. Webb Hubbell, *Friends in High Places*, p. 234.
341. Webb Hubbell, *Friends in High Places*, p. 65.
342. Dan Moldea, *A Washington Tragedy: How the Death of Vince Foster Ignited a Political Firestorm*, p. 387.
343. Carl Bernstein, *A Woman in Charge*, p. 338.
344. Carl Bernstein, *A Woman in Charge*, p. 339.
345. Ronald Kessler, *The Secrets of the FBI*, p. 108.
346. Ronald Kessler, *The Secrets of the FBI*, p. 108.
347. Ronald Kessler, *The Secrets of the FBI*, p. 109.
348. Ronald Kessler, *The Secrets of the FBI*, p. 110.
349. Hillary Clinton, *Living History*, p. 175.
350. Sander Hicks. "Hillary's Secrets." http://www.rense.com/general80/hll.htm accessed November 27, 2014.
351. Dan Moldea, *A Washington Tragedy: How the Death of Vince Foster Ignited a Political Firestorm*, p. 204 .
352. Christopher Ruddy, *The Strange Death of Vince Foster: An Investigation*, back flap.
353. Hillary Clinton, *Living History*, p. 174.
354. Chris Ruddy, *The Strange Death of Vince Foster: An Investigation*, p. 113.
355. Chris Ruddy, *The Strange Death of Vince Foster: An Investigation*, p. 113.
356. Barbara Walters interview of Hillary Clinton. *20/20*. January 12, 1996.
357. Ibid.
358. Michael Kellet, *The Murder of Vince Foster*, p. 99.
359. Michael Kellet, *The Murder of Vince Foster*, p. 100.
360. Michael Kellet, *The Murder of Vince Foster*, p. 101.
361. Marinka Peschmann, *Following Orders: The Death of Vince Foster, Clinton White House Lawyer*, p. 104.
362. Marinka Peschmann, *Following Orders: The Death of Vince Foster, Clinton White House Lawyer*, p. 105.
363. Michael Kellet, *The Murder of Vince Foster*, pp. 22–23.

364. Dan Moldea, *A Washington Tragedy: How the Death of Vince Foster Ignited a Political Firestorm*, p. 196.

365. Ambrose Evans-Pritchard, *The Secret Life of Bill Clinton: the Unreported Stories*, p. 134.

366. Michael Kellet, *The Murder of Vince Foster*, p. 153.

367. Michael Kellet, *The Murder of Vince Foster*, p. 154.

368. Michael Kellet, *The Murder of Vince Foster*, p. 155.

369. Michael Kellet, *The Murder of Vince Foster*, p. 28.

370. Michael Kellet, *The Murder of Vince Foster*, pp. 28–29.

371. Michael Kellet, *The Murder of Vince Foster*, p. 31.

372. Dan Moldea, *A Washington Tragedy: How the Death of Vince Foster Ignited a Political Firestorm*, p. 200.

373. Marinka Peschmann, *Following Orders: The Death of Vince Foster, Clinton White House Lawyer*, p. 130.

374. Matthew MacAdam. "Vince Foster." http://www.crimelibrary.com/notorious_murders/celebrity/vincent_foster/8.html accessed November 20, 2014.

375. Michael Kellet, *The Murder of Vince Foster*, p. 24.

376. Michael Kellet, *The Murder of Vince Foster*, p. 115.

377. Michael Kellet, *The Murder of Vince Foster*, p. 147.

378. Michael Kellet, *The Murder of Vince Foster*, p. 36.

379. Michael Kellet, *The Murder of Vince Foster*, p. 39.

380. Michael Kellet, *The Murder of Vince Foster*, p. 39.

381. Ambrose Evans-Pritchard, *The Secret Life of Bill Clinton: the Unreported Stories*, p. 144.

382. Chris Ruddy, *The Strange Death of Vince Foster: An Investigation*, back flap.

383. Chris Ruddy, *The Strange Death of Vince Foster: An Investigation*, p. 93.

384. Michael Kellet, *The Murder of Vince Foster*, p. 41.

385. Michael Kellet, *The Murder of Vince Foster*, p. 51.

386. Marinka Peschmann, *Following Orders: The Death of Vince Foster, Clinton White House Lawyer*, p. 121.

387. http://www.fbicover-up.com/photos/fosterkeys.htm accessed November 29, 2014.

388. Hillary Clinton, *Living History*, p. 175.

389. Ambrose Evans-Pritchard, *The Secret Life of Bill Clinton: the Unreported Stories*, p. 186.

390. Chris Ruddy, *The Strange Death of Vince Foster: An Investigation*, p. 106.

391. http://content.time.com/time/nation/article/0,8599,4717,00.html accessed November 20, 2014.

392. L. D. Brown, *Crossfire*, p. 46.

393. Chris Ruddy, *The Strange Death of Vince Foster: An Investigation*, p. 102.

394. Chris Ruddy, *The Strange Death of Vince Foster: An Investigation*, p. 103.

395. Chris Ruddy, *The Strange Death of Vince Foster: An Investigation*, p. 104.

396. Chris Ruddy, *The Strange Death of Vince Foster: An Investigation*, p. 103.

397. Chris Ruddy, *The Strange Death of Vince Foster: An Investigation*, pp. 106–107.

398. Ambrose Evans-Pritchard, *The Secret Life of Bill Clinton*, p. 209.

399. http://en.wikipedia.org/wiki/Ken_Starr accessed November 24, 2014.

400. Ambrose Evans-Pritchard, *The Secret Life of Bill Clinton*, p. 160.

401. Ambrose Evans-Pritchard, *The Secret Life of Bill Clinton*, p. 160.

402. Ambrose Evans-Pritchard, *The Secret Life of Bill Clinton*, p. 161.

403. Ambrose Evans-Pritchard, *The Secret Life of Bill Clinton*, p. 166.

404. Ambrose Evans-Pritchard, *The Secret Life of Bill Clinton*, p. 164.

405. Ambrose Evans-Pritchard, *The Secret Life of Bill Clinton*, p. 164.

406. Ambrose Evans-Pritchard, *The Secret Life of Bill Clinton*, p. 167.

407. http://www.law.cornell.edu/uscode/text/18/1512 accessed November 27, 2014.

408. Ambrose Evans-Pritchard, *The Secret Life of Bill Clinton*, p. 172.

409. Ambrose Evans-Pritchard, *The Secret Life of Bill Clinton*, p. 173.

410. *Failure of the Public Trust.* http://www.fbicover-up.com/Miquel/Miquel.htm accessed December 3, 2014.

411. Ambrose Evans-Pritchard, *The Secret Life of Bill Clinton*, p. 175.

412. Ambrose Evans-Pritchard, *The Secret Life of Bill Clinton*, p. 177.

413. Ambrose Evans-Pritchard, *The Secret Life of Bill Clinton*, p. 177.

414. http://www.prorev.com/knwltn.htm accessed November 28, 2014 .

415. *Failure of the Public Trust.* http://www.fbicover-up.com/press/index.htm accessed November 28, 2014.

416. *Failure of the Public Trust.* http://www.fbicover-up.com/Miquel/Miquel.htm accessed December 3, 2014.

417. Thomas Defrank. "CARTER RIPS CLINTON ON 'DISGRACE' OF PARDON." *New York Daily News*. February 22, 2001. Web. May 28, 2015.

418. Thomas Defrank. "CARTER RIPS CLINTON ON 'DISGRACE' OF PARDON."*New York Daily News*. February 22, 2001. Web. May 28, 2015.

419. http://en.wikipedia.org/wiki/Marc_Rich.

420. Ibid.

421. Jordan, Hamilton. "The First Grifters." *Wall Street Journal*. February 20, 2001. Web. May 28, 2015.

422. Lewis, Neil A. "The Nation: Pardon Me. Please.; Lobbying for Forgiveness." *New York Times*. February 24, 2001. Web. May 28, 2015.

423. Labaton, Stephen. "Hillary Clinton Turned $1,000 Into $99,540, White House Says." *New York Times*. March 29, 1994. Web. May 28, 2015.

424. Babcock, Charles R. "Hillary Clinton Futures Trades Detailed." *Washington Post*. May 27, 1994. Web. May 28, 2015.

425. Ibid.

426. John M. Broeder. "Hillary Clinton's Futures Trades Unusual, Experts Say." *Los Angeles Times*. March 31, 1994. Web. May 28, 2015.

427. Angie Cannon. "Hillary Clinton Invested $1,000, Netted $100,000 Through Trading." *Seattle Times*. May 30, 1994. Web. May 28, 2015.

428. Brad Fox. "10 Scandals Involving Hillary Clinton You May Have Forgotten."*Media Research Council*. March 10, 2015. Web. May 28, 2015.

429. Suzi Parker, *Salon*, "Blood Money," http://www.salon.com/1998/12/24/cov_23news/ accessed October 30, 2014.

430. http://www.encyclopediaofarkansas.net/encyclopedia/entry-detail.aspx?entryID=3732 accessed October 20, 2014.

431. http://www.encyclopediaofarkansas.net/encyclopedia/entry-detail.aspx?entryID=3732 accessed October 20, 2014.

432. http://www.encyclopediaofarkansas.net/encyclopedia/entry-detail.aspx?entryID=3732 accessed October 20, 2014.

433. http://www.encyclopediaofarkansas.net/encyclopedia/entry-detail.aspx?entryID=3732 accessed October 20, 2014.

434. Michael Sullivan, *Blood Trail*, inside rear book flap.

435. Suzi Parker. "Blood Money." *Salon*. http://www.salon.com/1998/12/24/cov_23news/ accessed October 30, 2014.

436. Suzi Parker. "Blood Money." *Salon*. http://www.salon.com/1998/12/24/cov_23news/ accessed October 30, 2014.

437. Suzi Parker. "Blood Money." *Salon*. http://www.salon.com/1998/12/24/cov_23news/ accessed October 30, 2014.

438. Suzi Parker. "Blood Money." *Salon*. http://www.salon.com/1998/12/24/cov_23news/ accessed October 30, 2014.

439. Suzi Parker. "Blood Money." *Salon*. http://www.salon.com/1998/12/24/cov_23news/ accessed October 30, 2014.

440. *World Net Daily*, "'Blood Trail' Author's Clinic Burns," May 21, 1999. http://www.wnd.com/1999/05/3696/ accessed October 30, 2014.

441. Suzi Parker, *Salon*. "Dumping Scandal: The Export of Bad Blood." http://www.salon.com/1999/02/25/news_185/ accessed October 30, 2014.

442. Candice Jackson, *Their Lives: The Women Targeted by the Clinton Machine*, p. 31.

443. Candice Jackson, *Their Lives: The Women Targeted by the Clinton Machine*, p. 32.

444. Candice Jackson, *Their Lives: The Women Targeted by the Clinton Machine*, p. 32.

445. *Globe*. Interview with Danney Williams. 2013.

446. *Globe*, February 18, 1992.

447. *Globe*, February 18, 1992.

448. George Carpozi, *Clinton Confidential: The Unauthorized Biography of Bill and Hillary Clinton*, p. 174.

449. *Globe*, February 18, 1992.

450. "Bill's Secret Son Begs to Meet Dying Dad." *Globe*, May 13, 2013.

451. *Globe*, February 18, 1992.

452. *Globe*, February 18, 1992.

453. *Globe*, February 18, 1992.

454. "Clinton's Bi-racial son story is not over" http://www.clevelandchallenger. com/clintons-bi-racial-son-story-is-not-over/ accessed December 4, 2014.

455. *NewsMax*. "Racist Cover-Up in Story of Clinton's 'Illegitimate Son?'" December 15, 1998.

456. George Carpozi, *Clinton Confidential: The Unauthorized Biography of Bill and Hillary Clinton*, p. 174.

457. George Carpozi, *Clinton Confidential: The Unauthorized Biography of Bill and Hillary Clinton*, p. 180.

458. *London Daily Telegraph*. January 8, 1999. http://prorev.com/whtwtrm.htm accessed December 7, 2014.

459. *NewsMax*. "Stephanopoulos Used Threat to Stifle Clinton Son Story." December 28, 1998.

460. *NewsMax*. "Stephanopoulos Used Threat to Stifle Clinton Son Story." December 28, 1998.

461. Joyce Milton, *The First Partner: Hillary Rodham Clinton*, p. 217.

462. http://fatherhood.hhs.gov/pclinton95.htm.

463. *NewsMax*. "News on the President's Secret Son." November 2, 1998.

464. *NewsMax*. "Racist Cover-Up in Story of Clinton's 'Illegitimate Son?'" December 15, 1998.

465. http://prorev.com/whtwtrm.htm accessed December 7, 2014.

466. http://www.drudgereportarchives.com/dsp/specialReports_pc_carden_detail.htm?reportID=%7BB5E2DC5F-DCB0-4A4A-AD05-95EF060CBA36%7D accessed December 7, 2014.

467. Bill Clinton. President's Radio Address. June 17, 2000. http://www.presidency. ucsb.edu/ws/?pid=58649.

468. Bill Clinton. President's Radio Address. June 17, 2000. http://www.presidency. ucsb.edu/ws/?pid=58649.

469. http://www.presidency.ucsb.edu/ws/?pid=58649.

470. http://www.presidency.ucsb.edu/ws/?pid=58649.

471. "Off Color 'Joke' is a Hot Potato." *New York Post*. December 10, 2007. http:// nypost.com/2007/12/10/off-color-joke-is-a-hot-potato.

472. http://www.alllaw.com/calculators/childsupport/arkansas accessed December 6, 2014.

473. Larry Nichols, *The Larry Nichols Story*, p. 95.

474. Larry Nichols, *The Larry Nichols Story*, p. 95.

475. *Cleveland Challenger*. "Clinton's Bi-Racial Son Story is Not Over." February 22, 2013. http://www.clevelandchallenger.com/clintons-bi-racial-son-story-is-not-over.

476. *Cleveland Challenger*. "Clinton's Bi-Racial Son Story is Not Over." February 22, 2013.

477. Larry Sabato, Robert Lichter, Mark Stencel, *Peepshow: Media and Politics in an Age of Scandal*, p. 55.

478. Celina Durgin. "Here's How Little Chelsea Clinton Cares About Money, In Dollars." *National Review.* June 24, 2014.

479. Ibid.

480. Webb Hubbell, *Friends in High Places*, p. 14.

481. http://en.wikipedia.org/wiki/Hillary_Rodham_Clinton accessed December 12, 2014.

482. Samantha Chang. "Chelsea Clinton's stunning plastic surgery before and after." http://www.examiner.com/article/chelsea-clinton-s-stunning-wedding-makeover-weight-loss-plastic-surgery accessed December 9, 2014.

483. http://www.celebrityplasticsurgery24.com/chelsea-clinton-plastic-surgery accessed December 9, 2014.

484. Webb Hubbell, *Friends in High Places*, p. 84.

485. Texe Marrs, *Big Sister is Watching*, p. 52.

486. Edward Klein, *The Truth about Hillary*, p. 62.

487. Edward Klein, *The Truth about Hillary*, p. 63.

488. Christopher Andersen, *Bill and Hillary: The Marriage*, p. 143.

489. Gennifer Flowers, *Passion and Betrayal*, pp. 41–42.

490. http://www.dailymail.co.uk/news/article-2424555/Bill-Clintons-mistress-Gennifer-Flowers-Wed-today-wasnt-Chelsea.html accessed December 12, 2014.

491. Texe Marrs, *Big Sister is Watching*, p. 52.

492. http://www.thedailybeast.com/articles/2013/02/07/dick-morris-s-fox-exit-latest-fall-and-rise-of-a-political-survivor.html accessed December 11, 2014.

493. Rafe Klinger, "Hillary's Gay Roommate," *Globe*, May 3, 2004.

494. http://www.rightwingwatch.org/content/sandy-rios-floats-rumor-hillary-clinton-lesbian.

495. http://www.rightwingwatch.org/content/fischer-america-will-never-elect-saggy-old-woman-hillary-clinton-president accessed December 12, 2014.

496. Luke Ford. "Hillary and Huma—A Dark Unseen Scandal Star." October 30, 2007. http://www.lukeford.net/blog/?p=1031 accessed December 11, 2014.

497. Michelle Cottle. *New York* magazine. August 13, 2007.

498. Michael Goodwin. "2 More Suspect Clinton Donors." *New York Post.* June 7, 2015.

499. John Gartner, *In Search of Bill Clinton: A Psychological Biography*, pp. 77–78.

500. David Maraniss, *First in His Class: A Biography of Bill Clinton*, p. 28.

501. Nigel Hamilton, *Bill Clinton: an American Journey*, p. 33.

502. John Gartner, *In Search of Bill Clinton: A Psychological Biography*, p. 19.

503. John Gartner, *In Search of Bill Clinton: A Psychological Biography*, p. 73.

504. John Gartner, *In Search of Bill Clinton: A Psychological Biography*, p. 74.

505. John Gartner, *In Search of Bill Clinton: A Psychological Biography*, p. 72.

506. John Gartner, *In Search of Bill Clinton: A Psychological Biography*, p. 76.

507. John Gartner, *In Search of Bill Clinton: A Psychological Biography*, pp. 77–78.

508. John Gartner, *In Search of Bill Clinton: A Psychological Biography*, p. 82.

509. Texe Marrs, *Big Sister is Watching You*, p. 51.

510. Dan Merica and Alexandra Jaffe. "Hillary Clinton: 'I Used One Email for Convenience.'" CNN.com.

511. Michael S. Schmidt. "Hillary Clinton used Personal Email Account at State Department, Possibly Breaking Rules." *New York Times*. March 2, 2015.

512. Patrick Howley. "Left-Wing Writer Max Blumenthal Helped Craft Hillary's 'Youtube Video' Benghazi Explanation." *Daily Caller*. May 27, 2015.

513. Rowan Scarborough. "Obama-Clinton Benghazi Narrative Rebutted by Defense Department Report." *Washington Times*. May 19, 2015.

514. Jerry Zeifman. "Hillary's Crocodile Tears in Connecticut." February 8, 2008.

515. New York Post Editorial Board. March 30, 2015.

516. John Fund. *National Review*. March 29, 2015.

517. Meghan Keneally, Liz Kruetz, Shushanah Walshe. ABC News. March 16, 2015.

518. *New York Times*. March 14, 2015. p. A1.

519. Meghan Keneally, Liz Kruetz, and Shushanah Walshe. ABC News. March 16, 2015.

520. Ibid.

521. Ibid.

522. Ibid.

523. Derek Hunter. "Carville 'I Suspect' Hillary didn't want Congress 'rifling through her emails.'" *Daily Caller*. March 15, 2015.

524. Ron Fournier. "Hillary Clinton: Congenital Rule-Breaker." *National Journal*, April 30, 2015.

525. "Bill Clinton defends foundation, says nothing 'sinister' at work." *FOXNEWS*. May 4, 2015.

526. Michael Fishel. "State Department says No Undue Influence After Foreign Gifts to Clinton Foundation." ABCNews. May 4, 2015.

527. Geoff Earle. *New York Post,* March 12, 2015.

528. Ibid.

529. Washington Free Beacon Staff. "Hillary Contradicts Bill's Claim that he has never used email." *Washington Free Beacon*. March 10, 2015

530. Laura Meckler. "Bill Clinton Still Doesn't Use Email." *Wall Street Journal*. March 10, 2015.

531. Joe Tacopino. "Hillary had second secret email address." *New York Post*. May 19, 2015.

532. Peter Schweizer, *Clinton Cash*, p. 8.

533. Ibid. p. 13.

534. Jonathan Allen. "Republicans ask White House about Clinton's Broken Charity Promise." Reuters. March 25, 2015.

535. Ibid.

536. Sarah Westwood. "Most Firms that gave to the Clinton Foundation also lobbied State Department." *Washington Examiner*. February 25, 2015.

537. Ron Fournier. *National Journal.* March 8, 2015.

538. Mariah Blake. "How Hillary Clinton's State Department Sold Frackng to the World." *Mother Jones.* September/October 2014 issue.

539. Ibid. p. 113.

540. Mark Tapscott. *Washington Examiner.* March 16, 2015.

541. Matthew Cunningham-Cook. *International Business Times.* April 16, 2015.

542. Peter Nicholas. *Wall Street Journal* February. 19, 2015.

543. Jonathan M. Katz. *Politico Magazine.* May 4, 2015.

544. FoxNews.com. April 24, 2015.

545. Ron Fournier. "The Proof of the Clintons' Wrongdoing." *National Journal.* April 27, 2015.

546. David Sirota and Andrew Perez. "Clinton Foundation Donors Got Weapons Deals From Hillary Clinton's State Department." *International Business Times.*

547. Ibid.

548. Ibid.

549. Michael Allan McCrae. "Clinton, Giustra push back against New York Times' Uranium One story." Mining.com. April 23, 2015.

550. Peter Schweizer, *Clinton Cash,* p. 29

551. Jo Becker and Mike McIntire. "Cash Flowed to Clinton Foundation amid Russian Uranium Deal." *New York Times.* April 23, 2015.

552. Douglas Birch. R. Jeffrey Smith. "U.S. Unease About Nuclear Weapons Fuel Takes Aim At A South African Vault." *Washington Post.* March 14, 2015.

553. Jo Becker and Mike McIntire. "Cash Flowed to Clinton Foundation amid Russian Uranium Deal." *New York Times.* April 23, 2015.

554. Matthew Boyle. Breitbart News. April 23, 2015.

555. Andrew Rafferty. "Romney: Clinton Foundation Donations 'Looks Like Bribery.' NBCNEWS. April 24, 2015.

556. Hannah Thoburn. "Russia Building Nuclear Reactors-and influence-around the globe." Reuters. April 29, 2015.

557. David Von Drehle. "Mills: A Brand New Legal Star on the Rise." *Washington Post.* January 21, 1999.

558. Isabel Vincent and Melissa Klein. "Clinton Confidant Cuts Ties with the Formidable Family." *New York Post.* June 21, 2015.

559. Glazov, Jaime. "Huma Abedin, Islamic Connection and Willful Blindness." Frontpagemag.com. August 21, 2012.

560. Paige Lavender. "Hillary Clinton: I Regret saying we were 'Dead Broke.'" *Huffington Post.* July 29, 2014.

561. Michael Goodwin. "In Bed with the Clintons." *New York Post.* May 17, 2015

562. Clinton Global Initiative Report February 2015.

563. Ezra Klein. "One Tweet that shows the Insane Rates Hillary Clinton got Paid for Speeches." *Vox.* May 19, 2015.

564. Rosallind S Helderman and Tom Hamburger. "Clinton Foundation Reveals Up To $26 Million In Additional Payments." *Washington Post.* May 21, 2015.

565. Von Drehle, David. "The Clinton Way." *Time.* March 23, 2015.

566. Jonathan Allen. "Hillary Clinton Personally took money from companies that thought to influence her." *Vox.* May 15, 2015.

567. Mike McIntire and Raymond Hernandez. "Company Finds Clinton Useful, and Vice Versa." *New York Times.* April 12, 2006.

568. Jonathan Allen. "Hillary Clinton Personally took money from companies that thought to influence her." *Vox.* May 15, 2015

569. *Politics.* February 18, 2015.

570. Rosalind S. Helderman and Thomas Hamburger. *Washington Post*, February 25, 2015.

571. Mike Allen. "Rand Paul: Foreign Donations to Clinton Foundation 'Thinly Veiled Bribes.'" *Politico.* March 20, 2015.

572. Ibid.

573. Cameron Joseph. "Clinton Foundation Takes Check from Moroccan government-owned Company." *Daily News.* April 9, 2015.

574. Kenneh Vogel. *Politico.* May 15, 2015.

575. Michael Goodwin. "2 More Suspect Clinton Donors." *New York Post.* June 7, 2015

576. Ed Morrisey. HotAir.com. November 20, 2014.

577. Peter Schweizer, *Clinton Cash.*

578. Ibid.

579. Ibid.

580. Richard Johnson. "Staff Quit Clinton Foundation over Chelsea." *New York Post.* May 18, 2015.

581. Ibid.

582. Jonathan Martin. "Republicans Paint Clinton as Old News for 2016 Presidential Election." *New York Times.* June 29, 2013.

583. Catherine Thompson. "Drudge Suggests Hillary is 'Holding a Walker' on People Magazine Cover." *TPM.* June 2, 2014.

584. Margaret Wheeler Johnson. "Calling Hillary Clinton Old on Twitter isn't Cool, but it is Working in her favor." *Huffington Post.* April 13, 2015.

585. "Bill's Dementia Nightmare!" *Globe.* June 22, 2015. 6–7

586. http://www.breitbart.com/big-government/2015/03/04/hillary-clintons-long-history-of-hiding-documents.

BIBLIOGRAPHY

In order to understand the Clintons, one must educate oneself on their wildly dysfunctional "Jerry Springer Show" lifestyles. In writing this book, we used a robust bibliography in an attempt to understand the Clintons and their abuse of women and also men.

Some of the most important books on the Clintons are the ones that detail the Clinton-Bush connection in the CIA drug trade of Iran-Contra. This is a verboten topic across the political spectrum because an in-depth examination of this topic would utterly wipe out both the Clintons and the Bushes.

There have been many good examinations of the Bush-Clinton CIA drug connection. One of the most important books on American politics that has been written in the past twenty-five years is Daniel Hopsicker's *Barry and the Boys: the CIA, the Mob and America's Secret History*. This seminal work was written in 2001, but lawsuits delayed its publication until 2006. A lot of very powerful people did not want this book to be published, and that is precisely why you should read it. It examines the life and death of CIA drug smuggler Barry Seal.

Other good Iran-Contra books to read are efforts by L. D Brown (who was very close to Bill Clinton), Al Martin (who worked closely with Jeb Bush and Oliver North), Chip Tatum (who worked closely with Oliver North and Vice President G. H. W Bush), and Terry Reed, whose classic book *Compromised* examines both sides of the Bush-Clinton CIA drug connection. Terry Reed also worked with Oliver North. Read Bo Gritz, and you will understand why Ross Perot was so incensed at U.S. government drug smuggling. Cele Castillo was an honest DEA agent working in Guatemala in the 1980s when he stumbled across Contra drug smuggling at Ilopango Airport in El Salvador, and he also had a memorable experience with Vice President G. H. W. Bush, which Castillo details in his book. Mitchell and Burdick's book on cigarette boat king Don Aronow covers the friendship of a man involved in the drug trade with the Bushes. The reporting of Gary Webb has been vindicated with the movie *Kill the Messenger*. It was too bad the *NY Times*, the *LA Times*, and the *Washington Post* tried to move heaven and earth to debunk Webb's stellar reporting.

The legendary Rodney Stich, who is in his nineties now, has several informative books that are classics in the genre of official governmental crime: *Defrauding America* and *The Drugging of America* are two of them. Stich was an FAA whistleblower, and over the years, operatives from CIA, DEA, FBI, and other governmental agencies have come to him when these whistleblowers become targets of an often illegal governmental operation that has gone awry. Ambrose Evans-Pritchard wrote a classic book on it, titled *The Secret Life of Bill Clinton: The Unreported Stories*. "Unreported" means censored or covered up in the MSM, which is precisely why you should read this book. Evans-Pritchard has some great chapters on the murder of Jerry Parks and the very suspicious circumstances of the death of Vince Foster. Bill Clinton's cocaine use is also detailed.

The information in the following books is funny, sad, and extremely disturbing, especially when one ponders the role this pair plays on the stage of national and international politics.

—Robert Morrow

Aldrich, Gary. *Unlimited Access: An FBI Agent Inside the Clinton White House.* Washington, DC. Regnery Publishing, 1998.

Allen, Jonathan and Amie Parnes. *HRC: State Secrets and the Rebirth of Hillary Clinton.* New York: Crown Publishers, 2014.

Andersen, Christopher. *American Evita: Hillary Clinton's Path to Power.* New York: HarperCollins, 2004.

Andersen, Christopher. *Bill and Hillary: The Marriage.* New York: William Morrow and Company, Inc., 1999.

Anonymous (Joe Klein). *Primary Colors: A Novel of Politics.* Great Britain: Vintage, 1996.

Barr, Bob. *The Meaning of Is: the Squandered Impeachment and Wasted Legacy of William Jefferson Clinton.* Atlanta: Stroud & Hall Publishers, 2004.

Bernstein, Carl. *A Woman in Charge: The Life of Hillary Rodham Clinton.* New York: Alfred Knopf, 2007.

Biesada, Rick. *Angry White Male and the Horse He Rode In On.* Unknown City: 1st Books Library, 2001.

Bossie, David. *Hillary: The Politics of Personal Destruction.* Nashville, TN: Thomas Nelson, 2008.

Bozell, L. Brent III. *Whitewash: What the Media Won't Tell You About Hillary Clinton, But Conservatives Will.* New York: Crown Forum, 2007.

Bresnahan, David. *Cover Up: The Art and Science of Political Deception.* West Jordan, UT: David M. Bresnahan, 1998.

Bresnahan, David. *The Larry Nichols Story: Damage Control: How to Get Caught with Your Pants Down and Still Get Elected President.* Midvale, UT: Camden Court Publishers, Inc., 1997.

Brock, David. *Blinded by the Right: The Conscience of an Ex-Conservative.* New York: Crown Publishers, 2002.

Brock, David. *The Seduction of Hillary Clinton.* New York: The Free Press, 1996.

Brown, Floyd. *"Slick Willie:" Why America Cannot Trust Bill Clinton.* Annapolis, MD: Annapolis Publishing Company, Inc.: 1992.

Brown, L.D. *Crossfire: Witness in the Clinton Investigation.* San Diego: Black Forest Press, April, 1999.

Browning, Dolly Kyle. *Perjuries of the Heart: A True Story.* Dallas: Direct Outstanding Creations Corporation, 1999.

Brummett, John. *High Wire: From the Backroads to the Beltway: the Education of Bill Clinton.* New York: Hyperion, 1994.

Burdick, Thomas and Charlene Mitchell. *Blue Thunder: How the Mafia Owned and Finally Murdered Cigarette Boat King Donald Aronow*. New York: Simon and Schuster, 1990.

Carpenter, Amanda. *The Vast Right-Wing Conspiracy's Dossier on Hillary Clinton*. Washington, DC: Regnery Publishing, 2006.

Carpozi, George Jr. *Clinton Confidential: The Climb to Power: The Unauthorized Biography of Bill and Hillary Clinton*. Del Mar, CA: Emery Dalton Books, 1995.

Cashill, Jack and James Sanders. *First Strike: TWA Flight 800 and the Attack on America*. Nashville, TN: Thomas Nelson, Inc., 2003.

Castillo, Celerino III and Dave Harmon. *Powderburns: Cocaine, Contras & the Drug War*. Buffalo, NY: Mosaic Press, 1994.

Chafe, William H. *Bill and Hillary: The Politics of the Personal*. New York: Farrar, Straus and Giroux, 2012.

Charney, Milton. *Murder, Mass Murder and Involvement in 9/11*. Unknown City: Evidence First Publishing, 2008.

Clarke, John and Patrick Knowlton, and Hugh Turley. *Failure of the Public Trust: Proof of FBI and OIC Cover-Up in the Independent Counsel's Probe into the Death of Deputy White House Counsel Vincent W. Foster*. Unknown City: McCabe Publishing, 1999.

Clinton, Bill. *My Life*. New York: Alfred Knopf: 2004.

Clinton, Hillary Rodham. *Hard Choices*. New York: Simon and Schuster, 2014.

———. *It Takes a Village: and Other Lessons Children Teach Us*. New York: Simon and Schuster, 1996.

———. *Living History*. New York: Simon and Schuster, 2003.

Clinton, Roger. *Growing Up Clinton: The Lives, Times and Tragedies of America's Presidential Families*. Arlington, TX: The Summit Publishing Group, 1995.

Clinton Investigative Commission. "Report to Congress: Implications of White House Involvement in the Death of Vince Foster." Annandale, VA: Clinton Investigative Commission, 1997.

Conason, Joe and Gene Lyons. *The Hunting of the President: The Ten-Year Campaign to Destroy Bill and Hillary Clinton*. New York: St. Martin's Press, 2000.

Coulter, Ann. *High Crimes and Misdemeanors: The Case Against Bill Clinton*. Washington, DC: Regnery Publishing, 1998.

BIBLIOGRAPHY

Davidson, James Dale. *Who Murdered Vince Foster?: And Why the Biggest Political Scandal in History is Also the Biggest Financial Story of Our Lifetimes.* Baltimore: Strategic Investment Limited Partnership, 1996.

Des Barres, Pamela. *Let's Spend the Night Together: Backstage Secrets of Rock Muses and Supergroupies.* Chicago: Chicago Review Press, 2007.

Dumas, Ernst, editor. *The Clintons of Arkansas: An Introduction by Those Who Know Them Best.* Fayetteville: University of Arkansas Press, 1993.

Evans-Pritchard, Ambrose. *The Secret Life of Bill Clinton: The Unreported Stories.* Washington, DC: Regnery Publishing, 1997.

Felsenthal, Carol. *Clinton in Exile: A President Out of the White House.* New York: William Morrow, 2008.

Fick, Paul. *The Dysfunctional President: Understanding the Compulsions of Bill Clinton.* Secaucus, NJ: Citadel Press Book, 1998.

Flaherty, Peter and Timothy Flaherty. *The First Lady: A Comprehensive View of Hillary Rodham Clinton.* Lafayette, LA: Vital Issues Press, 1996.

Flowers, Gennifer. *Passion & Betrayal.* Del Mar, CA: Emery Dalton Books, 1995.

Freeh, Louis. *My FBI: Bringing Down the Mafia, Investigating Bill Clinton, and Fighting the War on Terror.* New York: St. Martin's Press, 2005.

Gartner, John. *In Search of Bill Clinton: A Psychological Biography.* New York: St. Martin's Press, 2008.

Gergen, David. *Eyewitness to Power: the Essence of Leadership Nixon to Clinton.* New York: Touchstone, 2000.

Gerth, Jeff and Don Van Natta, Jr. *Her Way: The Hopes and Ambitions of Hillary Rodham Clinton.* New York: Little, Brown and Company, 2007.

Gibbs, Nancy and Michael Duffy. *The President's Club: Inside the World's Most Exclusive Fraternity.* New York: Simon and Schuster, 2012.

Gillon, Steven. *The Pact: Bill Clinton, Newt Gingrich, and the Rivalry that Defined a Generation.* New York: Oxford University Press, 2008.

Gottlieb, Alan. *She Took a Village: The Unauthorized Biography of Hillary Rodham Clinton.* Bellevue, WA: Merril Press, 1993.

Graham, Michael. *Clinton & Me: How Eight Years of a Pants-Free Presidency Changed My Nation, My Family and My Life.* Columbia, SC: Pinpoint Press, 2000.

Grant, George. *Hillarious: The Wacky Wit, Wisdom & Wonderment of Hillary Rodham Clinton.* Franklin, TN: Adroit Press, 1992.

Green, Melrose Larry. *Why the Clintons Belong in Prison.* California: Bookman Publishing & Marketing, 2004.

Greenberg, Paul. *No Surprises: Two Decades of Clinton-Watching*. Washington, DC: Brassey's, 1996.

Gormley, Ken. *The Death of American Virtue: Clinton v. Starr*. New York: Crown Publishers, 2010.

Gritz, James "Bo." *Called to Serve: Profiles in Conspiracy from John F. Kennedy to George Bush*. Sandy Valley, NV: Lazarus Publishing, May, 1991.

Gross, Michael. *Model: The Ugly Business of Beautiful Women*. New York: Warner Books, 1995.

Hagood, Wesley. *Presidential Sex: From the Founding Fathers to Bill Clinton*. New York: Carol Publishing Group, 1995.

Halper, Daniel. Clinton, Inc.: *The Audacious Rebuilding of a Political Machine*. New York: HarperCollins, 2014.

Hamilton, Nigel. *Bill Clinton: An American Journey: Great Expectations*. New York: Random House, 2003.

———. *Bill Clinton: Mastering the Presidency*. New York: Public Affairs, 2007.

Harris, John F. *The Survivor: Bill Clinton in the White House*. New York: Random House, 2005.

Hitchens, Christopher. *No One Left to Lie To: The Values of the Worst Family*. London: Verso, 1999.

Hopsicker, Daniel. *Barry & 'the Boys:' the CIA, the Mob and America's Secret History*. Venice, FL: MadCow Press, 2001.

Hubbell, Webb. *Friends in High Places*. New York: William Morrow and Company, 1997.

Isikoff, Michael. *Uncovering Clinton: A Reporter's Story*. New York: Random House, 1999.

Jackson, Candice E. *Their Lives: The Women Targeted by the Clinton Machine*. Los Angeles: World Ahead Publishing, 2005.

Kellet, Michael. *America Needs Your Verdict*. Columbia, MD: CLS Publishing, 1999.

———. *The Murder of Vince Foster*. Columbia, MD: CLS Publishers, 1995.

Kellet, Michael C. *Phantoms of the World Stage: The Clintons Tell the Truth*. Unknown City: Evidence First Publishing, 2006.

Kelley, Virginia. *Leading With My Heart*. New York: Simon & Schuster, 1994.

Kessler, Ronald. *Inside the White House: The Hidden Lives of the Modern Presidents and the Secrets of the World's Most Powerful Institution*. New York: Pocket Books, 1996.

———. *The First Family Detail: Secret Service Reveal the Hidden Lives of the Presidents*. New York: Crown Forum, 2014.

———. *The Secrets of the FBI*. New York: Crown Publishers, 2011.

BIBLIOGRAPHY

Klein, Edward. *Blood Feud: the Clintons vs. the Obamas*. Washington, DC: Regnery Publishing, 2014.

———. *The Truth About Hillary: What She Knew, When She Knew It, and How Far She'll Go to Become President*. New York: Sentinel, 2005.

Klein, Joe. *The Natural: The Misunderstood Presidency of Bill Clinton*. Great Britain: Coronet Books, 2002.

Kopel, David B. and Paul H. Blackman. *No More Wacos: What's Wrong With Federal Law Enforcement and How to Fix It*. Amherst, NY: Prometheus Books, 1997.

Kuiper, Thomas D. *"I've Always Been a Yankees Fan:" Hillary Clinton in her Own Words*. Los Angeles: World Ahead Publishing, 2006.

Leveritt, Mara. *The Boys on the Tracks: Death, Denial, and a Mother's Crusade to Bring Her Son's Killers to Justice*. New York: Thomas Dunne Books, 1999.

Limbacher, Carl. *Hillary's Scheme: Inside the Next Clinton's Ruthless Agenda to Take the White House*. New York: Crown Forum, 2003.

Limbaugh, David. *Absolute Power: The Legacy of Corruption in the Clinton-Reno Justice Department*. Washington, DC: Regnery Publishing, 2001.

Lowinger, Paul. *The Clintons Meet Freud: A Psychohistory of Bill, Hillary and Chelsea*. San Francisco: Knoll Press, 2004.

Lyons, Gene. *Fools for Scandal: How the Media Invented Whitewater*. New York: Franklin Square Press, 1996.

Maraniss, David. *First in His Class: A Biography of Bill Clinton*. New York: Simon and Schuster, 1995.

Marrs, Texe. *Big Sister Is Watching You*. Austin, TX: Living Truth Publishers, 1993.

Martin, Al. *The Conspirators: Secrets of an Iran-Contra Insider*. Pray, MT: National Liberty Press, 2002.

Matrisciana, Patrick. *The Clinton Chronicles Book*. Hemet, CA: Jeremiah Books, 1994.

McAuliffe, Terry. *What a Party! My Life Among Democrats: Presidents, Candidates, Donors, Activists, Alligators, and other Wild Animals*. New York: Thomas Dunne Books, 2007.

McDougal, Jim and Curtis Wilke. *Arkansas Mischief: The Birth of a National Scandal*. New York: Henry Holt, 1998.

McDougal, Susan. *The Woman Who Wouldn't Talk: Why I Refused to Testify Against the Clintons & What I Learned in Jail*. New York: Carroll & Graf Publishers, 2003.

Milton, Joyce. *The First Partner: Hillary Rodham Clinton*. New York: William Morrow, 1999.

Moldea, Dan. *A Washington Tragedy: How the Death of Vincent Foster Ignited a Political Firestorm*. Washington, DC: Regnery Publishing, 1998.

Moore, Carol. *The Davidian Massacre: Disturbing Questions about Waco which Must be Answered*. Franklin, TN: Legacy Communications, 1995.

Morris, Dick. *Because He Could*. New York: HarperCollins, 2004.

———. *Rewriting History*. New York: ReganBooks, 2004.

Morris, Roger. *Partners in Power: The Clintons and Their America*. New York: Henry Holt and Co., 1996.

Nichols, Larry. *The Genie is out of the Bottle!: Even if the Clintons Leave, Their System of Controlling Our Country Will Remain*. Conway, AR: Larry Nichols, 1999.

Novak, Robert. *The Prince of Darkness: 50 Years Reporting in Washington*. New York, NY: Crown Publishing, 2007

Oakley, Meredith. *On the Make: The Rise of Bill Clinton*. Washington, DC: Regnery Publishing, 1994.

Odom, Richard. *Circle of Death: Clinton's Climb to the Presidency*. Lafayette, LA: Huntington House Publishers, 1995.

Olson, Barbara. *Hell to Pay: The Unfolding Story of Hillary Rodham Clinton*. Washington, DC: Regnery Publishing, 1999.

———. *The Final Days: The Last, Desperate Abuses of Power by the Clinton White House*. Washington, DC: Regnery Publishing, 2001.

Oppenheimer, Jerry. *State of a Union: Inside the Complex Marriage of Bill and Hillary Clinton*. New York: HarperCollins, 2000.

Patterson, Robert "Buzz." *Dereliction of Duty: The Eyewitness Account of How Bill Clinton Compromised America's National Security*. Washington, DC: Regnery Publishing, 2003.

Poe, Richard. *Hillary's Secret War: The Clinton Conspiracy to Muzzle Internet Journalists*. Nashville, TN: WND Books, 2004.

Peschmann, Marinka. *Following Orders: The Death of Vince Foster, Clinton White House Lawyer*. Canada: One Rock Ink Publishing, 2012.

———. *The Whistleblower: How the Clinton White House Stayed in Power to Reemerge in the Obama White House and on the World Stage*. Canada: One Rock Ink Publishing, 2011.

Posner, Gerald. *Citizen Perot: His Life and Times*. New York: Random House, 1996.

Radcliffe, Donnie. *Hillary Rodham Clinton: A First Lady for Our Times*. New York: Warner Books, Inc., 1993.

———. *Hillary Rodham Clinton: The Evolution of a First Lady*. New York: Warner Books, Inc., 1999.

Reagan, Michael. *Making Waves: Bold Exposes from Talk Radio's Number One Nighttime Host*. Nashville, TN: Thomas Nelson, Inc., 1996.

Reavis, Dick. *The Ashes of Waco: An Investigation*. New York, Simon & Schuster, 1995.

Reed, Terry and John Cummings. *Compromised: Clinton, Bush and the CIA*. New York: S.P.I. Books, 1994.

Reel, Guy. *Unequal Justice: Wayne Dumond, Bill Clinton, and the Politics of Rape in Arkansas*. Buffalo, NY: Prometheus Books, 1993.

Renshon, Stanley. *High Hopes: The Clinton Presidency and the Politics of Ambition*. New York: Routledge, 1998.

Ruddy, Christopher and Carl Limbacher, Jr., editors. *Bitter Legacy: NewsMax Reveals the Untold Story of the Clinton-Gore Years*. West Palm Beach, FL: NewsMax.com, 2001.

———. *Vincent Foster: The Ruddy Investigation*. Unknown City: United Publishing, 1996.

Ruddy, Christopher. *The Strange Death of Vincent Foster: An Investigation*. New York: The Free Press, 1997.

Sanders, James. *Altered Evidence: Flight 800: How and Why the Justice Department Framed a Journalist and His Wife*. Dallas: Offset Paperback Mfrs., 1999.

———. *The Downing of TWA Flight 800: The Shocking Truth Behind the Worst Airplane Disaster in U.S. History*. New York: Zebra Books, 1997.

Schippers, David. *Sellout: The Inside Story of President Clinton's Impeachment*. Washington, DC: Regnery Publishing, 2000.

Schweizer, Peter. *Clinton Cash: The Untold Story of How and Why Foreign Governments and Businesses Helped Make Bill and Hillary Rich*. New York: HarperCollins, 2015.

———. *Do As I Say (Not as I Do): Profiles in Liberal Hypocrisy*. New York: Doubleday, 2005.

Sheehy, Gail. *Hillary's Choice*. New York: Random House, 1999.

Slate, Chuck. *Hillary: America's First Dictator*. Victoria, BC, Canada: Trafford, 2004.

Smith, I.C. *Inside: A Top G-Man Exposes Spies, Lies, and Bureaucratic Bungling Inside the FBI*. Nashville, TN: Nelson Current, 2004.

Smith, Sally Bedell. *For Love of Politics: Bill and Hillary Clinton: The White House Years*. New York: Random House, 2007.

Stich, Rodney. *Defrauding America: Encyclopedia of Secret Operations by the CIA, DEA, and other Covert Agencies*. Alamo, CA: Diablo Western Press, 1998.

Stich, Rodney. *Drugging America: A Trojan Horse*. Alamo, CA: Silverpeak Enterprises, 2006.

Stone, Roger. *Nixon's Secrets: The Rise, Fall, and Untold Truth about the President, Watergate and the Pardon*. New York: Skyhorse Publishing, 2014.

Starr, Ken. *The Starr Report: The Official Report of the Independent Counsel's Investigation of the President*. Rockland, CA: Forum, 1998.

Stewart, James. *Blood Sport: The President and His Adversaries*. New York: Simon & Schuster, 1996.

Sullivan, Michael. *Blood Trail*. Ottawa, IL: Jameson Books, 1998.

Stone, Deborah and Christopher Manion. *"Slick Willie" II: Why America Still Cannot Trust Bill Clinton*. Annapolis, MD: Annapolis-Washington Book Publishers, Inc., 1994.

Taie, Sanders Gaillar. *Living Lies: A Response to Hillary Clinton*. Laredo, TX: We-Publish.com, 2003.

Tatum, Gene "Chip." *The Tatum Chronicles*. Unknown City: Gene Tatum, 1996.

Thomas, Gordon. *Gideon's Spies: The Secret History of the Mossad*. New York: Thomas Dunne Books, 2005.

Thorn, Victor. *Hillary (and Bill): The Sex Volume*. State College, PA: Sisyphus Press, 2008.

———. *Hillary (and Bill): The Drugs Volume*. State College, PA: Sisyphus Press, 2008.

———. *Hillary (and Bill): The Murder Volume*. State College, PA: Sisyphus Press, 2008.

Troy, Gil. *Hillary Rodham Clinton: Polarizing First Lady*. Lawrence, KS: University Press of Kansas, 2006.

Tyrrell, R. Emmett Jr. *Boy Clinton: The Political Biography*. Washington, D.C.: Regnery, 1996.

Tyrrell, R. Emmett Jr. *Madame Hillary*. Washington, D.C.: Regnery Publishing: 2004.

———. *The Clinton Crack-Up: The Boy President's Life after the White House*. Nashville, TN: Thomas Nelson, Inc., 2007.

———. *The Impeachment of William Jefferson Clinton: a Political Docu-Drama*. Washington, DC: Regnery Publishing: 1997.

Walden, Gregory. *Our Best Behavior: The Clinton Administration and Ethics in Government*. Indianapolis, IN: Hudson Institute, 1996.

Warner, Judith. *Hillary Clinton: The Inside Story*. New York: Signet, 1999.

Watson, Kevin. *The Clinton Record: Everything Bill and Hillary Want You to Forget!* Bellevue, WA: Merril Press, 1996.

Webb, Gary. *Dark Alliance: The CIA, The Contras and the Crack Cocaine Explosion*. New York: Seven Stories Press, 1999.

Whitehead, David Jr. *99 Things Hillary Hopes You Forgot About*. Austin, TX: Prevailing Publications, 2007.

Willey, Kathleen. *Target: Caught in the Crosshairs of Bill and Hillary Clinton*. Los Angeles: WND Books, 2007.

Williams, Thomas. *I Hate Hillary: All the Reasons Why Hillary Just Isn't Right*. Naperville, IL: Sourcebooks Hysteria, 2008.

Wilson, Ann. *Bill Clinton: Friend or Foe?* St. Clair, MO: J.W. Publishing, 1994.

Woodward, Bob. *Shadow: Five Presidents and the Legacy of Watergate*. New York: Simon & Schuster, 1999.

Wright, Stuart, editor. *Armageddon in Waco: Critical Perspectives on the Branch Davidian Conflict*. Chicago: University of Chicago Press, 1995.

Zeifman, Jerry. *Hillary's Pursuit of Power*. USA: Xlibris Corporation, 2006.

———. *Without Honor: The Impeachment of President Nixon and the Crimes of Camelot*. New York: Thunder's Mouth Press, 1995.

INDEX